MEDIEVAL WARFARE

READINGS IN MEDIEVAL CIVILIZATIONS AND CULTURES: XXI

series editor: Paul Edward Dutton

MEDIEVAL WARFARE

A READER

edited by

KELLY DEVRIES AND MICHAEL LIVINGSTON

UNIVERSITY OF TORONTO PRESS
Toronto Buffalo London

Toronto Buffalo London
utorontopress.com
Printed in Canada

Library and Archives Canada Cataloguing in Publication

Title: Medieval warfare : a reader / Kelly DeVries, Michael Livingston, editors.
Names: DeVries, Kelly, 1956–, editor. | Livingston, Michael, 1975–, editor.
Description: Series statement: Readings in Medieval Civilizations and Cultures; XXI | Includes bibliographical references and index.
Identifiers: Canadiana 2019011424X | ISBN 9781442636705 (hardcover) | ISBN 9781442636699 (softcover)
Subjects: LCSH: Military art and science—History—Medieval, 500–1500—Sources. | LCSH: Military history, Medieval—Sources.
Classification: LCC U37 .M43 2019 | DDC 355.0094/0902—dc23

We welcome comments and suggestions regarding any aspect of our publications—please feel free to contact us at news@utorontopress.com or visit our internet site at utorontopress.com.

North America
5201 Dufferin Street
North York, Ontario, Canada, M3H 5T8

2250 Military Road
Tonawanda, New York, USA, 14150
ORDERS PHONE: 1-800-565-9523
ORDERS FAX: 1-800-221-9985
ORDERS E-MAIL: utpbooks@utpress.utoronto.ca

UK, Ireland, and continental Europe
NBN International
Estover Road, Plymouth, PL6 7PY, UK
ORDERS PHONE: 44 (0) 1752 202301
ORDERS FAX: 44 (0) 1752 202333
ORDERS E-MAIL: enquiries@nbninternational.com

University of Toronto Press acknowledges the financial assistance to its publishing program of the Canada Council for the Arts and the Ontario Arts Council, an agency of the Government of Ontario.

Canada Council for the Arts | Conseil des Arts du Canada

ONTARIO ARTS COUNCIL
CONSEIL DES ARTS DE L'ONTARIO
an Ontario government agency
un organisme du gouvernement de l'Ontario

Funded by the Government of Canada | Financé par le gouvernement du Canada | Canada

FSC www.fsc.org MIX Paper from responsible sources FSC® C016245

CONTENTS

ACKNOWLEDGEMENTS

The editors wish to thank their friends and colleagues in the field who made suggestions regarding the selection of sources for this reader. We wish to thank, too, Loyola University Maryland for its financial support in bringing this book to press.

At its heart, a reader such as this inevitably reflects the experiences of its editors: it is what we know. We owe a deep gratitude, therefore, to those who have taught us, mentored us, and challenged us. While no list could ever be sufficient to name them all, we wish to highlight in particular the impact of John France, who has been a powerful and inspiring guide to a wide generation of medieval scholars. Perhaps even more importantly, he has been a friend. This one is for you, John.

GENERAL INTRODUCTION

The modern world seems not to like a peaceful Middle Ages. From films to television shows, from games to other aspects of our mass media, our culture has been taught to read the Middle Ages as a bloodied and brutal epoch—a time of sword and shield, horse and harness, death and destruction.

There was indeed, as this reader in your hands will show, much of that. But there was also, it should be said at the outset, times of peace and prosperity, happiness and health.

Still, human beings, as near as we can tell, have always been trying to kill each other. This fact, regrettable though it is, makes war one of the few constants of history. There have always been wars, so anyone wishing to understand the human experience of any individual period of history would do well to study the motives and mechanisms, impacts and institutions of warfare within it. And the Middle Ages, because it reaches across such a particularly dynamic period of history, makes for a truly productive field in which to examine the subject of armed conflict.

A MILITARY MIDDLE AGES

The Middle Ages, perhaps more obviously than most of the arbitrary chronological periods of history, is a label that no one living within it would have recognized. No one thought they lived in a world that was "medieval." They were living in what was, for them, the modern world; it was only in hindsight (and with no small amount of bias) that people began to view it as a "middle" time between other historical periods.

So how do we define the Middle Ages? To keep the numbers easy for students to remember, we could identify the Middle Ages as the Euro-centric experience of the thousand years between 500 and 1500. This is a convenient and traditional definition, to be sure, but it is difficult to imagine that anyone, anywhere in Europe woke up on the first day of 1501 with any sense that a new era in history had dawned. Seeking dates with sharper edges, we could arguably pinpoint the end of the Middle Ages as the fall of Constantinople in 1453. That was essentially the end of what was left of the Roman Empire—a sensible enough breaking point—yet one could easily argue that the idea of Rome had been on life support long enough to have been declared dead long before the mighty walls of that city fell. Christopher Columbus's 1492 arrival in the New World very clearly shook the Old World, even if in truth the Vikings had beaten him to North American shores by some five centuries. And what about the cultural upheavals tied to the invention of the printing press, which had printed more books within 100 years of its appearance than had been written in all the millennia before? Each of these radical shifts could be said to mark the end of one era and the beginning of another, and even if the wide range of medievalists around the world could somehow manage to pick one final answer for the end date of the period—and we cannot—we would still only have half the definition: we face the very same issues, after all, in defining the starting date for the period—which includes still more dates for the fall of the Roman Empire. More troublesome, what happens when we push the boundaries of our perspective beyond the soft borders of the European experience of the world? After all, how do we even define Europe?

To put it simply, if there are *any*, there are *many* Middle Ages. The Middle Ages is a period inevitably defined by context: the political Middle Ages is different from the economic Middle Ages; the Euro-centric is different from the global; the social is different from the cultural.

This reader is focused on warfare: a military Middle Ages. As a result, we have defined this particular Middle Ages as the widely experienced European period lasting from the invasions of the Goths, Vandals, and Huns in the fourth and fifth centuries to the full realization of the power of gunpowder in warfare. Though history rarely offers moments of truly radical change—history is far more organically modulating shades of gray than stark alterations of black to white—we have associated these shifts with the Battle of Adrianople in 378 and the Siege of Rhodes in 1522. We freely concede that these dates are a minority definition, but they have also been intentionally chosen to provide us with the broadest reach possible; however you define the medieval period, we hope you can find it within these pages.

A NEW VIEW OF WAR

Traditionally, a book such as this would have focused almost exclusively on military actions, recounting battles on land and sea, describing sieges, and perhaps making a few gestures toward the theories and the logistics of warfare. Gathering together readings to encompass the human experience of warfare in even this fairly limited way—from 378 to 1522, from the sands of Egypt to the fjords of Scandinavia, from the shores of the Atlantic to shores of the Holy Land—would be a daunting assignment that we would inevitably fail. No book could possibly capture such a totality, much less one that could be carried in a student's backpack.

Making matters even more difficult for ourselves, we have chosen to broaden the scope of this volume far beyond such traditional limitations. There is certainly much within these pages for readers expecting descriptions of the medieval Preparations for War (Part Two) and the Waging of War (Part Three). If we have done our work well, readers will find in these sections the "classic" battles, events, and theories that they would expect in a book such as this, along with more than a few unexpected surprises. We have consciously framed this core of conflict, however, with a wide range of vibrant and informative sources on the Casualties of War (Part One) and the Outcomes of War (Part Four).

Our decision to foreground this material is not taken lightly. In deviating from traditional expectations, we realize that we are establishing a moral backbone for the volume that might induce a set of challenging questions that could otherwise go unasked. This, we believe, is a good and necessary thing. Too often, the real and horrible human costs of warfare are lost in the focus upon the lauding or demonizing of its leaders and the moving of colored blocks around clean and unbloodied maps. Likewise, a focus on the fighting man can too-frequently neglect his life when returned from war—not to mention the lives left behind back home or buried in foreign soil abroad. Highlighted both within these sections and its conflict core, as well, are the rarely illumined roles of women and the diversity of gender experiences in medieval warfare. These matters, too, are overdue their incorporation into studies of war.

Several additional goals have driven our selection of the 139 readings included here. Perhaps chief among them has been to show how the conduct of warfare changed dramatically across the 1,144 years between the blood spilled at Adrianople and the blood spilled at Rhodes. Most obviously, gunpowder introduced a radical new technological force of arms, but there were other massively significant changes across the period, too, such as the adoption of Germanic warfare tactics (and personnel) into Roman legionary practices, the dramatic rise of the longbow, or the introduction of ordinances to regulate recruitment, leadership, and discipline. It is perhaps inadvisable to use terms like "revolution" to describe such changes, but we cannot ignore their very real impacts on warfare: though gradual in development, the shifting modes of warfare could be vastly different from one end of the period to the other. We have worked hard to make our selections of readings reflect such changes across the period, though it is an unfortunate truth for historians (and for us as editors) that sources prior to the eleventh century are typically more spare in detail than those that come in the later Middle Ages. As such, despite our efforts, readers will no doubt observe that the early Middle Ages is less well represented here.

Another of our goals is to spread our selections beyond the geographical axis of England and France. While we recognize that the audience for this book is likely to be most interested in the military history of Europe from a Western European perspective, we have attempted to search out sources from further afield wherever possible—while nevertheless including a core of selections that will maintain the book's usefulness for classes in Western European history of one kind or another.

In sum, the diverse sources we have selected for this reader aim both to respect a past historiography and to encourage future study for student and scholar alike.

RECOMMENDED READING

The editors recommend the following overview volumes on warfare in the Middle Ages, which will do much to provide additional contexts for the readings herein:

- DeVries, Kelly, and Robert Douglas Smith. *Medieval Military Technology.* 2nd edition. Toronto: University of Toronto Press, 2012.
- Nicholson, Helen. *Medieval Warfare.* New York: Palgrave Macmillan, 2004.
- Rogers, Clifford J. *Soldiers' Lives through History: The Middle Ages.* Westport, CT: Greenwood Press, 2007.
- Verbruggen, J.F. *The Art of Warfare in Western Europe during the Middle Ages: From the Eighth Century to 1340.* Trans. S. Willard and R.W. Southern. 2nd edition. Woodbridge, UK: The Boydell Press, 1997.

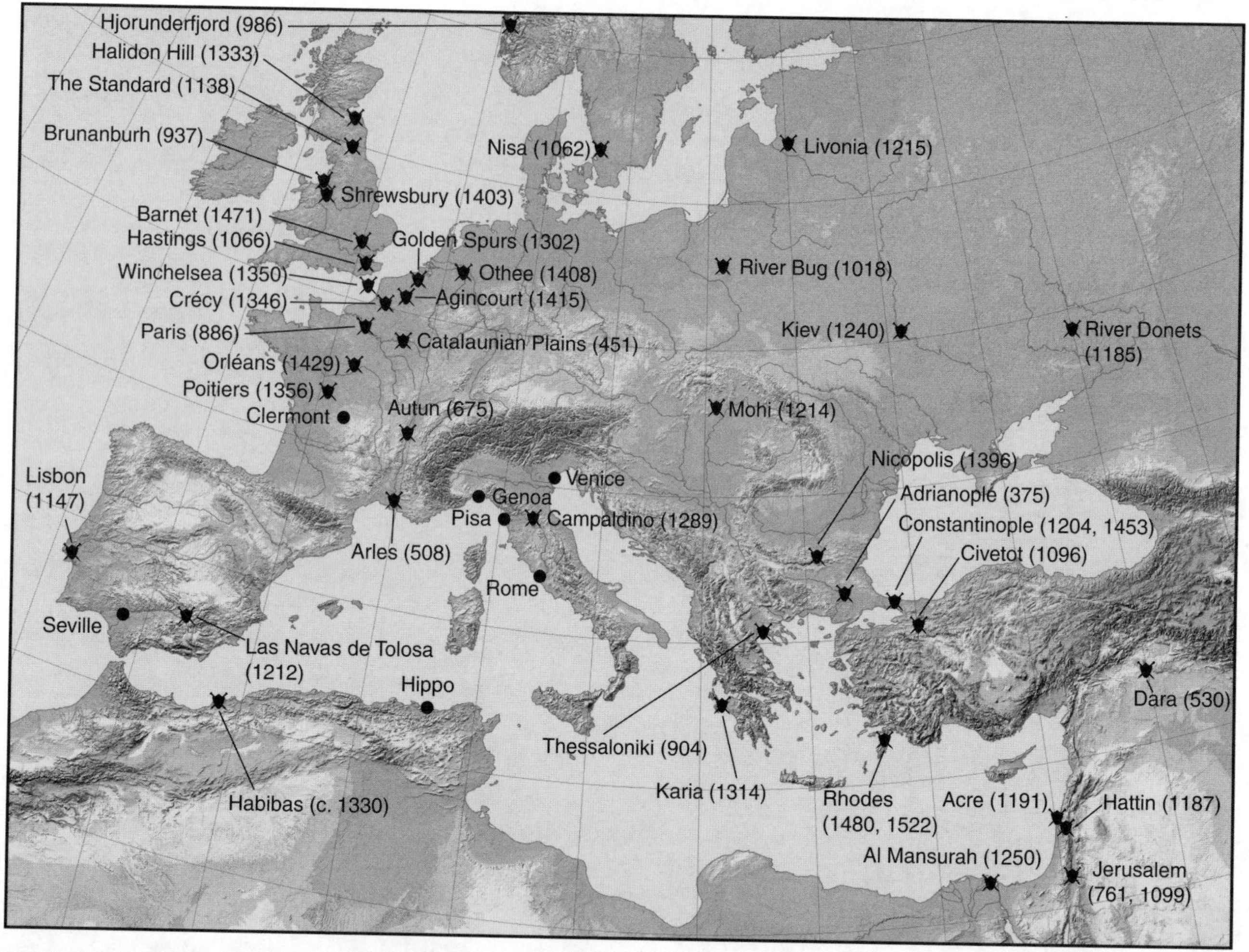

Relief map of Europe, showing the location of battles and other major sites mentioned in this book.

PART ONE

THE CASUALTIES OF WAR

A. THOSE WHO MOURNED

1. ON THE THURINGIAN WAR (AFTER 561)

Though published as a work of Venantius Fortunatus, this 172-line poem appears instead to be the work of his friend, Saint Radegund of Thuringia; if so, it is the first commentary on warfare written by a woman in medieval history. Despite its brevity, her poem, about one of the wars between Merovingian kings, is a powerful statement about the devastation of armed conflict, vividly describing the destruction not just to the buildings and landscapes but also to the people fallen and left behind. Sometimes, she suggests, it can be harder to survive this type of violence than to die.

Source: trans. Jo Ann McNamara, "Radegund, Queen of the Franks and Abess of Poitiers (ca. 525–587)," in *Sainted Women of the Dark Ages*, ed. Jo Ann McNamara, John E. Halborg, and E. Gordon Whatley (Durham, NC: Duke University Press, 1992), pp. 65–66.

Oh, sad state of war, malevolent destiny
  that fells proud kingdoms in a sudden slide!
The roofs that stood so long in happiness are broken
  to lie fallen beneath the vast charred ruin.
The palace courts, where art once flourished
  are vaulted now with sad, glowing ashes.
Towers artfully gilded, then shone golden-red,
  now drifting ashes blur the glitter to pallor.
The captive maid given to a hostile lord, her power fell,
  from the heights of glory to the lowest depths.
The entourage of servants, standing resplendent, her youthful peers
  where dead is a day, besmirched with funeral ashes.
The bright attendant halo of powerful ministers,
  now lie still without tomb or funeral service.
The conquering flame belching, reddens the gold hair of her beloved
  while the milk-white woman lies on the ground.
Alas, the corpses lie shamefully unburied on the field,
  an entire people, strewn in a common grave.

Not Troy alone must mourn her ruins:
  the Thuringian land suffered equal slaughter.
The matron was rapt away, with streaming hair, bound fast
  without even a sad farewell to the household gods.
Nor could the captive press a kiss on the threshold
  nor cast one backward glance toward what was lost.
A wife's naked feet trod in her husband's blood
  and the tender sister stepped over the fallen brother.
The boy torn from his mother's embrace, his funeral plaint
  hung on her lips, with all her tears unshed.
So to lose the life of a child is not the heaviest lot,
  gasping, the mother lost even her pious tears.
I, the barbarian woman, seek not to count these tears,
  nor to keep afloat in the melancholy lake of all those drops.
Each one had her own tears: I alone have them all,
  anguish is private and public both to me.
Fate was kind to those whom the enemy struck down.
  I, the sole survivor, must weep for them all.
Not only must I mourn the near ones who died:
  I also grieve for those still blessed with life.
My face often moistened, my eyes are blurred,
  my murmurs are secret but my care unstilled.

2. WULF AND EADWACER (c. 1000)

War leaves victims far beyond the battlefield. Just one such story might lie behind "Wulf and Eadwacer," a brief poem widely considered to be one of the most enigmatic works in Old English—and perhaps of the Middle Ages entirely. Various readings have been given to its mystery, but one of the most common is that it is the lament of a woman whose life and love have been fractured by war.

Source: trans. Michael Livingston, from the *Exeter Book*, Dean and Chapter Library of Exeter Cathedral, MS 3501, fols. 100v–101r.

To my people it is as if one gives them an offering:
They desire to take him if he comes against the threat.
  It is different with us.
Wulf is on one isle, I on another;
That island is fast, surrounded by fens;
Blood-thirsty men are there on the isle:

They desire to take him if he comes against the threat.
It goes differently with us.
I dogged the far-wanderings of my Wulf with expectations:
When the weather was rainy, and I sat grief-withdrawn,
When the battle-bold forequarters laid down by me;
There was joy to me in that, yet it was also hateful to me.
Wulf, my Wulf, my expectations of you
Caused sickness, your infrequent visits,
A mourning spirit—though not through starvation.
Do you hear, wealth-watcher? Our ready whelp
Wulf bears to the wood.
Man easily rends apart that which was never assembled:
The riddle of us together.

3. A CRUSADER'S LAMENT (1096–1300)

This moving lament, ostensibly written by a departing crusader, reveals the deep emotional pain of a soldier who must leave his home and his love behind as he departs for battle on foreign shores. The journey would be long—just getting there would take months—and the probability of return slim. A soldier could be slain in battle, but just as easily die from accident, disease, or deprivation. Likely, he would never see his home or family again. No matter his dedication to the cause, and his dreams of eternal rewards, the realities of loss in this world torment him.

Source: trans. Michael Livingston, from Joseph Bédier and Pierre Aubry, *Les chansons de croisade* (Paris: Honoré Champion, 1909), pp. 283–85.

To have a perfect joy in paradise
I must leave that land I love so much,
Where she lives whom I am thankful for each day—
her body gentle and lithe, her face fresh and lovely.
My heart surrenders all to her,
Yet my body must depart from her:
I am leaving for that place where God suffered death
To ransom us on a Friday.
Sweet love, I have a great sorrow in my heart
Now that I must leave you in the end,
One with whom I've found such goodness, such kindness,
Such joy and solace—everything to please me!
But Fortune by her power has made me

Exchange my joy for a sadness and pain
That I'll feel for you for many days and nights.
In this way will I go to serve my Creator.
No more than an infant can suffer hunger-pains—
And no one can scold him for crying about it—
Do I believe that I have the power to stay away
From you, whom I would kiss and embrace.
Nor do I have the strength of abstinence:
One hundred times a night I'll recall your face!
I took such pleasure in holding your body,
That when I have it no more, I'll die of desire.
Benevolent God, if for you I must thus leave
The country where she is, whom I love so much,
I ask you to give us heavenly joy for all time,
My love and me, through your mercy.
And give to her the power to love me,
That she won't forget me in my long sojourn,
Because I adore her more than anything in the world;
I'm in such pitiable sorrow that my heart breaks.
Beautiful Isabel, I commend you to God.
No longer can I remain with you.
Into pagan lands, among a miscreant people,
I must thus leave for the love of God.
To save my soul, I go with good intent,
But remember well, beautiful and gentle love,
That if we died for loving loyally,
I wouldn't survive to see the port of the sea.
For just as the flower blooms from the branch,
The great pain that torments me springs from you.
But, should I come back, I swear by saintly relics,
That it will be to serve and honor you.
I sing of loyal love where I have my intent,
Nor do I wish for my heart to repent;
But I wish it known to my lord of Gisors
That loyal love is the highest of honors.

4. DESTRUCTION FROM THE HUNDRED YEARS WAR (1361)

In this excerpt from a 27 July 1361 letter urging his countrymen to support the Treaty of Brétigny (1360), King Jean II of France describes the destruction his country had experienced through the first decades of the Hundred Years War. For all the horror that he decries, Jean II's hope for a lasting peace would not be achieved. The Hundred Years War would re-erupt within nine years of the treaty's ratification and last until 1453.

Source: trans. Michael Livingston, from *Procès-verbal de délivrance à Jean Chandos*, ed. A. Bardonnet (Niort, France: Clouzot, 1869), pp. 14–17.

The wars that have endured so long—between our very dear lord and father formerly the king of France [Philip VI], while he was living, and after his death between us on the one side and the king of England our brother [Edward III], who has claimed to have a right to this realm on the other side—have brought great damages not only to us and to you, but to all the people of our realm and of the neighboring realms and to all Christendom, as you yourselves know well. Because in these wars many deadly battles have been fought, people slaughtered, churches pillaged, bodies and souls destroyed, young girls and virgins deflowered, respectable wives and widows dishonored, towns, manors, and buildings burned, and robberies, cruelties, and ambushes committed on the paths and roads. Justice has failed, the Christian faith has chilled, and commerce has died, and so many other evils and horrible things have followed from these wars that they cannot be spoken, numbered, or written down. And not only these two realms, but the other realms of Christendom, too, have sustained many afflictions and irreparable damages.

B. THOSE WHO FOUGHT

5. RIDDLES ON ARMAMENTS (c. 1000)

The widespread familiarity with the implements of warfare in Anglo-Saxon England is suggested by the fact that they are the subject of several riddles preserved in the famous Exeter Book. *The solutions to the two riddles provided here are commonly understood to be "shield" and "bow."*

Source: trans. Michael Livingston, from *The Exeter Book*, in *Anglo-Saxon Poetic Records: A Collective Edition*, vol. 3, ed. George Philip Krapp and Elliot Van Kirk Dobbie (New York: Columbia University Press, 1936).

Riddle 5

Alone I am,   wounded by iron,
Battered by blades,   battle-work sated,
Weary of swords.   Often I see war,
Fighting so fierce;   no hope I foresee:
I won't be spared   from the struggle's heat
Until I am eaten   entirely by men.

The hammered blades will batter me on,
Hard-edged and sharp, the hand-work of smiths,
Biting my lips. I ever abide
A contest more cruel. Never could I find
Among town's folk a leech fine enough,
Who could with herbs heal my harsh wounds:
Gashes from the edge grow ever greater
By deadly strikes both day and night.

Riddle 23

"Wob" is my name, meant back to front.
Beautiful I am, shaped for the battle.
Whenever I'm bent there flies from my bosom
A venomous dart. Very eager I am
To drive from afar that deadly foe.
When my master who most knows my shape
Lets go my limb, I am longer than I was—
Until I spit forth that death-blended spew,
Fell-to-all poison that first I pulled in.
This thing I quip no man withdraws quick
If it flings from me and touches him free;
He purchases with all his power
A fatal drink, a full atonement.
Unbound I obey not a single one
Until skillfully strung: so say what I am named.

6. MASSACRE AT CIVETOT (1096)

Unanticipated by Urban II when he called the First Crusade at the Council of Clermont in 1095 (doc. 14), preachers, the most famous of which was known as Peter the Hermit, took the pope's message to the general populace. Inflamed by the same spirit as nobles and other soldiers, thousands—largely peasants—joined together in the so-called People's Crusade and marched to the Holy Land. By a cruel act of fate, their arrival at Constantinople preceded that of the soldiers. The Byzantines fed the fanatical mob and transported them across the Bosporus where they split into linguistic groups, the Germans and the Franks. There they met the Muslim army of Kilij Arslan. Though women were an essential part of most military campaigns in the Middle Ages, few accounts record their presence. Here Albert of Aachen, in his History of the Journey to Jerusalem, *tells the story of the battle of Civetot, a disastrous defeat that ended the People's Crusade. Aside from underscoring the superiority of the Muslim forces over the rag-tag Christian army, Albert's recounting makes note of the women and children who were present on the ill-fated expedition.*

Source: trans. James A. Brundage, *The Crusades: A Documentary Survey* (Minneapolis: Marquette University Press, 1962), pp. 31–36.

The Turkish prince and leader Kilij Arslan, when he heard of the arrival of the Christians ... gathered together fifteen thousand of his Turks from all over Asia Minor and Khurasan. His troops were highly skilled in warfare and were extremely dextrous archers, using bows made either of horn or bone. Two days after they had assembled, a considerably exaggerated report of the German victories was brought from afar to the city of Nicaea. Kilij Arslan's sorrow and wrath were further magnified by the stories about the Germans, by the loss of his fortress, and by the defeat and expulsion of his garrison.

At sunrise on the third day, therefore, Kilij Arslan and all his forces set out from their encampment at Nicaea ... [against] the Germans ... The first groups of the Turkish force assailed and beat down the Germans so decisively that the Germans, who fought back ferociously, were unable to hold their defensive positions and were forced from the walls and battlements by a heavy hail of arrows. The poor unprotected Germans then took shelter in the stronghold from the Turkish missiles. When the Turks saw that they had forced the Germans back from the walls and battlements, they prepared to make their way over the walls. The Germans within the fort, however, were still striving anxiously to save their own lives. Some of the Germans brought up their lances to stave off the entering Turks, while others fought them back with swords and double-edged axes. In the face of this resistance the Turks dared not continue the assault.

Since they had not cowed the Germans by showering them with a hail of arrows, the Turks now assembled all kinds of wood at the gate of the fort. They kindled it and it burst into flames. A number of buildings within the compound were also ignited. At length the flames and heat grew so intense that some of the Germans were consumed, while others, hoping for safety, leaped from the walls. The Turks outside the walls slaughtered the fugitives with swords. They took captive about two hundred whose youthful features and bodies made them attractive. All the rest were killed by arrows or by the sword.

When Kilij Arslan and his men had withdrawn with their German captives, following this dreadful fray, the news of the slaughter of the Germans reached Peter [the Hermit]'s camp. The spirits of the group were greatly dampened by the defeat of their comrades. Moved by the misfortunes of their companions, they took frequent counsel with one another to decide whether to set out immediately to revenge their comrades' slaughter or to wait for Peter, who had left some time before to journey to the Emperor at Constantinople, where he sought better marketing conditions for his men.

In their councils with one another, Walter the Penniless held out against a foray to avenge their brethren until the situation was clarified and until the return of Peter, on whose advice they would act. Walter's plan quieted the people for eight days, while they awaited Peter. Peter, however, was unable to secure the Emperor's permission to return.

On the eighth day a hundred Turkish soldiers, men illustrious in the art of war, set out from Nicaea.... These Turks took it upon themselves that day to behead a great many Crusaders who were roving hither and yon in groups of ten or fifteen or a few more. When the rumor reached Peter's camp that the Turks were near and that they had beheaded the roaming Crusaders, the men refused to believe that the Turks had come so far away from Nicaea. Some of the Crusaders advised, however, that they give chase to the Turks, were any discovered in that vicinity.

Meanwhile, when the truth became known, a tumult arose among the people. All the infantrymen called together Walter the Penniless, Rainald of Breis, Walter of Breteuil, and Fulk of Orleans, who were the leaders of Peter's army. They asked the leaders whether they should all rise up against the insolence of these Turks, but the leaders forbade any attacks until they could consult Peter upon his return. The master of the infantry, Geoffrey Burel, listened to their replies and then asserted that the timid were scarcely worthy as much as brave knights in battle. He made a harsh speech in which he repeated his charges and rebuked the men who forbade the troops to follow the Turks and to revenge their brethren. The army leaders, on the other hand, were unable to bear any longer the charges and insults of Geoffrey and of their own followers. Deeply moved by wrath and indignation, the leaders agreed to set out against the Turkish snares and plots, no matter what the cost. There was no delay. All the cavalry and infantry troops throughout the camp were ordered to arise at the first light of dawn on the fourth day. They were then to sound on their horns the signals to assemble for battle. Only the sick and those without weapons were left in the camp, together with a countless number of women. Twenty-five thousand armed infantrymen and five hundred armored knights were assembled and started on their way to the city of Nicaea in order to avenge their comrades by provoking Kilij Arslan and the other Turks to battle. The army was divided and was arranged in six divisions, with the standard bearers marching on the right and left flanks of the group. Peter was still absent and his wishes were unknown.

The army marched barely three miles from the gate of the stronghold at Civetot, making its way noisily with loud boasts and much shouting through mountain and forest. Suddenly Kilij Arslan and his whole reprehensible army entered the forest from the other side. The enemy were coming from Nicaea to make a surprise attack upon the Frankish camp and thus to slaughter and annihilate with swords those who were unprepared and unwary. When Kilij Arslan heard the noise made by the advancing Christians he was very anxious to know who was responsible for the uproar, for he was quite unaware of the

Christians' intentions. As soon as he learned that the Crusaders were there, he addressed his men:

"The Franks, whom we were going to trap, are here. Undoubtedly they are on their way to attack us. Let us, therefore, withdraw from the forest and the mountains into the open plains. There we can engage them freely in battle, while they can find no place of refuge." Kilij Arslan's directions were carried out without delay, and in deep silence they left the forest and mountains.

The Franks, of course, were unaware of Kilij Arslan's arrival. They came out of the forest and mountains with much shouting and noise-making. Then, for the first time, they gazed in amazement at Kilij Arslan's forces standing in battle formation in the midst of the plain, covering them for battle. When the Franks caught sight of them, they began to comfort one another in the name of the Lord. They sent on ahead two divisions which included five hundred knights.

Kilij Arslan, when he saw the two divisions advance, at once loosened the reins of his horse and unleashed his men. Their unheard-of shouting terrified and stupefied the Catholic knights. Then the Turks sent a shower of arrows into the midst of the two divisions. As a result of this, the scattered survivors of those divisions were separated from the multitude which followed them.

The rest of the Crusading army had not yet marched out of the forest when they heard the clash of aims and the cruel attack of the shouting Turks. The Crusaders assembled in one group on the narrow path by which they were travelling and tried to block and hold the path through the mountains. Meanwhile, the two divisions which the Turks had broken up and divided from their Christian companions, found that they could not return to the forest and mountains and so began to take the road to Nicaea. All at once, they turned around and, shouting loudly, they flew back into the midst of the Turks. Knights and foot soldiers encouraged one another, and in a short time, they had killed two hundred Turks. The Turks saw that the force of the Christian cavalry was grinding down their men. Accordingly, they shot arrows which wounded the horses of the Crusaders. Thus the strongest of Christ's athletes were turned into foot soldiers.

Walter the Penniless was struck by seven arrows through his mail coat and belly and was laid to rest there. Rainald of Breis and Fulk of Chartres—men famous in their own country—suffered a similar martyrdom when they were destroyed by the enemy and died, though not without a great slaughter of Turks. Walter of Breteuil, the son of Waleran, and Geoffrey Burel, the master of the infantry, escaped by taking flight through the bramble and bush. This whole group withdrew from the fight, assembled, and fled by a narrow path. When it became known that they had fled and forsaken the rest all the men took flight, speedily hurrying back toward Civetot on the same road by which they had come, but now they were scarcely able to defend themselves from the enemy.

The Turks, accordingly, rejoined in the good fortune of their success and victory. They beheaded the piteous handful of Crusaders, whom they followed for three miles, killing them as they went along, all the way into Peter's camp. They entered the camp and found there the feeble and the sick, clerics, aged women, monks, and infants. All of these they destroyed with swords, irrespective of age. They took alive only those delicate girls and nuns whose appearance and figures appealed to them, as well as some beardless youths of attractive appearance. They carried off to Nicaea the money, clothing, mules, horses, and all the other valuables, along with the tents.

On the seashore, alongside the aforementioned town of Civetot, there was an old deserted fort and to this place three thousand of the Crusaders took flight, entering the crumbling fort in the hope of defending themselves there. Since there were no gates or defensive works, they used their shields for a gate, while they cleverly piled up rocks at the entrance for they were afraid and bereft of help. They fought for life itself, defending themselves from the enemy only with spears, the wooden bow, and stone missiles. The Turks, since they were able to accomplish only a part of their plan to kill those within the fort, surrounded the structure, which was roofless, and shot arrows into the air. When the arrows dropped down out of the sky, they hit the defenders, killing the poor wretches. The rest of the men, when they saw this, were forced to consider surrendering, for a great many are reported to have been wounded and killed there in this fashion. They feared even crueler treatment from these godless men, however, and so neither arms nor force would bring them to leave the fort.

Now the sun had marked midday when the three thousand men had entered the fort and had been besieged by the Turks. They defended themselves vigorously, not by the cleverness of their strategy, but because they were fighting for life itself. At last, during the night, a loyal, Catholic, Greek messenger was able to sail across the sea to find Peter, who was in the royal city. The messenger reported the dangers besetting the Crusaders and the devastation and destruction of the rest. When Peter learned of the dangers to his men and of the tragedy of those who had been annihilated, he went, weeping and grieving, to beseech the Emperor in Christ's name to assist those wretched Crusaders, the few who were left out of so many thousands. He begged the Emperor not to allow his anguished men to be destroyed and consumed by such executioners.

The Emperor heard Peter's report of the defeat and besieging of the Crusaders and was moved to pity. He summoned his Turcopoles and all the nations of his realm and ordered them to cross the straits to assist the fugitive and besieged Christians and to drive the assaulting Turks from the siege. When the Turks got wind of the Emperor's command, they marched away from the fort, taking their Christian captives and much booty with them. And so the surrounded and besieged Crusading soldiers were freed from these godless men.

7. BATTLE OF WAUN GASEG (c. 1410)

First-person accounts of military actions during the Middle Ages are relatively rare, which makes this deft, light-hearted poem all the more remarkable: Welsh poet Llywelyn ab y Moel mocks his own actions (or inactions) during an engagement at "Waun Gaseg," which has been tentatively identified as a location in Radnorshire. Llywelyn had joined the rebellion of Owain Glyndŵr during its last years, when it was largely reduced to a guerilla campaign of preying on the English from forest and mountain hide-outs.

Source: trans. John K. Bollard, in *Owain Glyndŵr: A Casebook,* ed. Michael Livingston and John K. Bollard (Liverpool: Liverpool University Press, 2013), pp. 129–33.

We were fine today,
a ready war band, on the brow of the hill,
strong, faultless fine folk,
setting out with fair, resolute determination,
with the intent of getting—splendid portent—
the greatest news about Owain.
We held, before any dull-witted complaint,
a discussion before engaging in battle,
declaring our purpose of sharing
the profit if the host was slain.
All those of eager sort gave
their oath, before seeing the men,
that they would not ever—they would deserve fame—
retreat from the field, because of an attack.
And as we were thus, after a song of praise,
debating about abundant fame,
behold, we could see close by us,
set loose amongst us—strange was the turn of events—
along the bracken-covered slope,
horses, more than a hundred of them,
and with them—grounds for complaint—
a high, piercing cry.
A splendidly advantageous harsh tune was raised
(an odious French badger-keeper leers,
ape's jawbone playing a tabor)
from a clarion louder than a mighty gun.

Disheartened spirit, sally with no losses,
we, for our part, after our earlier words,
had no intent, along the moorland,
to stay in the battle for a moment,
or to have a trial of arms—swift scattering attack—
or to use a cuirass until we fled!
The host that we had angered
was there in great numbers chasing us.
They were energetic in chasing us;
they chased us across nine streams,
the pick of men from Caer Wysg's fort,
a goat chase, heady in their attire.
A sorry turn of events, a blow to our pride,
it was painful for us to see—I am a witness—
at Waun Gaseg, unbloodied bundle,
the spears of our men in the grass.
As for me—sad bravado—
I gained an advantage from the battle,
making at breakneck speed
for a ravine with a great host behind me,
and all of them pointing me out fleeing,
recognizing me there.
Dull-witted, on the slope of a big mountain,
is a man with unstained cuirass—unfortunate event!
Because of this—summons without encounter—
let them return, when they wish;
I'll be damned if they see me
and my unbloodied cuirass in the hollow on the Waun!

8. PITY THE VETERAN SOLDIERS (c. 1420)

The plight of neglected war veterans—frequently wounded in mind or body—was a recurrent issue throughout the Middle Ages (as it is today). Here, the poet Thomas Hoccleve writes an impassioned plea for the current generation of knights not to forget their too-often destitute and potentially disabled forebears.

Source: trans. Michael Livingston, from Thomas Hoccleve, *The Regiment of Princes*, ed. C.R. Blyth (Kalamazoo, MI: Medieval Institute Publications, 1999).

O fickle world! Alas, your variance!
How many gentlemen may men now see,

Who before in the old wars of France,
Honored were, and held most fondly
For their prowess in arms, and plenty
Of friends had in youth, and now, for shame,
Alas, their fellowship is crooked and lame.
Now age decrepit shuts away favor,
That flowery youth in his season conquered;
Now all forgotten is the manly labor
Through which so often they their foes a-feared,
Now be those worthy men beaten with the rod
Of need, alas! And none has for them pity;
Pity, I believe, is buried, by my honesty.
If she be dead, God have her soul, I pray;
And so shall more hereafter pray, I know.
He who pretends to have the highest nobility;
If he lacks her, shall well figure and know
That cruelty, her foe, may for just a brief row
Permit him to live in any wealth;
A compassionate heart, to body and soul is health.
You old men of arms who know
By sight and by report their worthiness,
Let not such misfortune those men overthrow!
Show them your manly kindness!
You young men who engage in prowess
Of arms, honor your old forefathers you should;
Help them yourselves, or procure for them some good!
Knighthood, awake! You sleep too long;
Your brother, you see, nears death in neglectfulness;
Awake, and sorrow upon his pains so strong!
If you hereafter come into such distress
You would also long for relief;
You are not certain what to you will befall:
Wealth is slippery; beware lest you fall!
...
God wills that the needy be relieved;
It is one of the works of mercy;
And since those men who were in arms decreed,
Are into poverty fallen, truly
You men of arms ought especially
To help them: alas! have you no piteous blood
That might stir you to do for them some good?

C. THOSE WHO FEARED

9. AFTER THE SIEGE OF ARLES (507–508)

Caesarius was the Catholic bishop of Arles when the city, then controlled by Visigoths, was besieged by a Frankish and Burgundian army. The besiegers were Catholic, while those besieged were mostly Arian Christians, so there is some question in other sources about Caesarius's collaboration with his city's enemies, although he was welcomed back to his position following the Ostrogothic raising of the siege after several months. In an early sermon following the siege, Caesarius describes the suffering of common people caught in the midst of such a vicious military action.

Source: trans. M.M. Mueller, Caesarius of Arles, *Sermons*, vol. 1 (Washington, DC: Catholic University of America, 1956), pp. 331–32.

But since dire calamity struck our eyes at the time of the siege and now afflicts them in time of death, and scarcely anyone survives to care for the bodies of men who have died and need burial, consider also those evils which we have borne through the just judgement of God, when entire provinces were led into captivity, mothers of families abducted, pregnant women carried off, little children torn from arms and thrown into the road, half-dead, while their nurses are not permitted to keep living children or to bury the dead. On all sides there is great agony and grief. One bewails her little child thrown to the birds and dogs; another fears to offend her barbarian master. Fear and horror equally continue to torture hearts. Burdens are placed on their shoulders; their spirit is worn out from great torments, their body exhausted by heavy loads. Wicked savage power especially demanded of such women that one who knew she was mistress of many slaves suddenly grieved that she was a servant of the barbarians and without wealth. [...] The barbarians demanded hard services of delicate, noble women without any compassionate pity. While we see and behold such calamities, the noise of their shouting rises to our ears from those who lost their husbands or parents in that siege. Is the flesh of men unfeeling, even if stony feelings are found in some men? Who would not grieve upon hearing and seeing this, and in the person of those who were struck bewail himself rather than them?

10. DEVASTATION OF VILLAGES (1215)

Following set-backs in the Middle East with the failure of the Third Crusade to recapture Jerusalem and of the Fourth Crusade to even reach the Holy Land (although it did conquer the Byzantine capital of Constantinople), several crusades were launched against closer non-Catholic foes. The largest and longest of these was into Northeastern Europe.

Such wars, fought between religious opponents, were always bloody. But, as can be read in the chronicle of eyewitness Henry of Livonia, this crusade—led and manned mostly by the military monastic order of the Teutonic Knights—was particularly ruthless.

Source: trans. James A. Brundage, Henricus Lettus, *The Chronicle of Henry of Livonia*, ed. James A. Brundage (New York: Columbia University Press, 2003), pp. 144–47.

Meanwhile, the Saccalians and the Ungannians had also come into the land of the Letts with a great army. They besieged the fort of Autine, and the Brothers of the Militia [non-knightly associates of the Teutonic Knights], wishing to fight with them, left Wenden. When the Saccalians and Ungannians got word of this, they, too, fled. They came to Tricatia toward evening and found that Thalibald had come back from the hiding places of the forest for a bath. They seized him and cruelly burned him, still alive, before a fire, threatening to kill him unless he would show them all of his money. He showed them fifty *oseringi*, but, nevertheless, they burned him. He said: "If I were to show you all my money and all my sons' money, you would burn me nonetheless," and he would show them no more. They put him again into the fire, therefore, and roasted him like a fish, until he gave up the spirit and died. Since he was a Christian and one of the number of faithful Letts, we hope that his soul is gladly rejoicing for such a martyrdom in eternal happiness in the company of the holy martyrs. The Esthonians returned to their own land and the Lord reduced their plan to nothing. Then Rameke and Drivinalde, the sons of Thalibald, seeing that their father was dead, were greatly angered at the Esthonians. They and their friends and relatives collected an army of Letts, and the Brothers of the Militia from Wenden and other Germans went with them. They entered Ungannia, despoiled all the villages, and delivered them to the flames. They burned alive all the men they could capture in revenge for Thalibald. They burned down all the forts, so that they would have no refuge in them. They sought out the Ungannians in the dark hiding places of the forests and the Ungannians could hide from them nowhere. They took them out of the forests and killed them and took the women and children away as captives. They drove off the horses and flocks, took many spoils, and returned to their own land. As they returned, other Letts again met them on the road and they marched into Ungannia. What the former had neglected, the latter performed. For these men went to the villages and provinces to which the others had not come and whoever had escaped from the earlier men could not escape from these. They seized many people, killed all the men, and dragged away the women and children as captives. They took away with them the flocks and much loot. As they returned, again they met other Letts on the road, prepared for an expedition into Ungannia; they, too, wished to take booty. They also sought to kill men in revenge for their parents and relatives who had earlier been killed by the Esthonians. They proceeded into

Ungannia, which they despoiled no less than the former army had and they took no fewer captives than the earlier ones had. They seized the people who were coming out of the forests to their fields or villages for food. Some they burned, while they cut the throats of others. They inflicted various tortures upon them, until the Esthonians showed them all their money and until they led them to all the hiding places of the woods and delivered the women and children into their hands. But even so the hatred of the Letts was not slaked. After carrying off the money and all the possessions, the women and children, at last they took life, too, the only thing left. They crossed all of the provinces up to the Mother of Waters at Dorpat and spared no one. They killed all of the males, took the women and children captive, and took revenge upon their enemies. Then they joyfully returned to their homes with all their loot. Likewise Berthold of Wenden with his men, Theodoric the bishop's brother with his knights and servants, and the sons of Thalibald with their Letts gathered together. They went with an army into Ungannia and seized many of the Esthonians, who had earlier escaped from the Letts, and killed them. They burned the villages which remained and whatever had been done incompletely by the first groups was carefully completed by them. They went around through all the provinces and, crossing the Mother of Waters, they went up to Waiga. They ravaged and burned the villages no less in the land across the river. They killed the men, took the women and children, and after doing all the harm they could, they returned to Livonia. They arranged for still other men to return immediately to Ungannia and to do similar harm to the Ungannians and when they came back they sent still others in turn. The Letts did not stop nor did they allow the Esthonians in Ungannia to rest. They did not have any rest themselves, until during that same summer, devastating the land with nine armies, they made it so deserted and desolate that now neither men nor food were found there. Their aim was to fight long enough so that either those who were left would come to seek peace and baptism or they would be completely wiped out from the earth. It came to pass that by now the sons, in order to avenge their father, had killed over a hundred men, either by burning them alive or by various other tortures. These were in addition to the innumerable others whom each of the Letts, Germans, and Livonians had slaughtered.

11. LOCAL ATROCITIES (1358)

Following the Black Death of 1347–48, their number of soldiers having declined so that sieges and battles became more risky endeavors, the English began following a new strategy in the Hundred Years War, the chevauchée. *This was a raid—sometimes fast moving, sometimes lingering in places for weeks—in which troops were let loose to terrorize the non-combatant population through pillage, destruction, and murder.* Chevauchées *were powerfully effective in causing terror, as described in this account by Hugues de*

Montgeron, a rural prior in the diocese of Sens. But they did not, as hoped, draw French armies from the protection of the high and thick walls of their large cities.

Source: Clifford J. Rogers, "By Fire and Sword: *Bellum Hostile* and Civilians in the Hundred Years' War," in *Civilians in the Path of War*, ed. Mark Grimsley and Clifford J. Rogers (Lincoln: University of Nebraska Press, 2002), pp. 48–49.

In the year of our Lord 1358 the English came to Chantecocq and captured the castle on Halloween. The same evening they burned almost all of the town and then brought the whole countryside under their control, ordering the towns, both great and small, to ransom all their possessions—namely, bodies, goods, and movables—or else they would burn the houses. This they did in many places. Confounded and completely terrorized in this fashion, many of the people submitted to the English, paying them ransom money and agreeing to provide them with cash, flour, oats, and many other necessary supplies, if they would stop for a while the aforementioned torments because they had already killed many men in different places. Some they shut up in dark dungeons, threatening them daily with death, and continually making them suffer with whippings, wounds, hunger, and deprivation beyond belief. But others had nothing with which to pay ransom or were unwilling to submit to the power of the English. To escape from their hands these people made themselves huts in the woods and there ate their bread with fear, sorrow, and every misery. But the English learned of this and resolutely sought out these hiding places, searching numerous woods and putting many men to death there.... [I] put together a hut in the woods of les Queues and stayed there with many of my neighbors, seeing and hearing every day about the vicious and wicked work of our enemies: namely, houses burned and many dead left lying like animals throughout the villages and hamlets. Seeing and hearing such things, I decided on December sixteenth to go to the city and stay there. But it happened that very night that these accursed English found their way to my hut so quietly that, in spite of the watchfulness of our sentinels, they almost captured me while I was asleep. But by God's grace and through the help of the blessed Virgin Mary I was awakened by the noise they made and escaped naked, taking nothing with me because of my haste except a habit with a hood. Crossing into the middle of the swamp I stayed there, trembling and shivering in the cold, which was then very great, while my hut was completely despoiled.

12. THE POOR IN WAR (1425)

Non-combatants who suffered in war included the poor laborers who worked the fields that armies would plunder for food or destroy for spite or strategic purposes. That these people were often forcibly conscripted into the war effort—to fight or, more likely, to labor in digging trenches, building bridges, foraging, or other necessary tasks—is shown in the repeated discussions in military manuals about whether it is appropriate or not. Christine de Pisan provides an answer.

Source: trans. Sumner Willard, Christine de Pizan, *The Book of Deeds of Arms and of Chivalry*, ed. Charity Cannon Willard (Philadelphia: Pennsylvania State University Press, 1999), pp. 171–72.

Here Inquiry Is Made Regarding the Right to Seize in Enemy Territory Simple Peasants Who Are Not Engaged in Warfare

I ask you whether a king or prince, when warring against another, even though the war may be just, has the right to overrun the enemy land and take prisoner all manner of people, including common people, that is, peasants, shepherds, and such like; it would appear not. Why should they bear the burden of the profession of arms, of which they know nothing? It is not for them to pass judgment about war; common people are not called on to bear arms; rather, it is distasteful to them, for they say they want to live in peace and ask no more. They should be free, it seems to me, just as all priests and churchmen are, because their estate is outside military activity. What honor can accrue to a prince in killing, overrunning, or seizing people who have never borne arms nor could make use of them, or poor innocent people who do nothing but till the land and watch over animals?

To this I would answer with a supposition like this: Let us suppose that the people of England wishes not to aid their king in injuring the king of France, and the French fell upon them instantly, with right and reason on his side. In accordance with lawful practice they should not in any way cause bodily harm to, or injure the property of, such people or those who did not come to aid the king, offering either goods or counsel. But if the subjects of that king or of another in a similar situation, be they poor or rich, farmers or anything else, give aid and comfort to maintain the war, according to military right the French may overrun their country and seize what they find, that is to say, prisoners of whatever class, and all manner of things, without being obliged of any law to return the same. For if a war is judged by the counselors of both kings or princes, the men-at-arms are free to dominate each other. And occasionally the poor and simple folk, who do not bear arms, are injured—and it cannot be otherwise, for weeds cannot be separated from good plants, because they are so close together that the good ones suffer. But in truth it is right that the valiant and good gentlemen-at-arms must take every precaution not to destroy the poor and simple folk, or suffer them to be tyrannized or mistreated, for they are Christians and not Saracens. And if I have said that pity is due some, remember that not less is due the others; those who engage in warfare may be hurt, but the humble and peaceful should be shielded from their force.

PART TWO

THE PREPARATIONS FOR WAR

A. THEORIES OF WAR

1. Just War

13. THE JUST WAR (BEFORE 430)

Few figures did more to shape the intellectual traditions of the Christian West than Saint Augustine of Hippo (d. 430), who in his numerous influential treatises covered a multiplicity of theological, ethical, and even political topics. Excerpted here is a sample of his commentary on whether the precepts of Christianity allow an individual to engage in violence if it is for the state or the church. Augustine's opinions in favor of necessary force—building on both biblical and ancient authorities—rather than uncompromising pacifism did much to define the flexible doctrine of "just war" for Christendom.

Source: trans. Richard Stothert, in *Augustine: The Writings against the Manichaeans, and against the Donatists*, vol. 4, ed. P. Schaff, *The Nicene and Post-Nicene Fathers*, 1st Ser. (Buffalo: The Christian Literature Company, 1897), pp. 300–03; revised.

73. According to the eternal law, which requires the preservation of natural order, and forbids the transgression of it, some actions have an indifferent [that is, neutral] character, so that men are blamed for presumption if they do them without being called upon, while they are deservedly praised for doing them when required. The act, the agent, and the authority for the action are all of great importance in the order of nature. For Abraham to sacrifice his son of his own accord is shocking madness. His doing so at the command of God proves him faithful and submissive....

74. ... [The] account of the wars of Moses will not excite surprise or abhorrence, for in wars carried on by divine command, he showed not ferocity but obedience; and God, in giving the command, acted not in cruelty, but in righteous retribution, giving to all what they deserved, and warning those who needed warning. What is the evil in war? Is it the death of some who will soon die in any case, that others may live in peaceful subjection? This is mere cowardly dislike, not any religious feeling. The real evils in war are love of violence, revengeful cruelty, fierce and implacable enmity, wild resistance, and the lust of power, and such like; and it is generally to punish these things,

when force is required to inflict the punishment, that, in obedience to God or some lawful authority, good men undertake wars, when they find themselves in such a position as regards the conduct of human affairs, that right conduct requires them to act, or to make others act, in this way. Otherwise John [the Baptist], when the soldiers who came to be baptized asked, "What shall we do?" would have replied, "Throw away your arms; give up the service; never strike, or wound, or disable anyone." But knowing that such actions in battle were not murderous, but authorized by law, and that the soldiers did not thus avenge themselves, but defended the public safety, he replied, "Do violence to no one, accuse no one falsely, and be content with your wages." ... Again, in the case of the centurion who said, "I am a man under authority, and have soldiers under me: and I say to one, 'Go,' and he goes; and to another, 'Come,' and he comes; and to my servant, 'Do this,' and he does it," Christ gave due praise to his faith; he did not tell him to leave the service. But there is no need here to enter on the long discussion of just and unjust wars.

75. A great deal depends on the causes for which men undertake wars, and on the authority they have for doing so; for the natural order, which seeks the peace of humankind, ordains that the monarch should have the power of undertaking war if he thinks it advisable, and that the soldiers should perform their military duties in behalf of the peace and safety of the community. When war is undertaken in obedience to God, who would rebuke, or humble, or crush our human pride, it must be allowed to be a righteous war; for even the wars which arise from human passion cannot harm the eternal well-being of God, nor even hurt his saints; for in the trial of their patience, and the chastening of their spirit, and in bearing fatherly correction, they are rather benefited than injured. No one can have any power against them but what is given him from above. For there is no power but of God, who either orders or permits. Since, therefore, a righteous man, serving perhaps under an ungodly king, may do the duty belonging to his position in the state in fighting by the order of his sovereign—for in some cases it is plainly the will of God that he should fight, and in others, where this is not so plain, it may be an unrighteous command on the part of the king, while the soldier is innocent, because his position makes obedience a duty—how much more must the one be blameless who carries on war on the authority of God, of whom everyone who serves him knows that he can never require what is wrong?

76. If it is supposed that God could not enjoin warfare, because in after times it was said by the Lord Jesus Christ, "I say unto you, that you resist not evil: but if anyone strike you on the right cheek, turn to him the left also," the answer is that what is here required is not a bodily action but an inward disposition.... Thus the name martyrs, which means witnesses, was given to those who, by

the will of God, bore this testimony, by their confessions, their sufferings, and their death. The number of such witnesses is so great that, if it pleased Christ ... to unite them all in one army, and to give them success in battle, as he gave to the Hebrews, what nation could withstand them? What kingdom would remain unsubdued? But as the doctrine of the New Testament is that we must serve God not for temporal happiness in this life, but for eternal felicity hereafter, this truth was most strikingly confirmed by the patient endurance of what is commonly called adversity for the sake of that felicity. So in the fullness of time the Son of God ... sends his disciples as sheep in to the midst of wolves, and bids them not fear those that can kill the body, but cannot kill the soul, and promises that even the body will be entirely restored, so that not a hair shall be lost. Peter's sword he orders back into its sheath, restoring, as it was before, the ear of his enemy that had been cut off. He says that he could obtain legions of angels to destroy his enemies, but that he must drink the cup which his Father's will had given him. He sets the example of drinking this cup, then hands it to his followers, manifesting thus, both in word and in deed, the grace of patience....

78. It is therefore mere groundless calumny to charge Moses with making war, for there would have been less harm in making war of his own accord, than in not doing it when God commanded him. And to dare to find fault with God himself for giving such a command, or not to believe that a just and good God did so, shows, to say the least, an inability to consider that in the view of divine providence, which pervades all things from the highest to the lowest, time can neither add anything nor take away; but all things go, or come, or remain according to the order of nature or what is deserved in each separate case, while in humans a right will is in union with the divine law, and ungoverned passion is restrained by the order of divine law; so that a good person wills only what is commanded, and a bad one can do only what he is permitted, at the same time that he is punished for what he wills to do unjustly.

14. THE CALL TO CRUSADE (1095)

As the Seljuk Turks spread across Anatolia all the way to Nicaea following the battle of Manzikert, the Byzantine Empire looked west for help in regaining what had been lost, as well as defending what remained. In 1074, Pope Gregory VII attempted to gather a crusade in response (doc. 45), but it failed to materialize. Responding to further pleas from the beleaguered Byzantines, a new pope would achieve what Gregory did not. On 27 November 1095, at the close of a church council at Clermont in France, Pope Urban II issued a call to "holy war" that would be of key importance to the launching of the First Crusade. Five different renditions of Urban's speech survive; the account provided here is from Robert the Monk, who may have been present at the council. Urban's call achieved a response even he could not have foreseen, as an estimated 100,000 answered it, setting off for the Holy Land less than a year later. Only about a quarter of those would make it all the way to Jerusalem, but in capturing the city they accomplished what the by then deceased pontiff Urban had asked for.

Source: trans. Oliver J. Thatcher and Edgar Holmes McNeal, *A Source Book for Mediæval History: Selected Documents Illustrating the History of Europe in the Middle Ages*, ed. Oliver J. Thatcher and Edgar Holmes McNeal (New York: Charles Scribner's Sons, 1905), pp. 516–21; revised.

In 1095 a great council was held at Auvergne, in the city of Clermont. Pope Urban II, accompanied by cardinals and bishops, presided over it. It was made famous by the presence of many bishops and princes from France and Germany. After the council had attended to ecclesiastical matters, the pope went out into a public square, because no house was able to hold the people, and addressed them in a very persuasive speech, as follows:

"O race of Franks, O people who live beyond the mountains [that is, from Rome], O people loved and chosen by God, as is clear from your many deeds, distinguished over all other nations by the situation of your land, your catholic faith, and your regard for the holy church, we have a special message and exhortation for you. For we wish you to know what a grave matter has brought us to your country. The sad news has come from Jerusalem and Constantinople that the people of Persia [that is, the Seljuk Turks], an accursed and foreign race, enemies of God, 'a generation that set not their heart aright, and whose spirit was not steadfast with God' [Ps. 78:8], have invaded the lands of those Christians and devastated them with the sword, rapine, and fire. Some of the Christians they have carried away as slaves; others they have put to death. The churches they have either destroyed or turned into mosques. They desecrate and overthrow the altars. They circumcise the Christians and pour the blood from the circumcision on the altars or in the baptismal fonts. Some they kill in a horrible way by cutting open the abdomen, taking out a part of the entrails and tying them to a stake; they then beat them and compel them to walk until all their entrails are drawn out and they fall to the ground. Some they use as targets for their arrows. They compel some to stretch out their necks, and then they try to see whether they can cut off their heads with one stroke of the sword. It is better to say nothing of their horrible treatment of the women. They have taken from the Byzantine Empire a tract of land so large that it takes more than two months to walk through it. Whose duty is it to avenge this and recover that land, if not yours? For to you more than to other nations the Lord has given the military spirit, courage, agile bodies, and the bravery to strike down those who resist you. Let your minds be stirred to bravery by the deeds of your forefathers, and by the efficiency and greatness of Charlemagne, and of Louis [the Pious] his son, and of the other kings who have destroyed Turkish kingdoms and established

Christianity in their lands. You should be moved especially by the holy grave of our Lord and Savior which is now held by unclean peoples, and by the holy places which are treated with dishonor and irreverently befouled with their uncleanness.

"O bravest knights, descendants of unconquered ancestors, do not be weaker than they, but remember their courage. If you are kept back by your love for your children, relatives, and wives, remember what the Lord says in the Gospel: 'He that loveth father or mother more than me is not worthy of me' [Matt. 10:37]; 'and everyone that hath forsaken houses, or brothers, or sisters, or father, or mother, or wife, or children, or lands for my name's sake shall receive a hundredfold and shall inherit everlasting life' [Matt. 19:29]. Let no possessions keep you back, no solicitude for your property. Your land is shut in on all sides by the sea and mountains and is too thickly populated. There is not much wealth here and the soil scarcely yields enough to support you. On this account you kill and devour each other, and carry on war and mutually destroy each other. Let your hatred and quarrels cease, your civil wars come to an end, and all your dissensions stop. Set out on the road to the holy sepulcher, take the land from that wicked people and make it your own. That land which, as the scripture says, is flowing with milk and honey, God gave to the children of Israel. Jerusalem is the best of all lands, more fruitful than all others, as it were a second paradise of delights. This land our Savior made illustrious by his birth, beautiful with his life, and sacred with his suffering; he redeemed it with his death and glorified it with his tomb. This royal city is now held captive by her enemies, and made pagan by those who know not God. She asks and longs to be liberated and does not cease to beg you to come to her aid. She asks aid especially from you because, as I have said, God has given more of the military spirit to you than to other nations. Set out on this journey and you will obtain the remission of your sins and be sure of the incorruptible glory of the kingdom of heaven."

When Pope Urban had said this and much more of the same sort, all who were present were moved to cry out with one accord, "God wills it! God wills it! (*Deus vult! Deus vult!*)" When the pope heard this he raised his eyes to heaven and gave thanks to God, and, commanding silence with a gesture of his hand, he said: "My dear brethren, today there is fulfilled in you that which the Lord says in the Gospel, 'Where two or three are gathered together in my name, there I am in the midst' [Matt. 18:20]. For unless the Lord God had been in your minds you would not all have said the same thing. For although you spoke with many voices, nevertheless, it was one and the same thing that made you speak. So I say unto you, God, who put those words into your hearts, has caused you to utter them. Therefore let these words be your battle cry, because God caused you to speak them. Whenever you meet the enemy in battle, you shall all cry out, 'It is the will of God, it is the will of God.' And we do not command the old or weak to go, or those who cannot bear arms. No women shall go without their husbands, or brothers, or proper companions, for such would be a hindrance rather than a help, a burden rather than an advantage. Let the rich aid the poor and equip them for fighting and take them with them. Clergymen shall not go without the consent of their bishop, for otherwise the journey would be of no value to them. Nor will this pilgrimage be of any benefit to a layman if he goes without the blessing of his priest. Whoever therefore shall determine to make this journey and shall make a vow to God and shall offer himself as a living sacrifice, holy, acceptable to God [Rom. 12:1], shall wear a cross on his brow or on his breast. And when he returns after having fulfilled his vow he shall wear the cross on his back. In this way he will obey the command of the Lord, 'Whosoever doth not bear his cross and come after me is not worthy of me' [Luke 14:27]."

15. TAKE HER HUSBAND, PLEASE (1212)

In the early months of 1212, King Alfonso VIII of Castile endeavored to recruit Count Raymond IV of Toulouse to join him on a military campaign that would come to fruition at the battle of Las Navas de Tolosa in July, a resounding victory for the Christians against the Muslims in Iberia (doc. 72). To mark the occasion, the troubadour poet Guilhem Adémar wrote a short poem, three stanzas of which are here translated into prose, voicing his own enthusiasm for the men of Toulouse joining in the fight ... for far different reasons.

Source: Colin Smith, *Christians and Moors in Spain: 1195–1614* (Warminster, UK: Aris and Phillips, 1989), p. 13.

Now, by my faith, I sailed my ship into the goodly harbour of salvation, giving up lead and tin and changing my silver into pure gold. For one of the loveliest ladies in the world has promised—to my enormous pleasure—to grant me her love and to give me a kiss; so noble is she that a king would be honoured by that.

And so I count myself very fortunate and would not envy any other man alive, if one evening my lady would receive me in the place of her husband, dressed or naked, stretched out at her side. Never would so much favour be done to a man of my station if it were granted to me, while kissing her and holding her in my arms, to gaze on her white, rounded, willowy, smooth body.

If King Alfonso, whom the Almohads fear, and the best Count in Christendom, mobilize their forces—since they have not yet set out—in the name of God, they would perform a great service against the pagan treacherous Saracens, provided that one of them takes with him the lord her husband, who keeps [my lady] shut away in his possession; they have not so far sinned in any way which could not be forgiven them [by such a goodly act].

16. HOW WE DIE (1481)

On 6 February 1481 Giulio Acquaviva, an Italian nobleman and general, was killed by Ottoman forces at Minervino di Lecce. In a letter of condolence to Giulio's son, Andrea Matteo, the poet Michael Tarchaniota Marullus, who had fought alongside his father, writes of a soldier making a good end of life.

Source: Carol Kidwell, *Marullus: Soldier Poet of the Renaissance* (London: Duckworth, 1989), pp. 102–03.

Neither right nor the laws of mortals affect the gods. Fierce fortune carries everything away according to its whim. Pious Byzantium and Christian Rome both fell to the enemy. Only their glory survives.

Honour lives, good deeds and the strivings of men. Fame and noble exploits escape the hostile flames. Acquaviva's achievements will live through the ages, celebrated by poets; they will be on everybody's lips. This is what great-hearted heroes should strive for. No one must violate a noble death with complaints. Let the enemy die in a soft bed in a woman's embraces! War and death are for men.

What good is it to count one's birthdays? He has lived long enough who is not ashamed of his past life.... There is nothing more certain for mortals than the last hour. Sooner or later there is a single road to be followed.... The best part of life is the end you make of it. Happy is the man who has been given the opportunity to die well. But if anyone thinks of the misfortunes of men and the successions of struggles and so many ugly hurts in a brief life then, with me, he will think that it is not the last moments, but the very conception of mortal man that is a cause for tears.

Death is the debt we owe nature.... Therefore, do not lament, Matteo, moderate your grief.... Remember your responsibilities, to your brother, your friends, your wife. See how many people depend on you, how great a burden is placed on your shoulders.... Give your people their rights and live long in your lands. Your father dwells in the stars, as he deserves.

II. Regulating War

17. DECLARATION OF A TRUCE OF GOD (1063)

During times of peace, European rulers, together with the Catholic Church, found it difficult to control those who had chosen to pursue an occupation of arms and were now out of work. Among the attempts to pacify this militarized segment of society was the Truce of God. This declaration of 1063, made between Drogo, bishop of Thérouanne, and Baldwin, duke of Hainaut, exemplifies the provisions such a truce attempted to enforce. Yet, it would not be until Pope Urban II's pronouncement of the First Crusade at Clermont in 1095 (doc. 14), and its overwhelming success at recruitment for warfare in the Middle East, that European militarism was curtailed and controlled.

Source: trans. Oliver J. Thatcher and Edgar Holmes McNeal, *A Source Book for Mediæval History: Selected Documents Illustrating the History of Europe in the Middle Ages*, ed. Oliver J. Thatcher and Edgar Holmes McNeal (New York: Charles Scribner's Sons, 1905), pp. 417–18; revised.

Drogo, bishop of Thérouanne, and count Baldwin [duke of Hainault] have established this peace with the cooperation of the clergy and people of the land.

Dearest brothers in the Lord, these are the conditions which you must observe during the time of the peace which is commonly called the truce of God, and which begins with sunset on Wednesday and lasts until sunrise on Monday.

1. During those four days and five nights no man or woman shall assault, wound, or slay another, or attack, seize, or destroy a castle, burg, or villa, by craft or by violence.
2. If anyone violates this peace and disobeys these commands of ours, he shall be exiled for thirty years as a penance, and before he leaves the bishopric he shall make compensation for the injury which he committed. Otherwise he shall be excommunicated by the Lord God and excluded from all Christian fellowship.
3. All who associate with him in any way, who give him advice or aid, or hold converse with him, unless it be to advise him to do penance and to leave the bishopric, shall be under excommunication until they have made satisfaction.
4. If any violator of the peace shall fall sick and die before he completes his penance, no Christian shall visit him or move his body from the place where it lay, or receive any of his possessions.
5. In addition, brethren, you should observe the peace in regard to lands and animals and all things that can be possessed. If anyone takes from another an animal, a coin, or a garment, during the days of the truce, he shall be excommunicated unless he makes satisfaction. If he desires to make satisfaction for his crime he shall first restore the thing which he stole or its value in money, and shall do penance for seven years within the bishopric. If he should die before he makes satisfaction and completes his penance, his body shall not be buried or removed from the place where it lay, unless his family shall make satisfaction for him to the person whom he injured.
6. During the days of the peace, no one shall make a hostile expedition on horseback, except when summoned by the count; and all who go with the count shall take for their support only as much as is necessary for themselves and their horses.

7. All merchants and other men who pass through your territory from other lands shall have peace from you.
8. You shall also keep this peace every day of the week from the beginning of Advent to the octave of Epiphany and from the beginning of Lent to the octave of Easter, and from the feast of Rogations [the Monday before Ascension Day] to the octave of Pentecost.
9. We command all priests on feast days and Sundays to pray for all who keep the peace, and to curse all who violate it or support its violators.
10. If anyone has been accused of violating the peace and denies the charge, he shall take the communion and undergo the ordeal of hot iron. If he is found guilty, he shall do penance within the bishopric for seven years.

18. CRITICISM OF THE SECOND CRUSADE (1149)

From the failures of the Second Crusade was born a strand of bitterness toward the very notion of crusading. While monastic annals frequently recorded only the name of that year's pope and abbot, and little else, an anonymous annalist at the monastery of Würzburg utilized this platform to vent his frustrations about the recent crusade. The annalist rationalizes defeat by specifically attacking the clergy, especially the crusade-recruiting preachers who enticed too many pilgrims who were unskilled in warfare, unprepared for the ensuing financial hardship, or driven by desires not in keeping with pure-hearted spiritual devotions. In the following years this annal returned to its single-lined record of papal and abbatial names.

Source: trans. James A. Brundage, *The Crusades: A Documentary Survey* (Milwaukee, WI: Marquette University Press, 1962), pp. 121–22.

God allowed the Western church, on account of its sins, to be cast down. There arose, indeed, certain pseudo prophets, sons of Belial, and witnesses of anti-Christ, who seduced the Christians with empty words. They constrained all sorts of men, by vain preaching, to set out against the Saracens in order to liberate Jerusalem. The preaching of these men was so enormously influential that the inhabitants of nearly every region, by common vows, offered themselves freely for common destruction. Not only the ordinary people, but kings, dukes, marquises, and other powerful men of this world as well, believed that they thus showed their allegiance to God. The bishops, archbishops, abbots, and other ministers and prelates of the church joined in this error, throwing themselves headlong into it to the great peril of bodies and souls.... The intentions of the various men were different. Some, indeed, lusted after novelties and went in order to learn about new lands. Others there were who were driven by poverty, who were in hard straits at home; these men went to fight, not only against the enemies of Christ's cross, but even against the friends of the Christian name, wherever opportunity appeared, in order to relieve their poverty. There were others who were oppressed by debts to other men or who sought to escape the service due to their lords, or who were even awaiting the punishment merited by their shameful deeds. Such men simulated a zeal for God and hastened chiefly in order to escape from such troubles and anxieties. A few could, with difficulty, be found who had not bowed their knees to Baal, who were directed by a holy and wholesome purpose, and who were kindled by love of the divine majesty to fight earnestly and even to shed their blood for the holy of holies.

19. CURSE ON THOSE WHO REQUIRE THE MAKING OF ARMS (1374)

Eustache Deschamps was a French poet and diplomat, who was made huissier d'armes *to Charles V in 1372. Whether the following poem—in which he curses those who would require him to make arms—is pertinent to that service, or who indeed it is that he blames for the requirement, whether French, English, or otherwise, is not known. Terms left in italics within the translation are various types of staff weapons of the late fourteenth century that have no equivalent modern English translation.*

Source: trans. Michael Livingston and Kelly DeVries, from Eustache Deschamps, *Oeuvres complètes de Eustache Deschampes*, vol. 7, ed. Gaston Raynaud (Paris: Firmin Didot et cie, 1891), pp. 34–36.

From evil daggers from Bordeaux,
And swords from Clermont,
Crossbow bolts and knives
Made from Milanese steel,
To small axes beaten to strength by hammers,
Croquepois, iron lanceheads,
Short spears that can be thrown or thrust,
Fauchards, long swords, *guisarmes*—
He can keep his money,
Whoever would require me to make arms!
From cannons, using both stones and quarrels,
Espringales, Greek fire,
Engines, catapults, wall-breakers
Which when discharged let projectiles fly,
To perilous bows that pierce so deep
And are so suddenly loosed,
At so great a distance,
And always land with sorrow and tears—

In grief, in despair,
Who would require me to make arms?
From maces from Damascus, flails,
Pikes that the Flemings use,
Haucepiez that are so fast,
Lead hammers that disfigure bodies,
Axes, spears that are called javelins,
To sharp glaives without hope
Of healing, thus would it kill or wound
Those, or you who are with those arms!
They cause damage to honor and courage,
Who would require me to make arms!
L'envoy
Princes, with anvils and hammers,
Of copper, bronze, wood,
iron, enchantments, or charms,
Let it reach through to your entrails
And gut you like pigs,
Those who would require me to make arms!

20. WYCLIF AGAINST WAR (1375)

Much was written during the Middle Ages justifying war. Very few regarded warfare as evil, only that the motives for fighting it might be evil. Among those most vehemently anti-war was the English theologian John Wyclif, who wrote during the Hundred Years War. Already deemed a heretic during his life, but protected by his connections with the English royal family, Wyclif's judgments about warfare were simple and direct: it came from Satan, and anyone fighting in a war was doing his bidding.

Source: trans. Michael Livingston, from *Society at War: The Experience of England and France During the Hundred Years War*, ed. Christopher Allmand, 2nd ed. (Woodbridge, UK: Boydell Press, 1998), pp. 37–38.

But yet, argues the Antichrist to maintain men's fighting, nature teaches that men should by strength stand against their enemies. Since an adder by its nature bites a man who treads upon it, why should we not fight against our enemies? For otherwise they will destroy us, and damn their own souls. And thus, for love, we chastise them, as God's Law teaches us. But yet, since our enemies will assail us, unless we assail them beforehand, since we love ourselves better, we should attack them first, and thus we shall have peace.

Here I think that the devil deceives many men through the falseness of his reasons, and by his false principles. For is there a man who has wit who cannot see this deceit? If it is lawful by strength to stand against violence, then it is lawful to fight with men who stand against us. Well I know that angels stand against devils, and many men by strength of law stand against their enemies; and yet they neither kill them nor fight with them. And wise men of the world withhold their strengths, and thus vanquish their enemies without a single stroke, and men of the Gospel vanquish by patience and come to rest and to peace through suffering death. So also we must do, if we keep charity; though men seize our lordship, or our goods, we should suffer in patience—yes, even if they do to us more. These are the counsels of Christ. But here the world complains and says that in this matter their realms will be destroyed. But here belief teaches us, since Christ is our God, that thereby should our realms be established and our enemies vanquished. Perhaps many men will lose their worldly riches. But what harm comes from that, since in the state of innocence all men commonly lacked such lordship. The fiend takes examples from serpents of venom, and by a bare manner teaches men to fight; but many other examples of patience from beasts should teach us to suffer to get far more good. A devil's conscience rules him who concludes from this that if he were thus patient his enemies will kill him. As if a man would say that if he kept Christ's counsel, the devil would destroy him, for he is greater than Christ. And if we fight thus for love, it is not love of charity; for charity seeks not physical goods in this life by common goods in heaven through virtuous patience. I well know that worldly men will scorn this advice; but men who would be martyrs for the love of God will hold with its meaning, and they will have more belief, for they have more charity and are better connected to God. A deceit of love is with men who fight, as there is a feigned, false love with the fiends of Hell. But at Judgment Day shall men know who fights thus for charity; for it seems no charity to ride against your enemy well-armed with a sharp spear upon a strong courser. Even the kiss of (Judas) Iscariot was more a token of charity. God's law teaches men to come first in deeds of charity and works of honor; but I read not in God's law that Christian men should come first in fighting or battle—rather in meek patience. This is the means through which we will have God's peace.

21. END THE HUNDRED YEARS WAR (1395)

Peace in any medieval war was difficult to obtain and even more difficult to maintain. Even if the causes of the conflict could be thoroughly addressed, years of fighting had produced other problems which also needed to be solved. This rather unique and very emotional letter, written in 1395 from the cleric Jean de Montreuil to John Beaufort, earl of Somerset, is an appeal to end the Anglo-French war after 60 years of fighting: Montreuil's plea is filled with classical and biblical references as to why peace should be sought. That the war would become known as the Hundred Years War indicates its lack of success.

Source: James Bruce Ross and Mary M. McLaughlin, ed., *The Portable Renaissance Reader* (Harmondsworth, UK: Penguin, 1953), pp. 65–69.

You will wonder, illustrious and most magnificent prince, how it has happened that I, a man of modest birth and as completely French as a man of my clerical rank can be, should presume to write to you, a prince of the highest and most noble royal line of Britain, and related to that of Spain. Know then that I speak the truth, I do not lie; I am moved to do this by the glorious renown of your name, which has reached not only those close to you and the great of this world, but also more distant peoples and those of lowly condition, proclaiming you a distinguished lover of truth and peace and justice. From earliest boyhood I have always admired and cultivated such men, and I have ever followed them with the greatest affection, but my desire to praise them is greater, I fear, than my ability.

The subject about which I am going to write also moves me, namely peace, encompassing all good in a single monosyllable [that is, *peace*]. I am further inspired, most kind prince, by the fact that I have heard that you love letters, and especially that you often meditate upon the Sacred Scripture, qualities which are certainly deserving of praise, and that you are also vigorous in action; in fact, that you excel in all things, although very many modern nobles despise the knowledge of letters, and spurn what was once to other men both honourable and glorious. Were not Alexander of Macedon, King David, Joshua, Judas Maccabeus, and the wise Solomon and the Queen of Saba [Sheba], who came from the ends of the earth in order to acquire knowledge, were not Julius Caesar, and Augustus, and the other Caesars, and, among the Christians, Charlemagne and very many other most powerful kings and nobles (whom I shall not mention because of their number and because I think that you have read the works of history more thoroughly than I)—were not all these deeply devoted to letters, and at the same time men of action? Indeed, in the first age men very seldom advanced to the highest dignities if they had not been instructed and perfected in liberal studies. May, therefore, that age return which then and for this reason was called golden. But, in order not to prolong my plea, let me come now, O kindest of princes, to what it is that I long for.

There have now elapsed, as I have gathered from our elders, almost sixty years in which the most extensive war has raged between our kings [the Hundred Years War], and with such hostility that one ruler—and this I call to mind with the most bitter sorrow that it could be true of those joined by so strong a bond of kinship—that one ruler strives to destroy the other rather than to crush the infidel [that is, the Muslims]. In these unbelievers and servants of Satan, this enmity inspires exultation and rejoicing; indeed, it fosters not a little, they say, the increase and progress of their most wicked religion and the weakening of our own most true law and faith. And it is not to be doubted that, if one of our kings should turn against the infidel attacks like those which he directs against his fellow ruler, besides the service which would be rendered to Christ crucified, he would deserve glory, fame, and praise which would endure through all time, and he would be able to conquer more lands and possessions than the most noble kingdoms of both rulers now encompass or possess. As the most elegant of poets writes, the great sequence of the ages would begin anew for me; I would take up a more exalted theme. But if I wish to relate the evils which follow from the war that now rages, I am compelled to exclaim with Vergil: "What opening words shall I choose first?" ...

For who shall describe the slaughter, especially of so many nobles of the highest rank and even of kings? Who shall tell of the robbery and the burning even of sacred places? Who shall set forth the sacrilege, the raping, the violence, the oppression, the extortion, the plundering, the pillaging, the banditry, and the rioting? Finally, to embrace many crimes in a few words, who will portray the inhuman savageries ... committed in this horrible and most cruel war? Indeed, as Sallust says, how can I relate things which no one would believe unless he had seen them? How can these crimes be exaggerated enough, even if, as Vergil says, there were a hundred tongues and a hundred mouths? But who, most sweet Jesus, will tell with dry eyes how children are snatched from the embraces of their parents, some slain on the very bosoms of their mothers, and others cruelly slaughtered at their parents' feet, how mothers and daughters are subjected to enemy lust, how many people of the highest rank are carried off into servitude, and how many are put up for sale like animals? O savage spirits, O cruel deeds, O men forsaken by humanity! ...

But who, I say, if he has not a heart of iron, shall refrain from tears when he describes or hears the cries of so many infants, languishing and dying of hunger and cold on the breasts of their mothers, among brambles and thornbushes.... Some, alas, were born prematurely, to be devoured by their own mothers after the manner of cattle, a thing horrible to relate! They were finally driven to this by the madness of hunger and desperation. Many of these innocents, moreover, lay half dead or dying from the mangling of vultures, and were slain and destroyed by the fangs of wild beasts, and many others—alas, how dreadful!—were greedily devoured by savage wolves. O heavens, O earth, O Neptunian seas, as the venerable Terence exclaimed, indeed I may call on all the elements! So now it comes back to this: why have we been born in times when Christians so cruelly persecute Christians and cause them to die such monstrous deaths? For if a just man will hardly be saved, what an entrance to hell have you made for your souls, O you who die in such acts! Truly you little heed, you heed not at all, the command of our Saviour, Jesus, saying to you: "Thou shalt not kill, thou shalt not commit adultery, thou shalt not steal," forbidding all these crimes under pain of perpetual damnation.

For these reasons, most high prince and lord, and because a far more favourable opportunity to make peace offers itself now than ever before, I beg, pray, and beseech you to consider very carefully, through your devotion to the good of the commonwealth, the many arguments that plead the cause of peace, ... so that by your intervention such a wholesome, necessary, and beautiful end may be achieved and these kingdoms may rest in the sweetness of peace and tranquility. Consider the truce which has been made for a period of four years; this offers the image and likeness of peace, an interval of time in which you will be able to exhort and urge your king, a man of good will, and others who are, with you, of his own most noble blood, to seek those things which are for the peace of Jerusalem. I say Jerusalem, since from the most glorious peace of kings the reformation of the holy Church, our best mother, may follow without delay; she is truly our best mother, in that when we were born, receiving us in the embrace of sincerity, she conferred upon us the water of regeneration in holy baptism....

Withdraw then from your other cares, and devote yourself to this purpose as your manly portion, exhorting your king and highest lord, and other princes and lords of his blood and yours, to this end, which I know our king, now that we have suffered every horror, is also most willing and ready to seek, even to the jeopardizing of his body and his goods. Then finally, when peace has been made among kings, let peace be made also, by their efforts, in the Church of God, for no one will resist them if they agree in this one purpose. Then will this age flourish and its spirit grow strong.

B. TRAINING FOR WAR

22. VEGETIUS ON FORTIFICATIONS AND SIEGE PREPARATION (c. 388)

Massively popular across the Middle Ages, Vegetius' Epitome *is one of the most studied arts of war in Europe—though how present it was in the minds of actual military commanders in the field remains a disputed question. His instructions in Book IV on the importance of building and stocking fortifications in preparation for a siege, however, speak well to reality across the Middle Ages.*

Source: adapted by Michael Livingston, from Vegetius, *The Military Institutions of Vegetius*, trans. John Clarke (London: W. Griffin, 1767), pp. 169–77.

1. Natural and Artificial Fortification

Cities and castles are fortified either by natural or by artificial works, or by both, which is still more complete: by nature, when situated on a high or steep place, or surrounded by the sea, marshes, or rivers; by artificial works, when enclosed with ramparts and ditches. When a place is to be built, the surest way is to take every advantage of ground; for in a level and uniform situation, nothing can be done but by mere dint of industry and labor. We see, however, ancient cities built in open plains, which, notwithstanding the disadvantage of ground, have been rendered impregnable by artificial works and labor.

2. The Walls of Cities

The ancients never build their walls in straight lines, that disposition exposing them too much to the violence of the ram, but with angles going in and out with towers at the extremities. If an enemy attempts to fix scaling ladders or advance machines to a wall of this construction, he is seen in front, in flank, and almost in rear, and is in a manner surrounded by the defences of the place.

3. Ramparts

A rampart, to have sufficient strength and solidity, should be thus constructed. Two parallel walls are built at the distance of twenty feet from each other; and the earth, taken out of the ditches, is thrown into the space between them and well rammed down. The inner wall should be lower than the outer, to allow an easy and gradual ascent from the level of the city to the top of the rampart. A ram cannot destroy a wall thus supported by earth, and, in case the stone-work should by some event be demolished, the mass of earth within would resist its violence as effectually.

4. Portcullises and Gates

To secure the gates of a city from fire, they should be covered with raw hides and plates of iron. But the ancient invention is the best for this purpose: it is a barbican built in front of the gate, with a portcullis and the entrance surrounded by iron rings and ropes. If the enemy enters the barbican, the portcullis is let down, and the enemy is at the mercy of the besieged. The wall above the gate should also be perforated in several places, so that water may be poured down to extinguish fires when needed.

5. Ditches

The ditches around a city should be very broad and deep, so that the besiegers may not easily fill them up, and that an effectual stop may be put to mines by the quantity of water they contain. For the depth of the ditch and the water that fills it are the two principal obstructions to these kinds of subterranean works.

6. Methods of Protecting the Garrison

There is good reason to fear the showers of arrows that could drive the besieged from the defences of the place, whereby the enemy can gain an opportunity of fixing their ladders and mounting the ramparts: the largest possible number of the garrison should therefore be provided with armor and shields for security against the danger. They should also be covered with a curtain of coarse cloth or hair mats, hung around the ramparts and thus forming a double parapet. This breaks the force of the arrows, which do not easily pierce any fluctuating and yielding material. Another solution is to fill frames of wood, called *metallae*, with stones, and then carefully set them up between the battlements. As the enemy climbs up their scaling ladders, and they approach any part of the parapet, they are overwhelmed by the showers of stones that are tipped onto their heads.

7. Provisions Necessary During a Siege

We shall present the several methods of attack and defence in their proper places, but for now we shall observe that there are in general two ways of attacking a place. One, when the besiegers endeavor to make themselves masters of it by repeated assault and by storming it. The other, when they cut off the supplies of water and every kind of provision, in order to reduce it by famine. By following this second method they tire out the besieged at leisure and without running any risk. To provide security against the danger, on the least suspicions of such designs of the enemy, provisions of every kind must be carefully conveyed into the place, so that they may have even more than they need themselves—and the besiegers are forced to retire for want of subsistence. Hogs and all other animals that cannot be kept alive within the place are to be salt-cured, so that the bread may hold out longer by the distribution of meat. All sorts of poultry may be kept without any great expense, and they are very useful for the sick. Above all, a sufficient provision of forage is to be laid in for the horses. And what cannot be carried into the city must be burned. Wine, vinegar, grain, and fruits of all kinds must be stocked in abundance, and nothing can be left behind that may be serviceable to the enemy. As for the gardens of the city, public and private, pleasure as well as profit will induce the inhabitants to take great care of them [to produce food]. But it will be of little service to amass large quantities of provisions, unless from the very beginning of the siege they are distributed by proper officers with prudence and frugality. For never has a garrison that led a frugal diet in times of plenty been in danger from starving. The besieged have even sometimes found themselves under the necessity of turning the old men, women, and children out of the city, lest a lack of provisions might force the garrison to surrender.

8. Military Stores

Quantities of bitumen, sulphur, liquid pitch, and incendiary oil must be provided to burn the machines of the besiegers. To make arms, the magazines must be stored with iron, steel, and coals, together with wood proper for spears and arrows. The round stones found in rivers, those of the heaviest kind that are most suitable for use in slingers, are to be carefully collected and piled up in heaps on the ramparts and towers. The smallest are thrown by the sling, the staff-sling, or by the hand; those of the middle size by the onagers; and the heaviest and roundest are laid along the parapets to be rolled down upon the assailants in order to crush them in pieces and demolish their machines. Large wheels are likewise made of green wood, or smooth cylinders are cut out of strong trees to be rolled along with great ease: when suddenly thrown down steep places, these destroy men, horses, and everything in their way. Beams, planks, and iron nails of all sizes, are to be provided for the construction of machines to oppose against those of the enemy—especially as it is often necessary to raise the height of the ramparts or parapets by expeditiously adding new works to prevent their being overtaken by the moving towers of the besiegers.

9. Cords for the Engines

A sufficient quantity of cords of sinews is to be provided, since without them the onagers, balistae, and other [torsion] engines are of no service. The hairs of the manes and the tails of horses are also fit for this use. And we are taught by the experience of our ancestors that women's hair will serve equally for this purpose in cases of necessity. At the siege of the capitol, the [torsion] engines became unserviceable by continual use when the supply of cords failed; the Roman women voluntarily cut off their hair and gave it to their husbands to repair the engines, who thereby repulsed the enemy. Thus, by giving up the ornamentation of their hair, these virtuous ladies preserved their own and their husbands' liberty. Hair-cloths and raw hides must also be provided to cover the balistae and other engines.

10. Precautions Against Shortage of Water

Perpetual springs within the walls are of the utmost advantage to a city. But where nature has denied this convenience, wells must be sunk, however deep, until you come to water, which must be drawn up by ropes. Some fortresses are built upon mountains or rocks, the situation of which is so dry that they are forced to fetch water from springs that rise below outside the walls, and to secure access to it by ranged weapons from the ramparts and towers. If the vein of water below the place is out of reach of their weapons, a small fortification, called a *burgus*, should be erected between the place and the spring, with archers and engines therein to defend the men sent for water. Besides this, cisterns are to be made, to receive the rainwater from the roofs, in all the public and many of the private buildings. A garrison which uses its water only for drinking, without scarcity, cannot be easily reduced to extremity by thirst.

11. Methods of Making Salt

If besieged in a maritime city, and you are in need of salt, the sea-water should be poured into broad troughs and reservoirs, and the heat of the sun will harden it into salt. If your access to the water should be cut off by the enemy, as sometimes happens, you may collect the sands scattered at a distance by winds and waves, and wash them with fresh water, which the sun will also convert into salt.

23. RULE OF THE TEMPLARS (1135–1165)

Following the success of the First Crusade, with Antioch, Jerusalem, and other Holy Land sites captured, many crusaders returned to Europe leaving numbers too few to effectively rule and defend these places, let alone carry out new conquests. One of the solutions was the formation of monastic military orders, fighting monks. One of the most famous of these was the military order of the Knights Templar, founded around 1119, with papal recognition received in 1128. Similar to other monastic institutions, the Templars followed a Rule, regulations to keep their members in line. The earliest version of its Primitive Rule (the first official regulations), in Latin, dates to about 1129; a French version, excerpted below, was written between 1135 and 1147. The Hierarchical Statutes of the order, also excerpted below, were composed around 1165.

Source: trans. J.M. Upton-Ward, *The Rule of the Templars* (Woodbridge, UK: Boydell Press, 1992), pp. 21–22, 35, 58–60.

The Primitive Rule

9. You who renounce your own wills, and you others serving the sovereign king with horses and arms, for the salvation of your souls, for a fixed term, strive everywhere with pure desire to hear matins [that is, the morning service] and the entire service according to canonical law and the customs of the regular masters of the holy city of Jerusalem. O you venerable brothers, similarly God is with you, if you promise to despise the deceitful world in perpetual love of God, and scorn the temptations of your body: sustained by the food of God and watered

and instructed in the commandments of our Lord, at the end of the divine office, none should fear to go into battle if he henceforth wears the tonsure.

10. But if any brother is sent through the work of the house and of Christianity in the East—something we believe will happen often—and cannot hear the divine office, he should say instead of matins thirteen paternosters; seven for each hour and nine for vespers. And together we all order him to do so. But those who are sent for such a reason and cannot come at the hours set to hear the divine office, if possible the set hours should not be omitted, in order to render to God his due.

The Manner in Which Brothers Should Be Received

11. If any secular knight, or any other man, wishes to leave the mass of perdition and abandon that secular life and choose your communal life, do not consent to receive him immediately, for thus said my lord St. Paul: ... "Test the soul to see if it comes from God." Rather, if the company of the brothers is to be granted to him, let the Rule be read to him, and if he wishes to studiously obey the commandments of the Rule, and if it pleases the master and the brothers to receive him, let him reveal his wish and desire before all the brothers assembled in chapter and let him make his request with a pure heart....

On the Commitment of Sergeants

67. As the squires and sergeants who wish to serve charity in the house of the Temple for the salvation of their souls and for a fixed term come from diverse regions, it seems to us beneficial that their promises be received, so that the envious enemy does not put it in their hearts to repent of or renounce their good intentions....

Hierarchical Statutes

How the Brothers Form the Line of March

156. When the convent wishes to ride, the brothers should not saddle up, nor load the baggage, nor mount, nor move from their places unless the marshal has the order called or commands it; but tent pegs, empty flasks, the camping axe, the camping rope and fishing net may be put on the horses before the order to load the baggage is given. And if any brother wishes to speak to the marshal he should go to him on foot, and when he has spoken to him he should return to his place; and he should not leave his place before the order to mount is given for as long as his companions are in camp.

157. When the marshal has the order to mount called, the brothers should look over their campsite so that nothing of their equipment is left behind, and then they should mount and go quietly with their troop, at a walk or amble, their squires behind them, and position themselves in the line of march if they find an empty place for themselves and their equipment; and if he does not find it empty, he may ask the brother who had taken it, who may give it to him if he wishes, but need not if he does not wish to. And when they have joined the line of march each brother should give his squire and his equipment a place in front of him....

159. No brother should leave his troop to water his horses or for anything else, without permission; and if they pass by running water in peaceful territory, they may water their horses if they wish; but they may not endanger the line of march. And if they pass by water whilst on reconnaissance, and the standard bearer passes by without watering the horses, they should not do so without permission; and if the standard bearer stops to water his horses, they may do likewise without permission. And if the alarm is raised in the line of march, the brothers who are near the shout may mount their horses and take up their shields and lances, and keep calm and await the marshal's order; and the others should go towards the marshal to hear his command.

160. When there is a war and the brothers are lodged in an inn or established in camp, and the alarm is raised, they should not leave without permission, until the banner is taken out; and when it is taken out they should all follow it as soon as possible, and they should not arm or disarm without permission; and if they are lying in ambush or guarding pasture, or somewhere they are reconnoitering, or they are going from one place to another, they should not remove bridle or saddle or feed their horses without permission.

How Brothers Should Go in a Squadron

161. When they are established in squadrons, no brother should go from one squadron to another, nor mount his horse nor take up his shield or lance without permission; and when they are armed and they go in a squadron they should place their squires with lances in front of them, and those with horses behind them, in such a way that the marshal or the one who is in his place commands; no brother should turn his horse's head towards the back to fight or shout, or for anything else, while they are in a squadron....

163. And if it happens by chance that any Christian acts foolishly [in battle], and any Turk attacks him in order to kill him, and he is in peril of death, and anyone who is in that area wishes to leave his squadron to help him, and his conscience tells him that he can assist him, he may do so without permission, and then return to his squadron quietly and in silence....

When the Marshal Takes Up the Banner to Charge

164. When the marshal wishes to take the banner on God's behalf ... the marshal should order up five or six or up to ten knight brothers to guard him and the banner; and these brothers should overwhelm their enemies all round the banner, to the best of their ability and they should not leave or go away; rather they should stay as near to the banner as they can, so that, if necessary, they may assist it. And the other brothers may attack in front and behind, to the left and the right, and wherever they think they can torment their enemies in such a way that, if the banner needs them they may help it, and the banner help them, if necessary....

168. And if it happens that the Christians are defeated, from which God save them, no brother should leave the field to return to the garrison, while there is a piebald banner [that is, a Templar banner] raised aloft; for if he leaves he will be expelled from the house forever. And if he sees that there is no longer any recourse, he should go to the nearest Hospital or Christian banner if there is one, and when this or the other banners are defeated, henceforth the brother may go to the garrison, to which God will direct him.

24. PRACTICE ARCHERY, NOT GAMES (1363)

By 1363 English longbows had proven themselves effective in several battles on land—Falkirk (1298), Halidon Hill (1333), Crécy (1346), and Poitiers (1356)—and at sea—Sluys (1340) and Winchelsea (1350). However, archery was a skill, requiring extensive training and practice. As the supply of skilled archers began declining throughout the fourteenth century, English leaders began to develop a fear that numbers would continue to dwindle. The answer was laws such as this royal decree from 1363.

Source: trans. Michael Livingston, from *Foedera*, vol. 3, ed. Thomas Rymer (London: A. & J. Churchill, 1739), p. 79.

The king to the sheriff of Kent, greetings:

The people of our realm, high-born and low-born alike, in the past would come together to practice archery in their games—through which our realm is well known to have gained much honor and profit and advantage in our military actions, thanks be to God! Yet now that very skill has almost totally been forsaken. Those same people give themselves over to the throwing of stone, wood, and iron; others to playing ball with hand, foot, and stick; others to dog- and cock-fighting; and still others to shameful and even less useful, less strength-testing games. As a result, it appears that our realm—God forbid!—will soon be devoid of archers.

Wishing to establish a suitable remedy for this matter, we hereby order that you would make a proclamation—in all places in your county, whether in liberties or not, wherever you consider proper—that every able-bodied man in the county, when he is unoccupied on feast days, shall use bows and crossbow (using arrows or bolts) in his games, and thus learn and practice the art of the bow.

Furthermore, each and everyone, from all our country, are prohibited—under penalty of imprisonment—from the throwing of stone, wood, or iron; playing ball with hand, foot, or stick; dog- and cock-fighting; or any other empty games, which can do nothing to strengthen them.

25. THE TRAINING OF BOUCICAUT (1409)

A young medieval nobleman was trained to fight from childhood on. To become a celebrated warrior, such as Jean II Le Maingre, known mostly by the name Boucicaut, whose early training is detailed in his anonymous biography, certainly required bravery and talent, but it also needed skills that were honed by constant tutoring and practice. As Boucicaut lived in a time of war, he also apprenticed on campaigns.

Source: trans. Craig Taylor and Jane H.M. Taylor, *The Chivalric Biography of Boucicaut, Jean II Le Meingre* (Woodbridge, UK: Boydell Press, 2016), pp. 29–31.

VI: Here We Explain How Even at a Young Age, Boucicaut Was Determined to Follow Arms, and How He Began to Take Part in Expeditions

In this way, and willy-nilly, the young Boucicaut was kept at court with the dauphin, so much so that he found it more and more frustrating. So he started to pester everyone to be allowed to leave and bear arms—which he ardently wished, since he thought himself strong and hardy enough to exchange heavy blows with lance and sword, and to carry the weight of arms. He complained so vociferously about it that the king heard how determined he was, and how he had said that if no-one was prepared to give him arms he would simply go and serve whatever nobleman would give him horses and armour, because he simply did not wish to remain at court. The king was delighted to see such determination at so young an age, and such resolve to achieve chivalric renown, and was sure that he would take after his chivalrous father; and although the king delayed giving him what he wanted because he was so young, nevertheless Boucicaut acquired such a reputation and was so insistent that, in the end, it was agreed he should be armed. So the king had everything he needed supplied to him, and furnished him with excellent horses; he also allowed him first-rate attendants and a generous allowance, and sent him so equipped to the company of [Louis II] the duke of Bourbon who greeted him enthusiastically; Bourbon, in concert with [John the Fearless] the duke of Burgundy, was about to join battle with the English under [Humphrey Stafford] the duke of Buckingham, who was harrying the kingdom of France. And the two French dukes and their companies inflicted frequent damage on Buckingham, so much so that in the end he retreated back to England having made little progress in France. On this expedition, the young Boucicaut began to show evidence of his courage and daring, for in skirmishes and encounters with the enemy he threw himself into battle with such abandon that there was no-one more intrepid, to such an extent that everyone was amazed that someone so young could be so courageous. He would have been prepared to do even more, but his attendants prevented him from indulging in even more dangerous enterprises. The duke of Bourbon himself, who was very fond of the boy because of his friendship with his valiant father, became more and more fond of him because of the signs he showed of the valiant knight he would become; from that time on he was pleased to find the boy in his company. After this expedition, Bourbon and Burgundy returned to Paris, and Boucicaut with them. He was warmly received by the king and his son the dauphin, who had heard how he had proved his bravery and his determination.

VII: Here We Tell of the Physical Exercises Boucicaut Undertook in Order to Become Hardened to Arms

And this was not all that the noble young Boucicaut did. He declared that he would no longer be detained at court, and that henceforth he would be master of his own fate; he saw himself as already a grown man, who needed to perform as others did. So very soon he left Paris and went to Guyenne with the Marshal Louis de Sancerre who was about to lay siege to the castle of Montguyon—and now we shall recount how Boucicaut conducted himself on that expedition.

So unwavering was he in the pursuit of arms that no hardship was too great; privations that would have seemed intolerable to others gave him great pleasure, for even in periods of respite, he could not take it easy. So instead, he would train himself to leap fully armed onto his horse's back, or on other occasions he would go for long runs on foot, to increase his strength and resistance, or he would train for hours with a battle-axe or a hammer to harden himself to armour and to exercise his arms and hands, so that he could easily raise his arms when fully armed. Doing such exercises gave him a physique so strong that there was no other gentleman in his time who was so proficient—for he could do a somersault fully armed but for his bascinet, and he could dance equipped in a coat of mail.

Item: he could leap fully armed onto his courser, without putting his foot in a stirrup.

Item: he could leap up from the ground onto the shoulders of a tall man mounted on a large horse, simply by grabbing the man's sleeve in one hand.

Item: by placing one hand on the saddlebow of a great courser and the other between its ears, he could vault between his arms over the horse, holding its mane.

Item: if two plaster walls, the height of a tower, stood an arm's width apart, he could climb up them using just feet and hands, no other aid, and without falling.

Item: fully armed in a coat of mail, he could climb right to the top of the underside of a scaling ladder leaning against a wall, simply swinging from rung to rung by his two hands—or without the coat of mail, by one hand only.

These things are absolutely true—and indeed he trained his body so hard in so many other exercises that it would be difficult to find his like. And when he was at home, he would never tire of competing with the other squires in throwing a lance and other warlike exercises. And this was how he behaved during the whole expedition, and he felt he could never be too prompt to take part in any skirmish. And when the army was besieging Montguyon, he was a part of every attack that took place, and he would hurry to be among the first to take part in any enterprise appropriate to a man of breeding. He would risk danger in a way that astonished everyone, and because of his bravery and courage, and his deeds, Marshal Sancerre became very fond of him, and said to his own followers: "If that boy lives, he will be remarkable man." And in the end, Montguyon fell, and a number of other castles and fortresses were rendered by agreement—after which the army returned to France.

26. HOW TO CONDUCT A SIEGE (c. 1425?)

Women participated in war when they needed to, generally if their spouse was dead or away. Few sought more significant roles. In the fifteenth century that changed. Not only did a French woman, Joan of Arc, lead an army to numerous victories and the crowning of Charles VII, but another, Christine de Pisan, wrote a widely read and well-respected treatise on conducting warfare. In it she utilized her wide range of military knowledge, gained from classical authors Vegetius and Frontinus, as well as her understanding of more contemporary tactics and technology. In this excerpt Christine instructs commanders on how to conduct a siege; of especial note is her inclusion of gunpowder weapons.

Source: trans. Sumner Willard, Christine de Pizan, *The Book of Deeds of Arms and of Chivalry*, ed. Charity Cannon Willard (Philadelphia: Pennsylvania State University Press, 1999), pp. 115–16.

When the time has come for the army to lay siege to a city or fortress, this is best done in the harvest season or shortly thereafter. If the commander in charge is wise, he will know that this is a profitable time for two reasons: one, that he will find more food in the fields; the other, that he will harm the enemy doubly, by the siege and by taking or preventing them from making a harvest of the grain and of other commodities. Thus the army in question will establish itself as near to the objective as possible. Before this they will have observed the layout and situation of the place, or will have been advised by others who are well informed, so that the siege will be undertaken to their advantage and they will know how to attack and place their machines.... If it is possible that the place can be besieged on all sides, it is all the more advantageous, but if there is a mountain or something that protects it, they will nevertheless establish themselves on all possible sides and will make trenches or palisades from one spot to another, so that those within cannot come out without risk.

Thus the besiegers will have made good trenches and fortified the position with strong stockades, like a true fortress, in order to oppose those who might come to raise the siege, or even those from within the walls, if they should come out to engage them. If they decide on scaling ladders, they will arrange as many as they think they will need in double ranks, and these will soon be raised against the walls, rolled there on good wheels attached to the ladders to make them slide better against the walls, and they will be strongly weighted below, if need be, so that they cannot be knocked down from above. Then straightaway they will begin the assault, strong and sharp on all sides. Likewise, they will provide sure defense on all sides and a good watch at all hours. Then they will decide by what means the place is most likely to be taken. If mining seems a good idea, they will immediately put in place the workmen they have brought along for the purpose to start digging in the earth. They will do this before the shelters are put in place, and this will be done so far away that those within the walls will in no way be able to see the men who are carrying out the dirt. This mine will be dug so deep that it will surpass the depth of the trenches and will be supported by strong wooden boards until the foundations of the walls or a lower depth have been reached. By this means they will find some way of entering, unless there is some impediment. While the mine is being dug, the wise commander will not be idle, but so that those within the walls can neither feel nor hear the miners, he will keep them busy with all sorts of assault so that the sounds, the activity, and the noise will keep their bodies as well as their ears occupied, for arrows thicker than flies from crossbows, bombards, cannon shots, the terrible din of stones being thrown by engines against the walls, the shouts of the attackers, the sound of trumpets, and the fear of those who may be scaling the walls will keep them sufficiently occupied.

Therefore, if it turns out that the miners can pierce the walls without being detected and get to the outer buildings of the castle, the men-at-arms will enter by that means and set fires everywhere; so the place will be taken. They will even have put dry wood against the walls, which they will set on fire so that all will collapse at one time. Then there will be a general entrance.

But if this plan cannot succeed, and if the place is very strong and well supplied, the wise commander who is determined must find a way to overcome the situation.

C. CHIVALRY

27. THE FUNCTION OF KNIGHTHOOD (1159)

While elite warriors had been celebrated since ancient time, the medieval concept of "knighthood" was still young in the twelfth century when John of Salisbury wrote the following, which is one of the earliest descriptions of what such a designation meant. Of course, loyalty to both God and lord were paramount.

Source: trans. John Dickinson, John of Salisbury, *Policraticus* (New York: Alfred A. Knopf, 1927), chap. 8; revised.

But what is the office of the duly ordained soldiery? To defend the Church, to assail infidelity, to venerate the priesthood, to protect the poor from injuries, to pacify the province, to pour out their blood for their brothers (as the formula of their oath instructs them), and, if need be, to lay down their lives. The high praises of God are in their throat, and two-edged swords are in their hands to execute punishment on the nations and rebuke upon the peoples, and to bind their kings in chains and their nobles in links of iron [that is, mail armor]. But to what end? To the end that they may serve madness, vanity, avarice, or their own private self-will? By no means. Rather to the end that they may execute the judgment that is committed to them to execute; wherein each follows not his own will but the deliberate decision of God, the angels, and men, in accordance with equity and the public utility ... For soldiers that do these things are "saints," and are the more loyal to their prince in proportion as they more zealously keep the faith of God; and they advance the more successfully the honor of their own valor as they seek the more faithfully in all things the glory of their God.

28. THE DECADENCE OF KNIGHTS (1250)

Life in Northern Italy changed considerably as the cities began to grow larger and more wealthy in the thirteenth century. Knights, whose power emanated from their castles and agricultural lands in the countryside, could not compete with the wealth of the towns and their leading citizens. Some knights tried to resist these changes, but others moved to the cities, even selling their titles to affluent burghers. This decline in the traditional knightly class drew criticism from some, including an Italian jurist, Odofredus (d. 1265), who perceives this decline to have resulted from their seeking comforts and not combat.

Source: Trevor Dean, *The Towns of Italy in the Later Middle Ages* (Manchester: Manchester University Press, 2000), p. 150.

For anyone to be a knight many things are needed. He should be of noble blood (the northern Europeans observe this), which means that tradesmen cannot be knights unless they obtain dispensation from a monarch ... He must be belted with a sword. He must be a bathed knight, as the Tuscans say. He must not wear fur at his neck as the Lombards do. He must swear on the divine gospels that he will not abandon his insignia [in battle]. This is said of knights who are chosen to go on military campaign, but those knights who are created today do not do such things ... Their instruments are dogs and hunting-birds.

29. BECOMING A KNIGHT (1352)

Geoffroi de Charny was already a knight of great renown when the Hundred Years War broke out in the 1337. Shaken at the poor performance of the French military in the early years of that war, he blamed the decline in French military training, chivalry, and honor. In response he wrote a number of critical treatises, including this excerpt from a Knight's Own Book of Chivalry, *attempting to restore French knights to their prior greatness. He would continue only to see defeat, however, as he was destined to die at the battle of Poitiers in 1356, while carrying the* Oriflamme, *a banner of reliquary significance that was said to have been borne by Charlemagne in his wars against the Saracens.*

Source: trans. Elspeth Kennedy, Geoffroi de Charny, *A Knight's Own Book of Chivalry* (Philadelphia: University of Pennsylvania Press, 2005), pp. 55–59.

How the Highest Standard in Deeds of Arms Is Achieved

16. ... It is embodied in those [nobles] who, from their own nature and instinct, as soon as they begin to reach the age of understanding, and with their understanding they like to hear and listen to men of prowess talk of military deeds, and to see men-at-arms with their weapons and armor and enjoy looking at fine mounts and chargers; and as they increase in years, so they increase in prowess and in skill in the art of arms in peace and in war; and as they reach adulthood, the desire in their hearts grows ever greater to ride horses and to bear arms. And when they are old enough and have reached the stage when they can do so, they do not seek advice nor do they believe anyone who wants to counsel them against bearing arms at the first opportunity, and from that time forward, on more and more occasions; and as they increase in years, so they increase in prowess and in skill in the art of arms for peace and for war. And they themselves, through their great zeal and determination, learn the true way to practice the military arts until they, on every occasion, know how to strive toward the most honorable course of action, whether in relation to deeds of arms or in relation to other forms of behavior appropriate to their rank.

Then they reflect on, inform themselves, and inquire how to conduct themselves most honorably in all circumstances. They do this quickly and gladly, without waiting for admonitions or exhortations. Thus it seems that such men have made a good reputation for themselves through their own efforts; in this way they double the good to be found in them, when from their own instinct and the will for good which God has given them, they know what is right and spare neither themselves nor what they own in their effort to achieve it. This can be apparent to us in the way that they come forward; for, at the outset, the first exercise in the use of arms which they can encounter is jousting, and they are eager to do it. And when God by his grace grants them frequent success in jousting, they enjoy it, and their desire to bear arms increases. Then after jousting, they learn about the practice of arms in tournaments, and it becomes apparent to them and they recognize that tournaments bring greater honor than jousting for those who perform well there. Then they set out to bear arms in tournaments as often as they can. And when, by God's grace, they perform well there, joyfully, gladly, and openly, then it seems to them that tournaments contribute more to their renown and their status than jousting had done; so they no longer take part in jousts as often as they were wont to do, and go to tournaments instead. Their knowledge increases until they see and recognize that the men-at-arms who are good in war are more highly prized and honored than any other men-at-arms. It therefore seems to them from their own observation that they should immediately take up the practice of arms in war in order to achieve the highest honor in prowess, for they cannot attain this by any other form of armed combat. And as soon as they realize this, they give up participating so frequently in exercising their skill at arms in local events and take up armed combat in war. They look around, inquire, and find out where the greatest honor is to be found at that particular time. Then they go to that place and, in keeping with their natural good qualities, are keen to discover all the conditions of armed combat in war, and cannot be satisfied with themselves if they do not realize to the full their wish to find themselves there and to learn.

How to Study the Art of War

17. They want to observe and to find out how to set up an expedition to attack and fight one's enemies, and to observe the deployment of light horsemen, the deployment of men-at-arms and foot soldiers, and the best way to advance in a fine attack and to make a safe and honorable withdrawal, when it is the time to do so. And when they have observed that, they then will not be content until they have been present at and learned about the defense of castles and walled towns: how they can be held, guarded, and provisioned against both enemy

attack and siege, and against all advances against them which can be made; what should be done in relation to an encounter from within. And they still do not want to give up at this point, even though they have achieved great honor in this form of the practice of arms; they always want to learn more because they hear people talk about how one can lay siege to walled towns and castles. Then they do their best to seek out the places where such sieges are going on. And when they come there, they take great pleasure in seeing how a siege is set up to surround the town or castle, how the *battifol* are made to block the way out for the besieged, and to exert more pressure on them, how mining is carried out under the cover of devices such as sows, *buyres*, cats, and belfries [siege machines to protect miners digging below them], and other matters, such as how to mount an attack on the walls, to climb up on ladders, and to pierce the walls and to enter and take by force. They are then glad when God by his grace has granted that they should have been there, observed, and performed well during this military operation. And the more these men see and themselves perform brave deeds, the more it seems to them, because of the high standards their natural nobility demands of them, that they have done nothing and that they are still only at the beginning. And as a result of this, they are still not satisfied, for they have heard talk as to how one should fight on the battlefield, men-at-arms against others, and they hear those who were there recall the great exploits that good warriors achieved there; then it seems to them that they have seen and done nothing if they do not take part in such a noble form of military activity as a battle. They therefore take pains to travel to different places and to endure great physical hardship in their journeys through many countries across land and sea. And when, through the grace of God, they find out and witness such supremely noble affairs as battles were they also to be granted the grace and favor of performing great deeds, then such men should indeed thank Our Lord and serve him for the kindness he has shown them and the assistance he has given in their continuance of these military pursuits. And when they recognize what a great benefit and honor it is, this increases their determination to strive to seek out opportunities for such deeds of arms. And when they are fortunate enough to find them, this is very good; and he who is the most fortunate in often taking part in them and in doing his duty well in his own region and in others is of that much greater worth than those who have done less. The question which is the better of two revolves around the honors, of which one is more worthy than the other. Every man who does well in this military vocation should be prized and honored, and one should observe those who are best and learn by listening to them and by asking about what one does not know, for they ought rightly to know better how to explain, teach, and advise than the others, for they have seen and known, taken part in, experienced, and proved themselves in all forms of armed combat in which good men have learned and learn how to excel. It therefore follows that they should know how to speak about everything that concerns armed combat and many other matters. And in relation to such talk, some might argue over and question which might be the kind of person from whom one might derive the greatest benefit. Would it be the impoverished companions who make and have made a name for themselves in the manner explained above, or would it be the great lords who want to make their reputation and have done so in the same way, and are of equal worth in wisdom and in conduct, and in skill and performance in combat? It seems to me that one can give a good answer to this question, for the impoverished fighting companions rightly deserve esteem and praise, those who with their limited resources set out to make such strenuous efforts and exertions, through which they achieve such noble prowess and such great understanding that the renown of their exploits spreads everywhere, which, up until then, had been held to be of little account, nor would they ever have won this reputation if they had not first had the courage to set about achieving the good deeds of arms spoken of above. And from this honor they gained recognition, rise in status, profit, riches and increase in all benefits. It is, therefore, more necessary for them, in their own interest, to perform and have performed these above-mentioned noble deeds than it is for great lords who have no need to go anywhere to become known, as their rank ensures that they are well known; nor do they need to travel about in order to be served and honored, as their rank entitles them to this; nor can necessity move them to go forth in search of financial gain, for they already have considerable riches. Nor do they have any great need after this to travel abroad in search of pleasure or entertainment, for they can have as much as they want in their own land and territory. One should therefore take far greater account of undertakings involving physical hardship and danger which the great lords are prepared to and do embark on of their own free will without any need to do so other than to achieve personal honor, with no further expectation of any reward for the money and effort which they devote to performing these great deeds of arms; these enterprises should be valued more than those of men who expect some profit or advancement or rise in status as a reward for the honor which they have won or are winning.

30. PEACE-TIME JOUSTS AT SAINT-INGLEVERT (1390)

Tournaments were meant as spectacles in the Middle Ages: they often included parades, feasts, melees, jousts (on horseback), and duels (on foot). Certainly they were meant to display martial feats, but those became increasingly less important than the overall theater of the event. Private jousts, however, such as what is described by Jean Froissart at Saint-Inglevert in 1390, were not meant for large crowds or any amount of pomp or pageantry; they were simply games to display martial skills, and they could only legitimately occur during peacetime, where foes were not conceived of as enemies. At Saint-Inglevert, three young but already renowned French knights took advantage of a lull in the Hundred Years War to challenge any and all to joust with them. A large number of English knights and squires answered their call. Froissart, one of the great observers and reporters of historical events, gives a very detailed eyewitness account of each and every joust. Several of the more repetitious ones have been removed for brevity.

Source: trans. Kelly DeVries, from Jean Froissart, *Chroniques*, in *Oeuvres de Froissart*, vol. 14, ed. Henri Marie Bruno Joseph and Baron Kervyn de Lettenhove (Brussels: V. Devaux, 1867–77), pp. 108–50.

In this season, the truce between England and France was maintained on sea and land by both kings and their subjects ...

It happened at this time ... that three knights ... took their arms to Saint-Inglevert, near Calais: namely, Sir [Jean II Le Maingre] Boucicaut the younger, the lord Reginald de Roye, and [Jehan] the lord de Saimpi, who made preparations to fulfil their engagement. These jousts were made known and publicized, especially in the kingdom of England, where the news was well received, and greatly excited many knights and squires—young adventurers who wanted to joust and were confident in what they could do. They would be ashamed not to go across the sea with their horses to a place near Calais and joust with them.

I will name some of those who were most eager in these conversations. The first was Sir John Holland, earl of Huntingdon, Sir John Courtenay, Sir John Traicton, Sir John Goulouffre, Sir John Roussel, Sir Thomas Scorabonne, Sir William Clifton, Sir William Clinton, Sir William Taillebourg, Sir Godfrey de Seton, Sir William de Haquenay, Sir John Bolton, Sir John Arundel, Sir John d'Ambreticourt, Sir John Beaumont, and many other knights, more than one hundred. They said, "Let us prepare ourselves to go near to Calais; for these French knights only placed themselves in our lands for these games, to bring us to them. Certainly they have done this well and are good. Let us go, and fulfill their need."

This became so well known in England that many who did not want to joust wanted to go to see what happened now. So all these knights and squires, pleasing themselves and others, came to Calais, and the great lords who held estates there sent their purveyances and armors of peace and war for their horses [armor for peace (jousting armor) was heavier and more rigid than armor for war], when the appointed term was approaching for the jousts. Sir John Holland, brother to the king, was the first to cross the sea, and more than sixty knights and squires with him. They came to Calais and took up quarters.

At the beginning of the charming month of May, the three young French knights who were to joust at Saint-Inglevert, after sending news throughout France, England and Scotland, first traveled to Boulogne-sur-Mer, where they stayed for I know not how many days, and then left and came to the monastery of Saint-Inglevert. On their arrival, they learned that a large number of English knights and squires had come to Calais. This gave them much joy, and they got to work: they sent word to the English, and on a pasture in between Calais and Saint-Inglevert they pitched three very beautiful and very rich vermilion-colored pavilions. Before each were suspended two targes [jousting shields] with the coats of arms of the lords, one for peace and one for war. It was ordered that any desiring of jousting should touch, or send to have touched, one or both of these targets according to their pleasure; they would be summoned and delivered to the joust, according to what had been requested ...

On 21 May, as it had been noted and proclaimed, the three knights were properly armed and their horses already saddled according to the laws of the tournament. And that day all the knights and squires in Calais went there, wishing either to joust or to see the jousts. They rode until they came to the place, and they drew themselves to one side. The place where the joust was held was beautiful and large, green with grass and plants.

Sir John Holland was the very first who sent his squire to touch the war-target of Sir Boucicaut. This done, Sir Boucicaut went immediately from his pavilion fully armored. He mounted his horse and took his targe and good lance, strong and well steeled. The two knights took their distances. After they had eyed each other, they spurred to full gallop, coming one onto the other without sparing anything. Sir Boucicaut hit the earl of Huntingdon in such a way that his lance pierced his targe and the iron point scraped along his arm—although without causing a wound—and passed by his head. Afterwards the knights rode to the end and stopped in good order. This joust was well praised. In the second joust, they hit each other only slightly and did no harm. The horses refused a third joust [as there was no barrier between the jousters, the horses often shied away rather than charging at each other]. The men spurred the horses forcefully, very forcefully. The earl of Huntingdon wished to joust and was angry as he expected that Boucicaut would retake his lance, but he did not. Boucicaut only showed that he did not want to joust further.

When the earl of Huntingdon saw this he sent his squire to touch the lord de Saimpi's targe of war. He was never going to refuse and immediately came out of his pavillion and mounted his horse, taking his targe and lance. When the earl saw that he was not going to refuse but was ready, he enthusiastically spurred his horse, and the lord de Saimpi did likewise. They couched their lances and each aimed his lance at the other, but one horse crossed in front of the other. They still connected; however, because the horses crossing caused problems, the earl was unhelmed. Returning to his host, he was re-helmed and again took his lance. And the lord de Saimpi did the same. Having once more taken their lances, they galloped at each other, both hitting in the middle of their targes, so that they would have been unhorsed had they not clutched the horses tightly with their legs. They returned each to his place, where they refreshed themselves for a short while, catching their breath.

Sir John Holland, who had a great desire to win honor at these jousts, took up his lance again, attached his targe and spurred his horse; the lord de Saimpi, seeing this, did not refuse him, but came against him on the right. The two knights hit the steel helmets of each other with their war-lances so strongly and directly that sparks of fire flew from them. In this pass, the lord de Saimpi lost his helmet; but the two knights rode on very proudly and returned to their places.

This joust was much praised, and the English and French said that these knights, the earl of Huntingdon, Sir Boucicaut, and the lord de Saimpi, had jousted very well, without letting up nor causing damage. The earl wanted another pass with his lance for the love of his lady, but it was refused him. So Sir John Holland departed, for he had run six lances with such honor and grace that he gained praise from all sides.

Then appeared a young and gallant English knight, called the earl-marshal, who sent, according to the regulations, for the war-targe of Sir Reginald de Roye to be touched. This done, Sir Reginald came from his pavilion fully armed, and mounted his horse that was all ready for him. He attached the targe to his neck and shoulder, and he took up his lance. At the starting distance, the two knights spurred their horses with great force, and they came at each other. But the joust failed because of the swerving of their horses, which made the men very angry. In the second pass Sir Reginald de Roye was hit and his lance broken. At the third pass, they met with such force that sparks of fire flew from their helmets, and the earl-marshal was unhelmed. He rode by and returned proudly, and he did not joust more that day as he had done enough.

The lord of Clifford, appearing to be a very valiant knight, and cousin to the late Sir John Chandos, of famed renown ... called again to joust with Boucicaut. But Boucicaut did not place his helmet on and told the lord of Clifford that he preferred to joust with another. So Lord Clifford sent his squire to touch the targe of the lord de Saimpi, who came out from his pavilion, mounted his horse—which was all ready—took his targe and lance, and prepared for the joust. They came at each other with great force and hit each other with a full shot. The lord of Clifford broke his lance into three pieces against the targe of the lord de Saimpi. And the lord de Saimpi hit his helmet and knocked it off, and both continued to their places. The lord of Clifford returned to his men and did no more that day, because they said he had honourably and valiantly borne himself.

After that came a gallant knight of great desire called Sir Henry Beaumont, and he sent to touch the targe of Sir Boucicaut.... The two knights spurred their horses with great force and charged each other. The lord Beaumont did not manage his lance well, and hit Boucicaut wide. But Sir Boucicaut struck him with his lance on the middle of his targe so that it knocked him to the ground, and he continued riding past. Beaumont was raised up by his attendants and remounted on the horse. So he took himself before the lord de Saimpi and prepared to joust with the knights. They jousted twice well and courteously without causing damage to each other.

Sir Peter of Courtenay, who was anxious to engage and to run six lances, ordered a squire to touch the three targes of war with a rod. This was a surprise, and he was asked what he intended. He replied, that he wished to joust with each of the French knights, if nothing prohibited him from doing so, and he asked that they please agree to his request. And thus they agreed. Sir Reginald de Roye came out first; he took his targe and his lance and prepared to joust. They spurred their horses with enthusiasm, and positioned themselves correctly to hit one another without laying up. But the first pass failed as their horses refused, and they were very frustrated and returned to their places without causing damage. Afterwards they spurred their horses and couched their lances, and they did not fail in this second joust but hit each other with great force. Sir Reginald unhelmed the English knight and rode to the end and returned to his place. He stayed there because he had done his two passes.

Sir Peter of Courtenay was re-helmed and returned in good condition. So the lord de Saimpi came out to joust, and the two rode from their sides against each other. Their lances, however strong and straight, were broken on their helmets. They took new lances and spurred their horses and came at each other with great force. The lord de Saimpi hit Sir Peter Courtenay askance because of his horse, and did little; but Sir Peter hit him on his helmet and unhelmed him. So he rode well and proudly to the end and returned to his place.

Then Sir Boucicaut came out to complete the wish of Sir Peter of Courtenay. He took his lance and spurred his horse, and Sir Peter did the same against him. They hit each other's targe with such a strong and direct blow that their horses stopped in their tracks. But no damage had been caused to either. In the second pass they unhelmed each other.

The six passes completed, Sir Peter of Courtenay asked whether one of the knights might go again, but he was refused and told that they were done for the day. So Sir Peter of Courtenay rested.

An English knight, called Sir John Goulouffre, came forward, fully armed, with his targe on his neck and his lance in his hand. He sent his squire to touch the war-targe of Sir Reginald de Roye, who answered the challenge to joust. They spurred their horses with great force and charged each other. They hit their helmets strongly and directly, but neither were unhelmed nor broke their lances. Their horses refused to run the second pass, to their great frustration. In the third pass they struck their targes and broke their lances. They were supplied with others. In the fourth pass they came onto each other too widely and without contact. The fifth pass was very well done, for they were both unhelmed, and so they proudly rode to their own sides.

Afterwards came Sir John Rousseau, a capable and valiant knight from England, well traveled and known in many lands. He ordered his squire to touch the targe of the lord de Saimpi. The knight responded that he was ready, armed, mounted, and had his targe on his neck. When given his lance he took it and left his place, spurring his horse, with the English knight against him. Their lances hit full on the targes, with such a force that the horses stopped. The two knights swerved away from the course and returned each to their place. Without a long break, they again spurred their horses and charged at each other, but when they approached the horses swerved and they were unable to hit each other. So the two knights were very frustrated, and they returned for another pass. They spurred their horses and couched their lances. And the steel tips struck the visors of their helmets so strongly and directly that the two were unhelmed. They rode on proudly; the English knight returned to his companions and would not joust again that day.

Sir Thomas Schoenhorne, a young knight, but of good enthusiasm, sent his squire to touch the war-targe of Sir Boucicaut. The knight was ready to respond, for he was armed and on horseback; his targe was on his neck, and he was leaning on his lance, waiting only for an adventure. And when he was requested to joust, he raised his lance, and looked to see what the English knight was doing. He saw that he was petting his horse, and so he did likewise. They spurred their horses and charged. They couched their lances and just as they were about to hit they could not as their horses decided not to. They were very frustrated and had to return each to their own places. And they thought better how to steady their horses better when they came again to joust. After a short break they spurred their horses, trying to keep them in line. The light on their helmets went back and forth. Sir Reginald [*sic*, this was actually Boucicaut] broke his lance, and while the English knight did not break his lance he used it so well and grandly that he unhelmed Sir Boucicaut so forcefully that blood burst from his nose. Thus Sir Boucicaut retired to his pavillion and would not joust more that day.

Although evening was approaching, Sir Thomas Schoenhorne did not want to stop jousting until he had completed his number of passes. He sent his squire to touch the war-targe of the lord de Saimpi, who was completely prepared to meet him, armed and mounted, with his targe on his neck, so he came forward. The two knights spurred their horses and charged straight on and hit each other on the top of the helmet, but they did not connect with the lances glancing off. They passed by each other. It was said by many who saw the joust that had the point hit the targes, one or both would have been hurt and been knocked to the ground. This joust finished, they made ready to joust again, spurring on their horses, charging each other and hitting their targes dead on. The English lance fractured in three pieces. But the lord de Saimpi hit so forcefully and directly that he drove the English knight to the ground. He was quickly helped by his men to his side ...

On Tuesday, after saying mass and eating and drinking, all those who intended to joust, and those who wished to see them, left Calais, and rode together as a very orderly company to the place were the jousts had been held before, and there, when the English arrived, the French were already ready to receive them. The day was bright, clear, and hot enough to be pleasant ...

A squire called Lancaster went forward. He sent to touch the targe of Sir Boucicaut, who responded that he was ready as he was mounted on his horse with his targe buckled on his neck. He called for his lance and placed it in its rest [the "lance-rest," a bar attached to the jouster]. They charged at each other with great force and hit their helmets so strongly, iron connecting with steel, that it caused flames of fire to leap off; it was astonishing that they were not unhelmed. They rode on and returned each to their own places. They did not stay long before returning to spurring on their horses and charging, each hitting his opponent's targe: but their horses swerved, which meant that the joust was not very pretty nor very strong, though they could do nothing about it. They returned for a third pass, and their blows were placed well on the helmets, and the Englishman was unhelmed. He went on bareheaded except for his coif and would not joust any more that day ...

Then came Sir Godfrey de Seta, a gallant knight. He jousted well, which could be seen that day by his horse and the way he held his lance, and he had a great desire to joust and sent a squire to hit the war-targe of Sir Reginald de Roye. That knight responded that he was ready, mounted with his targe on his neck. He took his lance and prepared to joust well. The two knights who wished to joust charged and hit strongly on their targes. The lances were strong and did not break; the horses pushed hard, their thighs and legs shuddering as they were halted. So they returned to their sides without having to throw their lances on the ground. They rode proudly back to face each other, putting their lance in their rests and spurring their horses, which were good and healthy. So they charged each other, but their horses swerved before they could encounter each other. They passed too wide to make contact, and they dropped their lances. These were taken by those who were present and returned. The knights put them in their rests and spurred their horses, because they did not want to spare each other because they were heated. The English knight hit Sir Reginald de Roye on the top of his helmet and gave him a very strong blow without damaging him; but Sir Reginald de Roye gave him so strong and direct a hit on his targe ... that pierced through it as well as striking his left arm on the outside. The lance broke and the end fell to the ground, the middle sticking through his targe and the point into his arm. The knight, however, did not turn around but returned proudly to his place. His companions attended to him, and the lance and iron tip were removed from his arm; the blood was stopped and it was bandaged. Sir Reginald returned to his companions, and there remained, leaning on a lance that had been given him. Sir Reginald was much praised by his companions, and by the English, for this joust. No one said anything bad to him, as to how the knight was wounded, for such are jousts: to one they can be good, to another bad, especially when neither wanted to spare the other.

An English squire, named Blacquet, sent to touch the war-targe of the lord de Saimpi, who was already, mounted on his horse with his targe buckled onto his neck. So he took his lance and responded to the squire with a joust as he had demanded. They spurred their horses, and couched their lances under their arms. The first blow each hit the helmets very strongly but their points glanced off and their lances were lost. So they returned each to his place. They were given lances, placed them in their rests, and spurred their horses with great force, showing that they wanted to do well. But during the approach their horses swerved, which meant that they hit very weakly. They rode on to the end of the course and each went to their places. They did not rest long. When they had their lances and placed them in their rests they spurred and came together in a joust. Blacquet hit the lord de Saimpi a very hard blow with his lance on the top of his helmet. Saimpi struck him much harder on the visor, and he unhelmed him, such that the buckle to which the helmet was attached at the rear was broken and it fell. They rode on and the squire returned to his companions, not intending to joust again that day. The lord de Saimpi remained on his horse, leaning on his spear, but he was told to wait until he should be asked to joust again ...

Thomelin Messiden, a young English squire, well and proudly fully armed, with a great desire to joust, sent to touch the targe of Sir Boucicaut. The knight was all ready and responded, grasping his lance. Both spurred their horses and charged. This first blow hit, glancing off their helmets without doing any damage. They returned to their places but did not stay and again spurred. In this joust they both hit the targes very powerfully and directly. Thomelin Messiden broke his lance and shivered. Sir Boucicaut's blow was so direct that it knocked him to the ground over the rear of his horse. Those on his side ran across to him, raised and carried him off. He did not joust again that day ...

Another squire, named Sequaqueton, came forward, an able man-at-arms and a good joust. He sent to touch the war-targe of Sir Reginald de Roye, who replied that he was prepared: mounted on his warhorse, targe on his neck, and lance in his hand. The two spurred their horses and came at each other. They hit the targes with powerful blows, sparing nothing. Sequaqueton bore himself well without falling, which was marveled at because Sir Reginald had hit him in such a way that he had bent him across the crupper of his horse. He raised himself, and proudly rode on, although he had lost his lance. He took another and placed it in its rest, spurring his horse. Sir Reginald did the same. So they came and charged, giving each other's helmets very strong hits that made sparks of fire fly from them. The blows were beautiful, but they did no damage. They rode on and returned each to his side, and they repaired to their posts. They went for a third pass. In this joust, Sequaqueton was very strongly unhelmed, and almost fell from his horse, as he staggered. But he was strengthened and recovered once he was back on his feet. He returned to his companions and did not joust further this day.

Nor did any others, as evening approached, and it was now late. The English came together, and departing as a company returned to Calais, as did the French to Saint-Inglevert.

You must know, though I have made no mention of it before, that King Charles [VI] of France very much held the view that he should not miss seeing these jousts at the time that they were held between Calais and Saint-Inglevert. He had a lively spirit and very much enjoyed seeing new things. He told me that he would he would have been very angry if he had not seen these jousts, from the very first to the last ones. With him was the lord of Garensières, who came with a company, who were all disguised ...

Tuesday became Wednesday....

Another English squire, who was called John Scot, came forward and sent to have the war-targe of the lord de Saimpi touched. The knight responded, as he was in good order and all ready to joust. They took their lances and placed them in their rests, then they each spurred their horses and charged. They gave their targes such solid blows that their horses stopped, but their lances, being strong, neither broke nor fell out of their hands. They each returned to their sides until ordered to joust a second time, which was also beautiful and well done. The lord de Saimpi hit on the helmet, but John Scot did better, unhelming him before riding on. For this joust the squire was honored by his men. The lord de Saimpi was soon re-helmed, and that same hour he took his lance and put it in his rest. They spurred and charged with great violence. They hit the targes with great blows. John Scot was knocked out of his saddle. Thus the lord de Saimpi gained revenge against the English squire. The squire was raised and carried off by his companions. He did no more for the day ...

Another squire from England, called John Marshal, completely armed, came forward to joust and sent to touch the war-targe of Sir Boucicaut. The knight responded that he was all ready, and waiting for nothing other than to joust. He took his lance and put it in the rest. The two knights spurred their horses, each holding and running with great power. They couched their lances. They hit each other on the targes without sparing, but caused little damage. Their lances were dropped, and they rode to the end of the course. When they had returned each to their places and grabbed other lances, they placed them in their rests, secured their targes, and spurred their horses. Coming on to each other, they hit on the helmets, giving great blows, and rode on carrying their strong lances. When they had ridden to the end of the course and come to their places, they rested a little and considered how they might deliver a strong blow. They both spurred their horses and gave such powerful blows on their targes that their horses were stopped. Though they had suffered these hard blows, they came against each other again. John Marshal hit Boucicaut's targe in such a way that his lance was broken into three pieces, and Boucicaut's blow hit the top of his Marshal's helmet in such a way that he was unhelmed and driven back onto the rear of his horse. The squire rode on without falling, and when he had reached the end of the course, he returned to his companions who said he had performed well. He did not joust further this day ...

After this a very gallant knight from the county of Hainaut, along the border, called Ostrevan, a good jouster, offered himself. Since his youth he had been raised in England at the court of King Edward [III], and his name was Sir Jean d'Aubricourt, and brother to that excellent knight, Sir Eustache d'Aubricourt.... The knight was completely equipped for the joust, and sent one of his squires to touch the war-targe of Sir Reginald de Roye. The knight responded that he was all ready and mounted on his horse. They took their places and acknowledged one another. They took their lances and put them in their rests before spurring on their horses. So they came at each other with great power and delivered a direct hit onto the helmets so strong that sparks of fire flew. The knights' blows were impressive but caused no damage. Both rode on proudly to the end of the course and returned to their places. They did not rest for long before they spurred their horses and aimed at the other's targe. As they approached they couched their lances and charged against each other. It was marvelous that they did not hit at the same time, for they were two courageous jousters, and proud. They did not fear pain, death nor peril. The shock of the blow delivered to the targes was such that the horses rose up on their front feet and they staggered; nevertheless, the two knights rode on, their lances destroyed, and returned to their own places. They received new lances, placed them in their rests, aimed at the targes, and spurred their horses. They charged each other and hit very strongly on their helmets. Sir Jean d'Aubricourt rode very proudly to the end of the course and afterwards returned to his place. Sir Reginald went to his companions and showed that he did not wish to joust more that day ...

The English saw that evening was approaching, so they gathered together and departed from that place, riding in a company and returned to Calais, each to his inn. During the evening they talked about and discussed the many feats of arms between themselves and the French. The French also returned to Saint-Inglevert, but they were quiet.

When the morning of Thursday, the fourth day of the week, arrived, the English who were at Calais realized that there were many of their companions, knights and squires, who had not jousted, and who had purposely come across the sea to do so. So they said that any who wished to joust should do so or not be among the company. All the lords were in agreement, and that Thursday they returned to Saint-Inglevert, wanting all who wished to be able to joust. After mass and breakfast they mounted their horses and left Calais in a company. They rode until they came to the place where the jousts were to be made. The three French knights had arrived at their pavilions and were making all the preparations, accompanied by those on their side who served them and those who wanted to see the jousts.

The first at the place, an English knight, named Sir Godfrey d'Estas ... was completely and proudly armed. He sent a squire to touch the war-targe of Sir Boucicaut, who immediately left his pavilion armed and prepared to respond to the request to joust. His horse was ready and he mounted it. He was handed his lance and placed it in the rest. The other knight already had his. They regarded each other and then spurred their horses with great power. Their first blows hit the helmets with great force, but their lances glanced off, and they continued to the end of the course and returned each to his place. They had still held onto their lances; so they spurred their horses. As they approached, they couched their lances and came one onto the other. The second blows were delivered onto the targes with such great force that their lances broke, otherwise they would have hurt each other. They rode on and returned each to their place, where they received new lances. When they had taken these, they placed them in their rests and aimed at the targes. They spurred their horses and powerfully charged each other, hitting the visors of the helmets so well and strongly that both were unhelmed. They rode on and returned each to his companions. The English knight did nothing more this day, for he was told that he had performed valiantly, and should let others joust ...

Afterwards a Bohemian knight came forward, named Sir Here-hance (or Herehauce) [probably Herr (sir) Hans], who was in the court of the queen of England. He was held to be a good jouster, strong and proud ... When he had come onto the course, he was asked with which of the three he wished to tilt: he replied, "With Boucicaut." An English squire was sent, according to the rules, to touch Sir Boucicaut's war-targe. That knight was ready and mounted on his warhorse. He responded that this was the reason he had been summoned. He buckled on his targe and grasped his lance, placing it in the rest, and indicated he was ready to the knight, who was also ready to joust, his targe on his neck and his lance in his fist. They spurred their horses with great force and charged each other. They hoped to deliver good blows, but that did not happen: the Bohemian knight, illegally [according to the rules this was an unfair blow] hit the helmet of Sir Boucicaut. The English saw well his illegitimate hit and that because of this he would lose his arms and horse, should the French wish. The French and English held a long conversation together on this unfair stroke, but finally the three knights pardoned it, the better to please the English. Here-hance asked as a favour that he might be permitted to make one more pass. He was asked with whom of the three did he want to do this with. He sent to touch the war-targe of Sir Reginald de Roye. That knight, who was waiting in his pavilion, for he had not jousted that day, came out all ready and said that he wished to do what had been asked. Sir Reginald mounted his horse, buckled his targe on, took his lance given him and placed it in its rest. He focused his gaze entirely on the goal of attacking the Bohemian. The two spurred their horses at the same moment, and approaching they couched their lances and hit directly on the targes. But Sir Reginald de Roye, who at the time was one of the strongest and firmest jousters in France, hit in such a way that the Bohemian flew completely off and fell so severely onto the ground that those who saw it thought he was dead. Sir Reginald continued on to the end of the course and returned to his place. Here-hance was lifted in great pain by his attendants, who brought him back. The English were in agreement that he deserved what had happened to him due to the uncourteous way he had jousted in his first pass, and that he was not to joust further that day ...

Afterwards, another English squire, a tall, handsome man, seated well on his horse came forward, prepared to joust. He was called Janequin Scrop. He sent to touch the war-targe of the lord de Saimpi. The knight responded, as he was standing before his pavilion, armed and mounted. He was given his lance and placed it in its rest. The two spurred their horses and, couching their lances, came one on the other with great violence. Yet the first blow failed because the horses swerved, which very much frustrated them. Returning each to his place, they did not rest for long. They spurred their horses and couched their lances, seemingly putting themselves in position to have a good joust. They came at each other and hit so strongly high on their helmets that sparks flew. They rode on having lost only their lances. New lances were brought to their places as they desired. These were offered to them; they grabbed them and placed them in their rests. Then they couched them and spurred their horses. They charged each other with great force and hit their targes. Janequin Scrop broke his lance, while the lord of Saimpi held his so strongly that the squire was driven off the horse. He rode on to the end of the course, and then returned to his place. Janequin Scrop was raised from the ground and taken by his attendants. He did no more that day ...

Then came forward another English squire, called Nicolas Lam, well and handsomely armed in complete armor, having a very great desire to joust and show his skill in arms that day. He sent to touch the war-targe of the lord de Saimpi. The knight was ready to respond and came out immediately, mounted, with his targe emblazoned with his arms on his neck. He took his lance and put it in its rest ... At the same time the English squire did the same. They both spurred their horses and while charging couched their lances; they both delivered a direct hit, and these were so strong on their targes that, had their lances not broken, they would have been hurt and unhorsed. But they held so well that they did not fall. They rode on to the end of the course before going to their places. When given new lances, they took them and placed them in their rests, and then they spurred their horses. In their second pass they delivered such great blows on their helmets that sparks of fire flew, but no other damage was done, for the lances had crossed. They rode on, finished the course, and returned each to his place. They did not rest long before both spurred their horses and couched their lances. Before doing so they had considered well where to aim, as they did not want to fail to attack one another. The third pass of the joust was good, as they hit high on the visors of the helmets so strongly and directly that the points of the lances penetrated and stuck. Both were unhelmed so cleanly that the lacings of the helmets broke and they flew over the rear of their horses. The jousters held so well to the horse that they did not fall. They rode on and finished the course in good array, returning to their companions. These had picked up the helmets and carried them back to their places.

For this day the jousts had ended, for no one came forward from the English side. The earl of Huntingdon, the earl-marshal, the lord Clifford, the lord Beaumont, Sir John Clifton, Sir John d'Aubricourt, Sir Peter Shoenehorne, and all the knights who had jousted these four days, waited in a company for the French lords, and thanked them greatly for their pleasures. They said, "All the knights and squires of our company who wished to joust have done so; so we take our leave of you, returning to Calais on our way to England. We know well that whomever might wish to joust with you and to show their skill in arms will find you here for thirty days according to your proclamation. We return to England, assuring you that all the knights and squires will tell anyone who asks us about these jousts to come and see them."

"Many thanks," replied the three knights. "They shall be made welcome, and jousted with as you have been. We thank you very much for the courtesy you have shown us."

Thus in a sweet and friendly state the English departed from the French at Saint-Inglevert and returned to Calais. On Saturday morning they boarded passenger vessels. They had a good wind and came to Dover by midday.

31. THE DECLINE OF CHIVALRY (1483–1485)

The violence of the Wars of the Roses brought an end to the lives of many nobles and knights. Their sons would fill their places, and when they were killed, their grandsons. In some families three generations of knights met their end; some noble dynasties did not recover. It was not just lives that were affected, but also the practice and ideals of chivalry. William Caxton appended his own thoughts on the sad state of chivalry at the end of the fifteenth century and on ways to return it to its former glory in the conclusion of his 1483–85 translation of Ramon Llull's famous late thirteenth-century book on chivalry—originally written in Catalan, although here Caxton seems to suggest he used a French translation. There is some irony in the fact that Richard III died at the battle of Bosworth not long after this book was published; his reputation remains one of the most ruthless of English monarchs, and not at all as Caxton describes him here.

Source: trans. Michael Livingston, from *Society at War: The Experience of England and France During the Hundred Years War*, ed. Christopher Allmand, 2nd ed. (Woodbridge, UK: Boydell Press, 1998), pp. 29–30.

Here ends *The Book of the Order of Chivalry*, which has been translated from the French and into English at the request of a gentle and noble squire by me, William Caxton, dwelling at Westminster beside London, in the best manner that God allowed me, and in accordance with the copy that the said squire delivered to me. This book is not requisite for every common man to have, but it is for noble gentlemen who by their virtue intend to come and enter into the noble order of chivalry, which in these latter days has been used according to this book heretofore written but forgotten, and the practices of chivalry not used, honored, nor exercised as it has been in ancient times. In those times the noble acts of the knights of England that used chivalry were renowned through the entire world; just to speak of those before the Incarnation of Jesus Christ, were there ever any found like Brennius and Belinus, that from Great Britain, now called England, unto Rome and far beyond conquered many kingdoms and lands, whose noble acts remain in the old histories of the Romans? And since the Incarnation of Our Lord, behold that noble king of Britain, King Arthur, with all the noble knights of the Round Table, whose noble acts and noble chivalry occupy so many large volumes that it is hard to believe.

O, you knights of England, where is the custom and usage of noble chivalry that was used in those days? What do you do now but go to the baths and play at dice? And some, not well advised, use not honest and good rules—against all orders of knighthood. Leave this! Leave it and read the noble volumes of the Holy Grail, of Lancelot, of Galahad, of Tristram, of Perys de Forest, of Percival, of Gawain, and many more. There shall you see manhood, courtesy, and gentility. And look, in latter days, at the noble acts since the Norman Conquest, as in the days of King Richard the Lionheart; Edward I and III, and his noble sons; Sir Robert Knolles; Sir John Hawkwood; Sir John Chandos; and Sir Walter Manny—read Froissart! And also behold that victorious and noble King Henry V, and the captains under him, his noble brethren, [Thomas] Montagu, the earl of Salisbury, and many others whose names since gloriously by their virtuous nobility and the acts that they did in the honor of the order of chivalry. Alas, you do nothing but sleep and relax, and are all completely disconnected from chivalry. I would ask you a question, if I should not displease: how many knights are there now in England that have the usefulness and the ability of a knight, that is to say, that he knows his horse, and his horse knows him? He must be ready at a moment to have all things that are proper for a knight: a horse that is compliant and broken after his hand, his armor and harness sound and fitting, and so forth, et cetera. I suppose a due search could be made, and however many should be found who lack, the more pitiful it would be. I wish it pleased our sovereign lord that twice or thrice in a year, or at the least once, he would call for jousts of peace, just so that every knight should have horse and harness, and also the use and craft of a knight, and also to tourney one against one, or two against two, and the winner to have a prize, a diamond or jewel such as should please the prince. This should cause gentlemen to resort to the ancient customs of chivalry, to great fame and renown, and also to be always ready to serve their prince when he shall call them, or have need. So let every man who is come from noble blood and intends to come to the noble order of chivalry read this little book, and do thereafter in keeping the lore and commandments contained herein. And then I do not doubt that he shall attain to the order of chivalry, et cetera. And thus this little book I present to my redoubted, natural, and most dread sovereign lord, King Richard III, king of England and of France, to the end that he command this book to be had and read to other young lords, knights, and gentlemen within this realm, that the noble order of chivalry be hereafter better used and honored than it has been in latter days. And thereby he shall do a noble and virtuous deed. And I shall pray to Almighty God for his long life and prosperous welfare, that he may have victory over all his enemies and, after this short and transitory life, that he have everlasting life in heaven, where there is joy and bliss, world without end, Amen.

D. FINANCING WAR

32. MILITARY OBLIGATIONS OF LANDHOLDERS (743)

In the early Middle Ages, "obligations" filled military ranks. Lords were granted lands on which their peasants would keep them wealthy enough to provide military service with a retinue of professional soldiers when needed by a superior lord or king. Lands granted to a holder in return for military service were called precaria. *These grants had an important part in the evolution of the general social organizations loosely defined as "feudalism." When greater numbers or financing were needed for an army, lands could be confiscated, even from the churches, and granted to lords. One of the earliest instances of this practice is provided here: the capitulary of Lestinnes, from the hand of Carloman,*

Charlemagne's uncle, in 743. Although established in this document, few pecaria were ever returned to their previous owners.

Source: trans. Oliver J. Thatcher and Edgar Holmes McNeal, *A Source Book for Mediæval History: Selected Documents Illustrating the History of Europe in the Middle Ages*, ed. Oliver J. Thatcher and Edgar Holmes McNeal (New York: Charles Scribner's Sons, 1905), p. 357.

Because of the threats of war and the attacks of certain tribes on our borders, we have determined, with the consent of God and by the advice of our clergy and people, to appropriate for a time part of the ecclesiastical property for the support of our army. The lands are to be held as *precaria* for a fixed rent; one solidus, or twelve denarii, shall be paid annually to the church or monastery for each *casata* [farm]. When the holder dies the whole possession shall return to the church. If, however, the exigency of the time makes it necessary, the prince may require the *precarium* to be renewed and given out again. Care shall be taken, however, that the churches and monasteries do not incur suffering or poverty through the granting of *precaria*. If the poverty of the church makes it necessary, the whole possession shall be restored to the church.

33. THE SALADIN TITHE AND CRUSADER ORDINANCES (1188)

Saladin's victory in the battle of Hattin (doc. 71) and his subsequent conquest of Jerusalem sent shockwaves throughout Europe. Among those answering the call for another crusade were the kings Henry II of England and Philip II Augustus of France: setting aside their own conflicts, they agreed to fight for the Holy Land and established a new kind of tax, popularly called the Saladin Tithe, to finance the coming crusade. The French king would eventually repeal the deeply unpopular tax, but, as seen below, Henry passed it via ordinance in 1188, along with a series of directives for would-be crusaders. After Henry's death in 1189, his successor Richard I the Lionheart agreed to uphold his predecessor's vow to go on crusade: as he prepared to depart in 1190, he passed further regulatory ordinances for those who would sail with him to the Holy Land.

Sources: trans. Henry Thomas Riley, *The Annals of Roger de Hoveden*, vol. 2 (London: H.G. Bohn, 1853), pp. 79–81, 140–41, 160–63; revised.

Ordinances of 1188

... Henry [II], king of England, after he had thus taken the cross, came to Le Mans, where on his arrival, he gave orders that everyone [in his kingdom] should give one-tenth of his revenues in the present year, and one-tenth of his chattels, as alms in a subsidy to the land of Jerusalem. The following articles were excepted from the levy: the arms, horses, and garments of men-at-arms, and the horses, books, clothes, vestments, and all kinds of sacred vessels belonging to the clergy, and also all kinds of precious stones belonging to either the clergy or the laity. Excommunication was pronounced beforehand by the archbishops, bishops, and rural deans, in each parish, against anyone who would not lawfully pay his aforementioned tithe in the presence and at the assessment of those whose duty it was to be present there.

Furthermore, the said money was to be collected in each parish in the presence of the priest of the parish, the rural dean, one Templar, one Hospitaller, one member of the household of our lord the king, one yeoman of the baron's household, his clerk, and the clerk of the bishop. And if anyone should give less, according to their conscientious assessment, than he ought to give, four or six lawful men of the parish were to be chosen, who, on oath, were to state the amount that he ought to have stated, on which he would be bound to add the amount by which it was deficient. Clerks, however, and knights who would take the cross, were not to pay any such tithes; but the revenues from their demesnes, and whatever their vassals should owe as their due, were to be collected by the above named persons, and to be remitted to them untouched.

... It was also enacted by the kings [of France and England], and the archbishops, bishops, and other princes of the land ... that no one [among the crusaders] should swear profanely, and that no one should play at games of chance or at dice; and no one was after the ensuing Easter to wear beaver, or grey fur, or sable, or scarlet; and all were to be content with two dishes [at a meal]. No one was to take any woman with him on the pilgrimage, unless, perhaps, some laundress accompany him on foot, about whom no suspicion could be entertained; and no person was to have his clothes in rags or torn....

34. POLL TAX (1379)

War is expensive. Even if systems of levy (or outright enslavement) mitigated the cost of some of the personnel, there remained enormous costs in their arms and armor, their foodstuffs, their encampments, and the transports to move it all. Medieval armies were often paid for through a combination of plunder rights, loans against treasures, and various forms of taxation on the populace. Among the most common taxes in this regard was the poll tax, which was essentially a tax on the value of an individual's movable goods—with churchmen, the poor, and specific other groups of individuals often exempt. In 1377 a more expansive poll tax was passed in England with an aim of gathering funds for the war against France: outside of a narrower range of exempt persons (churchmen and beggars), citizens over the age of 14 paid a single tax of a groat (4d). Two years later, the poll tax of 1379 introduced a far more complex method of military fundraising: the age was raised to 16, and taxes were broken down by social class. This taxation document, provided here, enables us to observe how a war-bound medieval England saw itself—or at least how government accountants saw it. The unpopularity of these taxes, and a third passed in 1381, is among the reasons for the bloody summer of the Peasants' Revolt that year.

Source: Alec R. Myers, ed., *English Historical Documents, Volume IV: 1327–1485* (London: Eyre and Spottiswoode, 1969), Parliamentary Roll III, document 50, p. 57.

The Duke of Lancaster and Duke of Brittany, each one ... 10 marks
Also, each earl of England ... £4
Also, each widowed countess of England, the same as an earl ... £4
Also, each baron and banneret, or knight of equal wealth ... 40s
Also, each widowed baroness shall pay as the baron, etc. ... 40s
Also, each bachelor and each squire who by the statute ought to be a knight ... 20s
Also, each widowed lady, wife of a bachelor or squire, according to her condition ... 20s
Also, each squire of less estate ... 6s 8d
Also, each widow of such a squire or merchant of sufficient means ... 6s 8d
Also, each squire possessing neither land nor rent nor castles, who is in service or under arms ... 3s 4d
Also, the chief prior of the hospital of St John [that is, the Hospitallers], as the baron ... 40s
Also, each commander of this order of England, as a bachelor ... 20s
Also, each other brother knight of the said order ... 13s 4d
Also, all the other brothers of the said order, each as a squire without possessions ... 3s 4d
Also, each justice, as well of one bench as the other, and those who have been justices of the same benches, and the chief baron of the exchequer, each ... 100s
Also, each sergeant and greater apprentice at law ... 40s
Also, other apprentices who follow the law, each ... 20s
Also, all the other apprentices of less estate, and attorneys, each ... 6s 8d
Also, the mayor of London, who pays as an earl ... £4
Also, the aldermen of London, each as a baron ... 40s
Also, all the mayors of the large towns of England, each as a baron ... 40s
Also, the other mayors of the other smaller towns, according to the condition of their estate ... 20s, 10s, or ½ mark
And all the aldermen of the large towns, and the great merchants of the realm, pay as bachelors ... 20s
Also, other merchants of sufficient means ... 13s 4d

Also, all the lesser merchants and artificers who have profit of the land, according to the condition of their estate ... 6s 8d, 3s 4d, 2s, 12d, or 6d
Also, each sergeant and franklin of the country, according to his estate ... 6s 8d or 40d
Also, the farmers of the manors, benefices, and granges, merchants of cattle and of other small merchandise, according to their estate ... ½ mark, 40d, 2s, or 12d
Also, all the advocates, notaries, and married solicitors pay as sergeants of the law, apprentices of the law, and attorneys, each according to his estate ... 40s, 20s, or ½ mark
Also, married pardoners and summoners, each according to his estate ... 3s 4d, 2s, or 12d
Item, all the hostlers who do not belong to the estate of merchant, each according to his estate ... 40d, 2s, or 12d
Also, each married man, for: Himself and his wife, who do not belong to the above named estates, above the age of sixteen, except veritable beggars ... 4d
And each single man and woman of such condition and above the said age ... 4d
Also, each foreign merchant, of whatsoever estate he may be, pays according to his condition as other residents.

And these payments above named shall be levied from no person except in the place where he is living and nowhere else. And be it remembered that the sums above named which are not definitely determined shall be assessed at the discretion of the assessors and controllers appointed for this purpose. And that the collectors of the subsidy above named shall have as the days of payment the feast of St John the Baptist next coming and the feast of St Peter ad Vincula next ensuing after that.

E. OUTFITTING FOR WAR

I. Individual

35. RENTING A SUIT OF ARMOR (1248)

Purchasing armor was a large expense for a young knight. Yet without looking the part, he would never be respected as a knight. An option, as is seen in this French contract from 1248, was to rent his armor.

Source: L. Blancard, ed., *Documents inédits sur le commerce de Marseille au Moyen Age*, vol. 2 (Marseilles: Barlatier-Feissat, Père et Fils, 1884), p. 305, in Roy C. Cave and Herbert H. Coulson, ed. *A Source*

Book for Medieval Economic History (Milwaukee, MI: The Bruce Publishing Co., 1936; repr., New York: Biblo & Tannen, 1965), pp. 110–11.

July 27th. In the year of the Incarnation of the Lord 1248.

I, Bonfils Manganelli, of Gaeta, acknowledge and confess to you, Atenoux Pecora, of Gaeta, that I have taken and received from you a certain suit of armor at a rent of seventeen solidi in mixed money now current in Marseilles, which seventeen solidi I have already paid you, renouncing all claims, etc. This armor I should take on the next voyage I am to make across the sea, for the price mentioned, at your risk and for your profit, going across the sea and returning to Marseilles. But if, on the completion of the said voyage, I should make another voyage with the said armor, I promise to pay you by this agreement, as hire for the said armor, one augustal of gold, and on the return from the said voyage to pay you that augustal and to return the armor or its value, namely seventy solidi in mixed money now current in Marseilles, if by chance the armor should be lost through my fault. Or I promise to bring the said armor to your profit under pledge of all my goods, present and future, renouncing the protection of all laws, etc. Witnesses, etc.

36. THE ARMING OF SIR GAWAIN (c. 1360)

Sir Gawain and the Green Knight, *while fanciful in its tale of a seemingly immortal Green Knight and the Arthurian knight who seeks him to pay a lost wager, is nevertheless grounded in the historical realities of its composition. Here, Sir Gawain arms himself before departing Camelot, revealing the poet's remarkably accurate portrait of a contemporary knight dressed in plate armor.*

Source: trans. Michael Livingston, from *Sir Gawain and the Green Knight*, ed. J.R.R. Tolkien and E.V. Gordon (Oxford, Clarendon Press, 1967), pp. 16–18.

He dwells there all that day, and dresses in the morn,
Asks early for his arms, and all at once were brought.
First a rug of Toulouse was spread over the floor,
Piled over with gilded gear that gleamed;
The brave man steps upon it, and handles the steel,
Dubbed in a doublet of a dear-bought Tars,
And then a well-crafted hood and collar, closed up high,
That with a bright white fur was lined within.
Then they set the steel shoes upon the man's feet,
His legs were lapped in steel with lovely greaves,
Then hinged plates, polished to a sheen,
About his knees were fastened with knots of gold;
Then fine cuisses, fitted to his form,

Enclosed his thick thighs, attached with thongs;
And then the decorated suit of bright steel rings
Encased that hero in costly clothes,
And well-burnished braces upon both his arms,
With elbow guards goodly and gay, and gloves of plate,
And all the fine gear that might be useful
    At that time;
  With a rich surcoat,
  Gold spurs to wear with pride,
  A sure, sheathed sword swinging
  From a silken sash at his side.

When he was set in arms, his harness was rich:
The least latch or loop gleamed with gold.
Thus harnessed he went to hear his mass,
Offered and honored at the high altar.
Then he comes to the king and to his court,
Rightly asks his leave from the lords and ladies;
And they kissed and escorted him, commended him to Christ.
By then Gringolet was ready, and rigged with a saddle
That gleamed in finery with many gold fringes,
Every nail was brand new, for that special occasion;
The bridle was barred, bound with gold bright;
The decoration of its breastpiece and its proud skirts,
The crupper and the caparison, matched the saddle-bow;
And all were adorned with rich red-gold nails,
That glittered and glint with the gleam of the sun.
Then he holds up his helmet and hastily kisses it,
Which was stoutly stapled with a stuffed lining.
It sat high on his head, fastened behind,
With a light cloth over the ventail,
Embroidered and bound with the best gems
On the broad silken border, and birds were on the seams,
Like popinjays painted preening between
Turtle-doves and true-loves interlaced so thick:
As many birds as had been thereabout in seven winters
    in the town.
  The circlet was even more prized
  Which surrounded his crown,
  A devise of diamonds
  That were both bright and smoked.

37. MARGARET PASTON TO HER HUSBAND (1449)

As the Hundred Years War turned against the English in the 1440s, political divisiveness spread throughout the kingdom. It would be another decade before the Wars of the Roses would begin, but already rebellions from the nobles to the peasants had begun, most placing the blame on the declining military fortunes of Henry VI, who had been king since he was only a couple of months old. One of the families caught up in this turmoil was the Pastons. While her husband, John, was away, Margaret Paston—as many medieval noble women did in similar circumstances—became responsible for the defense of their house and lands. Of special interest is her knowledge of effective defensive arms (including gunpowder weapons), both those owned by the family as well as others she felt ought to be purchased.

Source: trans. Michael Livingston, from *The Paston Letters,* vol. 1, ed. James Gairdner (Edinburgh: John Grant, 1910), pp. 82–83.

Rightly honored husband [John Paston], I recommend myself to you and pray that you will get some crossbows, windlasses to bind them with [to retract the stiff string of the crossbow], and quarrels. Your houses here are so low-ceilinged that no man may shoot out with a longbow—though we have ever so much need!

I suppose you should have such things from Sir John Fastolf, if you would send to him. Also I would ask you to get 2 or 3 short poleaxes [staff weapons] to keep beside the doors, and also many jacks [cloth covered armor made of small plates sewn onto fabric], if you can.

Patrick and those with him are deeply afraid that you would enter again upon them, and they have gathered a great ordinance within their house, as it is told to me. They have made bars to bar the doors crosswise, and they have made wickets on every corner of the house to shoot out from—both with bows and with hand-held guns. The holes that are made for hand-held guns are scarcely knee-high from the floor, and they've made five such holes. No man can shoot out from them with regular bows.

Perry fell into fellowship with William Hasard at Querles' [home], and he told him that he would come and drink with Patrick and his people. Querles said he should be welcome, and after noon he went there to see what they were doing and what company they had with them. When he came there, the doors were speared shut [fastened], and there was no one with them but Marioth, Capron and his wife, and Querles' wife, and another man in black who spoke somewhat haltingly—I suppose by his words that it was Norfolk of Gemingham. Perry spied all these aforesaid things. And Marioth and his company had a lot of big talk that shall be told to you when you come home.

I pray that you will vouchsafe to buy for me one pound of almonds and one pound of sugar, and that you will buy some frieze to make children's gowns;

you shall have the best prices and best choices from Hay's wife, so I'm told. And also please a yard of broad cloth of black for a hood for me ... for there is neither good cloth nor good frieze in this town. As for the children's gowns, once I have them, I will make them well.

The Trinity have you in His keeping, and send you Godspeed in all your matters.

II. Militia

38. FLORENTINE MILITIA REQUIREMENTS (1260)

Il libro di Montaperti, *from which the following is excerpted, was written in 1260—possibly by the philosopher Brunetto Latini—to prepare Florence (supporting the Guelphs) for war against neighboring Siena (supporting the Ghibellines). Siena would win a monumental, but hardly decisive battle at Montaperti (giving the* libro *its later title): within 30 years Siena was aligned with and under the leadership of Florence, and within 50 years the Ghibellines would be out of power in northern Italy. Both opposing armies in the battle were composed largely of citizen militia, for cavalry, infantry, and archer troops. This document explains the arms and armor each Florentine militia member was to provide, as well as the financial penalties incurred were they not to do so. As can be seen in the 1474 Troyes inventory (doc. 40), by the end of the Middle Ages city arsenals would provide militias with most of their required arms and armor.*

Source: trans. Kelly DeVries, from *Il libro di Montaperti (An. 1260)*, ed. Cesare Paoli (Florence: G.P. Vieusseux, 1889), pp. 373–74. The editors wish to thank Niccolò Capponi for suggesting this document to them.

Item, that any free cavalryman of the Commune of Florence, both the city and the county of Florence, ought to own and is obligated to carry and have in the present army a saddle for his warhorse; a horse covering; either a breastplate or coat of mail; greaves or mail leggings; a steel cap; a coat of plates or coat of mail [for the thighs]; a lance; a shield, either a targe or a broad shield. And whoever disobeys this and thus does not carry and have in the army said arms ... shall be condemned and fined, for the saddle 20 *solidi* of small florins; for the covering 60 *solidi*; for the breastplate or coat of mail 100 *solidi*; for the greaves or mail leggings 20 *solidi*; for the steel cap 20 *solidi*; for the lance 20 *solidi*; for the shield, either the targe or broad shield 20 *solidi* of small florins.

Item, that any infantryman of the city of Florence, ought to own and is obligated to carry and have in the present army, a breastplate or coat of mail with plate gauntlets, or with plate gauntlets with mail sleeves; a steel cap or close-fitting helmet; a plate gorget or collar; a lance; a shield or large shield. And whoever disobeys this and does not carry or have in the army said arms ... shall be condemned and fined, for the breastplate or coat of mail with gauntlets or gauntlets and mail sleeves 20 *solidi* in small florins; for the cap or close-fitting helmet 10 *solidi*; for the gorget or collar 10 *solidi*; for the lance 10 *solidi*; for the shield or large shield 10 *solidi* in small florins.

Item, all crossbowmen and archers of the city and county of Florence ought to own and are obligated to carry or have in the present army all of the arms that are required and necessary for them, or suffer whatever penalty the Podesta [that is, the chief magistrate of Florence] wishes to give them.

39. PROVISIONS FOR THE OSTEND MILITIA (1436)

In 1436, after switching his support from England to France in the Hundred Years War, Philip the Good, duke of Burgundy, besieged English-held Calais. Despite its strong economic ties to England, much of Flanders joined the Burgundians in the fight. When the siege failed and Philip returned to Burgundy, Flemish militias were called out to guard against English retaliatory attacks. The local armed groups were given provisions by the communities they were from, including the militia described here, which took position on the seaside dunes outside Ostend.

Source: trans. Kelly DeVries, from Ed Vlietinck, "Le siège de Calais et les villes de la comté flamande," *Annales de la société d'emulation de Bruges* 40 (1890): 97, 99.

Item, on the eighth day of August, when the English fleet lay before the town, so was consumed on the dune by the aldermen and some of the burghers, in food and in drink totaling 13 l. 8 s.

Item, on the eighth day of August, when the English fleet lay before the town, so was given to our allies [that is, other nearby militia] 16 tonnes of beer, each tonne costing 3 l. 12 s., paying a total of 57 l. 12 s.

Item, paid for 6 tonnes of small beer consumed at the same time; paid for each tonne 20 s., 6 l.

Item, paid for bread sent to our allies at the above-mentioned time and consumed also by our townsmen, overall 8 l. 4 s.

Item, paid Pieter Lammaerd for powder and shot delivered by him at the same time, in total 4 l. 5 s....

Item, on the twenty-third day of August as our sailors and sergeants shipped all eastward to sail up to the English fleet, payment for victuals the following by name:

First, for 24 tonnes of beers, for each tonne 48 s.;

Item, for 6 measures of bread, for each measure 54 s.;

Item, for 2 tubs of butter, for each tub 6 l.;

Item, for bacon and for cheese, 7 l. 4 s.;

For fat and for candles, 36 s.; paid for all 94 l. 16 s.

40. TROYES ARSENAL (1474)

By the end of the fifteenth century, arsenals began supplying urban militias with their arms and armor. As this inventory from Troyes, France, shows, in 1474 the militia was well supplied, with the city purchasing more arms and armor to add to or replace those stores. Of special note is the number of gunpowder weapons in the arsenal, especially of hand-held guns, which almost double the number of bows and crossbows.

Source: trans. Kelly DeVries, from Philippe Contamine, "L'armement des populations urbaines à la fin du Moyen Âge: l'exemple de Troyes (1474)," in *Pages d'histoire militaire médiévale (XIVe–XVe siècles)* (Paris: l'Académie des Inscriptions et Belles-Lettres, 2005), pp. 65–78.

	Beffroi		Croncels		Comporté		S. Jacques		Sum		Total
		M*		M		M		M		M	
Complete armor	12	3	23	3	9		5		49	6	55
Brigandines	62	19	43	32	56	18	47		208	[69]	277
Plate torso armor	21	6	32		34	1	22		109	7	116
Banded torso armor	14	14	25		5		5		49	14	63
Haubergeons and mail-coats	62	5	45		42		50		199	5	204
Jacks	26		23		78		6		133		133
Salades [conical helmets covering face] and bicoquets [close-fitting helmets covering some face]	210	98	201	12	242		132		785	110	895
Helmets and bascinets	25		33		31		62		151		151
Hand-held guns	124		151		154		118		547		547

	Beffroi		Croncels		Comporté		S. Jacques		Sum		Total
		M*		M		M		M		M	
Cannons	3		2								5
Crossbows and cranequins	80	16	69		69		53		271	16	287
Bows			12		15		10		37		37
Vouges [type of staff weapon]	117	77	80	2	119		73		389	79	468
Axes and war-hammers	213	8	232		242		168		855	8	863
Swords	234		260		302		251		1047		1047
Mallets with iron, bronze, or lead heads	137		114		334		172		757		757
Javelins, guisarmes, partisans, and pikes [staff weapons]	86		53		53		9		201		201

*M = armament purchased from merchants during that year.

III. State

41. FORTIFICATIONS AT DARA (6th CENTURY)

By the beginning of the sixth century, the Byzantines recognized the need to improve the defense of their eastern border, especially as their generals felt that they did not have an adequate base to launch operations against the Persians. Thus, in 505, Emperor Anastasius I ordered the expansion and fortification of the frontier village of Dara (or Daras), just 18 kilometers, or 11 miles, from the frequently warred-over city of Nisibis, then under Persian control. According to the following account of Procopius, this work was hastily and shoddily done, so that Justinian I—the adopted son and successor of Justin I, himself successor to Anastasius—was forced to instigate an enormous program of fortification that included changing the course of the River Cordes.

Source: trans. H.B. Dewing and Glanville Downey, Procopius, *On Buildings*, Loeb Classical Library 343 (Cambridge, MA: Harvard University Press, 1940), pp. 97–115.

When the Persians retired from the territory of the Romans, selling to them the city of Amida, as I have related in the *Books on the Wars*, the Emperor Anastasius selected a hitherto insignificant village close to the Persian boundary, Dara by name, and urgently set about enclosing it with a wall and making it into a city which should serve as a bulwark against the enemy. But since it was forbidden in the treaty which the Emperor Theodosius once concluded with the Persian kingdom, that either party should construct any new fortress on his own land where it bordered on the boundaries of the other's land, the Persians, citing the terms of the peace, tried with all their might to obstruct the work, though they were hard pressed by being involved in a war with the Huns. So the Romans, observing that they were for this reason unprepared, pressed on the work of building all more keenly, being anxious to get ahead of the enemy before they should finish their struggle with the Huns and come against them. Consequently, being fearful by reason of suspicion of the enemy, and continually expecting their attacks, they did not carry out the building with care, since the haste inspired by their extreme eagerness detracted from the stability of their work. For stability is never likely to keep company with speed, nor is accuracy wont to follow swiftness. They therefore carried out the construction of the circuit-wall in great haste, not having made it fit to withstand the enemy, but raising it only to such a height as was barely necessary; indeed they did not even lay the stones themselves carefully, or fit them together as they should, or bind them properly at the joints with mortar. So within a short time, since the towers could not in any way withstand the snows and the heat of the sun because of their faulty construction, it came about that the most of them fell into ruin. So were the earlier walls built at the city of Dara.

The Emperor Justinian perceived that the Persians, as far as lay in their power, would not permit this outpost of the Romans, which was a menace to them, to stand there, but they would of course assault it with all their might, and would use every device to conduct siege operations on even terms with the city; and that a great number of elephants would come with them, and these would bear wooden towers on their shoulders, under which they would stand, supporting them like foundations; and worse still, that they would be led about wherever the enemy needed them and would bear a fortress which would follow along wherever, according to the judgement of their masters, it should happen to be needed; and that the enemy would mount these towers and shoot down upon the heads of the Romans inside the city, and attack them from a higher level; that, furthermore they would raise up artificial mounds against them, and would bring up all manner of siege-engines. And if any misfortune should befall the city of Dara, which was thrown out like an earthwork before the whole Roman

Empire and was obviously placed as a threat to the enemy's land, the disaster for us would not stop there, but a great part of the State would be seriously shaken. For these reasons he wished to surround the place with defences in keeping with its practical usefulness.

First of all he rendered the wall (which, as I have said, was very low and therefore very easy for an enemy to assault) both inaccessible and wholly impregnable for an attacking force. For he contracted the original apertures of the battlements by inserting stones and reduced them to very narrow slits, leaving only traces of them in the form of tiny windows, and allowing them to open just enough for a hand to pass through, so that outlets were left through which arrows could be shot against assailants. Then above these he added to the wall a height of about thirty feet, not building the addition upon the whole thickness of the wall, lest the foundations should be overloaded by the excessive weight which bore upon them, so that the whole work would suffer some irreparable damage, but he enclosed the space at that level with courses of stones on the outside and constructed a colonnaded stoa running all around the wall, and he placed the battlements above this portico, so that the wall really had a double roof throughout; and at the towers there were actually three levels for the men who defended the wall and repelled attacks upon it. For at about the middle of each tower he added a rounded structure (*sphairikon schêma*) upon which he placed additional battlements, thus making the wall three-storeyed.

Then he observed that it had come about that many of the towers, as I have said, had fallen into ruin in a short time, yet it was entirely out of the question to pull them down, since the enemy were constantly in the neighbourhood watching their opportunity and continually scouting to see whether they might not find some part of the defences dismantled at any time. But he hit upon the following plan. He left these towers in place, and outside each of them he cleverly erected another structure in the form of a rectangle, which was built securely and with every possible care, and thus, by means of a second set of defences, he safely enclosed those parts of the wall which had suffered. But one of the towers, called the "Tower of the Guard," he pulled down at a favourable moment and rebuilt so that it was safe, and everywhere he removed the fear which had arisen from the weakness of the circuit-wall. He also wisely added sufficient height, in due proportion, to the outerworks. And outside these he dug a moat, not in the way in which men are wont to make them, but only for a short distance and in a novel manner; and the reason for this I shall explain.

The greater part of the defences, as it happens, are in general unapproachable for an attacking party, since they do not stand on level ground and offer no favourable opportunity for assault to an approaching force; but they stand along a steep slope of a rough and precipitous character, where it is not possible for a mine to be dug or for any attack to be made. But on the side which is turned toward south, the soil is deep and soft and consequently easy to mine, so that it makes the city assailable on this side. So in that place he dug a crescent-shaped moat, with sufficient breadth and depth and extending to a great distance, and joined either end of this to the outworks and filled it amply with water, rendering it altogether impassable for the enemy; and on its inner side he set up another outerwork. On this the Romans take their stand and keep guard in time of siege, freed from anxiety for the circuit-wall and the other outerwork which is thrown out before the main wall. And it happened that between the main wall and the outerwork, at the gate which faces toward the village of Ammodius, there lay a great mound of earth, under cover of which the enemy were able to be in large measure unobserved while making mines against the city under the circuit-wall. This mound he removed from the spot and he cleared up the place thoroughly, and thus frustrated any secret attack on the wall by the enemy.

Thus did he construct these fortifications. He likewise made reservoirs for water both in the space between the circuit-wall and the outworks and also close by the church which is dedicated to the Apostle Bartholomew, situated toward the west. And a river also flows from a suburb of the city which is two miles distant from it and is called Cordes. On either side of it rise two cliffs which are exceedingly rugged. This river flows down between the heights on either side of it all the way to the city, carried along the bases of the mountains, and for just this reason it cannot be turned aside or tampered with by the enemy; for there is no flat ground where they might be able to turn it from its course. And it is drawn into the city in the following way. They have constructed a large channel extending out from the circuit-wall, and covered the mouth of the conduit with a great number of the thickest possible iron bars, some upright and some horizontal; and thus they have arranged that the water can enter the city without endangering the fortifications. In this way the water flows into the city and fills its reservoirs and then is conducted wherever the inhabitants wish, and finally flows out at another part of the city, the opening for its discharge being made like that by which it enters the city. And winding about the plain nearby, it used to make the city easy to besiege; for it was not a difficult matter, thanks to the bountiful supply of water, for the enemy to encamp there. So in order that this should not happen the Emperor Justinian took the situation under careful consideration, seeking diligently to find some remedy for the condition. And God provided the solution for the impossible problem which confronted him, settling the matter out of hand and saving the city without the least delay. This took place as follows.

One of the men serving in the army in this place, either in consequence of a dream or led to do it of his own accord, gathered a great throng of the workmen who were engaged in the building operations and bade them dig a long trench within the circuit-wall, shewing them a certain spot where he said that they would find sweet water welling up from the recesses of the earth. He made the pit in the form of a circle fifteen feet across and drove it down to a great depth. This pit proved to be the salvation of the city, not indeed by any foresight of these workmen, but an event here, which would have been a disaster, turned out entirely to the advantage of the Romans, all on account of the pit. For during this time extraordinarily heavy rains fell, and the river, which I just mentioned, rose in high flood before the circuit-wall and no longer flowed in its usual bed, and it became so swollen that neither the opening by which it entered the city nor the conduit could contain it as formerly. So it backed up and gathered its stream against the wall, rising to a great height and depth; in some places it was stagnant, but elsewhere it was rough and turbulent. Consequently it broke through the outer defences and levelled them at once, and it also carried away a great portion of the main wall, and forcing open the gates and flowing in a mighty stream it spread over practically the whole city, and it circulated through the market-place and the streets and even through the houses, sweeping onward a great mass of furniture and wooden utensils and other such objects; then plunging into this pit it disappeared underground. Not many days later it emerged near the confines of Theodosiopolis, reappearing in a place about forty miles from the city of Dara, and it was recognised by the objects which it had carried off from the houses of that city; for the whole of the rubbish came to light there. And since then, in times of peace and in prosperity, this river has flowed into the centre of the city and filled the storage-reservoirs with water to overflowing and then has been borne out of the city by the exits made for this purpose by those who built the city, as I have just explained. And it waters the land in that region and is always eagerly welcomed by all those who dwell round about. But whenever a hostile army comes up to besiege the city, they close the exits through the iron bars by means of sluice-gates, as they are called, straightway forcing the river, by this artificial constraint, to alter its course and change its exit, and they conduct it to the pit and the chasm which leads away from it. And as a result of this the enemy are hard pressed by lack of water and are compelled immediately to abandon the siege. Indeed Mirrhanes, the Persian general during the reign of Cabades, came there to lay a siege, but was compelled by all these difficulties to retire after no long time without having accomplished anything. And Chosroes himself, a long time later, came there for the same purpose with a great army and undertook to attack the city. But finding himself in straits for want of water, and viewing the imposing height of the circuit-wall, which he suspected was quite impregnable, he changed his purpose and departed, marching straight for the Persian territory, outwitted by the foresight of the Roman Emperor.

42. CONSTRUCTION OF SAPHET CASTLE (c. 1263)

Following the First Crusade, the crusaders who remained in the Holy Land built a number of stone fortifications throughout the lands they captured. With declining numbers, it would be easier to control these from a few garrisons protected by strong fortifications. From 1168 until its capture by Saladin following a year-long siege in 1188, the high mountain castle of Saphet was a crusader stronghold in the Holy Land. In 1240 Theobold I of Navarre, as part of the negotiations ending his part in the Barons' Crusade, regained the region; control of the site was handed over to the Knights Templar, who rebuilt the fortress under the encouragement of Benoît d'Alignan, bishop of Marseilles, as described in the account reproduced here. The castle would fall to Mamluk sultan Baybars in 1266.

Source: Hugh Kennedy, *Crusader Castles* (Cambridge: Cambridge University Press, 1994), pp. 190–98.

Since it is our firm and steadfast intention to be always zealous in those things which are to the honour of God and to dwell continually and chiefly on those which we perceive to be for the exaltation of the Faith and the Church; the edification of those around, the salvation of souls and the support of the Holy Land, we propose to set forth specially and principally when and why the castle of Saphet was begun and how it was built.

Why, When and How the Building of the Castle at Saphet Was Begun

A great army of Christians, among whom were the King of Navarre and Count of Champagne, the Duke of Burgundy, the Count of Brittany, the Count of Nevers and Forez, the Count of Montfort, the Count of Bar, the Count of Macon and many other counts and barons, arrived to support the Holy Land. In this army the knights with military equipment numbered more than 1,500 in addition to those who did not have sufficient military equipment and an almost uncountable multitude of crossbowmen and footmen. When they arrived at Jaffa and Ascalon and debated how they ought to proceed, certain nobles, trusting in their own strength and disregarding the advice of the Templars, Hospitallers and other churchmen and nobles of the country, left the army by night. And since they did not give glory to God, to whom victory belongs, but instead tried to take it for themselves, they were ignominiously defeated, many of them were captured and killed and the army was driven back to Jaffa in great confusion. There, in order to alleviate and mitigate the disaster, it was decided to rebuild the castle of Saphet, since they could not construct such a good work in the whole land. And so that the Master of the Temple could begin the work, they promised to give him 7,000 marks to pay for it and that the army would stay there for two months so that it could be built more safely and easily.

But when they returned to sandy Acre they forgot their promises and they did not go to build nor did they contribute anything towards it.... While [the bishop of Marseilles] was waiting for some days in Damascus as commanded by the Sultan, many people frequently inquired of him if Saphet was to be rebuilt....

Therefore when the bishop returned from Damascus, he carefully observed the land as far as Saphet and he did not see any fortress apart from Subeibe which was held by the nephew of the Sultan. When he reached Saphet he found there a heap of stones without any building where once there had been a noble and famous castle and there he was received with great joy by brother Rainhardus de Caro who was at that time the castellan there. But they had nowhere there to lay their head ...

When the bishop had inquired carefully about the surroundings and district of the castle and why the Saracens were so fearful of it being built, he found that if the castle were constructed, it would be a defence and security and like a shield for the Christians as far as Acre against the Saracens. It would be a strong and formidable base for attack and provide facilities and opportunities of making sallies and raids into the land of the Saracens as far as Damascus. Because of the building of this castle, the Sultan would lose large sums of money, massive subsidies and service of the men and property of those who would otherwise be of the castle and would also lose his own land casals [villages] and agriculture and pasture and other renders since they would not dare to farm the land for fear of the castle. As a result of this his land would turn to desert and waste and he would also be obliged to incur great expenditure and employ many paid soldiers [*stipendiarios*] for the defence of Damascus and the surrounding lands. In brief, he found from common report that there was no fortress in that land from which the Saracens would be so much harmed and the Christians so much helped and Christianity spread.

When the bishop heard this and similar opinions, he came to Acre and visited the Master of the Temple, Arnaud de Périgord, who was lying sick, and the Master asked him what he had seen and heard in Damascus. The bishop told him about what seemed more significant to him, what he had heard about how the Saracens were in fear and trembling and seeking reassurance about the building of the castle at Saphet. So with reference to what he had said, he began to persuade him forcefully and insistently that they should devote all their strength to build it quickly during the time of truce. But the Master said to him with a sigh, "Lord Bishop, it is not easy to build Saphet. Did not you yourself hear what the King of Navarre, the Duke of Burgundy and the counts and barons of the army promised about going to Saphet so that it could be built more securely and more rapidly, and how they would stay there for two months and give 7,000 marks for the building? In the end they did not pay a single penny for the building and you are saying that we should build the castle without a help from anyone?" ...

How the Bishop of Marseilles Persuaded the Master of the Temple and His Council to Build the Castle of Saphet

The following day the bishop came to the Master and asked him to call his council because he wished to speak to them about something important to him. When they came the bishop said to them, "Lords, I understand that your Order was first begun by holy knights who dedicated themselves totally to the protection of the Christians and attacks on the Saracens. Since they kept to this firmly and faithfully, the Lord exalted and favoured your Order with the Apostolic See and with kings and princes and today your Order is greatly celebrated and renowned with God and men. It seems to me that you should now follow the example of those holy knights. When I was in Damascus, I found out from many people that there is nothing else that the Saracens would fear as much as the building of Saphet, since it is said that with the building of that castle, the gates of Damascus are closed. We ourselves have seen and inspected the site and it is commonly known that it is not possible to build a castle or fortress in this land, by which Christianity can be so well defended and the infidelity of the Saracens attacked, as Saphet. Because of this I as your faithful friend, mindful of the honour of God, the salvation of souls and the promotion of your Order, ask, advise and demand that you, as faithful servants of God and devoted and strong knights, look back to the example of those first holy knights, who founded your Order and that, following the example of your founders, you offer you and yours to build the castle of Saphet, which will always remain such a threat to the infidels and such a defence to the faithful. I however do not have the money which would be sufficient for you for this work but I offer myself to make a pilgrimage there, if you want to build it. If however you don't want to, I will preach to the pilgrims and go there with them to build of rubble because there is there a big pile of stones, and I will make there a wall of dry stones to defend the Christians from the attacks of the Saracens!"

When he had heard this, the Master, as if laughing replied, "You are clearly determined what should be done!" and the bishop added, "May you and yours take good counsel and may the Lord be with you." And so he withdrew from them. The Lord, however, directed their council and they unanimously decided that the said castle should be rebuilt now while they were at truce with the Sultan of Damascus, because if it was put off, the building could easily be delayed.

The Joy at the Building of the Castle at Saphet

When it had been decided that Saphet should be built, there was great joy in the House of the Temple and in the city of Acre and among the people of the Holy Land. Without delay an impressive body of knights, serjeants, crossbowmen and other armed men were chosen with many pack animals to carry arms, supplies and other necessary materials. Granaries, cellars, treasuries and other offices were generously and happily opened to make payments. A great number of workmen and slaves were sent there with the tools and materials they needed. The land rejoiced at their coming and the true Christianity of the Holy Land was exalted.

The bishop of Marseilles himself came with those pilgrims he could bring and pitched his tents on the site of the synagogue of the Jews and the mosque of the Saracens so that by this he indicated and clearly showed that the castle of Saphet would be rebuilt to weaken the unfaithfulness of the infidels and strengthen and defend the faith of Our Lord Jesus Christ. When everything that was required for the beginning of so glorious a work was ready, after the celebration of Mass, the bishop came and gave a short sermon to encourage the devotion of those present, called on the grace of the Holy Spirit and, with a blessing and due solemnity, laid the first stone to the honour of Our Lord Jesus Christ and the exaltation of the Christian faith. On the stone he displayed a silver gilt jar full of money to support subsequent work. This was done in the year of the Lord 1240, on the third of the ides of December [11 December].

How a Well of Fresh Water Was Found Within the Castle of Saphet

Since there was a lack of water there and since it was brought from afar by many pack animals with labour and expense, the bishop sought for several days to find small springs to make a cistern to collect water in. A certain old Saracen man said to the bishop's steward, "If your lord gives me a tunic, I will show him a spring of fresh water within the castle." When he had promised him the tunic, he showed him the place where there is now a well over which there were ruins of towers and walls and many piles of stones. When they asked him again for a clear sign, he said that they would find a sword and a helmet of iron in the mouth of the well and so it was found to be. Because of this, they worked more determinedly and strenuously there until at length excellent flowing water was discovered in great abundance for the whole castle. The bishop stayed there until the castle was firmly established so that it could defend itself against the enemies of the faith. When he returned home he gave to the castle as if to his dearest chosen son ...

The Wonderful Construction of the Castle of Saphet

When, however, the same bishop returned to support the Holy Land ... on 4 of the Nones of October [4 October 1260], and came to visit Saphet, he found that, between the one journey when the bishop returned to Marseilles and the other by which he returned to Saphet, by the grace and providence of God and the energy and prestige of the brothers of the Temple, the castle had been built with such industry and such wonder and magnificence that its exquisite and excellent construction seemed to be made, not by man but rather by almighty God.

To understand this more fully and make it clearer: the castle of Saphet is situated almost half-way between the cities of Acre and Damascus, in Upper Galilee on a spur entirely surrounded by mountains and hills, sheer precipices, crags and rocks. From most directions it is inaccessible and impregnable because of the difficulties, hardships and narrowness of the roads. In the direction of Damascus, however, it has the river Jordan and the Lake of Genasereth (also known as the Sea of Galilee and the Sea of Tiberias) like a rampart and these are like natural fortifications at a distance. There are however there both inner and outer wonderful man-made fortifications and buildings to be admired.

It is not easy to convey in writing or speech how many fine buildings there are there: what fine and numerous defences and fortifications with ditches, which measure 7 cannas [15.4 m; a canna is 2.2 meters] in the depth of rock and six in width: what inner walls, 20 cannas [44 m] high and a canna and a half [3.3 m] thick at the top: what outer walls and trenches, 10 cannas [22 m] in height and 375 cannas [825 m] in circumference: what underground tunnels between the outer wall and the [inner] ditch with underground chambers round the whole castle for 375 cannas [825 m]: what casemates, which are called *fortie cooperte*, which are above the ditches and underneath the outer wall, where there can be crossbowmen with great balistas which defend the ditches and things near and far and cannot be seen by others from outside where they can be safe without any other protection: what towers and battlements where there are seven towers, of which everyone is 22 cannas [48.4 m] in height, 10 [22 m] in breadth, with walls 2 cannas [4.4 m] in thickness at the top: how many offices for all necessities: what number, size and variety of construction of crossbows, quarrels, machines and every sort of arms, and what effort and amount of expense in making them: what number of guards every day, what number of the garrison of armed men to guard and defend and repel enemies who were required there: how many workmen with different trades, how much and what expenses are made to them daily. It is not suitable to pass by in silence such famous, such exceptional, such magnificent and such necessary works done and needing to be done for the honour of God and the exaltation of the Christian name, for the bringing down of the infidel and the building up of the faithful but at least to proclaim some of them to encourage the devotion and compassion of the faithful.

The Massive Daily Expenses for Guarding the Castle of Saphet

For the honour therefore of Our Lord Jesus Christ and to show the devoted strength and immense need of the holy knights of the Order of the Temple, and to encourage devotion and compassion and to kindle the charity of the Christian faithful towards the Order and the castle, we will detail the expenses which the house of the Temple made there for building. For as we asked and carefully inquired from the senior men and through the senior men of the house of the Temple, in the first two and a half years, the house of the Temple spent on building the castle of Saphet, in addition to the revenues and income of the castle itself, eleven hundred thousand Saracen bezants, and in each following year more or less forty thousand Saracen bezants. Every day victuals are dispensed to 1,700 or more and in time of war, 2,200. For the daily establishment of the castle, 50 knights, 30 serjeants brothers, and 50 Turcupoles are required with their horses and arms, and 300 crossbowmen, for the works and other offices 820 and 400 slaves. There are used there every year on average more than 12,000 mule-loads of barley and corn apart from other victuals, in addition to payments to the paid soldiers and hired persons, and in addition to the horses and tack and arms and other necessities which are not easy to account.

The Excellence of the Castle of Saphet

To show the excellence of the castle so that so much work does not seem useless, burdensome, dispensible and insufficient, or unfit for habitation, it should be noted that the castle of Saphet has a temperate and healthy climate, rich in gardens, vines, trees and grass, gentle and smiling, rich and abundant in the fertility and variety of fruit. There figs, pomegranates, almonds and olives grow and flourish. God blesses it with rain from the sky and richness from the soil and abundance of corn, vines, oil, pulses, herbs and choice fruits, plenty of milk and honey, and pastures suitable for the feeding of animals, glades, trees and woods for making lime-kilns and for cooking plentiful foods, very good stone quarries in the place for building work and irrigation from springs and large cisterns to water animals and irrigate plants, not only outside the castle, but even within where very good fresh water abounds and several great cisterns suitable for any purpose.

There are there twelve water-mills outside the castle and many more powered by animals or wind and more than enough ovens, as is appropriate. Nor is anything lacking for the nobility and needs of the castle; there are various sorts of hunting and various sorts of plentiful fish in the River Jordan, the Sea of Galilee, the Lake of Genasereth and the Great Sea, from other places whence fresh or salt fish can be brought daily.

Among the other excellent features which the castle of Saphet has, it is notable that it can be defended by a few and that many can gather under the protection of its walls and it cannot be besieged except by a very great multitude; but such a multitude would not have supplies for long since it would find neither water nor food, nor can a very great multitude be near at the same time and, if they are scattered in remote places, they cannot help one another.

The Usefulness of the Castle and the Surrounding Places Which Are Attached to It

You can realise how useful and necessary the castle is to the whole of the Christian lands and how harmful it is to the infidels by the experience of those who know that before it was built the Saracens, Bedouin, Khwarazmians and Turkmen used to make raids to Acre and through other lands of the Christians. By the building of the castle of Saphet, a bulwark and obstacle was placed and they did not dare to go from the River Jordan to Acre, except in very great numbers, and between Acre and Saphet loaded pack animals and carts could pass safely and agricultural lands could be worked freely. Between the River Jordan and Damascus, on the other hand, the land remained uncultivated and like a desert for fear of the castle of Saphet, whence great raids and depredations and layings waste are made as far as Damascus. There the Templars won many miraculous victories against the enemies of the Faith, which are not easy to recount since a great book could be written about them.

However it should not be omitted that below the castle of Saphet in the direction of Acre, there is a town or large village where there is a market and numerous inhabitants and which can be defended from the castle. In addition the castle of Saphet has under its lordship and in its district, more than 260 casals, which are called *ville* in French, in which there are more than 10,000 men with bows and arrows in addition to others from whom it is possible to collect large sums of money to be divided between the castle of Saphet and other Orders and barons and knights to whom the casals belong, and from whom little or nothing could be collected before the building of Saphet, nor would it be collected today if the castle had not been built since all were in the possession of the Sultan and other Saracens....

43. A WEAPONS DOWRY (1449)

James II had become king in 1437 at age five following the assassination of his father, James I. In preparing to wed ten years later, he looked toward the continent for a suitable bride. Negotiations with the powerful Philip the Good, duke of Burgundy, led to a 3 July 1449 marriage between James II and Philip's great-niece, Mary of Guelders. As part of Mary's dowry, Philip sent the following weapons, in what may be the only weapons dowry given during the Middle Ages. James would die in 1460: in looking down at the firing of a cannon, the removeable chamber flew out and decapitated the king. We do not know if it was one the dowry cannons that did the deed.

Source: trans. Kelly DeVries, from Joseph Garnier, *L'artillerie des ducs de Bourgogne d'après les documents conservés aux archives de la Cote-d'Or* (Paris: Honoré Champion, 1895), pp. 130–31.

Hereafter follows the artillery which was sent in five galleys, which the duke had built in Antwerp in the years 1448 and 1449, and which were taken to the queen of Scotland, Mary of Guelders, wife of James II, in Scotland. Duke Philip himself had negotiated this marriage.

Firstly.

50 brigandines [cloth-covered armor made of plates] covered in black fustian.
33 garde-bras [shoulder and arm armor] of the same color.
87 brigandines for the Scots.
Item for the Scots, 649 salades [conical helmets with face covering].
Item 480 swords for these Scots.
Item 126 steel crossbows.
Item 36 martinets called baudré to hold those crossbows.
Item 428 lances with stops and points.
Item 81 gisarmes [staff weapons].
Item 130 pavises, both large and small.
Item 115 cases of crossbow bolts, containing 30,000 crossbow bolts.
Item 5,000 large crossbow bolts and 5,000 half-size large crossbow bolts.
Item 10 cases of bows, containing 400 bows.
Item 17 cases of arrows, containing 9,600.
Item 22 iron veuglaires and 64 chambers for those veuglaires [medium-sized gunpowder artillery].
Item 46 iron couleuvrines [hand-held gunpowder weapons].
Item 5 barrels of powder, as much for couleuvrines as for veuglaires.
Item 4 barrels of Antwerp rope.
Item 16 winches.
Item 400 stones for the veuglaires.
Item 6,000 caltrops.

F. RECRUITING AND OBLIGATIONS

44. CHARLEMAGNE'S WAY OF RAISING TROOPS (801–811)

The recruitment of men to fight in wars is among a ruler's most important duties. The few willing to serve rarely fill required numbers. By 804 Charlemagne's Holy Roman Empire was the largest political entity in Europe. He needed both to defend against incursions from outside, as well as continue his conquest of neighbors, primarily non-Catholics the emperor targeted for conversion, by force if necessary. The following provisions are taken from three capitularies and one letter to an abbot from the few sources that reveal some of the regulations and methods used by Charlemagne to raise soldiers and guarantee appropriate arms and armor for his armies in the early ninth century.

Source: James Harvey Robinson, ed., *Readings in European History* (Boston: Ginn and Company, 1904), pp. 135–37; revised.

Capitulare Italicum (801), On Those Who Refuse to Serve in the Army

If any free man, out of contempt for our command, shall have presumed to remain at home when the others go to war, let him know that he ought to pay the full *hari bannum* [a fine for refusing to join the army] according to the law of the Franks—that is, sixty *solidi*. Likewise, also, for contempt of single capitularies which we have promulgated by our royal authority—that is, any one who shall have broken the peace decreed for the churches of God, widows, orphans, wards, and the weak shall pay the fine of sixty *solidi*.

If any one shall have shown himself so contumacious or haughty as to leave the army and return home without the command or permission of the king—that is, if he is guilty of what we call in the German language *herisliz*—he himself, as a criminal, shall incur the peril of losing his life, and his property shall be confiscated for our treasury.

Capitulare Missorum De Exercitu Promovendo (808), On the Military Obligations of Landowners

Every free man who has four *mansi* of his own property [each manse equals about 135 acres], or as a benefice from any one, shall equip himself and go to the army, either with his lord, if the lord goes, or with his count. He who has three *mansi* of his own property shall be joined to a man who has one *mansus*, and shall aid him so that he may serve for both. He who has only two *mansi* of his own property shall be joined to another who likewise has two *mansi*, and one of them, with the aid of the other, shall go to the army. He who has only one *mansus* of his own shall be joined to one of three men who have the same and shall aid him, and the latter shall go alone; the three who have aided him shall remain at home.

Capitulare Aquisgranense, On the Supplying of Armies

Concerning going to the army: the count in his county under penalty of the ban, and each man under penalty of sixty *solidi*, shall go to the army, so that they come to the appointed muster at that place where it is ordered. And the count himself shall see in what manner they are prepared; that is, each one shall have a lance, shield, bow with two strings, and twelve arrows. And the bishops, counts, and abbots shall oversee their own men and shall come on the day of the appointed muster and there show how they are prepared.

The equipments of the king shall be carried in carts, also the equipments of the bishops, counts, abbots, and nobles of the king; flour, wine, pork, and victuals in abundance, mills, adzes, axes, augers, slings, and men who know how to use these well. And the marshals of the king shall add stones for these on twenty beasts of burden, if there is need. And each one shall be prepared for the army and shall have plenty of all utensils. And each count shall save two parts of the fodder in his county for the army's use, and he shall maintain good bridges and good boats.

Charlemagne's Letter to Abbot Fulrad, Summoning Him for Military Service

In the name of the Father, Son, and Holy Spirit, Charles, serene and august, crowned by God great and pacific emperor, and by God's mercy king of the Franks and the Lombards, to Fulrad the Abbot:

Be it known to you that we have decided to hold our general assembly for this year in the eastern part of Saxony, on the river Bode, at the place which is called Straßfurt. Wherefore we do command you that you come to this place with the full quota of men, well armed and equipped, on the fifteenth day before the Kalends of July, which is seven days before the feast of St. John the Baptist. Then shall you come to the aforesaid place, with your men ready, so that you can go in military array in any direction where our command shall send you.

You shall have arms and gear, and warlike instruments, and food and clothing. Each horseman shall have a shield, lance, sword, dagger, bow, and quivers with arrows. In the carts you shall have implements of divers kinds: axes, planes, augers, boards, spades, iron shovels, and other tools of which an army has need. In the carts you must also have supplies of food for three months, dating from the time of the assembly, and arms and clothing for a half year. We order you to attend carefully to all these things so that you may proceed peacefully to the aforesaid place. For through whatever part of our realm your journey shall take you, you shall not presume to take anything but fodder, food, and water. Let the men of each one of your vassals march along with the carts and horsemen, and let the leader always be with them until they reach the aforesaid place, so that the absence of a lord may not give to his men an opportunity of doing evil....

45. POPE GREGORY PLEADS FOR MATILDA TO LEAD A CRUSADE (1074)

The 1071 defeat of Byzantine imperial forces by the Seljuk Turks at the battle of Manzikert—which left the Byzantine emperor a prisoner and his realm in turmoil—sent shockwaves through the West. Just three short years later, at the Byzantines' request, the newly anointed Pope Gregory VII made a general call to Christian princes to unite Christendom against the Muslim threat. Gregory also sent a personal letter to Matilda, the increasingly powerful margravine of Tuscany. The high military and political regard in which she was held is made clear by the pope's pleading that she and Adelaide, the wife of Holy Roman Emperor Henry IV (against whom Gregory would face off in the Investiture Controversy), might do more than anyone else to help the cause. While this bears striking similarities with Pope Urban II's successful call for the First Crusade just 21 years later (doc. 14), Gregory's call to the princes and Matilda went unanswered.

Sources: trans. Oliver J. Thatcher and Edgar Holmes McNeal, *A Source Book for Mediæval History: Selected Documents Illustrating the History of Europe in the Middle Ages*, ed. Oliver J. Thatcher and Edgar Holmes McNeal (New York: Charles Scribner's Sons, 1905), pp. 512–13; trans. Ephraim Emerton, *The Correspondence of Pope Gregory VII, Selected Letters from the Registrum*, Records of Civilization (New York: Columbia University Press, 1932, repr. 1990), pp. 60–61.

General Letter to Christian Princes

Gregory, bishop, servant of the servants of God, to all who are willing to defend the Christian faith, greeting and apostolic benediction.

We hereby inform you that the bearer of this letter, on his recent return from across the sea [from Palestine], came to Rome to visit us. He repeated what we had heard from many others, that a pagan race had overcome the Christians and with horrible cruelty had devastated everything almost to the walls of Constantinople, and were now governing the conquered lands with tyrannical violence, and that they had slain many thousands of Christians as if they were but sheep. If we love God and wish to be recognized as Christians, we should be filled with grief at the misfortune of this great empire [the Byzantine] and the murder of so many Christians. But simply to grieve is not our whole duty. The example of our Redeemer and the bond of fraternal love demand that we should lay down our lives to liberate them. "Because he has laid down his life for us: and we ought to lay down our lives for the brethren," [1 John 3:16]. Know, therefore, that we are trusting in the mercy of God and in the power of his might and that we are striving in all possible ways and making preparations to render aid to the Christian empire [the Byzantine] as quickly as possible. Therefore we beseech you by the faith in which you are united through Christ in the adoption of the sons of God, and by the authority of St. Peter, prince of apostles, we admonish you that you be moved to proper compassion by the wounds and blood of your brethren and the danger of the aforesaid empire and that, for the sake of Christ, you undertake the difficult task of bearing aid to your brethren [the Byzantines]. Send messengers to us at once inform us of what God may inspire you to do in this matter.

Personal Letter to Matilda

How serious my intention and how great my desire to go overseas and with Christ's help carry succor to the Christians who are being slaughtered like sheep by pagans, I hesitate to say to some persons lest I seem to be moved by too great fickleness of purpose. But to you, my most dearly beloved daughter, I have no hesitation in declaring any of these matters; for I have more confidence in your good judgment than you yourself could possibly express.

Therefore, when you have read the letter which I have written to the faithful beyond the Alps, pray use your utmost efforts to furnish whatever aid and counsel you can in the service of your Creator. If, as some say, it is beautiful to die for one's country, it is most beautiful and glorious indeed to give our mortal bodies for Christ, who is life eternal. I am convinced that many men-at-arms will support us in this work, that even our empress will be willing to go with us to those parts and to take you with her, leaving your mother here to protect our common interests, so that with Christ's help we may be safe in going. If the empress will come, her prayers joined with yours may rouse many to this work. And I, provided with such sisters, would most gladly cross the sea and place my life, if need be, at the service of Christ with you whom I hope to have forever at my side in our eternal home. Pray and send me word as soon as possible of your decision in this matter and also of your coming to Rome, and may Almighty God deign to grant you his blessing, leading you from strength to strength, that our universal mother may long rejoice in you.

46. LEVY OF TROOPS FOR THE WARS IN BOHEMIA (1422)

Although more and more reliant on waged professional and paid mercenary soldiers, in the fifteenth century many armies continued to use forces levied for service out of "feudal" obligation, as seen in this Holy Roman Imperial muster of 1422 to raise troops to fight the Hussites rebels in Bohemia. Some of these obligations were based on centuries-old legal tradition, with both secular and ecclesiastical lords expected to provide and arm soldiers.

Source: *Translations and Reprints from the Original Sources of European History*, vol. 3, published for the Department of History of the University of Pennsylvania (Philadelphia: University of Pennsylvania Press, 1897–1907), pp. 8–11; revised.

[The Electors]. Archbishops: Mainz 50 [men-at-arms] with swords, Cologne 40 with swords, Trier 40 with swords. The Count Palatine 50 with swords. Saxony 20 mounted men-at-arms. Brandenburg 50 with swords.

The Bishops. The archbishop of Magdeburg 30 swordsmen, 10 archers. Bishop of Hildesheim 5 swordsmen, 5 archers. That of Würzburg 20 swordsmen. That of Bamberg 20 swordsmen. That of Eichstätt 10 swordsmen. That of Strasbourg 10 swordsmen. That of Constance 8 swordsmen. That of Basel 2 swordsmen. That of Chur 2 swordsmen. That of Besançon 6 swordsmen. That of Augsburg 2 swordsmen. That of Metz 6 swordsmen. That of Toul 3 swordsmen. That of Verdun 6 swordsmen. That of Lausanne 6 swordsmen. That of Speyer 8 swordsmen. That of Worms 2 swordsmen. That of Verdun 3 swordsmen, 6 men-at-arms. That of Schwerin 8 swordsmen, 8 men-at-arms. That of Halberstadt 6 swordsmen, 6 men-at-arms. That of Bremen 10 swordsmen, 10 men-at-arms. That of Commin 6 swordsmen, 6 men-at-arms. That of Regensburg 5 swordsmen. That of Münster 10 swordsmen.

Dukes and lay princes. Duke of Lorraine 20 swordsmen. Duke of Bar 20 swordsmen. Duke of Savoy 50 swordsmen. Margrave of Baden 10 swordsmen. Landgrave of Hesse 20 swordsmen, 10 men-at-arms. Duke Otto of the Leina 10 swordsmen, 10 men-at-arms. Erich of Braunschweig 5 swordsmen, 5 men-at-arms. Duke Otto of Hirschberg 5 swordsmen, 5 men-at-arms. Bernhard and William of Braunschweig with their cities namely, Braunschweig and Lüneburg, 10 swordsmen, 10 men-at-arms. John of Mecklenburg 10 swordsmen, 10 men-at-arms. Albrecht of Mecklenburg 10 swordsmen, 10 men-at-arms. Children of Duke Ulrich with the country of Stuttgart 10 swordsmen, 10 men-at-arms. Otto and Casimir of Szozrcin 20 swordsmen, 12 men-at-arms. Vladislaf of Wolgast 15 swordsmen, 12 men-at-arms. Erich of Saxe-Lauenberg 3 swordsmen, 6 men-at-arms. Louis of Ingolstadt in Bavaria 16 swordsmen. Ernest and William of Bavaria 10 swordsmen. Henry of Bavaria 20 swordsmen. John of Bavaria 10 swordsmen. Stephen of Bavaria 5 swordsmen. Otto of Bavaria 5 swordsmen. Adolphus of Cleves 20 swordsmen. Duke of Berg 6 spearmen. The bishop of Utrecht, with Deventer, Kempten, Zwolle, and Utrecht, 40 swordsmen.

Lords and counts in the Netherlands. The duke of Jülich, and the knights of Jülich and Guelders, and the four cities of Romunde, Nijmwegen, Arnhem and Zutphen 60 swordsmen. The three cities of Brabant 100 swordsmen. The cities of Liège 100 swordsmen. Standard bearers, knights, and men of Holland 60 swordsmen. Standard bearers, knights, and men of Hainault, the cities of Hainault, the count of Namur 20 swordsmen. Lords and knights of Flanders, the cities of Flanders 20 swordsmen.

Counts and lords. Gerhard, count of Mark 3 swordsmen. William count of Ravensburg 2 swordsmen. Count of Tecklenburg 2 swordsmen. Count of Riedenburg 1 swordsman. Lord of Lippe 2 swordsmen. Lord of Dippoldswalde

1 swordsman. Count of Bentheim 1 swordsman. Count of Schaumburg 1 swordsman. Count of Oldenburg 1 swordsman. Frederick and William of Henneberg 4 swordsmen. Count of Rheineck 2 swordsmen. Count of Kastel 2 swordsmen. Count of Hohenlohe 2 swordsmen. Count of Weinsberg 2 swordsmen. Count of Heideck 1 swordsman. Otto Erich of the Heist 6 swordsmen. Count of Würtemberg 20 swordsmen. Count of Schauen 15 swordsmen. Margrave of Rötteln 3 swordsmen. Margrave of Toggenburg 5 swordsmen. Conrad of Freiburg 5 swordsmen. Hugo master of the Order of St. John [that is, the Hospitallers] 10 swordsmen. Christopher of Wenden 6 swordsmen, 6 men-at-arms. Albrecht and George of Anhalt 5 swordsmen, 5 men-at-arms. Bernhard of Anhalt 4 swordsmen, 4 men-at-arms. Bernhard of Rheinstein, 3 swordsmen, 3 men-at-arms. Count of Wernigerode 4 swordsmen, 4 archers. Emich of Leinigen 3 swordsmen. Frederick of Leinigen 2 swordsmen. Philipp of Nassau 4 swordsmen. John of Sponheim 5 swordsmen. Frederick of Veldenz 3 swordsmen. John and Frederick, counts of the Rhine 2 swordsmen. Philipp and Emich, lords of Oberstein, 2 swordsmen. Lord of Hohenfels 1 swordsman. Nicholas Vogt of Holstein 1 swordsman. John of Katzenellenbogen 8 swordsmen. Adolphus of Nassau 2 swordsmen. William of Wieden 3 swordsmen. Philipp and Salentin lord of Isenburg 3 swordsmen. John of Wieden, Reinhard, lord of Westerburg 2 swordsmen. Dietrick, lord of Runkel 1 swordsman. John and Henry, counts of Nassau lord of Bilstein 2 swordsmen. Bernhard and John brothers, count Solms 3 swordsmen. John of Wittgenstein 1 swordsman. Rupert of Virneburg 2 swordsmen. Gottfried Eberhard, lord of Eppstein 4 swordsmen. Reinhard, lord of Hanau 3 swordsmen. Dieter, lord of Büdegen 3 swordsmen. Michael of Wertheim 1 swordsman. William of Eberstein 1 swordsman. Lords of Arbergen 3 swordsmen. William of Blankenstein 1 swordsman. John, lord of Schleiden 1 swordsman. Frederick of Moers 4 swordsmen. John, lord of Heimsberg 4 swordsmen. Walrave of Moers 1 swordsman. William Craft, lord of Saffenburg 1 swordsman. John, lord of Rodemachern 2 swordsmen. John and Gottfried, lord of Ziegenhain 2 swordsmen. Henry of Waldeck, and the others of Waldeck 4 swordsmen. John Henry of Vinstigen 2 swordsmen. The lord of Wibelkoben 1 swordsman. Shenk Eberhard, Schenk Conrad and Schenk Conrad the younger, of Ehrenbach 3 swordsmen. Conrad, lord of Bickenbach 1 swordsman. The lord of Neuenahr 1 swordsman. Eberhard of Lindburg, lord of Hartenburg 2 swordsmen. Count of Limburg 1 swordsman. The lord of Hahn 2 swordsmen. John of Saarwerden 1 swordsman. The Brothers of Bitsch 1 swordsman. Count of Salm 1 swordsman.

The Abbots. The abbot of Fulda 6 swordsmen. The abbot of Weissenburg 2 swordsmen. The abbot of Zelle 1 swordsman. The abbot of Mürbach 3 swordsmen. The abbot of Maulbronn 5 swordsmen. The abbot of Einsiedeln 2 swordsmen. The abbot of Biebenhausen 3 swordsmen. The abbot of Salem 5 swordsmen. The abbot Alb 2 swordsmen. The abbot of Kemptem 2 swordsmen. The abbot of

Schaffhausen 2 swordsmen. The abbot of Petershausen 2 swordsmen. The abbot of Kinzing 2 swordsmen. The abbot of Weingarten 4 swordsmen. The abbot of Elchingen 2 swordsmen. The abbot of St. Blasien 2 swordsmen. The abbot of Balbeuren 2 swordsmen. The abbot of Zwiefalten 2 swordsmen. The abbot of Isni 1 swordsman. The abbot of Saint George 1 swordsman. The abbot of Saint John 1 swordsman. The abbot of Pfaeffers 1 swordsman. The abbot of Königsbrünn 1 swordsman. Prior to Schussenried 2 swordsmen.

The cities. The confederates of Berne, Lucerne, Zurich, Freiburg in Vaud 250 horse. Constance, Lindau, Buchhorn, Ravensburg, Ueberlingen, Zelle am Unter See, Diessenhofen, 50 swordsmen and 200 mounted men. Schaffhausen, Waldshut, Lauffenberg, Säckingen, Rheinfelden, Winterthür, Rapperswil, Frauenfeld 26 men-at-arms. Kempten, Isny, Wangen, Leutkirch, Memmingen, Augsburg, Biberach, Pfullendorf, Kaufbeuren, Ulm, Giengen, Nordlingen, Bopfingen, Aalen, Gmünd, Dünkelsbühl, Esslingen, Reutlingen Rottweil, Weil, Buchau, 100 swordsmen and 100 men-at-arms. Halle 12 swordsmen and 12 men-at-arms. Heilbronn, Wimpfen Weinsberg 24 mounted men armed. Basle 16 swordsmen. Strassburg Muhlhausen, Colmar, Münster in St. Gregorienthal, Kaiserberg, Dürkheim, Schlettstadt, Oberehnheim, Roshein, Hagenau, Weissenburg, 30 swordsmen. Freiburg, Neuenberg Breisach, Kenzingen Endingen 10 swordsmen. Verden 10 swordsmen. Kaufmansarburg 3 swordsmen. Treves 4 swordsmen. Metz 20 swordsmen. Toul 10 swordsmen. Speyer Worms and Mainz 24 swordsmen. Cologne, Aachen 30 swordsmen. Dortmund 6 swordsmen. Frankfurt 15 swordsmen. Friedberg 2 swordsmen. Gelnhausen 3 swordsmen. Wetzlar 2 swordsmen. Nuremberg 30 swordsmen, 30 men-at-arms. Rothenburg 12 swordsmen, 12 men-at-arms. Windsheim 5 swordsmen, 6 men-at-arms, Weissenburg in Franconia 5 swordsmen, 5 men-at-arms. Schweinfurt 5 swordsmen, 5 men-at-arms. Regensburg 15 swordsmen, 15 men-at-arms. Lübeck 30 swordsmen, 30 men-at-arms. Hamburg 15 swordsmen, 15 men-at-arms. Mühlhausen [Saxony] 3 swordsmen, 6 men-at-arms. Nordhausen 15 swordsmen, 10 men-at-arms. Aschesleben 10 swordsmen, 6 men-at-arms. Halberstadt 10 swordsmen, 10 men-at-arms. Quedlinburg 10 swordsmen, 10 men-at-arms. Sum total, 754 swordsmen and 777 mounted horse from the cities.

47. INDENTURE OF WAR (1415)

By the end of the thirteenth century, military recruitment by traditional "obligation" was coming to an end. The soldiers raised by obligation (the feudal levy) were comparatively inexperienced and unprepared, and incapable of facing larger, experienced, skilled, and well-trained forces. New methods of recruitment, such as the indenture, soon replaced the levy. The example below was made in 1415 between King Henry V and Sir Thomas Tunstall regarding service in the upcoming campaign (whether it would be into Guienne or, as happened, into northern France had not yet been determined). Incorporated in the agreement was the soldier's rate of pay—all soldiers were paid at this time—as well as shares of booty.

Source: trans. Adam Chapman, "Indenture Between Henry V and Sir Thomas Tunstall, 29 April 1415," *University of Southampton Humanities Research Blog*, posted 26 October 2013, http://blog.soton.ac.uk/humanitiesresearch/history-2/2013/10/indenture-between-henry-v-and-sir-thomas-tunstall-29-april-1415/.

This indenture made between the king our sovereign lord on the one hand, and Sir Thomas Tunstall on the other, bears witness that the said Thomas is bound towards our lord the king to serve him for a whole year on the expedition (*voiage*) which the lord king will make, God willing, in his own person, into his duchy of Guienne, or into his kingdom of France. The year will begin on the day of the muster to be made of the men of his retinue at a place which will be informed to him within the month of May next by the lord king, if he is then ready to make the said muster. Thomas shall have with him in the expedition for the whole year six men-at-arms, himself included, and 18 mounted archers. He will take wages for himself of 2 shillings per day. If Thomas goes to the duchy of Guienne in the company of the king, then he shall take as wages for the whole year for each of the men-at-arms, 40 marks, and for each of the archers, 20 marks. In the event that Thomas goes in the company of the king into the kingdom of France, he shall take as wages for each man-at-arms 12d per day, and for each of the archers, 6d per day, during the year. If the expedition is to France, then Thomas shall take the customary regard for himself and his men-at-arms, that is, according to the rate of 100 marks for 30 men-at-arms each quarter. Of the wages of the territory of Guienne, Thomas will be paid for half of the first quarter at the making of this indenture, and the other half when he makes muster ready to go to Guienne if the King goes there or sends him there. If it happens that, after the muster, the king does not go to his duchy of Guienne, but does go to the territory of France, then Thomas shall be paid as much as shall be owing to him for the said quarter above the sum received by him, as mentioned above, for the wages and regard, both for himself as for the men-at-arms and archers crossing to France.

For surety of payment for the second quarter, the lord king will have delivered to Thomas on 1 June next, as pledge, jewels which, by agreement with Thomas, are worth as much as the value of the wages or wages and regard for that quarter. These jewels Thomas shall be bound to return to the lord king at the time he wishes to redeem then within a year and a half and one month following the receipt of the said jewels. It shall be permissible for Thomas or anyone else to whom he delivers the jewels to dispose of them after the end of the said month at their pleasure without prevention by the king or his heirs, according to the contents of the letters patent under the great seal to be granted to Thomas in this matter.

For the third quarter, Thomas shall be paid for himself and his retinue within six weeks after the beginning of it, according to the rate of the wages or wages with regard, as the case requires, for the last quarter of the year, if the king, our lord, does not by halfway through the third quarter give such surety to Thomas for the payment as he might reasonably accept, then at the end of the third quarter, Thomas shall be acquitted and discharged towards the lord king of the agreements specified in this present indenture.

Thomas shall be obliged to be ready at the sea coast with his men well mounted, armed and arrayed as appropriate to their rank, to make muster on 1 July next, and later, after their arrival overseas, Thomas will be obliged to muster men of his retinue before such a person or persons as it may please the lord king to appoint and assign, and as often as Thomas shall be reasonably required to do so. Thomas shall have shipping for himself and his retinue, their horses, harness and provisions, at the expense of the king, and also return shipping, like others of his rank in the expedition. If it happens that Thomas is given orders to the contrary before he crosses the sea, he shall be bound to serve the king wherever it pleases the latter, for the same sum of money, with the said men-at-arms and archers, according to the rate of wages accustomed in the territory to which they shall be ordered by the lord king, except for those who die, if any do, in the mean time.

If it happens that the adversary of France, or any of his sons, nephews, uncles or cousins, or any king of any kingdom or his lieutenant, shall be captured in the expedition, the lord king shall have the Adversary or other person of the ranks mentioned above who are captured, and shall make reasonable composition with Thomas or the person who has effected the capture. With reference to other profits of gains of war the lord king shall have the third part of the gains of Thomas as well as the third of a third of a part of the gains of prisoners, booty, money, all gold, silver and jewels worth more than 10 marks.

In witness of these matters, Thomas has affixed his seal on the half of the indenture remaining with the king. Given at Westminster 29 April the third year of our lord king.

PART THREE

THE WAGING OF WAR

A. PLANS AND RULES

48. BARBAROSSA'S RULES OF THE ARMY (1158)

Soldiers were, by the nature of their occupation, almost always "looking for a fight." At war, the presence of enemies generally provided outlets for this bellicosity, but at peace, on garrison duty, or even just when camped at a siege or on campaign, their nature sometimes got the better of their self-control. The result was strict rules of behavior, like those established by Emperor Frederick I Barbarossa in 1158 to keep order but not destroy a soldier's desire to fight.

Source: trans. Charles Christopher Mierow, *The Deeds of Frederick Barbarossa* (New York: Columbia University Press, 1953), pp. 202–04.

1) We have decreed and desire to have it strictly observed that no knight or sergeant shall presume to provoke strife. But if one man quarrel with another, neither shall utter the rallying cry of the camp, lest his people be incited thereby to battle. But if strife shall have started, no one shall run up with weapons (sword, spear, or arrows); but, clad in breast plate, shield, and helmet, let him bring to the fight nothing but staff with which to separate the combatants. No one shall shout the rallying cry of the camp save when seeking his quarters. But if a soldier shall cause strife by shouting out the rallying cry, all his accoutrement shall be taken from him, and he shall be expelled from the army. If a servant shall have done so, he shall be shorn, flogged and branded on the cheek, or his lord shall buy him off with all his accoutrement.
2) Whosoever shall have wounded anyone and deny it shall then have his hand cut off if the wounded man can convict him by two truthful witnesses, not related to him. But if witnesses are lacking and he wishes to clear himself by an oath, the accuser may, if he pleases, refuse to accept the oath and challenge him to a duel.
3) Whosoever kills anyone, and has been convicted by two truthful witnesses not related to the slain man, shall suffer death. But if witnesses are

lacking, and he wishes to purge himself by an oath, a close friend of the slain man may challenge him to a duel.

4) If a strange knight shall come peacefully to the camp, riding a palfrey, without shield and weapons, if anyone injure him, he shall be judged a violator of the peace. But if he come to camp riding a charger, with a shield slung from his neck and a lance in his hand, if anyone injure him he has not broken the peace.

5) A soldier who has despoiled a merchant shall make twofold restitution for what he has taken, and swear that he did not know he was a merchant. If he be a servant, he shall be shorn and branded on the cheek, or his lord shall restore the plunder on his behalf.

6) Whosoever sees anyone robbing a church or a market ought to prevent him, yet without strife; if he cannot prevent him, he should bring accusation against the guilty man in court.

7) No one is to have a woman in his quarters; but he who dares to do so shall be deprived of all his accoutrement and be considered excommunicate, and the woman's nose shall be cut off.

...

12) If anyone set fire to a village or a house, he shall be shorn and branded on the cheeks and flogged.

...

14) If anyone injure another, charging that he has not sworn to keep the peace, he shall not be guilty of breaking the peace unless the other can prove by two satisfactory witnesses that he did swear to keep the peace.

...

16) Whoever finds a buried treasure may enjoy it freely. But if it is taken away from him, he shall not render evil for evil, shall not exact vengeance for the wrong done him, but shall lodge a complaint with the marshal in order to secure justice.

17) If a German merchant enters a city and buys goods and conveys them to the army and sells them at a higher price to the army, the chamberlain shall take away from him his entire stock and shall flog, shear and brand him on the cheek.

...

19) If a knight utters insults to a knight, he may deny it upon oath; if he does not deny it, he is to pay him a fine of ten pounds in that money current in camp at that time.

20) If anyone find vessels full of wine, let him drain off the wine so carefully that he will not break the vessels, or cut the bindings of the vessels, so that all the wine is not drained off, to the loss of the army.

21) If any fortress be taken, let the goods that are within be carried off, but do not let it be set on fire, unless the marshal commands do this.

This peace ordinance the archbishops, bishops, and abbots ratified, offering their right hands in token, and promised that violators of the peace would be chastised by the severity of the priestly office.

49. SPRING IS FOR WARFARE (1184–1188)

Troubadours, bards, minstrels, singers, and poets appeared in every court in medieval Europe. Their chief task was entertainment, although their songs were not just filled with romance, chivalry, and feats of arms, but often political and social commentary. Bertran de Born (c. 1140–1202), lord of Autofort, was one of the most famous French troubadours of the twelfth century, and he is the presumed author of the poem excerpted here, which emphasizes not only war's immediate horrors but also its influences on culture—as seen, for example, in the odd pairing of love-focused romance and death-oriented chivalric virtue. Whether the poem is an earnest ode to war or written in mock-praise of it might well depend on the reader.

Source: trans. Michael Livingston, from *The Poems of the Troubadour Bertran de Born*, ed. William D. Paden Jr., Tilde Sankovitch, and Patricia H. Stäblein (Berkeley: University of California Press, 1986), pp. 338–45.

It pleases me, the pleasant Spring,
when the leaves and flowers flourish.
It pleases me when I hear the fun
of the birds that ring
  their song through the woods.
It pleases me when I see pitched
the tents and pavilions in the meadows.
  And I feel great joy
when I see ranged across the fields
the armored knights and horses.
It pleases me when the foragers
drive the people and herds into flight.
It pleases me when I see in their wake
the many armed men running after them.
  And it pleases me in my heart
when I see strong castles besieged,
the palisades broken and smashed,
  and I see the army on the slope,
totally enclosed by ditches

made strong with bound-up stakes.
I am pleased, too, by a lord
when he is the first to charge
on horseback, armored, without fear.
By this he inspires his men
    to valiant duty.
When the ranks come together,
each man must be prepared
    to follow him with gladness,
for no man is respected
who hasn't taken and given many blows.
Maces and swords, helms with color,
shields smashed and scattered,
all this we see at the joining of battle,
and many vassals cut down—
    wandering wild
the horses of the dead and wounded.
And when he enters the battle,
    each man of good stock
thinking only of hacking heads and arms,
for it's better to die than to live having lost.
I tell you, for me there's no such savor
in eating or drinking or sleeping
as when I hear the cries of "Charge!"
sounding from both sides, and the noise
    of riderless horses in the shadows,
and the screams of "Help! Help!"
and I see falling into the ditches
    the small and great in the grass,
and the dead with splintered lances,
pennon-decked, pierced through their sides.
Love wants a knightly lover,
good with weapons and generous in service,
sweet of speech and a great giver,
who knows the proper thing to do and say,
    in or out of his estate,
as suits a man of his authority.
In company he should be amusing,
    courtly, and pleasant.
A lady who lies with such a lover
is thought clear of all her sins....

Lords, put to market your
castles and towns and cities
before you stop making war!

50. PAYMENT FOR CAMP WORKERS (1378)

Medieval armies contained more than leaders, knights, and soldiers. Especially at sieges there were large numbers of logistical specialists; the wages of some of these—carpenters, masons, quarriers, thatchers, and waggoners—are indicated in the following document concerning the French siege of Cherbourg in 1378. To give some perspective as to why these non-combatants would be there: for work on a cathedral or church at this time, carpenters and masons would be paid 1 sous a day, and for work on a castle 1½ sous a day.

Source: Christopher Allmand, ed., *Society at War: The Experience of England and France During the Hundred Years War*, 2nd ed. (Woodbridge, UK: Boydell Press, 1998), p. 64.

Audouin Chamieron, doctor of laws, bailiff of the Cotentin, and Jean des Ylles, bailiff there for our lord the king for the lands which [once] belonged to the king of Navarre, and at present acting on behalf of the king's general commissioners for the siege of Cherbourg, to Fouquet Tribout, receiver-general of the taxes for war imposed upon the dioceses of Avranches and Coutances for the sum given for the payment of engines, workmen and other equipment raised from the said region and taken to the siege of Cherbourg, greeting.

We have today seen the muster rolls of carpenters, masons, quarriers, thatchers, pioneers and waggoners from the viscounty of Avranches whom Jean Legey, viscount of Avranches, has brought to serve at the siege of Cherbourg, [these being] over and above the number already detailed for the management of the engines. In which muster there are twenty carpenters, twenty masons and quarriers, twenty-six thatchers and eight waggoners. We now order that, from the receipt of moneys obtained by you, you shall give them payment for the next ten days, including today; namely, for each of the carpenters, 3 shillings per day, which for the ten days for them all will amount to 30 pounds; to each mason and quarrier, 3 shillings which, for the ten days, will amount to 30 pounds; to each thatcher, 2 shillings and 6 pence per day which, for the ten days for them all, will be 32 pounds 10 shillings; to each waggoner, 10 shillings per day which, for the ten days for them all, will total 40 pounds *tournois*, in accordance with [the rate] at which they are evaluated in the said muster roll, to which this present order is annexed ... the total being 132 pounds 10 shillings, to be taken from your receipt.

Given at Carentan, under our seals, on the 12th day of November, 1378.

51. ORDINANCES OF A COMBINED ARMY (1385)

Having a common enemy—the English (even identified as such below)—forced the Scots and French together for much of the Hundred Years War. This agreement, made between the two in 1385, set regulations that their combined forces should follow: primarily, that battles were to be sought out, and, secondarily, sieges, but only if both armies agreed that the fortifications might fall, as well as rules of conduct to be followed by both armies' soldiers.

Source: Anne Curry, "Disciplinary Ordinances for English and Franco-Scottish Armies in 1385: An International Code?," *Journal of Medieval History* 37, no. 3 (2011): 293–94.

An ordinance made in the king's council concerning various articles and points to be considered and observed in the army being made by the French and Scots together.

This indenture or *lettre partie* contains and bears witness that at the beginning of the month of July 1385, the very noble and powerful prince Robert [II], by the grace of God king of Scotland, and his eldest son John [Stewart], earl of Carrick, with many other earls and barons of the realm of Scotland, and also the noble lord John de Vienne, admiral of France and lieutenant of the king of France in the regions of Scotland and England, with other nobles and valiant knights, lords of the realm of France, sent for this purpose by the king of France to the realm of Scotland, assembled at Edinburgh in order to take mutual advice on the matter of the war which is to be undertaken by consent against the king of England as common enemy and adversary of the kings of France and Scotland, came to consensus, after negotiation and discussion together at their leisure, concerning the campaign which was about to begin, in the agreement which follows:

To wit, that when they come to the marches of England on the day already assigned for their assembling, the 23rd day of this month, and have seen the castles which are at the entry into the marches, if they are of the opinion that these are easily assailable and winnable, they would commit to this, if they wished, by mutual consent. But since it might happen that they might have to give battle or where it seemed to them that the assault would be so hard and harmful that it might cause danger or loss of men, or men might be wounded which might weaken them when it came to battle, it would be agreed by common accord to pass on and make war, leaving aside such hazardous assaults in order to avoid the danger mentioned above, since those awaiting battle would not put themselves willingly to the assault, nonetheless on the way back it would be good to take advice from those of the frontiers and from those who might have certain understanding of the state and disposition of those within [the castles], and to do what seemed most expedient.

Once this was done and agreed in the said manner, certain ordinances were made and agreed to be set down in writing, and to be sealed and proclaimed in common.

(a) First, that, in passing towards the marches through the country of Scotland, no man should commit robbery or larceny, or take any booty, horses, equipment, victuals or other goods without the grace and willingness of those to whom these things belong, on pain of being beheaded.
(b) Item, that all persons who wished to come to the host wherever it may be, with merchandise and victuals to sell, should come in safety, and be able to come and go surely and safely, and no man should take anything without making payment or satisfaction, under the same penalty.
(c) Item, that whoever kills a man in the host, he shall be killed in return, and if an archer wounds a gentleman he will have his thumb or ear cut. And if a gentleman wounds another gentleman he should be arrested immediately and justice done according to the advice of the captains.
(d) Item, if any riot or dispute emerges between any of the men of France and Scotland that no one shall arm himself or rise up one against the other, but that those who have started the dispute on both sides should be arrested by the captains who will do justice in the matter. As for those who do not keep this ordinance, if he is a man-at-arms he shall lose his horse and equipment and, if he is an archer, his thumb or ear.
(e) Item, it is ordained that this same penalty and punishment should be maintained, upheld and carried out in the case of those who take their companions' lodgings and of those who do not keep the order which is made and established by the captains when the army is riding out or making war.
(f) Item, that all men, French and Scots, should have a badge at the front and the back, namely, a white cross of St Andrew. If his jack is white, or his tunic is white, he shall wear this white cross on a piece of round or square black cloth.
(g) If a Scot commits bad behaviour or offence in the French army, the captain in whose company this has been done will take those who have misbehaved and return them to his Scottish lord who ought to do right and justice. And similarly, if a Frenchman commits bad behaviour or offence in the company of Scots, the captain will take him and deliver him to his French lord to whom he belongs who will make amends and carry out justice.
(h) Item, that if any French or Scot brings an Englishman to the ground during the mounted pursuit, he who brings him to the ground will have half of his ransom so long as his action is acknowledged and proven.
(i) Item, that no man of arms, under pain of losing horse and equipment, or any archer, under pain of losing a hand or an ear, should lay or set fire to a church, or kill a woman or child, or take a woman by force.

52. BATTLE PLAN FOR AGINCOURT (1415)

This battle plan was apparently drawn up by French marshal Boucicaut in the days preceding the battle of Agincourt. The document seems to have been captured after the battle and remained lost in the English archives until rediscovered by Christopher Phillpotts in the early 1980s. Although clearly meant as a tactical plan for attacking Henry V's forces marching from Harfleur to Calais, it could not be used on the field where tradition says the French chose to fight the battle of Agincourt. This has left historians confused as to its purpose, without many examples to compare it with. In the following translation, superscript † indicates the individual died at Agincourt, while P indicates he was made prisoner.

Source: trans. Michael Livingston, from Christopher Phillpotts, "The French Plan of Battle During the Agincourt Campaign," *English Historical Review* 99, no. 390 (January 1984): 64–65.

This is the advice of the Lord Marshal [Boucicaut][P] and the lords who are with him—as commanded by the [dukes of] Alençon [Jean I][†] and Richemont [Arthur III, duke of Brittany][P] and the Lord Constable [Charles d'Albret, Comte de Dreux],[†] and submitted to the correction of these said lords—for the plan of the battle.

First, in the name of God, Our Lady, and Saint George, it is advised that there should be a large "battle" [*bataille*, a formation] that will serve as the vanguard. In this "battle" will be the constable and the marshal, with all of their men.

Also, in this same "battle" the banners of the constable and the marshal will be placed beside one another. That of the constable will be on the right side and that of the marshal on the left. On the right side will be all the men of the constable. On the left side will be all the men of the marshal.

Also, there should be another "battle" beside that one, in which there shall be the duke of Alençon, the count of Eu [Charles of Anjou],[P] and the other lords who are not otherwise listed. And if it happens that the English form up in only one "battle," these two [French] "battles" [must fight] together; if so, they can assemble all together.

Also, it is advisable that two large wings of foot-soldiers be made. The one on the right should be formed by Lord Richemont. With him in his company, aside from his own men, will be the lord of Combourg [Jean de Malestroit][†] and Lord Bertrand of Montauban.[†] The other [wing], which will be on the left, should be formed by the lord of Vendôme [Louis], the grand master of the king's household [Jehan de Montagu], [and the lord of] Jaligny [Guichard Dauphin].[†]

[Also,] the axes of the company and others who can be found elsewhere [should be with] the above two wings.

Also, all the archers of the whole company will stand before the two wings of foot-soldiers, where they will be commanded by the knights and squires appointed by the leaders of each wing, each on his own side.

Also, a "battle" of heavy horse should be formed from among the good men up to the number of 1,000 men-at-arms, at least. This "battle" will be led by the master of crossbowmen [David de Rambures], and he will be furnished up to this number from all the companies. This "battle" will hold itself outside all the other "battles" on the left edge, a little to the rear, and it will be sent to attack the archers and do all it can to break them. And when it charges out to ride down those archers, the "battles" of foot-men and the wings are to march in order to assemble together. So this "battle" will have half of all the varlets of the company, mounted on the best horses of their masters.

Also, another "battle" will be formed of two hundred mounted men-at-arms, along with the other half of all the varlets mounted on the best horses of their masters. This "battle" will be led by Lord Bosredon [Louis], and it will be sent to attack at the rear of the English "battle," against their varlets and their baggage and at the back of the English "battle." This "battle" will charge out when the master of crossbowmen sets out to go and attack the archers.

53. MAINTAINING DISCIPLINE (1419)

By 1419 Henry V had conquered much of Normandy, Maine, and the Ile-de-France. His army had become less of an invading and more of an occupying force. What had been tolerated on campaign, as far as the acquisition of food, fodder, and booty, would be tolerated no more, as the people these were once taken from by English soldiers were now subjects of the English king. In this statute Henry sets down the rules his army had to follow in order to maintain peace and civility with the people who lived on these newly occupied lands.

Source: trans. Michael Livingston, from *Society at War: The Experience of England and France During the Hundred Years War*, ed. Christopher Allmand, 2nd ed. (Woodbridge, UK: Boydell Press, 1998), pp. 93–95.

Here follows the statutes [of war of Henry V]. Although the great goodness and graciousness of the most high Creator has ordered and disposed that his subjects should be meek, charitable, and honest in their conversation, yet despite all that, unruly covetousness—mother of strife, enemy of peace, occasion of dispute and malice—engenders and breeds daily so great a debate among people that, unless justice does reprove and subdue their wicked assaults and powers, the universal good order of our Christian army will be completely destroyed, and with it the common wealth utterly undone through which we live and reign. Therefore laws and constitutions are ordained in order that the harmful appetite of man might be controlled under the rule of law, through which mankind is duly instructed to live honestly, to hurt no man, and to give every man what is his. And because our army must at all times, that is to say, both in peace and in war, be ruled and governed according to good order, and the common wealth maintained in prosperity—and also, on the other part, that the constable and marshal of our army may in the cases showed before them more discretely judge and discern—we, therefore, by the council of our lords, nobles, and gentlemen, have made certain statutes and constitutions, and caused them to be proclaimed openly in our army, commanding that each and every one of the captains in our said army have them in writing, so that our publishing of them may be taken for sufficient warning. Thus every one of our subjects in the said statutes and constitutions can pretend no ignorance....

To What Manner of Persons Men of War Shall Be Bound to Obey

We ordain moreover that all manner of men who are within our army, whatsoever their degree, status, condition, or country of origin, be dutifully obedient to our constable and marshal in all lawful and honest things, under pain of forfeiting their body and goods. Also, we command that all soldiers, and all those who receive wages from us and our realm, be likewise obedient unto their immediate captains and masters, keeping such watches and guard-duties that are put to them, or that shall be reasonably appointed into them; and that they not leave from the same watches and duties in any way whatsoever without special permission from their said captains and masters, under pain of arresting body and goods, until by the discretion and allowance of the marshal, the said captains or masters are fully content. Also, when scarcity occurs among provisions, or among horse-fodder, if the captains think it necessary to send to any village about for such supplies, we command that all manner of soldiers be ready to ride or go for the same at the assignment and ordinance of their aforesaid captains or masters; or else, if they be disobedient herein, that they be punished according to the penalty ordained in the statute written above. Moreover, regarding peddlers or food-sellers that otherwise ride with the army or come to our markets within to buy and sell there, we direct that they be obedient to the constable, the marshal, and clerk of market, as they would be to our own person. Also, we direct that all manner of bargains, fines, covenants, and treaties that are done within our army—in which one or both parties are from within our army—be shown and given final determination in our own courts at the judgment of the constable and marshal, or, in the absence of the marshal, whatsoever persons they might be.

54. HOW TO ATTACK VENICE (1517)

This entry in Marinus Sanudo's diary for 7 November 1517 wonderfully recounts the visit to Venice of Ali Bey, an Ottoman ambassador (whom Sanudo labels a spy). While visiting the Campanile (bell tower) of San Marco, a Venetian official bragged about how secure the Venetians were from attack, to which Ali Bey confidently suggested a number of approaches the Ottomans would be able to take.

Source: trans. Linda L. Carroll, *Venice,* Cità Excelentissima*: Selections from the Renaissance Diaries of Marino Sanudo,* ed. Patricia H. Labalme and Laura Sanguineti White (Baltimore: Johns Hopkins University Press, 2008), pp. 214–15.

This morning Alibei, the interpreter and ambassador of the sultan, arrived. Several elderly patricians were sent on barges to meet him, [along with] the heads of the Forty and the *savi ai ordeni* [that is, the commission on maritime commerce], to increase the size of the group, for of the many who were ordered to meet him twelve were absent. He was wearing a dolman of crimson velvet and a tunic of cloth of gold with a sable lining; part of his entourage was dressed in silk and part in scarlet. He had with him only seven men, however. Once he had entered the Collegia, he took his leave. The doge spoke gracious words to him of the good peace that our Signoria wants to maintain with his lord, saying that he respects his lordship more than all the others in the world and that he hopes that his lord has the same attitude toward our Signoria. He also hopes that, should something happen, [Ali Bey] would intercede to put things right with his lordship ... This Ali responded in part through the interpreter and in part on his own, for he knows Latin, saying that he will undertake every favorable office with his lord and that he wants to maintain the good peace. He touched on the idea that it would be wise to renew [the treaty] now, then took his leave. He was accompanied by the same gentlemen, and when the weather is right he will leave. His expenses have been taken care of, great friendship is being shown to him, and great honors have been paid him. He is a shrewd man and an evil one, and wherever he goes he spies for his lord.

Apropos of this, I wish to record that last Saturday, the last day of October, he wanted to climb the Bell Tower to see the city of St. Mark from it, saying that it had been so well restored. The *savi ai ordeni* were sent to accompany him, and a collation of malmsey wine and confections [*confeti*], etc., was prepared for him, and off he went. Once he was up there, he asked how one could approach the city by sea. He was told that it could be done with large ships by way of the two castles but that the port, or the channel, did not stay in the same place, that seasoned pilots were brought along to plumb it continuously, and that at times it represented a danger to ships and galleys and other large vessels. And he said, "If my lord came with 300 galleys to this port and armed the boats with good artillery, he would come inside." The *savi ai ordeni* said, "And then what? The inhabitants of the city would be there to oppose you." Then he said, "But couldn't you come by way of Chioza?" He was told that that would only work with small boats because of the shoals. Then he asked how far away dry land was, and he was told five miles to Liza Fusina and Mergera [Marghera]. Next he asked, "Don't your enemies come?" And he was told that they did. Then he asked, "Why don't they advance with their artillery loaded on rafts" and he said, "When my lord goes on an expedition, he has so many people with him that if each one carried just one bundle of sticks, he could make a bridge that would reach this city." The answer given to him was, "Those who would be defending the city would not let them get close, and ten would be enough against one hundred." Then he asked where Friuli was, on what side. It was shown to him. He remarked that one could ride horseback to a distance of only five miles from the city. And the *savi ai ordeni* said, "My lord ambassador, we are telling you that in this recent cruel war [of the League of Cambrai], in which all the kings of the world joined to defeat Venice, not a single man of this city died. Everything was accomplished with money and the deaths of foreign soldiers, and this city is still as packed as an egg with people, nor is it possible to conquer it," and other such words. Then they came down from the Bell Tower.

B. THE MARCH

55. ACCOUNTS OF THE THIRD CRUSADE (MID-1190s)

The western successes of the First Crusade in 1099—in which Christian forces seized much of the Holy Land, including Jerusalem—were short-lived. The outlying crusader county of Edessa fell in 1144, prompting the Second Crusade, which failed to restore it (though crusaders did make headway in Portugal; doc. 87). Then, in 1187, the Ayyubid sultan Saladin, who had been slowly making gains in the Holy Land, won an enormous victory over the Christian armies at the battle of Hattin (doc. 71). Soon, Jerusalem, too, was in his hands. European leaders responded with calls for a Third Crusade. England passed its "Saladin Tithe" (doc. 33), and armies formed up under Holy Roman Emperor Frederick I Barbarossa, King Philip II Augustus of France, and King Richard I the Lionheart of England, among others. Few of these men got along, and after Barbarossa drowned en route to the Holy Land, the tensions between Richard and Philip threatened the entirety of the enterprise—a concern running through the sources below. The first and third excerpts are from the Itinerary of the Pilgrims and Deeds of Richard, *one of the best sources for the Third Crusade. Compiled by one Richard, an English Augustinian canon, in the early thirteenth century, it is believed to be based on sources that include accounts by a Templar eyewitness and by Ambroise, a French cleric writing in the mid-1190s. The second account below is by the well-informed English historian Richard of Devizes. Both, being English, naturally focus on Richard the Lionheart.*

Source: trans. John Allen Giles, *Chronicles of the Crusades, Being Contemporary Narratives of the Crusade of Richard Coeur de Lion* (London: Henry G. Bohn, 1848), pp. 55–56, 60–64, 99–101, 151, 200, 206, 209–10, 217–21; revised.

[From the *Itinerary of the Pilgrims and Deeds of Richard*]

The [German] army now entered the Armenian territories: all rejoiced at having left a hostile kingdom, and at their arrival in the country of the faithful. But, alas! a more fatal land awaited them, which was to extinguish the light and joy of all.... On the borders of Armenia there was a place, surrounded on one side by steep mountains, on the other side by the river Selesius. While the packhorses and baggage were passing this river, the victorious emperor [Frederick Barbarossa] halted ... [and] in consequence of the packhorses crossing the river, became at last impatient of the delay; and wishing to accelerate the march, he prepared to cross the nearest part of the stream, so as to get in front of the packhorses and be at liberty to proceed. O sea! O earth! O heaven! the ruler of the [Holy] Roman Empire, ever august, in whom the glory of ancient Rome again flourished, ... was overwhelmed in the waters and perished! And though those who were near him hastened to his assistance, yet his aged spark of life was extinguished by a sudden though not premature death [at 67 or 68 years old]....

When his funeral rites had been performed, they left the fatal spot as soon as possible, bearing with them the body of the emperor adorned with royal magnificence, that it might be carried to Antioch. There the flesh, being boiled from the bones, reposes in the church of the apostolic see, and the bones were conveyed by sea to Tyre, to be transported from there to Jerusalem.... The [emperor's army], arriving at Antioch after many and long fastings, gave way too plentifully to their appetites, and [many] died of sudden repletion, and so ... the greater part of the great army perished, and most of the survivors returned to their own countries. A small body of them, ashamed to return, served under the emperor's son....

After Easter [1191] there arrived [at Acre] Philip, king of France, and not long after him, Richard, king of England.... Around [Acre] the besiegers lay in countless multitudes, chosen from every nation throughout Christendom and under the face of heaven, and well fitted for the labors and fatigues of war; for the city had now been besieged a long time, and had been afflicted by constant toil and tribulation, by the pressure of famine, and every kind of adversity, as we have before described. Moreover, beyond the besiegers was seen the Turkish army, not in a compact body, but covering the mountains and valleys, hills and plains, with tents, the colors of whose various forms were reflected by the sun.... King Richard beheld and counted all their army, and when he arrived in port, the king of France and a whole army of natives, and the princes, chiefs, and nobles, came forth to meet him and welcome him, with joy and exultation, for they had eagerly longed for his arrival....

The city of Acre, from its strong position, and its being defended by the choicest men of the Turks, appeared difficult to take by assault. The French had hitherto spent their labor in vain in constructing machines and engines for breaking down the walls, with the greatest care; for whatever they erected, at a great expense, the Turks destroyed with Greek Fire or some devouring conflagration....

King Richard was not yet fully recovered from [a] sickness; nevertheless, anxious for action, and strenuously intent upon taking the city, he made arrangements that his men should assault the city, in the hope that under divine providence he should succeed. For this purpose, he caused a hurdle to be made ... with the most subtle workmanship. This the king intended to be used for crossing over the trench outside the city. Under it he placed his most experienced crossbowmen, and he caused himself to be carried thither on a silken bed, to honor the Saracens with his presence, and animate his men to fight; and from it, by using his crossbow, in which he was skilled, he slew many with bolts and arrows. His sappers also dug a mine under the tower, at which a petraria [stone-throwing catapult] was directed; and having made a breach, they filled it with logs of wood and set them on fire; when, by the addition of frequent blows from the petraria, the tower fell suddenly to the ground with a crash.... [The assault continued and the city's inhabitants eventually agreed to surrender it.]

After this a great discord arose between the two kings.... Affairs being in this position, at the end of the month of July, within which the Turks had promised to restore the holy cross and receive back their hostages, a rumor spread among the army that the king of France, on whom the hope of the people rested, intended to return home and was making active preparations for his journey. Oh how wicked and how insulting a proceeding, while as yet so much work remained on hand to wish to go away, when his duty was to rule so large a multitude of people, and when his presence was so necessary to encourage the Christians to so pious a work.... The king of France alleged sickness as the cause of his return, and said that he had performed his vow as far as he was able.... It must not be denied, at the same time, that the king of France expended much labor and money in the Holy Land for the assaults on the city, and that he gave aid and assistance to very many, and that by the influence of his presence, he procured the more speedy execution and consummation of ... the capture of the city.... But when the inflexible determination of the king of France to return [home] became known to all, and his refusal to yield to the murmurs of his men, or their supplications to remain, the French would have renounced their subjection to him, if it could have been done.... But for all that, the king of

France hastened his voyage as much as possible, and left in his stead the duke of Burgundy, with a large number of men. Moreover, he begged King Richard to supply him with two galleys, and the king readily gave him two of his best; how ungrateful [Philip] was for this service was afterward seen.

King Richard was of the opinion that the king of France should enter into a covenant for the preservation of their mutual security; for they, like their fathers, regarded each other with mistrusts, under the veil of friendship, which even in the following generation never expelled fear. King Richard was therefore anxious with this uneasy feeling, and required an oath from the king of France to keep his faith not to do injury to his men or territory knowingly or purposely, while he, King Richard, remained in a foreign land; but if on any occasion any action [by Richard's vassals] that should appear reprehensible went unpunished, King Richard on his return should have forty days' notice before the king of France should proceed to obtain redress. The king of France took the oath which was required faithfully to observe all these conditions, and gave the duke of Burgundy and Count Henry as hostages, and five or more others, whose names are lost. How faithfully [Philip] kept his covenant and oath is very well known to all the world; for he had no sooner reached his own country, than he set it in commotion and threw Normandy into confusion [by attacking Richard's lands there]....

King Richard ... turned his attention to packing up the petrariae and mangonels [catapults] for transportation. For when the time had expired which had been fixed by the Turks for the restoration of the cross and the ransom of the hostages, after waiting three weeks, according to the conditions to see if Saladin would keep his word and covenant, the king regarded him as a transgressor, as Saladin appeared not to care about it at all; and perhaps this happened by the dispensation of God, so that something more advantageous might be obtained. But the Saracens asked for further time to fulfill their promise and make search for the cross....

When it became clearly evident to King Richard that a longer period had elapsed than had been agreed, and that Saladin was obdurate and would not bother to ransom the hostages, he called together a council of the chiefs of the people, by whom it was resolved that the hostages should all be hanged, except a few nobles of the higher class, who might ransom themselves or be exchanged for some Christian captives. King Richard, aspiring to destroy the Turks root and branch, and to punish their wanton arrogance, as well as to abolish the law of Mohammed, and to vindicate the Christian religion, on the Friday before the Assumption of the blessed virgin Mary, ordered 2,700 of the Turkish hostages to be led forth from the city and hanged [or beheaded]; his soldiers marched forward with delight to fulfill his commands and to retaliate, with the assent of divine grace, by taking revenge upon those who had destroyed so many of the Christians with missiles from bows and crossbows.... [The crusaders then moved toward Jerusalem, arriving in its vicinity in mid-1192, after much fighting and many delays.]

[From Richard of Devizes]

Richard, the king of the English, had already spent two years in conquering the region around Jerusalem, and during all that time no aid had been sent to him from any of his realms. Nor yet were his only and uterine brother John, count of Mortain, nor his justiciars, nor his other nobles, observed to take any care to send him any part of his revenues, and they did not even think of his return. However, the church prayed to God for him without ceasing. The king's army shrank daily in the promised land, and besides those who were slain by the sword, many thousands of people perished every month by the too sudden extremities of the nightly cold and the daily heat. When it appeared that they would all have to die there, everyone had to choose whether he would die as a coward or in battle.

On the other side, the strength of the infidels greatly increased, and their confidence was strengthened by the misfortunes of the Christians; their army was relieved at certain times by fresh troops; the weather was natural to them; the place was their native country; their labor, health; their frugality, medicine. Among us, on the contrary, that which brought gain to our adversaries became a disadvantage. For if our people had too little to eat even once in a week, they were rendered less effective for seven weeks after. The mingled nation of French and English fared sumptuously every day, at whatever cost, while their treasure lasted; and (no offense to the French) they ate until they were sick. The well-known custom of the English was continually kept up even under the clarions and the clangor of the trumpet or horn: with due devotion they drained their wine-cups to the dregs. The merchants of the country, who brought the victuals to the camp, were astonished at their wonderful and extraordinary habits, and could scarcely believe even what they saw to be true, that one people, and that small in number, consumed three times more bread and a hundred times more wine than that on which many nations of the infidels had been sustained, and some of those nations innumerable. And the hand of the Lord was deservedly laid upon them according to their merits. Such great lack of food followed their great gluttony, that their teeth scarcely spared their fingers, as their hands presented to their mouths less than their usual allowance. To these and other calamities, which were severe and many, a much greater one was added by the sickness of the king.

The king was extremely sick, and confined to his bed; his fever continued without intermission; the physicians whispered that it was an acute semitertian fever. And as they despaired of his recovery even from the beginning, terrible dismay was spread from the king's abode through the camp. There were few among the many thousands who did not consider fleeing, and the utmost confusion of dispersion or surrender would have followed, had not Hubert Walter, bishop of Salisbury, immediately assembled the council. By strenuous argument he won this concession: that the army should not break up until a truce was requested from Saladin. All the armed men stood in array more steadily than usual, and with a threatening look concealing the reluctance of their mind, they feigned a desire for battle. No one spoke of the king's illness, lest the secret of their intense sorrow should be disclosed to the enemy; for it was well known that Saladin feared the charge of the whole army less than that of the king alone; and if he should know that he was sick in bed, he would instantly pelt the French with cow-dung, and intoxicate the best of the English drunkards with a dose which should make them tremble....

[The Muslims eventually proposed a truce in these terms:] If it pleased King Richard, for the space of three years, three months, three weeks, three days and three hours, such a truce would be observed between the Christians and the infidels, that whatever either one party or the other in any way possessed he would possess without molestation to the end. During the interval the Christians would be permitted at their pleasure to fortify Acre only, and the infidels Jerusalem. All contracts, all commerce, every act and every thing would be mutually carried on by all in peace. [Saladin's brother] Saffadin himself was dispatched to the English as the bearer of this offer....

While King Richard was sick at Jaffa, word was brought to him that [Hugh III] the duke of Burgundy was taken dangerously ill at Acre. It was the day for the king's fever to take its turn, and through his delight at this report, it left him. The king immediately with uplifted hands imprecated a curse upon the duke, saying, "May God destroy him, for he would not destroy the enemies of our faith with me, although he had long served in my pay." ... [Eventually,] having resumed his strength of body more by the greatness of his mind than by repose or nourishment, he issued a command for the whole coast from Tyre to Ascalon, that all who were able to serve in the wars should come to fight at the king's expense. A countless multitude assembled before him, the greater part of whom were on foot. Having rejected them as useless, he mustered the cavalry and found scarcely 500 knights and 2,000 shield-bearers whose lords had perished. And not discouraged by their small number, he, being a most excellent orator, strengthened the minds of the fearful with a timely speech. He commanded that it be proclaimed through the companies that on the third day they must follow the king to battle, either to die as martyrs or to take Jerusalem by storm. This was the sum of his project, because as yet he knew nothing of the truce. For there was no one who dared even hint to him, when he had so unexpectedly recovered, that which they had undertaken without his knowledge, through fear of his death. However, Hubert Walter, bishop of Salisbury, took counsel with Count Henry concerning the truce and obtained his ready concurrence in his wishes. So having deliberated together how they might safely hinder such a hazardous engagement, they conceived of the one stratagem out of a thousand, namely, to try to dissuade the people from the enterprise. And the matter turned out most favorably; the spirit of those who were going to fight had so greatly failed even without dissuasion, that on the appointed day, when the king, according to his custom leading the van, marshaled his army, of all the knights and shield-bearers no more than 900 were found. On account of which defection, the king, greatly enraged, even raving, and gnawing the pine rod which he held in his hand, at length opened his indignant lips as follows: "O God!" said he, "O God, my God, why hast thou forsaken me? For whom have we foolish Christians, for whom have we English come hither from the furthest parts of the earth to bear our arms? Is it not for the God of the Christians? O fie! How good art thou to us thy people, who now are for thy name given up to the sword; we shall become a portion for foxes. O how unwilling should I be to forsake thee in so forlorn and dreadful a position, were I thy lord and advocate as thou art mine! In sooth, my standards will in future be despised not through my fault but through thine; in sooth, not through any cowardice of my warfare, art thou thyself, my King and my God, conquered this day, and not Richard thy vassal."

He spoke, and returned to the camp extremely dejected; and as a fit occasion now offered, Bishop Hubert and Henry, count of Champagne, approaching him with unwonted familiarity, as if nothing had yet been arranged, begged under diverse pretexts the king's consent for making such overtures to the infidels as were necessary. And thus the king answered them: "Since a troubled mind is usually more likely to thwart than to afford sound judgment—I, who am greatly troubled in mind, authorize you, whom I see to be calm of mind, to arrange what you shall think most proper for the good of peace." Having gained their desires they chose messengers to send to Saffadin upon these matters; Saffadin, who had returned from Jerusalem, was suddenly announced to be at hand. The count and the bishop went to meet him, and being assured by him of the truce, they instructed him how he must speak with the lord their king. Being admitted to an interview with the king as one who previously had been his friend, Saffadin could scarcely prevail upon the king not to destroy himself but to consent to the truce. For so great were the man's strength of body, mental courage, and entire trust in Christ, that he could hardly be prevailed upon not to undertake in his own person a single combat with a thousand of the choicest infidels, as he was destitute of soldiers. And as he was not permitted to attack, he chose this evasion, that, after a truce of seven weeks, the stipulations of the compact being preserved, it should remain for him to choose whether it were better to fight or to forbear. The two parties put their right hands to the final agreement, that they would faithfully observe it; and Saffadin, more honored than burdened with the king's present, went back again to his brother, to return at the expiration of the term for the final conclusion or breaking of the above truce.

Richard, king of England, held a council at Acre, and there prudently regulating the government of that state, he appointed his nephew, Henry, count of Champagne, on whom he had formerly conferred Tyre, to be captain and lord of the whole promised land. But he thought it proper to defer his consecration as king till he might perhaps be crowned at Jerusalem. King Richard, now thinking to return home, with the assistance of Count Henry appointed men for all the strongholds in his territories and found Ascalon alone without garrison or inhabitants, for lack of people. Wherefore, taking precaution that it might not become a receptacle of the infidels, he caused the ramparts and fortifications of the castle to be cast down.

The seventh day of the seventh week appeared, and behold Saffadin, with many emirs who desired to see the face of the king, drew near. The truce was confirmed on both sides by oath, with this provision being added to what had been previously agreed, that during the continuance of the truce no one, whether Christian or infidel, should inhabit Ascalon, and that all the fields pertaining to the town should still belong to the Christians. Hubert, bishop of Salisbury, and Henry, captain of Judaea, together with a numerous band, went up to Jerusalem to worship in the place where the feet of Christ had stood. And there was woeful misery to be seen—captive confessors of the Christian name, wearing out a hard and constant martyrdom; chained together in gangs, their feet blistered, their shoulders raw, their backsides goaded, their backs wealed they carried materials to the hands of the masons and stone-layers to make Jerusalem impregnable against the Christians. When the captain and bishop had returned from the sacred places, they endeavored to persuade the king to go up; but the worthy indignation of his great heart could not consent to receive by the courtesy of the infidels that which he could not obtain by the gift of God.

[From the *Itinerary of the Pilgrims and Deeds of Richard*]

[King Richard] urged the sailors to spread their canvas to the winds, so that they might the sooner cross over the expanse of sea that lay before them, ignorant indeed of the tribulations and sorrows that awaited him, and the calamities that he was to suffer from the treachery that had long before been transmitted to France, by which it was contrived that he should be wickedly thrown into prison [by Leopold V, duke of Austria], though he justly suspected no such evil in the service of God, and in so laborious a pilgrimage. O how unequally was he recompensed for his exertions in the common cause! His inheritance was seized by another [that is, his brother John], his castles in Normandy were unjustly taken [by Philip of France], his rivals made cruel assaults upon his rights without provocation, and he only escaped from captivity by paying a ransom to the emperor of Germany. To gather the money for his ransom, the taxes were raised to the uttermost; a large collection was levied upon all his land

... ; for the chalices and hallowed vessels of gold and silver were gathered from the churches, and the monasteries were obliged to do without their utensils; neither was this unlawful according to the decrees of the holy fathers, nay, it was even a matter of necessity, inasmuch as no saint, many though there be, ever during life suffered so much for the Lord as King Richard in his captivity in Austria and in Germany. He who had gained so many triumphs over the Turks was nefariously circumvented by the brethren of his own faith, and seized by those who agreed with him in name only as members of the creed of Christ.... But out of that captivity, by God's usual mercy, his own activity, and the care of his faithful servants, he was at length set at liberty for a large sum of money, because he was known to be a man of great power. At last restored to his native soil and the kingdom of his ancestors, in a short time he restored all to tranquility.

56. COSTS OF THE SEVENTH CRUSADE (1256)

Sometime between 1330 and 1332, a clerk for King Philip VI of France made a record of the expenses incurred by the Seventh Crusade, which was led by King Louis IX—who had been canonized as Saint Louis in 1297. At the time, Philip was planning to join King Edward III of England on a crusade, and he needed to know whether he could afford the endeavor. He could not. As the accounting revealed, the expenses of the Seventh Crusade were staggering: Louis spent perhaps five times the annual revenues of the crown on his venture. Adding the uncalculated human costs to the financial ones only emphasizes the mediocre results of the Seventh Crusade (doc. 78). The amounts given below are in livres tournois, shillings (20 to a livre), and pence (12 to a shilling).

Source: trans. Michael Livingston, from *Recueil des historiens des Gaules et de la France*, vol. 21, ed. Martin Bouquet (Paris: V. Palmé, 1840–1904), pp. 404, 513–14.

Total Expenses, 1247–56

Spent by St Louis, for the time across the sea from 1247 to 1256, for nine years: 1,537,570 livres tournois....

Yearly Expenses, 1251–52

Expenses for the household, for the war and shipping, from 1251 to 1252, for 351 days in the Holy Land:

Expenses for food ... 31,595 l. 11 s. 10 d.
Clothes and furs for the king ... 104 l. 12 s. 9 d.

Mantles for knights and clerics ... 312 l. 10 s. 0 d.
Harnesses and clothes for the same ... 12,910 l. 8 s. 11 d.
Gifts of robes and money ... 771 l. 10 s. 0 d.
Alms ... 1,515 l. 3 s. 9 d.
Crossbowmen and sergeants-at-arms for the household ... 4,494 l. 6 s. 6 d.
For 105 horses, packhorses, mules used by the household ... 1,916 l. 18 s. 11 d.
SUBTOTAL of expenses for the household of the king and queen for the time given ... 53,621 l. 2 s. 8 d.

Expenses for the war and for shipping for the time given:

Pay for the knights on wages ... 57,093 l. 17 s. 10 d.
Gifts and subsidies for knights not on wages ... 23,253 l. 18 s. 4 d.
Crossbowmen and sergeants on horse ... 22,242 l. 13 s. 6 d.
Payments for 264 horses ... 6,789 l. 17 s. 0 d.
Crossbowmen and sergeants on foot ... 29,575 l. 0 s. 6 d.
Carpenters, engineers, and other workers ... 689 l. 12 s. 3 d.
Common expenses (including 41,366 l. 14 s. 9 d. for workers in several oversea towns and 967 l. 13 s. 9 d. for the ransoming of prisoners) ... 66,793 l. 19 s. 6 d.
Spent on shipping ... 5,725 l. 15 s. 0 d.

SUBTOTAL for war and shipping for the time given ... 212,164 l. 13 s. 11 d.

TOTAL of the expenses for the household of the king and queen, and for the war and shipping, for the time given ... 265,785 l. 16 s. 7 d.

57. ARMY ON MARCH AND IN CAMP (1304)

Wounded during Philip IV (the Fair)'s Flemish campaign in 1304, French sergeant Guillaume Guiart wrote about his experiences, providing a rare glimpse of a soldier's life at war. Among his work is the 21,510-verse history of the French kings, Branche des Royaux Lignages, *which was written 1306–07. In the excerpts below, Guiart describes what he had witnessed of the chaos of an army on the march and in camp: the din of the people, horses, and carts all packed together, and the often-unnoted presence of the non-combatants who accompanied (and profited from) the hungry and thirsty soldiers.*

Source: trans. Michael Livingston, from *Recueil des historiens des Gaules et de la France*, vol. 22, ed. N. de Wailly and L. Delisle (Paris: V. Palmé, 1865), pp. 282–83.

At Arras is the king of France,
And many men of great power.
The town is full of men.
Eight days after the [Feast of] Magdalene,
It is ordered by the king, who will rule them all,
To cry and shout throughout the town
That the next day, at dawn,
All the men should be ready,
One and the other, large and small,
Who have come receiving wages,
As it had been arranged,
Should report into their constables' companies
Where each man is assigned and situated,
In order to move against their enemies;
And they pack the road tightly,
All of them following in an orderly manner
The marshals and their banner-bearers
Who go in the first position in front of the army.
After this the sergeants make a great gathering.
Throughout the morning the army gathers itself:
Those who will later go by the roads,
The men-at-arms go forward and back
In their troops, like sheep-herders,
As they issue out from the lodgings.
You would see the harnessing of carts with arms,
And the saddling of prized horses,
The loading of victuals on wheelbarrows,
And you would hear the rattling of carts,
The neighing of horses and blaring of trumpets,
The boys, who could not keep quiet,
Shouting and singing with joy.
I would do well to praise this last thing,
For can there be troubles on the road
If the heart is raised in joy?
Soldiers, who are provided with arms,
Prepared themselves to go against the Flemings
In order to do to them some misfortune.
But word is brought to the king
And to those who rest with him,
That his enemy turns aside;
What's more, all of them are fatigued!

The bridge at Vendin is recrossed;
There they desire that the French will find them
Such that they cannot advance against them:
There they are organized for war.
But one gave counsel to the king
That, if he wished to do harm to them,
They ought to search out another crossing;
At that place where their army is gathered up
He had no chance of defeating them,
The road is too difficult for them to attack.
For this reason the king decided, without delay,
To turn his army in a completely different direction.
The people who had already left Arras
Were stopped by a soldier,
Re-routed to the countryside of Fampoux.
Great is the noise when the army assembles;
The companies, troop to troop,
By way of Douai, issue from Arras;
They cover and fill the road,
Each one pressed against another,
These men who are armed and ready for war.
From Arras depart these dukes and counts,
Barons, castellans, and viscounts,
Sergeants of arms and seneschals.
The banners of the marshals,
Deployed against the wind,
Are in the first position up front.
A great multitude came after them,
All of them together, densely packed,
And this great host of barony,
Across mountains, valleys, plains,
No man could be found who could count them
Nor even imagine such a number,
Not in length nor in width!
God! how the saddled charger,
That the boy leads on the right side,
Shakes so proudly!
And with escutcheons on the saddles,
Golden horse bits and seat pads,
And bells and harness straps
On all the chargers I'm talking about,

Which were leaving so joyously,
They made a melodious sound.
The clerics chant motets; the militia dance;
The aged ones beg; the carters quarrel;
Young women chat and joke;
Sergeants hiccup; heralds cry;
Wagons with big barrels ramble;
Drums sound; horns trumpet loud;
Banners clatter and tremble;
Asses bray; horses neigh;
The arms of the armed made noise;
Scoundrels yell and boys argue.
All the surrounding country resounds
With the great din that they all make.
Constables and captains
Of the prestigious companies
Direct for them to lodge their goods,
Out of Arras, two good leagues;
And those to come follow their example,
In ordered fashion find their places.
With shovels and buckets
They deploy tents and pavilions,
As if in strong houses and halls,
Furnished with trunks and luggage.
Those on foot who do not have revenues,
Not a penny do they have for tents,
So they search out the limbs of trees:
There would you see little branches cut
And the sergeants dragging these
And bending them towards little saplings,
To make lodges and lean-to shelters
From the branches they have gathered up.
Before that would be a vast multitude
(If Guillaume Guiart doesn't lie)
You could see stretching out,
So many tents spread across the fields,
That more than a great league extends
The perimeter and the enclosure.
Among the others, by authority,
Are the tents the king establishes,
Pleasing, welcoming, and beautiful,

Around the outside of these,
A sergeant of the Orléanais who were there,
Standing armed guard with them each night;
With them a constable's company
Of the soldiers of Picardy.
In the host here and there, by the roads,
Are the diverse good people,
Who live by the work of their hands,
And who, for profit, accompany the army.
Here they make little furnaces and ovens
In ditches near the crossroads;
Many are there to make spits over fires;
There they cook tarts and pastries.
Barkeeps, to whom so many are in debt,
Bring barrels of wine in wagons,
Which to the soldiers who demand it
Watered down, even the dregs, they sell.
Others cry for their beers
Which are from Arras, as they say.
Here and there the aged ones echo,
Cry out their diverse calls,
The ones to sell cheeses,
Others white bread hard or tender.
These cooks set aside their pots;
Everyone's tents are filled with smoke.
The scoundrels, who carry their dice,
Will not cease to play their games.

58. ITINERARY OF THE CRÉCY CAMPAIGN (1346)

Though often neglected due to their simplicity in lacking narrative detail or poetic description, itineraries can be enormously valuable for the information they do provide about the strategy, tactics, and logistics of campaign routes, as well as the speed of an army on the move in foreign territory. These elements are clearly present in the so-called Cleopatra Itinerary (named for the manuscript in which it is found), which is one of two "simple" itineraries of the Crécy campaign that have survived. It also provides an excellent overview of one of the most famous campaigns in medieval history, including a brief account of its climactic battle on 26 August 1346.

Source: trans. Michael Livingston, from *The Battle of Crécy: A Casebook*, ed. Michael Livingston and Kelly DeVries (Liverpool: University of Liverpool Press, 2015), pp. 23–27.

These are the lodgings and the defeats that our lord the king made in the kingdom of France. It is to be noted: on 12 July he arrived at Saint-Vaast-la-Hougue, close to Barfleur, in Normandy; and the prince on that day was taken into the order of knighthood, together with other knights. Many people came upon the coast there, in order to defend the land; these were defeated and a large number of the men were killed. And the king remained there five days, until his men and his supplies had arrived. The following Tuesday [18 July] the king departed and lodged that night at Valognes, which town along with all the surrounding countryside was burned and destroyed. On Wednesday [19 July] the king lodged at Coigny. On Thursday, the Feast of Saint Margaret the Virgin [20 July], the king lodged in the fields outside of the town of Carentan, burning and destroying the surrounding countryside. On Friday [21 July] he lodged at Pont-Hébert, where he discovered that the Normans had torn down the bridge, in order to defend the crossing; and the king ordered the bridge repaired and he crossed the next morning. On Saturday, the Feast of Saint Mary Magdalene [22 July], the king lodged at Saint-Lô, which town had been deeply moated and barricaded and stocked with men-at-arms; and when they saw that our men approached them, they fled by another gate behind the city; the town and the surrounding countryside was captured and burned. On Sunday [23 July] he lodged at Cormolain. On the following Monday [24 July] the king lodged at Torteval-Quesnay. On Tuesday [25 July] he lodged at Maupertuis, on the Feast of Saint James. On Wednesday, Thursday, Friday, Saturday, and Sunday [26–30 July] the king lodged at Caen, which he discovered filled with men-at-arms and footmen; this town he captured and won by battle, and there were slain on that day a great number of men, and were captured the count of Eu, the constable of France; Tancarville, the chamberlain; along with 107 knights; not to mention the countless men who were killed. And there the leading citizens of the city of Bayeux came to offer peace, so that their town would not be burned and destroyed. On the following Monday [31 July] the king lodged at Troarn. On Tuesday [1 August] he lodged at Saint-Pierre-sur-Dives, the Feast of Saint Peter's Chains. On Wednesday and Thursday [2, 3 August] the king lodged in the city of Lisieux, where two cardinals came to the king, in order to negotiate a peace, and they were briefly answered. On Friday and Saturday [4, 5 August] the king lodged at Le Theil-Nolent near Le Neubourg. On Sunday [6 August] he lodged at Elbeuf on the Seine, where the cardinals came once more to the king, and there came with them an archbishop of France, and they were all answered. On the following Monday [7 August] the king lodged at Léry on the Seine; and that same day there was capture the castle of La Roche and the castle of Gaillon on the Seine, which were burned and destroyed along with the surrounding countryside. On Tuesday [8 August] the king lodged at Longueville near Vernon having passed by Pont-de-l'Arche; and the castle of Longueville was very full of men-at-arms, and they defended the castle well; but in the end it was taken by force and there many of the men-at-arms found inside the castle were killed. And when the men-at-arms that were within the town of Longueville saw that the men-at-arms inside the castle had been defeated, they issued out and fled by another gate, and a great many of them were killed; and our men seized and burned the town and all the surrounding countryside. On Wednesday [9 August] the king lodged at Bonnières-sur-Seine in fertile France. On Thursday on the Feast of Saint Lawrence [10 August] the king lodged at Épône on the Seine. On Friday and Saturday [11, 12 August] the king lodged at Fresnes-Ecquevilly on the Seine. On Sunday, Monday, and Tuesday [13–15 August] the king lodged at Poissy on the Seine, where he found the bridge destroyed; and the king immediately called for a halt, until the bridge could be repaired; and a large number of men-at-arms came against our baggage train there, their purpose to guard and defend the bridge and the passage; these were killed and a great many men were defeated, and the countryside was burned and destroyed all the way to Saint-Germain-en-Laye near Paris. On the following Wednesday [16 August] the king departed and lodged that night at Grisy-en-Vexin. On Thursday [17 August] he lodged at Auteuil. On Friday [18 August] he lodged at Troissereux in Picardie. On Saturday [19 August] he lodged at Sommereux. On Sunday [20 August] he lodged at Camps-en-Amiénois. On Monday and Tuesday [21, 22 August] the king lodged at Airaines in Picardie, and they captured the castle of Poix-de-Picardie by force of arms along the way, which was burned and destroyed with all the surrounding countryside. On Wednesday [23 August], on the day of Saint Bartholomew [24 August], the king lodged at Acheux-en-Vimeu. On Thursday [24 August] the king came to a ford of the river of the Somme, which was not far from Saint-Valery-sur-Somme toward Le Crotoy, and he discovered that all the bank on the other side of the river strengthened with cavalry and footmen, in order to defend the ford; these were defeated and a great number of men were killed, and that same night the king lodged beside the Forest of Crécy in Ponthieu. On Friday [25 August] the king lodged at another edge of the forest. The Saturday following the Feast of Saint Bartholomew [26 August] our lord the king came into the fields before the town of Crécy in Ponthieu; where he perceived the king of France was close to him, with all his forces and allies to fight. Between Nones [3 p.m.] and Vespers [usually between 4 p.m. and 6 p.m.] they assembled and they fought all that day and night until the next morning at Demi-prime, when, thanks be to God, the French were defeated, and the pursuit lasted more than 5 leagues. And in this defeat were slain the king of Bohemia, the duke of Lorraine, the archbishop of Sens, the bishop of Noyons, the Grand Prior of the Hospital of France, the count of Alençon, brother to the king of France, the count of Blois, the count of Flanders, the count of Namur and his brother the count of Harcourt, the count of Montbéliard, the count of Sauvay, the count of Auxerre, the count of Aumale, the count of Moreuil, the count of Grandpré, the count of Amartine [?], the count of Bar, the lord of Rosenburg, who was the most rich man in the realm after the king, the viscount of Trouard, Sir Jacques de Bourbon, brother of the duke of Bourbon, the lord of Cayeu, the lord of Saint-Venant, and many other men whose names are unknown. The following Sunday [27 August] the king lodged on the same field beside the Forest. On the following Monday [28 August] the king lodged at Valloire-Abbaye near Maintenay. On Tuesday [29 August] he lodged in the town of Maintenay. On Wednesday [30 August] he lodged at Saint-Josse in Ponthieu. On Thursday and Friday [31 August, 1 September] the king lodged at Neufchatel-Hardelot. On Saturday and Sunday [2, 3 September] the king lodged before Wissant. On the following Monday the king went to lodge before the town of Calais, on 4 September; and he will remain there until that town has been taken, with the aid of God, or the siege lifted by Philippe of Valois. And then came to Calais the counts of Warwick, of Arundel, and of Suffolk, with the good knights of the king's household, and they made a chevauchée all the way to Thérouanne; they gained victory and the city was burned and destroyed, with all the surrounding countryside; and 30 leagues they came and went, and a great number of men were killed, and they captured the archdeacon of the city, knights, and a great many others.

59. ARRAY OF VERONA (1386)

In trecento Northern Italy rival towns fought the largest wars for some of the smallest reasons, generally border disputes. Even if victorious, the costs of these conflicts almost always exceeded profits made. This can be clearly seen in Verona's war with Padua in 1386–87. That city's initial expenditures are listed in this catalogue of goods and men sent into that conflict. Verona would never recoup these expenses as Padua, aided by the employment of Sir John Hawkwood's mercenary army, would win the war at the battle of Castagnaro, on 11 March 1387. Yet, ironically, it would be the much larger city-states of Milan and Venice that would take advantage of the war and control both Verona and Padua within a year.

Source: trans. Niccolò Capponi, in Niccolò Capponi and Kelly DeVries, *Castagnaro, 1387: Hawkwood's Great Victory* (London: Osprey, forthcoming).

Array of the army of the magnificent and powerful lord sir Antonio Della Scala against the lord of Padua, this force moving on the 8th day of March 1386.

Wagons of bread ... 1,000
Wagons of wine ... 800
Wagons with other victuals ... 400

Wagons of sorghum and spelt ... 500
Wagons of arrows and bolts ... 300
Wagons of bombards and artillery, with all their apparatus and munitions ... 500
Wagons of tents and shacks ... 50
Wagons of bridges, ladders, bellows, shovels, levers, sawhorses, and other instruments ... 300
Wagons of balls for lanterns ... 200
Wagons of crossbows and pavises ... 50
Wagons of rushes and fascines ... 1,000
Carts of the aforementioned lord, courtiers and citizens ... 300
Wagons and apparels for all trades ... 50
Field fortifications (*bastie*) with all their necessities ... 4
Lances (*lanze*) of mounted soldiers, reviewed and paid for the whole month of March ... 2,500
Mounted crossbowmen ... 600
Foot crossbowmen ... 900
Infantry with "bolt-proof armor" ... 1,200
Armored horsemen with lances ... 300
Mounted pillagers (*sacardi*) ... 500
Infantry banners, with 25 [men] per banner ... 100
Trumpeters ... 46
Infantry of the Veronese county ... 5,400
Infantry from the Vicenza area ... 3,500
Sappers and miners ... 5,000

[The list continues with the gifts prepared by Antonio Della Scala to distribute to his victorious army, including fifty complete suits of armor, silverware, precious cloth, choice foreign wines, and 150 ounces (220 imperial ounces) of pearls "of various sizes."]

60. AGINCOURT: MARCH AND BATTLE (1415)

Within two years of Henry V's 1415 French campaign, which was highlighted by the battle of Agincourt, one of his men, possibly a royal chaplain, wrote the Gesta Henrici Quinti, *a narrative chronicle of the king's career to that point. Though deeply propagandistic, this eyewitness account is nevertheless invaluable for providing perspective on Henry V's remarkable victory in the face of odds, along with the increasing desperation of the English march that led to it. The excerpt below follows the campaign from the Somme to its most famous battle.*

Source: trans. Michael Livingston, from *Henrici Quinti, Angliae Regis, Gesta*, ed. Benjamin Williams (London: S. & J. Bentley and Henry Fley, 1850), pp. 46–56, 58–60.

Chapter 12

We withdrew from there [Péronne] on our march towards the River of Swords [Ternoise], leaving on the following Wednesday (23 October) the town of [Doullens] around one league away to our left flank. On the next day, Thursday (24 October), we were descending a valley in the direction of the River of Swords when our scouts and mounted guides reported to the king that an enemy many thousands strong was on the other side of the river, roughly one league to our right flank.

For this reason we crossed over the river as fast as we could. But when we gained the crest of the high ground on the other side, we saw, around a half-mile from us the grim ranks of the French emerging from higher up the valley: after some time, in columns, lines, and troops that were incomparably larger than our numbers, they took up a position over a half-mile opposite us, completely filling a very broad field like a innumerable swarm of locusts, controlling the moderately sized valley that lay between us and them.

Meanwhile, our king inspired his army with his very calm and undaunted manner, and he positioned them in lines and wings so that they could enter into battle immediately. Then each man who had not previously cleansed his conscience by confession obtained the armor of penitence. There was no shortage of men—only a shortage of priests.

Among the other things that I recorded as said at that time, a certain knight, Sir Walter Hungerford, prayed in the king's presence that he ought to have had, beyond the little company with he already had with him, ten thousand of the finest archers in England, who would have wished to be there with him. "Foolish talk," the king replied. "By God in Heaven, upon whose grace I have depended and in whom is my hope for an enduring victory, I would not add a single such man to the ones that I have, even if I could. For these men I have here with me are God's people, deemed worthy for me to have in this moment. Do you not believe that the Almighty, through these humble few, can defeat the opposing pride of the French, who boast of their great number and strength?" He said this as if were saying, "He can if he wants to do so." And, in my judgment, due to the true justice of God, no misfortune could befall a son of his with so great a faith, just as nothing befell Judas Maccabeus until he ceased to have faith: then, rightly, he fell into ruin.

After the scouts of the enemy had observed us for a little while—had considered our measure and small numbers—they withdrew to a field beyond a certain wood that was close to our left flank between us and them, where lay our road to Calais. Inferring that they would either circle around the wood in order to come upon him unexpectedly or circle around other woods in the area in order to surround us on every side, our king immediately moved his lines and positioned them so that they always faced the enemy.

Eventually, after more time had passed, we had nearly reached sunset. The French, seeming to recognize that a battle was not going to be fought—this was hardly possible with night approaching—occupied the farmsteads and scrub-fields nearby, intending to rest until morning.

When at last the light turned, and darkness had fallen between us and them, we heard the enemy encampment as we still remained on the field: each one of them called out, as was custom, for his fellow, servant, and friend who might have been separated in such a large crowd. Our men beginning to do likewise, the king ordered the whole army to silence, under the penalty of losing horse and harness if it was a nobleman who committed the offense or the loss of a right ear if it was a varlet or anyone of lower rank who presumed to violate the royal order, without hope of getting pardon. Then in silence he turned aside to a hamlet close by, where we had houses, although very few of them, and gardens and groves for our rest and a heavy rain for almost the whole night.

While our enemies noted our stillness and silence, thinking that our little numbers must be struck with fear and might be planning to flee in the night, they lit fires and set strong watches across the fields and paths. It was said that they considered themselves so secure from us that they cast dice for our king and his noblemen that night.

As dawn rose the next day, Friday on the Feast of Saints Crispin and Crispinian, 25 October, the French arrayed themselves in lines, columns, and wedges. In most terrifying numbers they took up a position in front of us in that said field, called Agincourt, across which ran our road to Calais. On each flank of their vanguard they set up cohorts of cavalry, many hundreds strong, to shatter our line and the strength of our archers. That vanguard was made of foot-men drawn from all their nobles and those they had chosen. A forest of spears and a horrifying number of gleaming helmets between them, with cavalry on its flanks, it was estimated that it was thirty times more men than all ours put together. Their rearguard and wings, troops and wedges, were all mounted as if more prepared to flee than to fight, but compared with our numbers they were like an uncountable multitude.

Meanwhile, after praising God and hearing Masses, our king made himself ready for the field, which was not far from his quarters, and established because of his few total numbers a single unit, positioning his vanguard as a wing on the right, commanded by the duke of York, and his rearguard as a wing on the left, commanded by Lord Camoys. He placed wedges of his archers into the battle line, and he caused them to fix stakes in front of them, just as he had previously arranged to do to prevent a cavalry charge. Perceiving this through the coming and going of scouts for one reason or another unknown to me (though God knows), the enemy facing us wisely held themselves back and came no closer to our lines.

With much of the day consumed in such delays, each army standing still and not taking one step towards the other, the king saw that the enemy multitude were refusing to make the assault he had expected them to make and thus stood blocking our way, either to disrupt our array or to infect our hearts with fear of their numbers—or, perhaps, they would impede our movement while awaiting reinforcements who were expected to arrive soon, or at least, knowing the desperate shortage of our supplies, they would defeat with hunger those whom they dared not engage with iron. So our king determined to move against them. He had previously ordered the army's baggage, together with the priests who were to perform [rites] and fervently pray for him and his men, to remain until the end of the battle in the same hamlet and confines in which he had been the night before; now he sent for it to be at the rear of the battle and not become spoils of the enemy, as the French pillagers were spying upon it from almost every side, proposing to assault it as soon as they saw the two armies engage. And, in the event, the moment the battle was begun, they fell upon the tail end of this baggage. Due to the sloth of the king's servants, the royal baggage was there, and they plundered valuable royal treasure, a sword, and a crown among other valuables, along with all of the bedding.

But once the king believed that nearly all his baggage had arrived at his rear, in the name of Jesus, to whom bends every knee in heaven, on earth, and in hell, and the glorious Virgin and St. George, he advanced against the enemy and the enemies advanced against him....

Chapter 13

After that, when the enemy was almost ready to attack, the French cavalry that had been positioned at the flanks charged against our archers who were positioned at each side of our army. But, as God willed it, under rains of arrows they were all quickly compelled to retreat to their rearguard, except for a very small number who ran, some dying, some wounded, among the archers and the trees, and, of course, the many men who were prevented from fleeing very far by the stakes driven into ground and the sharpness of missiles flying at both horses and riders.

The crossbows of our enemy, which were behind their men-at-arms and on their flanks, retreated in the face of the strength of our bows after an initial, hasty pull in which very few were injured.

When the men-at-arms on each side had approached each other nearly the same distance, the flanks of both lines—that is, ours and the enemy's—were immersed into the woods that were on each side of the armies. But the French nobles, who had previously advanced together in the front, so that they had almost come into contact with us, either fearing our missiles, whose might had pierced through the sides and visors of their helms, or to slam through our strength all the way to the standards, divided themselves into three parts, assaulting our battle-line at the three places where our standards were. In the first encounter of lances they threw themselves against our men, with such ferocity that they pushed them back almost the length of a lance.

Then in truth those of us looking on, who were to serve as chaplains, fell upon our faces in prayer before God's great mercy-seat, calling out in our despair that God might still remember us and the crown of England, and through the grace of His great generosity deliver us from this iron furnace and the dire death awaiting us. Yet God did not forget the multitude of prayers and supplications of England, by which, as it is devoutly believed, our men rapidly regained their strength, and through bold resistance, fought back the enemy until they had regained the lost ground.

Then the battle raged most fiercely, and our archers notched their arrows and shot the points into the flanks [of the enemy], ceaselessly renewing the fight. And when they had run out of arrows, snatching up the axes, stakes, swords, and spear-points that were scattered among them, they struck the enemy down, broke them, and cleaved them. For God, powerful and merciful, who is ever-wondrous in His works, who desired to show His mercy to us, and who was pleased that the crown of England should continue to remain invincible under the grace of our king, His soldier, and that little band, as soon as the lines had come together and the battle begun, increased the strength of our men who had been weakened and withered from lack of supplies, stripped them of their dread, and gave them fearless hearts. It had never been seen before, not even by our experienced men, that the English had ever attacked their enemies more boldly, fearlessly, or willfully: that same just Judge, who desired to pierce through the prideful multitude of the enemy with a thunderbolt of retribution, turned His face from them, broke their strength—bow, shield, sword, and formation. Nor had it ever been seen before, not recorded in any chronicle or history, that so many of the most select and strong soldiers made a stand so sluggishly, so disorderly, so fearfully, so unmanly. Indeed, fear and trembling took possession of them, for it was said in the army that there were some among them—even among their nobles—who surrendered that day more than ten times. Yet no one had time enough to take them as prisoners. Instead, almost all of them, without delay, without distinction of name, were put to death as soon as they were struck to the ground—whether by those who struck them down, by those who came after them, or by some hidden judgment of God, it isn't known.

Truly, God had struck them with another incurable blow. For when some of them fell at the front, killed at the joining of battle, so great was the uncontrolled violence and pressure of the many behind them that the living toppled upon the dead, and then those toppling upon the living were killed, too: as a result, in the three places where there was a strong force and the lines of our standards, there grew such a heap of dead men and those who lay crushed among them that our men climbed up those piles, which had grown taller than a man, in order to slaughter their enemies behind them swords, axes, and other weapons.

Finally, after two or three hours, their vanguard had been ripped through and broken apart, and the rest were forced to flee, our men began to tear those heaps apart and to separate the living from the dead, intending for the survivors to serve as collateral for ransom. But then, all at once—through what wrath of God it is unknown—a cry went up that the mounted rearguard of the enemy, which were still incomparable in number and fresh, were re-establishing their position and lines in order to ride over our little, weary host. Immediately, with no thought for the distinctions between them—except for the dukes of Orléans and Bourbon, certain other illustrious men in the royal battle-line, and a few others—the captives were killed by the swords of either their captors or the others who followed afterwards, so that they could not be disastrous to us into ruin in the coming battle.

Only a short time later, however, the enemy ranks, having tasted the bitterness of our missiles, and our king advancing close upon them, by God's will abandoned to us a field of blood along with their wagons and other carts, many of them loaded with supplies, missiles, lances, and bows....

Chapter 14

... But there was great joy among our people and great astonishment, because out of all our little band there were not found more than nine or ten men dead upon the field, except the illustrious and most wise prince, Lord Edward, duke of York, and Lord Michael, earl of Suffolk, a courageous young man, as well as two newly dubbed knights who were killed in the line of battle. Also Humphrey, our duke of Gloucester, the king's youngest brother and a valiant prince, took as well as he gave and was gravely wounded in the king's retinue. And little wonder, amid so many violently shaking swords, lances, and axes! Even so, after his arrival in Calais he quickly recovered. Praise God! ...

When our king, after the battle was done, had rested out of his humanity in the same place where he had the previous night, he resumed his march toward Calais on the next day, passing by that mound of duty (*pietatis*) and blood where the power of the French had fallen. And on Tuesday, the day after the feast of Saints Simon and Jude [29 October], he came to Calais. And on the Saturday after the feast of Saint Martin [16 November], when Lord Raoul De Gaucourt and the other captives from Harfleur had come, in accordance with their agreement, via the port of Dover he returned to England with his prisoners.

61. TRANSPORT OF ARTILLERY (1474)

During his reign as duke of Burgundy, 1467–77, Charles the Bold had the largest gunpowder artillery arsenal in all of Europe. In 1474 he needed to move a substantial train of this artillery from Luxembourg to Dijon so that it could be used in his ultimately unsuccessful siege of Neuss. The following order directs the transportation of the necessary materials, listing various gunpowder weapons (courtaux, serpentines, and bombards), their equipment, and the arms that would accompany them, along with the number of horses required to move it all.

Source: trans. Kelly DeVries, from Joseph Garnier, *L'artillerie des ducs de Bourgogne d'apres les documents conservés aux archives de la Côte-d'Or* (Paris: Honoré Champion, 1895), pp. 179–80.

State of that which seems to be necessary for the making and transporting of the artillery that our most redoubtable lord, M. the duke of Burgundy has ordered to be taken into Burgundy—to be taken into his said land of Burgundy under the direction of Estienne Ferroux by his commission to his government and army.

First:

To my said lord it is ordered to be taken two copper alloy courtaux presently at Luxembourg and for which it is suitable to take, 16 horses.

Item to take five medium and four small serpentines, that is to say that for the medium serpentines, three horses and for the small [ones] two, making 23 horses.

Item to take thirty casks of powder at the rate of five casks on each cart making six carts which makes 24 horses.

To take two hundred stone [shot] for courtaux at the rate of 40 stones on each [cart] of four horses making 20 horses.

To take the lead shot for the said 9 serpentines one and a half carts, 6 horses.

Item to take 2,500 bows, 2,700 dozen arrows, 6,000 strings, 11 carts which make 44 horses.

To take picks, hoes, spades, a cart with 4 horses.

To take grease, the bags of the saddler and of the cooper, a cart, 4 horses.

To take the bags of Estienne Ferroux and his aides by a commission of the receiver of the artillery, 6 horses.

To take into Burgundy a bombard to Dijon and to take which is needed no less than 24 horses.

To take a mantlet for this [bombard], ten carts are needed which makes 40 horses.

To take one carriage, 4 horses.

To take no less than one hundred stone [shot] for the said bombard at ten stones per cart with four horses making 40 horses.

It is necessary to take the bags of the carpenters their baskets and equipment, 4 horses.

To take the bags of the carters and other men of the said artillery, 4 horses.

To take the bags of the cannoneers two cart, 4 horses.

C. DECLARATION AND ORATION

62. ORATION AGAINST THE THURINGIANS (6th CENTURY)

The ability to inspire men to fight has long been an essential characteristic of a great military leader. There is, after all, a high probability that fighting may not be in a soldier's best personal interests. Throughout the pre-modern age—and well into our own—a key component of inspirational ability was the battlefield oration, an often emotional, rousing speech that can both rally the men and spur them into action. Here, Gregory of Tours records one such oration: a speech purportedly given by the Merovingian king Theuderic I, charging his men to fight against the nearby Thuringians. Hermanfrid, mentioned in the reading as king of Thuringians, was suspiciously murdered later in 632 when speaking with Theuderic.

Source: trans. Earnest Brehaut, Gregory of Tours, *The History of the Franks* (New York: Columbia University Press, 1916), book 3, chap. 7.

Be angry, I beg of you, both because of my wrong and because of the death of your kinsmen, and recollect that the Thuringians once made a violent attack upon our kinsmen and inflicted much harm on them. And they gave hostages and were willing to conclude peace with them, but the Thuringians slew the hostages with various tortures, and made an attack upon our kinsmen, took away all their property, and hung youths by the sinews of their thighs to trees, and cruelly killed more than two hundred maidens, tying them by their arms to the necks of horses, which were then headed in opposite directions, and being started by a very sharp goad tore the maidens to pieces. And others were stretched out upon the city streets and stakes were planted in the ground, and they caused loaded wagons to pass over them, and having broken their bones they gave them to dogs and birds for food. And now Hermenfred [king of the Thuringians] has deceived me in what he promised, and refuses to perform it at all. Behold, we have a plain word. Let us go with God's aid against them!

63. BATTLE OF THE STANDARD (1138)

Ostensibly moving in support of his niece Matilda, who had claimed the throne of England against King Stephen, but also no doubt seeing an opportunity to expand his own territories, King David I of Scotland invaded Yorkshire in 1138 during the horrific English civil war that has rightly been called the Anarchy. After some initial successes, the Scots met a group of northern barons and militia on 22 August on Cowpen Moor near Northallerton. While sometimes called the battle of Northallerton, the common name for the engagement is the battle of the Standard—named for a cart-mounted pole holding aloft a consecrated Host surrounded by church banners. This standard marked the gathering point for the Yorkshire defenders, and it was no doubt the place where pre-battle speeches were given. What follows is one chronicler's account of such a speech: a bishop's proclamation of the superiority of the Norman-blooded Englishmen who would indeed win the battle. Though likely imaginative regarding the actual words said on the field of battle, it is an excellent example of both an oration and the high-regard in which the Normans held themselves.

Source: trans. H.T. Riley, *The Annals of Roger de Hoveden*, vol. 1 (London: H.G. Bohn, 1853), pp. 231–33; revised.

While King Stephen was thus engaged in the southern parts of England, David, king of the Scots, led an innumerable army into England. By the advice and exhortation of Turstin, archbishop of York, the nobles of the north of England, went out to meet him, with William, the illustrious earl of Albemarle, and planted the standard or royal banner at Alverton, on Cutune Moor. As, in consequence of illness, the archbishop of York could not be present at the battle, he sent in his place Ralph, bishop of the Orkneys, who, standing in the midst of the army, on an elevated spot, addressed them to the following effect:

"Most illustrious nobles of England, Normans by birth—for when about to enter on the combat, it befits you to hold in remembrance your names and your birth—consider who you are, and against whom, and where it is, you are waging war; for then no one shall with impunity resist your prowess. Bold France, taught by experience, has quailed beneath your valor. Fierce England, led captive, has submitted to you. Rich Apulia, on having you for her masters, has flourished once again. Famed Jerusalem and illustrious Antioch have bowed themselves before you. And now Scotland, which of right is subject to you, attempts to show resistance, displaying a temerity not warranted by her arms, more fitted indeed for rioting than for battle. These are people, in fact, who have no knowledge of military matters, no skill in fighting, no moderation in ruling. There is no room then left for fear, but rather for shame, that those whom we have always sought on their own soil and overcome, reversing the usual order of things, have, like so many drunkards and madmen, come flocking into our country. This, however, I, a bishop, and the substitute for your archbishop, tell you, has been brought about by Divine Providence; in order that those who have in this country violated the temples of God, stained the altars with blood, slain his priests, spared neither children nor pregnant women, may on the same spot receive the appropriate punishment; and this most just resolve of the Divine Will, God will this day put in execution by means of your hands. Arouse your spirits then, you civilized warriors, and, firmly relying on the valor of your country—nay, rather on the presence of God—arise against these most unrighteous foes. And let not their rashness move you, because so many insignia of your valor cause no alarm to them. They know not how to arm themselves for battle; whereas you, during the time of peace, prepare yourselves for war, in order that in battle you may not experience the doubtful contingencies of warfare. Cover your heads then with the helmet, your breasts with the coat of mail, your legs with the greaves, and your bodies with the shield, that so the foeman may not find where to strike at you, on seeing you thus surrounded on every side with iron. Marching then against them thus, unarmed and wavering, why should we hesitate? On account of their numbers perhaps? But it is not so much the numbers of the many as the valor of the few that gains the battle. For a multitude unused to discipline is a hindrance to itself, when successful, in completing the victory, when routed, in taking to flight. Besides your forefathers, when but few in number, have many a time conquered multitudes; what then is the natural consequence of the glories of your ancestry, your constant exercises, your military discipline, but that though fewer in number, you should overcome multitudes? But now the enemy, advancing in disorder, warns me to close what I have to say, and rushing on with a straggling front, gives me great reason for gladness. I therefore in the place of the archbishop of you who are this day about to avenge the sins committed against the house of the Lord, against the priests of the Lord, and against your king under the Lord's protection, whoever of you shall fall fighting, do absolve him from all punishment for sins, in the name of the Father, whose creatures they have so shamefully and horribly slain, of the Son, whose altars they have polluted, and of the Holy Ghost, whose inspired ones, in their frenzy, they have slaughtered."

64. DECLARATION OF WAR AGAINST PHILIP II AUGUSTUS (1212)

Medieval "just war" doctrines often contained requirements that war be formally declared against an opponent. Despite this, very few of these declarations have survived. One of the most interesting is that written by Holy Roman Emperor Otto IV, a number of rebellious French lords, most notably Ferrand, count of Flanders and Hainaut, and William, count of Salisbury, the representative of King John of England. Ostensibly war was declared against the French king, Philip II (Augustus), but the declaration directs much of its blame at Pope Innocent III, who opposed Otto's reign, and the clergy. The war would be decided two years later, on 27 July 1214, when Philip annihilated the armies allied against him at the battle of Bouvines. Otto would be replaced as emperor by Frederick II, Innocent's choice, and most of the rebellious French lords would spend years in French confinement.

Source: trans. Peter Binkley and Kelly DeVries, "Medieval Declarations of War: An Example from 1212," in Kelly DeVries, *Guns and Men in Medieval Europe, 1200–1500: Studies in Military History and Technology*, vol. 2 (Aldershot, UK: Variorum, 2002).

Concerning ecclesiastical goods which should be expended for the public necessity; concerning the reformation of ecclesiastical priests; and concerning the war which is to be waged against the Pope and king of France. Made in the county of Valenciennes in the year 1212.

1. If it were not for the king of France, then we could be considered safe from any enemy in the whole world, and we could make the whole world subject to our swords. But this one person [the king of France] alone rendering disloyalty to us and always holding the cause of the clergy as if it were his own, the Roman Pope thus presumes to strike us with anathema and to absolve our nobles from their fealty to us. And, while he shows himself to be the friend of the king of Sicily [Frederick II], he dares to extend his forces into our empire, he who always raged against our people. And he presumes to disinherit King John himself who so generously rained money and wealth on us. Against him alone, therefore, it is expedient to resist with a complete endeavour. It is necessary that he first be restrained and subdued, who alone impedes our progress and opposes us. And whenever an enemy rises against us, he, too, becomes an enemy. With him overcome and subdued, we will easily conquer those who remain and bring the kingdom of France under our yoke and divide it according to our pleasure.
2. Moreover, it is necessary that we either depose or banish the clerics and monks whom Philip, the king of France, so elevates, loves, protects and defends with a vigilant heart, so that a few may remain for whom limited patrimony would suffice, and who may live only on a proffered benefice. Moreover, let the knightly-class receive the estates and great tithes and let those who care for the republic possess them and those who by fighting allow the people and the clergy to live in peace. Indeed, on that day when the Roman Pope rendered to us by the imperial diadem the first insignia [of rule], we published this law and ordered it, rendered in writing, to be observed firmly throughout the whole world: "Let the churches possess

only the tithes and proffered gifts, but let them relinquish the estates and farms to us, so that the people may live and the knightly-class may have their stipend from them."

3. Now, because the clergy does not obey me in this law, should we not reprove these people and freely take away from them the great tithes along with the estates? Can we not add a law to a law? Charles Martel, although he did not wish to remove the estates from the clergy, nevertheless took the tithes from them [in 733]. Hence will it not be permitted to us to take the estates from these same people with their tithes? Will it not be permitted to us—who compose laws and renew rights, who alone hold the power of the whole world—to bind the clergy to this law, so that those content with the small tithes and offerings may learn to be more humble and less proud? When we have renewed the laws, how much better, how much more commodious will the diligent knight have these newly tilled lands and the estates flowing with so many delights and so much wealth than this lazy species born to consume the fruits, which spend its time in leisure and lounges under a roof and in the shade, which lives without reason, whose every labour is in this, so that they may devote themselves to Bacchus and Venus, and for whom inebriation puffs up [their] necks with swollen drunkenness, and burdens [their] bellies with gluttony? Whence we, as soon as the Pope rebelled against us in the said law, snatched away Montfiascone, Aquapendente, Bitral, Radicofani, Villard-de-Lans, the castle at San Chirico Raparo, Bisterbius, Bissey-la-Cote and innumerable villages and castles by which rich Rome is surrounded which we still hold strongly and powerfully with arms against his will, and which we will hold for a long time; although he labors to overthrow our empire, and presumes to promise Frederick, the king of Sicily, our rights.

4. Then the nobles unanimously confirming the law in harmony, promise that there would be war, and all swear faithfully that they would heed what the Emperor said.

Signed Otto, Emperor Always Augustus of the Romans
Signed John, King of England, France and Ireland, by way of William, the Count of Salisbury
Signed Henry, Duke of Lotharingia and Brabant, Marquis of the Roman Empire
Signed Otto, Palatine Count of Burgundy
Signed Ferrand, Count of Flanders and Hainaut
Signed William, Count of Holland
Signed N., Count of Limburg

Signed N., Count of Barium
Signed Herves, Count of Nevers
Signed Peter, Count of Auxerre
Signed Henry, Count of Kuke
Signed Hugo, Baron of Boves

And many others, some nobles, some counts from Germany, from Hainaut, from Brabant and from Flanders signed. Enacted in the town of Valenciennes in the county of Hainaut, in the year of the incarnation of the Lord, MCCXII, in the year XV of our unconquered lord, Emperor Otto.

65. A KING'S CHALLENGE (1340)

In 1328, at the death of the childless King Charles IV of France, King Edward III of England was the closest heir to the French throne. But dusting off an early medieval legal code, the Salic Law, French nobles invalidated Edward's claim because his inheritance came through a woman, his mother, Isabella. Instead the nobles chose Philip, count of Valois, as their king Philip VI. This more than any single issue precipitated the Hundred Years War a decade later. Outside the city of Tournai in 1340, the two claimants to the throne found themselves potentially on the same battlefield for the first time. Edward, with a number of Low Countries allies, was already besieging the city when Philip arrived with an army and camped beyond their siegeworks. Edward wanted a battle, but the French king did not try to relieve the siege. Anxious to stir a fight that would prove his legitimacy, the English king challenged the French king to a duel, either between groups of selected soldiers or just the two of them: as an added point of provocation, he refused to address Philip as the king of France in his letter, having assumed that title himself. Philip turned down the challenge, and a short while later he retreated—though the city continued to hold out. Eventually, after three months, the English coalition broke apart and Edward returned to England defeated.

Source: trans. Michael Livingston, from *Society at War: The Experience of England and France During the Hundred Years War*, ed. Christopher Allmand, 2nd ed. (Woodbridge, UK: Boydell Press, 1998), pp. 102–04.

The Letter Sent from King Edward [III] to the French King

Edward, by the grace of God king of France and England and lord of Ireland, to Sir Philip de Valois.

For a long time we have exhorted you through messengers and manifold other ways to this end: that you should restore unto us and to do to us reason of our rightful inheritance of the realm of France, which you have for a long time occupied with great wrong. And for that, we see well that you intend to persevere in your injurious withholding from us without reason. In order to demand our rights we have entered into the land of Flanders as sovereign lord of the same and will pass into the country. Understand further that we have taken, with the help of our lord Jesus Christ, the rightful control of the said country and allied our people with them, beholding the right which we have in the heritage that you withhold from us with great wrong. And we are drawing ourselves toward you to make a short end of our rightful demand and challenge, if you dare approach us. And because so many and so great a power of men of arms have come on our part we may not long hold them together without great destruction of the people, which is a thing every good Christian man ought to eschew, especially a prince or someone else who has the governance of people. We therefore greatly desire that in a few days we may meet, and that—in order to limit the mortality of the people all the more—in the quarrel apparent between us the destruction of our challenge may stand in a trial between us two. This thing we offer unto you for the causes said above, remembering well the nobility of your person and your great wisdom and consideration. And in case you will not do that, then against our challenge be prepared to affirm the battle of yourself with a hundred persons of the most accomplished members of your party, and we will likewise do the same. And if you will not do the one nor the other, then you will assign a certain day before the city of Tournai to fight, strength against strength, within 10 days after the sight of these letters. We desire all the world to know regarding these things abovesaid that our desire is not for pride or for great arrogance; rather, it is so that our lord might set the more rest and peace among Christians, and so that that the enemies of God might be resisted and Christendom enhanced. The way that you will choose of these offers abovesaid, reply to us by the bearer of these letters, to him making hasty deliverance.

Given under our great seal at Espléchin near Tournai. In the year of grace 1340, 27 July.

The Answer of the French King

Philip, by the grace of God king of France, to Edward, king of England.

We have seen a letter sent to "Philip de Valois" brought to our court, in which were certain requests. And because the said letter came not to us, it appears by the substance of the letter that the said requests were not made to us. We therefore make no answer to you.

Nevertheless, because of what we understand by the said letter and otherwise that you have come armed into our realm of France—doing great damage to us our said realm and to the people, driven by an unreasonable will, disregarding that regard which a liegeman owes to his liege and sovereign lord, for you yourself are entered into our homage, acknowledging (as is reasonable) the king of France and promising obeisance such as a liegeman owes unto his sovereign lord, likewise having done so by your letters patent, sealed with your great seal, which we have here, and for which you should be obedient to us—our intent is such that, when we shall think it good, we shall chase you out of our realm to our honor and royal majesty, and to the profit of our people. And in doing this we have faithful hope in our lord Jesus Christ, from whom all good comes to us, since by your enterprise, which is in its desires unreasonable, a holy voyage over the sea has been prevented. A great number of Christian people have thereby been put to death, the service of God has been delayed, and the holy church unworshipped and unadorned with many great reverences. And in that, that you think to have the Flemings in your aid, we think ourselves assured that the good towns and commons will behave themselves in such ways towards us and our cousin, the earl of Flanders, that they will save their honor and loyalty. And in that, that they have misdone until now, is due to the evil counsel of such people who regard not the common weal of the people, but of their own profit only.

Given in the field of the priory of Saint-André beside Aire, under the seal of our secret signet in absence of our great seal, 30 July, the year of grace 1340.

66. JOAN OF ARC'S LETTER TO THE ENGLISH (1429)

Joan of Arc's confidence is remarked on by all who met her. That confidence comes through in a letter she dictated around 22 March 1429, before joining the French army at Orléans. At the time, she was under investigation by the professors at the University of Poitiers. Their judgment ascertained that Joan could *have been directed to Charles, the dauphin, from God. Of this there was no question by Joan, as expressed in this "declaration of war."*

Source: trans. Kelly DeVries, from *Procès de condamnation et de réhabilitation de Jeanne d'Arc, dite la Pucelle*, ed. Jules Quicherat, vol. 5 (Paris: Jules Renouard et Cie., 1841–49), pp. 95–98.

Jesus Mary

King of England, and you, duke of Bedford, who call yourself regent of the kingdom of France—and you, William de la Pole, count of Suffolk; John, Lord Talbot, and Thomas, sire of Scales, who call yourselves lieutenants of Bedford—do justice to the King of Heaven concerning he who is of royal blood: surrender to the Maid, who is sent by God, the King of Heaven, the keys of all the good cities [*bonnes villes*, used by Joan here, had an "official" designation] in France that you have taken and violated. She has come here on behalf of God, the King of Heaven, to claim the royal blood. She is fully ready to make peace, if you will do justice by giving up the lands that you hold in France. And with you, may the archers, gentlemen-at-war, and others who are before the good city of Orléans, go, for God's sake, back to your land. And if you do not do this, listen to the words of the Maid who will come for you soon to your very great sorrow: king of England, if you do not do this, I am a warlord [*chef de guerre*], and in whatever place that I meet your people in France, I will make them leave, willing or unwilling. If they are unwilling to obey, I will have them all killed. If they are willing to obey, I will show them mercy. I am sent on behalf of God, the King of Heaven, to kick you all out of France, man by man, to fight against all those who wish to commit treason, so that the kingdom of France is not further damaged. And you should have no other thought, for you will not hold the kingdom of France from God, the King of Heaven, the son of Saint Mary. But King Charles, the true heir, will hold it; because God, the King of Heaven, has shown it to be, as it was so revealed to the Maid, that he [Charles] will enter Paris in good company. If you do not wish to believe the words of God through the Maid, in whatever place that we find you, we will attack you. If you do not do justice, we will thus make such a great noise as has not been heard in France for a thousand years. And believe firmly that the King of Heaven will send more strength to the Maid, so that you will not be able to withstand all of the attacks by her and her good men-at-arms. Thus you will see who has the better right: the King of Heaven or you. Duke of Bedford, the Maid urges and requires you not to bring destruction on yourself, but to do justice, and come to this place where the French will do the best thing ever done for Christianity—if you make amends in the city of Orléans, if you make peace. But if you do not do so, a very great destruction will come upon you soon. Written on Tuesday of Holy Week (22 March 1429).

By the Maid.

D. THE FIGHT

I. ON LAND

67. BATTLE OF ADRIANOPLE (378)

The Romans certainly did not anticipate that upwards of 100,000 Gothic refugees would cross the Danube River as confederati *(people invited to settle in the Empire) in 376. When these settled in Thrace, the Romans were unable to feed their numbers, as promised, before crops could come in. Dire hunger and desperation resulted and Goths began raiding throughout the Balkans and Northern Anatolia looking for supplies. Emperor Valens decided to stop these raids with military force, but before reinforcements could arrive from the western part of the empire. The result was a devastating defeat and huge losses, including Valens, at the battle of Adrianople on 9 August 378. Ammianus Marcellinus, a contemporary soldier, although not an eyewitness, includes the most complete account of the battle in his* Roman History.

Source: trans. John C. Rolfe, *Ammianus Marcellinus*, vol. 3, Loeb Classical Library 331 (Cambridge, MA: Harvard University Press, 1939), pp. 463–83.

12. [Valens] had under his command a force made up of varying elements, but one neither contemptible, nor unwarlike; for he had joined with them also a large number of veterans, among whom were other officers of high rank and Trajanus, shortly before a commander-in-chief, whom he had recalled to active service. And since it was learned from careful reconnoitring that the enemy were planning with strong guards to block the roads over which the necessary supplies were being brought, he tried competently to frustrate this attempt by quickly sending an infantry troop of bowmen and a squadron of cavalry, in order to secure the advantages of the narrow passes, which were nearby. During the next three days, when the barbarians, advancing at a slow pace and through unfrequented places, since they feared a sally, were fifteen miles distant from the city, and were making for the station of Nice, through some mistake or other the emperor was assured by his skirmishers that all that part of the enemy's horde which they had seen consisted of only ten thousand men, and carried away by a kind of rash ardour, he determined to attack them at once. Accordingly, advancing in square formation, he came to the vicinity of a suburb of Hadrianopolis, where he made a strong rampart of stakes, surrounded by a moat ... Valens called a council of various of his higher officers and considered what ought to be done. And while some, influenced by Sebastianus, urged him to give battle at once, the man called Victor, a commander of cavalry, a Sarmatian by birth, but foresighted and careful, with the support of many others recommended that his imperial colleague be awaited, so that, strengthened by the addition of the [western] army, he might the more easily crush the fiery over-confidence of the barbarians. However, the fatal insistence of the emperor prevailed, supported by the flattering opinion of some of his courtiers, who urged him to make all haste in order that Gratian might not have a share in the victory which (as they represented) was already all but won.

... On the dawn of that day which is numbered in the calendar as the fifth before the Ides of August the army began its march with extreme haste, leaving all its baggage and packs near the walls of Hadrianopolis with a suitable guard of legions; for the treasury, and the insignia of imperial dignity besides, with the prefect and the emperor's council, were kept within the circuit of the walls. So after hastening a long distance over rough ground, while the hot day was advancing towards noon, finally at the eighth hour they saw the wagons of the enemy, which, as the report of the scouts had declared, were arranged in the form of a perfect circle. And while the barbarian soldiers, according to their custom, uttered savage and dismal howls, the Roman leader so drew up their line of battle that the cavalry on the right wing were first pushed forward, while the greater part of the infantry waited in reserve. But the left wing of the horsemen (which was formed with the greatest difficulty, since very many of them were still scattered along the roads) was hastening to the spot at swift pace. And while that same wing was being extended, still without interruption, the barbarians were terrified by the awful din, the hiss of whirring arrows and the menacing clash of shields; and since a part of their forces ... was far away and, though sent for, had not yet returned, they sent envoys to beg for peace. The emperor scorned these because of their low origin, demanding for the execution of a lasting treaty that suitable chieftains be sent; meanwhile the enemy purposely delayed, in order that during the pretended truce their cavalry might return, who, they hoped, would soon make their appearance; also that our soldiers might be exposed to the fiery summer heat and exhausted by their dry throats, while the broad plains gleamed with fires, which the enemy were feeding with wood and dry fuel, for this same purpose. To that evil was added another deadly one, namely, that men and beasts were tormented by severe hunger.

Meanwhile Fritigern [leader of the Gothic army], shrewd to foresee the future and fearing the uncertainty of war, on his own initiative sent one of his common soldiers as a herald, requesting that picked men of noble rank be sent to him at once as hostages and saying that he himself would fearlessly meet the threats of his soldiers and do what was necessary. The proposal of the dreaded leader was welcome and approved, and the tribune Aequitius, then marshal of the court and a relative of Valens, with the general consent was chosen to go speedily as a surety. When he objected, on the ground that he had once been captured by the enemy but had escaped from Dibaltum, and therefore feared their unreasonable anger, Richomeres voluntarily offered his own services and gladly promised to go, thinking this also to be a fine act and worthy of a brave man. And soon he was on his way [bringing] proofs of his rank and birth.... As he was on his way to the enemy's rampart, the [Gothic] archers and the targeteers, ... had rushed forward too eagerly in hot attack, and were already engaged with their adversaries; and as their charge had been untimely, so their retreat was cowardly; and thus they gave an unfavourable omen to the beginning of the battle. This unseasonable proceeding not only thwarted the prompt action of Richomeres, who was not allowed to go at all, but also the [returning] Gothic cavalry ... dashed out as a thunderbolt does near high mountains, and threw into confusion all those whom they could find in the way of their swift onslaught, and quickly slew them.

13. On every side armour and weapons clashed, and Bellona [the Roman goddess of war], raging with more than usual madness for the destruction of the Romans, blew her lamentable war-trumpets; our soldiers who were giving way rallied, exchanging many encouraging shouts, but the battle, spreading like flames, filled their hearts with terror, as numbers of them were pierced by strokes of whirling spears and arrows. Then the lines dashed together like beaked ships [galleys outfitted with rams], pushing each other back and forth in turn, and tossed about by alternate movements, like waves at sea.

And because the [Roman] left wing, which had made its way as far as the very wagons, and would have gone farther if it had had any support, being deserted by the rest of the cavalry, was hard pressed by the enemy's numbers, it was crushed, and overwhelmed, as if by the downfall of a mighty rampart. The foot-soldiers thus stood unprotected, and their companies were so crowded together that hardly anyone could pull out his sword or draw back his arm. Because of clouds of dust the heavens could no longer be seen, and echoed with frightful cries. Hence the arrows whirling death from every side always found their mark with fatal effect, since they could not be seen beforehand nor guarded against. But when the barbarians, pouring forth in huge hordes, trampled down horse and man, and in the press of ranks no room for retreat could be gained anywhere, and the increased crowding left no opportunity for escape, our soldiers also, showing extreme contempt of falling in the fight, received their death-blows, yet struck down their assailants; and on both sides the strokes of axes split helmet and breastplate. Here one might see a barbarian filled with lofty courage, his cheeks contracted in a hiss, hamstrung or with right hand severed, or pierced through the side, on the very verge of death threateningly casting about his fierce glance; and by the fall of the combatants on both sides the plains were covered with the bodies of the slain strewn over the ground, while the groans of the dying and of those who had suffered deep wounds caused immense fear when they were heard. In this great tumult and confusion the [Roman] infantry, exhausted by their efforts and the danger, when in turn strength and mind for planning anything were lacking, their lances for the most part broken by constant clashing, content to fight with drawn swords, plunged into the dense masses of the foe, regardless of their lives, seeing all around that every loophole of escape was lost. The ground covered with streams of blood whirled their slippery foothold from under them, so they could only strain every nerve to sell their lives dearly; and they opposed the onrushing foe with such great resolution that some fell by the weapons of their own comrades. Finally, when the whole scene was discoloured with the hue of dark blood, and wherever men turned their eyes heaps of slain met them, they trod upon the bodies of the dead without mercy. Now the sun had risen higher, and when it had finished its course through Leo, and was passing into the house of the heavenly Virgo [roughly several hours in midday], it scorched the Romans, who were more and more exhausted by hunger and worn out by thirst, as well as distressed by the heavy burden of their armour. Finally our line was broken by the onrushing weight of the barbarians, and since that was the only resort in their last extremity, they took to their heels in disorder as best they could.

While all scattered in flight over unknown paths, the emperor, hedged about by dire terrors, and slowly treading over heaps of corpses, took refuge with the lancers and the *mattiarii* [lightly armed Roman infantry], who, so long as the vast numbers of the enemy could be sustained, had stood unshaken with bodies firmly planted. On seeing him Trajanus cried that all hope was gone, unless the emperor, abandoned by his body-guard, should at least be protected by his foreign auxiliaries. On hearing this the general called Victor hastened to bring quickly to the emperor's aid the Batavi, who had been posted not far off as a reserve force; but when he could find none of them, he retired and went away. And in the same way Richomeres and Saturninus made their escape from danger.

And so the barbarians, their eyes blazing with frenzy, were pursuing our men, in whose veins the blood was chilled with numb horror: some fell without knowing who struck them down, others were buried beneath the mere weight of their assailants; some were slain by the sword of a comrade; for though they often rallied, there was no ground given, nor did anyone spare those who retreated. Besides all this, the roads were blocked by many who lay mortally wounded, lamenting the torment of their wounds; and with them also mounds of fallen horses filled the plains with corpses. To these ever irreparable losses, so costly to the Roman state, a night without the bright light of the moon put an end.

At the first coming of darkness the emperor, amid the common soldiers as was supposed (for no one asserted that he had seen him or been with him), fell mortally wounded by an arrow, and presently breathed his last breath; and he was never afterwards found anywhere. For since a few of the foe were active for long in the neighbourhood for the purpose of robbing the dead, no one of the fugitives or of the natives ventured to approach the spot. The Caesar Decius, we are told, met a similar fate; for when he was fiercely fighting with the barbarians and his horse, whose excitement he could not restrain, stumbled and threw him, he fell into a marsh, from which he could not get out, nor could his body be found. Others say that Valens did not give up the ghost at once, but with his bodyguard and a few eunuchs was taken to a peasant's cottage near by, well fortified in its second storey; and while he was being treated by unskilful hands, he was surrounded by the enemy, who did not know who he was, but was saved from the shame of captivity. For while the pursuers were trying to break open the bolted doors, they were assailed with arrows from a balcony of the house; and fearing through the inevitable delay to lose the opportunity for pillage, they piled bundles of straw and firewood about the house, set fire to them, and burned it men and all. From it one of the bodyguard leaped through a window, but was taken by the enemy; when he told them what had happened, he filled them with sorrow at being cheated of great glory, in not having taken the ruler of the Roman empire alive. This same young man, having later escaped and returned secretly to our army, gave this account of what had occurred....

Certain it is that barely a third part of our army escaped.

68. BATTLE OF DARA (530)

Wars between the Romans and the Persians had been fought since before the birth of Christ, with the Persians frequently coming out on top. This did not change when the empire split in two. In the early sixth century, threatened by Sassanid Emperor Kavadh I, Byzantine Emperor Justinian I sent one of his top generals, Belisarius, to defend the frontier with, and if possible extend it against, Persia. Initially defeated in battle, Belisarius regrouped in the fortified city of Dara, and restrategized. Though outnumbered, the Byzantines engaged and defeated the Sassanid forces in 530, which would leave time for Justinian to re-fortify the city (doc. 41). Procopius' account of the battle of Dara is fascinating not just for its descriptions of the tactics utilized by both the Byzantines (here called "Romans") and the Persians, but also for its details, such as the duel between two young men that preceded the full-scale fight.

Source: trans. H.B. Dewing, Procopius, *History of the Wars, Books I–II*, Loeb Classical Library 48 (Cambridge, MA: Harvard University Press, 1914), book 1, pp. 105–29; revised.

After this Emperor Justinian appointed Belisarius General of the East and bade him make an expedition against the Persians. And he collected a very formidable army and came to Dara. Hermogenes also came to him from the emperor to assist in setting the army in order, holding the office of magister; this man was formerly counsellor to Vitalianus at the time when he was at war with Emperor Anastasius. The emperor also sent Rufinus as ambassador, commanding him to remain in Hierapolis on the Euphrates River until he himself should give the word. For already much was being said on both sides concerning peace. Suddenly, however, someone reported to Belisarius and Hermogenes that the Persians were expected to invade the land of the Romans, being eager to capture the city of Dara. And when they heard this, they prepared for the battle as follows. Not yet July, far from the gate which lies opposite the city of Nisibis, about a stone's throw away, they dug a deep trench with many passages across it. Now this trench was not dug in a straight line, but in the following manner. In the middle there was a rather short portion straight, and at either end of this there were dug two cross trenches at right angles to the first; and starting from the extremities of the two cross trenches, they continued two straight trenches in the original direction to a very great distance. Not long afterward the Persians came with a great army, and all of them made camp in a place called Ammodios, at a distance of twenty stades [approximately 3.7 km or 2.3 miles] from the city of Dara. Among the leaders of this army were Pityaxes and the one-eyed Baresmanas. But one general held command over them all, a Persian, whose title was "mirranes" (for thus the Persians designate this office), Perozes by name. This Perozes immediately sent to Belisarius bidding him make ready the bath: for he wished to bathe there on the following day. Accordingly the Romans made the most vigorous preparations for the encounter, with the expectation that they would fight on the succeeding day.

At sunrise, seeing the enemy advancing against them, they arrayed themselves as follows. The extremity of the left straight trench which joined the cross trench, as far as the hill which rises here, was held by Bouzes with a large force of horsemen and by Pharas the Erulian with three hundred of his nation. On the right of these, outside the trench, at the angle formed by the cross trench and the straight section which extended from that point, were Sunicas and Aigan, Massagetae by birth, with six hundred horsemen, in order that, if those under Bouzes and Pharas should be driven back, they might, by moving quickly on the flank, and getting in the rear of the enemy, be able easily to support the Romans at that point. On the other wing also they were arrayed in the same manner; for the extremity of the straight trench was held by a large force of horsemen, who were commanded by John, son of Nicetas, and by Cyril and Marcellus; with them also were Germanus and Dorotheus; while at the angle on the right six hundred horsemen took their stand, commanded by Simmas and Ascan, Massagetae, in order that, as has been said, in case the forces of John should by any chance be driven back, they might move out from there and attack the rear of the Persians. Thus all along the trench stood the detachments of cavalry and the infantry. And behind these in the middle stood the forces of Belisarius and Hermogenes. Thus the Romans arrayed themselves, amounting to twenty-five thousand; but the Persian army consisted of forty thousand horse and foot, and they all stood close together facing the front, so as to make the front of the formation as deep as possible. Then for a long time neither side began battle with the other, but the Persians seemed to be wondering at the good order of the Romans, and appeared at a loss what to do under the circumstances.

In the late afternoon a certain detachment of the horsemen who held the right wing, separating themselves from the rest of the army, came against the forces of Bouzes and Pharas. And the Romans retired a short distance to the rear.

The Persians, however, did not pursue them, but remained there, fearing, I suppose, some move to surround them on the part of the enemy. Then the Romans who had turned to flight suddenly rushed upon them. And the Persians did not withstand their onset and rode back to their lines, and again the forces of Bouzes and Pharas stationed themselves in their own position. In this skirmish seven of the Persians fell, and the Romans gained possession of their bodies; thereafter both armies remained quietly in position. But one Persian, a young man, riding up very close to the Roman army, began to challenge all of them, calling for whoever wished to do battle with him. And no one of the whole army dared face the danger, except a certain Andreas, one of the personal attendants of Bouzes, not a soldier nor one who had ever practised at all the business of war, but a trainer of youths in charge of a certain wrestling school in Byzantium. Through this it came about that he was following the army, for he cared for the person of Bouzes in the bath; his birthplace was Byzantium. This man alone had the courage, without being ordered by Bouzes or anyone else, to go out of his own accord to meet the man in single combat. And he caught the barbarian while still considering how he should deliver his attack, and hit him with his spear on the right breast. And the Persian did not bear the blow delivered by a man of such exceptional strength, and fell from his horse to the earth. Then Andreas with a small knife slew him like a sacrificial animal as he lay on his back, and a mighty shout was raised both from the city wall and from the Roman army. But the Persians were deeply vexed at the outcome and sent forth another horseman for the same purpose, a manly fellow and well favored as to bodily size, but not a youth, for some of the hair on his head already shewed grey. This horseman came up along the hostile army, and, brandishing vehemently the whip with which he was accustomed to strike his horse, he summoned to battle whoever among the Romans was willing. And when no one went out against him, Andreas, without attracting the notice of anyone, once more came forth, although he had been forbidden to do so by Hermogenes. So both rushed madly upon each other with their spears, and the weapons, driven against their corselets, were turned aside with mighty force, and the horses, striking together their heads, fell themselves and threw off their riders. And both the two men, falling very close to each other, made great haste to rise to their feet, but the Persian was not able to do this easily because his size was against him, while Andreas, anticipating him (for his practice in the wrestling school gave him this advantage), smote him as he was rising on his knee, and as he fell again to the ground dispatched him. Then a roar went up from the wall and from the Roman army as great, if not greater, than before; and the Persians broke their formation and withdrew to Ammodios, while the Romans, raising the paean, went inside the fortifications; for already it was growing dark. Thus both armies passed that night.

[14] On the following day ten thousand soldiers arrived who had been summoned by the Persians from the city of Nisibis ... When Belisarius and Hermogenes ... saw the Persians advancing against them, they hastily drew up the soldiers in the same manner as before. And the barbarians, coming up before them, took their stand facing the Romans. But the mirranes did not array all the Persians against the enemy, but only one half of them, while he allowed the others to remain behind. These were to take the places of the men who were fighting and to fall upon their opponents with their vigor intact, so that all might fight in constant rotation. But the detachment of the so-called Immortals alone he ordered to remain at rest until he himself should give the signal. And he took his own station at the middle of the front, putting Pityaxes in command on the right wing, and Baresmanas on the left. In this manner, then, both armies were drawn up. Then Pharas came before Belisarius and Hermogenes, and said: "It does not seem to me that I shall do the enemy any great harm if I remain here with the Eruli; but if we conceal ourselves on this slope, and then, when the Persians have begun the fight, if we climb up by this hill and suddenly come upon their rear, shooting from behind them, we shall in all probability do them the greatest harm." Thus he spoke, and, since it pleased Belisarius and his staff, he carried out this plan.

But up to midday neither side began battle. As soon, however, as the noon hour was passed, the barbarians began the fight, having postponed the engagement to this time of the day for the reason that they are accustomed to partake of food only toward late afternoon, while the Romans have their meal before noon; and for this reason they thought that the Romans would never hold out so well, if they assailed them while hungry. At first, then, both sides discharged arrows against each other, and the missiles by their great number made, as it were, a vast cloud; and many men were falling on both sides, but the missiles of the barbarians flew much more thickly. For fresh men were always fighting in turn, affording to their enemy not the slightest opportunity to observe what was being done; but even so the Romans did not have the worst of it. For a steady wind blew from their side against the barbarians, and checked to a considerable degree the force of their arrows. Then, after both sides had exhausted all their missiles, they began to use their spears against each other, and the battle had come still more to close quarters. On the Roman side the left wing was suffering especially. For the Cadiseni, who with Pityaxes were fighting at this point, rushing up suddenly in great numbers, routed their enemy, and, crowding hard upon the fugitives, were killing many of them. When this was observed by the men under Sunicas and Aigan, they charged against them at full speed. But first the three hundred Eruli under Pharas from the high ground got in the rear of the enemy and made a wonderful display of valorous deeds against all of them and especially the Cadiseni. And the Persians, seeing the forces of Sunicas too already coming up against them from the flank, turned to a hasty flight. And the rout became complete, for the Romans here joined forces with each other, and there was a great slaughter of the barbarians. On the Persian right wing not fewer than three thousand perished in this action, while the rest escaped with difficulty to their army and were saved. And the Romans did not continue their pursuit, but both sides took their stand facing each other in line. Such was the course of these events.

But the mirranes stealthily sent to the left a large body of troops and with them all the so-called Immortals. And when these were noticed by Belisarius and Hermogenes, they ordered the six hundred men under Sunicas and Aigan to go to the angle on the right, where the troops of Simmas and Ascan were stationed, and behind them they placed many of Belisarius' men. So the Persians who held the left wing under the leadership of Baresmanas, together with the Immortals, charged on the run upon the Romans opposite them, who failed to withstand the attack and beat a hasty retreat. Thereupon the Romans in the angle, and all who were behind them, advanced with great ardor against the pursuers. But inasmuch as they came upon the barbarians from the side, they cut their army into two parts, and the greater portion of them they had on their right, while some also who were left behind were placed on their left. Among these happened to be the standard bearer of Baresmanas, whom Sunicas charged and struck with his spear. And already the Persians who were leading the pursuit perceived in what straits they were, and, wheeling about, they stopped the pursuit and went against their assailants, and thus became exposed to the enemy on both sides. For those in flight before them understood what was happening and turned back again. The Persians, on their part, with the detachment of the Immortals, seeing the standard inclined and lowered to the earth, rushed all together against the Romans at that point with Baresmanas. There the Romans held their ground. And first Sunicas killed Baresmanas and threw him from his horse to the ground. As a result of this the barbarians were seized with great fear and thought no longer of resistance, but fled in utter confusion. And the Romans, having made a circle as it were around them, killed about five thousand. Thus both armies were all set in motion, the Persians in retreat, and the Romans in pursuit. In this part of the conflict all the foot-soldiers who were in the Persian army threw down their shields and were caught and wantonly killed by their enemy. However, the pursuit was not continued by the Romans over a great distance. For Belisarius and Hermogenes refused absolutely to let them go farther, fearing lest the Persians through some necessity should turn about and rout them while pursuing recklessly, and it seemed to them sufficient to preserve the victory unmarred. For on that day the Persians had been defeated in battle by the Romans, a thing which had not happened for a long time. Thus the two armies separated from each other. And the Persians were no longer willing to fight a pitched battle with the Romans.

69. BATTLE AND AFTERMATH OF THE CATALAUNIAN PLAINS (551)

Though Attila is often given credit for the fall of the Roman Empire, most of the barbarian invasions of the empire had made their impact by the time he rose to the leadership of the Huns. Instead, Attila's reign brought a new phase of destructive raids, targeting not just Roman sites, but barbarian ones as well. His armies pillaged the Balkans, then part of the Eastern Empire, before turning toward the Western Empire. His invasions eventually took him as far as Orléans, which he besieged for two weeks without taking the city. He was ultimately drawn away by the approach of a Western Roman-Visigothic army led by Aetius, then Rome's greatest general. At a now lost location in the Catalaunian Plains, a huge battle was fought, leading to Attila's defeat. This account of what occurred during and following the battle, written later, by Jordanes, a Goth, contains the best narrative of the engagement.

Source: trans. Charles Christopher Mierow, *The Gothic History of Jordanes* (Princeton, NJ: Princeton University Press, 1915), pp. 106–14; revised.

The armies met in the Catalaunian Plains. The battlefield was a plain rising by a sharp slope to a ridge that both armies sought to gain, because an advantageous position is a great aid to victory. The Huns with their forces seized the right side. The Romans, Visigoths, and their allies seized the left. Then began a struggle for the still untaken crest. Theodoric with his Visigoths held the right wing [against Attila], and Aetius with the Romans held the left. On the other side, the battle line of the Huns was so arranged that Attila and his bravest followers were stationed in the center. In arranging them in this way the king had chiefly his own safety in view, since by his position in the very midst of his people, he would be kept out of the way of threatened danger. The wings of his army were formed of the innumerable peoples of the many tribes that he had subjected to his sway.... This crowd of kings—if we may call them so—and the leaders of these various nations hung upon Attila's nod like slaves. When he gave a sign even by a glance, without a murmur each was affixed with fear and trembling and did as he was bid. Attila alone was king of kings: leading all and concerned for all.

The struggle, as we mentioned, began for the most advantageous position. Attila sent his men to take the summit of the mountain, but he was outstripped by Thorismud [crown prince of the Visigoths] and Aetius, who in their efforts to gain the top of the hill reached higher ground and were able to use it to easily rout the Huns as they came up. When Attila saw his army was thrown into confusion by this event, he thought it best to encourage them with an extemporaneous address:

"Here you stand, after conquering mighty nations and subduing the world! It would be foolish for me to goad you with words, as if you are men who have not been proved in action. Let a new leader or an untried army resort to that. It would not be right for me to say anything common—nor right for you to listen—for what is war but your way of life? What is sweeter for a brave man than to seek revenge with his own hand? It is a right of nature to gilt the soul with vengeance. So let us attack the foe eagerly, for they are ever the bolder who make the attack. Despise this union of discordant races! To defend oneself by alliance is proof of cowardice. See, even before our attack they are smitten with terror! They seek the heights, they seize the hills, and, repenting too late, they clamor for protection against battle in the open fields. You know how slight a matter the Roman attack is. While they are still gathering in order and forming in one line with locked shields, they are checked, I will not say by the first wound, but even by the dust of battle. So into the fray with stout hearts, as is your habit. Despise their battle line! Attack the Alani! Smite the Visigoths! Seek swift victory in that spot where the battle rages. For when the sinews are cut the limbs will relax, and a body cannot stand when you have taken away its bones. Let your courage rise and your own fury burst forth! Now show your cunning, Huns, now your deeds of arms! Let the wounded exact in return the death of his foe. Let the unwounded revel in slaughter of the enemy. No spear shall harm those who are sure to live. And fate will take those who are sure to die into peace. And finally, why should fortune have made the Huns victorious over so many nations, unless it were to prepare them for the joy of this conflict? ... Who, moreover, made armed men yield to you, when you were as yet unarmed? Even a mass of federated nations could not endure the sight of the Huns. I am not deceived in the issue; here is the field so many victories have promised us. I shall hurl the first spear at the foe. If any can stand at rest while Attila fights, he is a dead man!"

Inflamed by his words they all dashed into the battle.

And although the situation was itself fearful, yet the presence of the king dispelled anxiety and hesitation. Hand to hand they clashed in battle, and the fight grew fierce, confused, monstrous, unrelenting—a fight whose like no ancient time has ever recorded. There were such deeds done that a brave man who missed this marvelous spectacle could not hope to see anything so astonishing all his life long. For if we may believe our elders, a brook flowing between low banks through the plain was greatly increased by the blood from the wounds of the slain. It was not flooded by showers, as brooks usually rise, but was swollen by a strange stream and turned into a torrent by the wash of blood. Those whose wounds drove them to slake their parching thirst drank water mingled with gore. In their wretched plight they were forced to drink what they thought was the blood they had poured out from their own wounds.

Here King Theodoric [the Visigoth], while riding by to encourage his army, was thrown from his horse and trampled underfoot by his own men, thus ending his days at a ripe old age. But others say he was slain by the spear of Andag of the host of the Ostrogoths who were then under the sway of Attila.... Then the Visigoths, separating from the Alani, fell on the horde of the Huns and nearly slew Attila. But he prudently took flight and immediately shut himself and his companions within the barriers of the camp, which he had fortified with wagons....

At dawn on the next day, when the Romans saw that the fields were piled high with corpses and that the Huns did not venture forth, they thought the victory was theirs. But they knew that Attila would not flee from the battle unless overwhelmed by a great disaster. Yet he did nothing cowardly, like one who is overcome, but with a clash of arms sounded the trumpets and threatened an attack. He was like a lion pierced by hunting spears, who paces to and fro before the mouth of his den and dares not spring—but ceases not to terrify the neighborhood by his roaring. In just this way this war-like king at bay terrified his conquerors. Therefore the Goths and Romans assembled and considered what to do with the vanquished Attila. They determined to wear him out by a siege, because he had no supply of provisions and was hindered from charging forth by a shower of arrows from the bowmen placed within the safety of the Roman camp. But it was said that the king remained supremely brave even in this extremity and had heaped up a funeral pyre of horse saddles, so that if the enemy should attack him he was determined to cast himself into the flames so that no one might have the glory of wounding him, and that the lord of so many races might not fall into the hands of his foes.

During this time, the Visigoths sought their king—and the king's sons their father—wondering at his absence when success had been attained. When, after a long search, they found him where the dead lay thickest, as happens with brave men, they honored him with songs and bore him away in the sight of the enemy....

Thorismud was eager to take vengeance for his father's death on the remaining Huns, being moved to this both by the pain of bereavement and the impulse of that valor for which he was known. Yet he consulted with the patrician Aetius (for he was an older man and of more mature wisdom) with regard to what he ought to do next. But Aetius feared that if the Huns were totally destroyed by the Goths, the Roman Empire would be overwhelmed. So he urgently advised him to return to his own dominions to take up the rule that his father had left: otherwise his brothers might seize their father's possessions and obtain the power over the Visigoths. In this case Thorismud would have to fight fiercely and, what is worse, disastrously with his own countrymen. Thorismud accepted the advice without perceiving its double meaning, but followed it with an eye toward his own advantage. So he left the Huns and returned to Gaul. Thus while human frailty rushes into suspicion, it often loses an opportunity of doing great things.

... Now when Attila learned of the retreat of the Goths, he thought it a ruse of the enemy—for so men are liable to believe when the unexpected happens—and remained for some time in his camp. But when a long silence followed the absence of the foe, the spirit of the mighty king was aroused to the thought of victory and the anticipation of pleasure, and his mind turned to the old oracles of his destiny.

... But Attila took occasion from the withdrawal of the Visigoths, observing what he had often desired—that his enemies were divided. At length feeling secure, he moved forward his array to attack the Romans. As his first move he besieged the city of Aquileia, the metropolis of Venetia, which is situated on a point or tongue of land by the Adriatic Sea.... The siege was long and fierce, but of no avail, since the bravest soldiers of the Romans withstood him from within.... [Attila] inflamed the hearts of his soldiers to attack Aquileia again. Constructing battering rams and bringing to bear all manner of engines of war, they quickly forced their way into the city, laid it waste, divided the spoil and so cruelly devastated it as scarcely to leave a trace to be seen. Then, growing bolder and still thirsting for Roman blood, the Huns raged madly through the remaining cities of the Veneti. They laid waste Mediolanum, the metropolis of Liguria, once an imperial city, and gave over Ticinum to a like fate. Then they destroyed the neighboring country in their frenzy and demolished almost the whole of Italy.

... While Attila's spirit was wavering in doubt between going and not going [to home], and he still lingered to ponder the matter, an embassy came to him from Rome to seek peace. Pope Leo himself came to meet him ... Then Attila quickly put aside his usual fury, turned back on the way he had advanced from beyond the Danube and departed with the promise of peace....

70. BATTLE OF HASTINGS (1066)

Few dates are more broadly known in the West than 1066: the year of the battle of Hastings. When the Anglo-Saxon king Edward the Confessor died without a direct heir in the first days of the new year, there were multiple claimants for the throne: Edgar Atheling was the grandson of King Edmund Ironsides, Duke William of Normandy insisted that Edward had promised him the throne, Harald Hardrada claimed the throne as his by right as king of Norway, and Harold Godwinson was the powerful earl of Wessex, who had served as Edward's right-hand man for more than a decade. Edgar was ignored, Harold

Godwinson was crowned, and Hardrada and William promptly raised armies to invade. Harold defeated Hardrada's army at the battle of Stamford Bridge on 25 September. Three days later, William's army landed on the south coast of England. After an extraordinary march, Harold and his Anglo-Saxon army met the Normans north of Hastings on 14 October, where Harold's death in battle turned the Norman duke into King William the Conqueror. The following account comes from William of Poitiers, a Norman apologist, but it paints what appears to be a reasonable picture of the famous engagement.

Source: trans. Ralph Henry Carless Davis and Marjorie Chibnall, *The Gesta Guillelmi of William of Poitiers*, ed. Ralph Henry Carless Davis and Marjorie Chibnall (Oxford: The Clarendon Press, 1998), pp. 115–17, 123–41.

9. The Battle Between Duke William and Harold, King of the English

The Normans, rejoicing after they had landed, occupied Pevensey with their first fortification, and Hastings with their second, as a refuge for themselves and a defence for their ships. Marius and Pompey the Great, each eminent for his astuteness and achievements, deserved a triumph, the former having brought Jugurtha in chains to Rome, the latter having forced Mithridates to take poison; but though daring to lead a whole army into enemy territory, each was chary of putting himself into danger away from the main army, with only a legion. It was their custom, as it still is the custom of leaders, to send out scouts, but not to go themselves on reconnaissance, being more concerned with preserving their own lives than with making provision for the army. But William was quick to investigate the region and its inhabitants with a company of no more than twenty-five knights. When he returned on foot because of the difficulty of the path (not without laughter; though the reader may laugh) he deserved genuine praise, for he carried on his own shoulders both his own hauberk and that of one of his followers, William fitz Osbern, renowned for his bodily strength and courage, whom he had relieved of this iron burden.

10. Robert, son of the noblewoman Guimara, who was a wealthy inhabitant of those parts and a Norman by birth, sent a messenger to Hastings to the duke, his lord and kinsman, with these words: "King Harold has fought with his own brother and with the king of the Norwegians, who passed for the strongest man living under the sun, and has killed both in one battle and destroyed huge armies. Encouraged by this success, he is advancing against you by forced marches, leading a strong and numerous troop; against him I consider that your men would be worth no more than so many wretched dogs. You are reckoned a prudent man; up to now you have always acted prudently in peace and war. Now I advise you, act circumspectly so as not to fall through rashness into a danger from which you will not escape. I urge

you: stay behind fortifications; do not offer battle for the time being." But the duke replied to the messenger, "For the message in which your lord wishes me to be cautious (although it would have been decent to give advice without insult) give him my thanks and this reply: 'I will not take refuge in the shelter of ditch or walls, but I will fight with Harold as soon as possible; nor do I lack confidence in the courage of my men to fight and destroy him with his men, if God so wills, even if I had only 10,000 men of the quality of the 60,000 I have brought with me.'"

...

14. Meanwhile experienced knights, who had been sent out scouting, reported that the enemy would soon be there. For the furious king was hastening his march all the more because he had heard that the lands near to the Norman camp were being laid waste. He thought that in a night or surprise attack he might defeat them unawares; and, in case they should try to escape, he had laid a naval ambush for them with an armed fleet of up to 700 ships. The duke hastily ordered all who could be found in the camp (for a large number of his companions had gone off foraging) to arm themselves. He himself participated in the mystery of the Mass with the greatest devotion, and strengthened his body and soul by receiving in communion the body and blood of the Lord. He hung around his neck in humility the relics whose protection Harold had forfeited by breaking the oath that he had sworn on them. Two bishops who had accompanied him from Normandy, Odo of Bayeux and Geoffrey of Coutances, were in his company, together with numerous clerks and not a few monks. This clerical body prepared for the combat with prayers. Anyone else would have been terrified by putting on his hauberk back to front. But William laughed at this inversion as an accident and did not fear it as a bad omen.

15. We do not doubt that the exhortation, brief because of the circumstances, with which he added still greater ardour to the valour of his troops, was outstanding, even though it has not been transmitted to us in all its distinction. He reminded the Normans that in many and great dangers they had always come out victorious under his leadership. He reminded them all of their fatherland, of their noble exploits and their great fame. Now they were to prove with their arms with what strength they were endowed, with what valour they were inspired. Now the question was not who should live and rule, but who should escape alive from imminent danger. If they fought like men they would have victory, honour, and wealth. If not, they would let themselves either be slaughtered, or captured to be mocked by the most cruel enemies—not to mention that they would bring on themselves perpetual ignominy. No way was open to flight, since their way was barred on one side by armed forces and a hostile and unknown country, and on the other by the sea and armed forces. It was not seemly for men to be terrified by numbers. Many times the English had

fallen, overthrown by enemy arms; usually, defeated, they had surrendered to the enemy; never were they famed for the glory of their feats of arms. Men who were inexpert in warfare could easily be crushed by the valour and strength of a few, especially since help from on high was not lacking in a just cause. Let them now dare and never yield, and they would soon rejoice in a triumph.

16. Now this is the well-planned order in which he advanced behind the banner which the pope had sent him. He placed foot-soldiers in front, armed with arrows and crossbows; likewise, foot-soldiers in the second rank, but more powerful and wearing hauberks; finally the squadrons of mounted knights, in the middle of which he himself rode with the strongest force, so that he could direct operations on all sides with hand and voice. If any author of antiquity had been writing of Harold's line of march he would have recorded that in his passage rivers were dried up and forests laid flat. For huge forces of English had assembled from all the shires. Some showed zeal for Harold, and all showed love of their country, which they wished to defend against invaders even though their cause was unjust. The land of the Danes (who were allied by blood) also sent copious forces. However, not daring to fight with William on equal terms, for they thought him more formidable than the king of the Norwegians, they took their stand on higher ground, on a hill near to the wood through which they had come. At once dismounting from their horses, they lined up all on foot in a dense formation. Undeterred by the roughness of the ground, the duke with his men climbed slowly up the steep slope.

17. The harsh bray of trumpets gave the signal for battle on both sides. The Normans swiftly and boldly took the initiative in the fray. Similarly, when orators are engaged in a lawsuit about theft, he who prosecutes the crime makes the first speech. So the Norman foot-soldiers closed to attack the English, killing and maiming many with their missiles. The English for their part resisted bravely each one by any means he could devise. They threw javelins and missiles of various kinds, murderous axes and stones tied to sticks. You might imagine that our men would have been crushed at once by them, as by a death-dealing mass. The knights came to their rescue, and those who had been in the rear advanced to the fore. Disdaining to fight from a distance, they attacked boldly with their swords. The loud shouting, here Norman, there foreign, was drowned by the clash of weapons and the groans of the dying. So for a time both sides fought with all their might. The English were greatly helped by the advantage of the higher ground, which they held in serried ranks without sallying forward, and also by their great numbers and densely-packed mass, and moreover by their weapons of war, which easily penetrated shields and other protections. So they strongly held or drove back those who dared to attack them with drawn swords. They even wounded those who flung javelins at them from a distance. So, terrified by this ferocity, both the footsoldiers and the Breton knights and

other auxiliaries on the left wing turned tail; almost the whole of the duke's battle line gave way, if such a thing may be said of the unconquered people of the Normans. The army of the Roman empire, containing royal contingents and accustomed to victory on land and sea, fled occasionally, when it knew or believed its leader to have been killed. The Normans believed that their duke and lord had fallen, so it was not too shameful to give way to flight; least of all was it to be deplored, since it helped them greatly.

18. For the leader, seeing a great part of the opposing force springing forward to pursue his men, rushed towards them, met them as they fled and halted them, striking out and threatening with his spear. Baring his head and lifting his helmet, he cried, "Look at me. I am alive, and with God's help I will conquer. What madness is persuading you to flee? What way is open to escape? You could slaughter like cattle the men who are pursuing and killing you. You are abandoning victory and imperishable fame, and hurrying to disaster and perpetual ignominy. Not one of you will escape death by flight." At these words they recovered their courage. He rushed forward at their head, brandishing his sword, and mowed down the hostile people who deserved death for rebelling against him, their king. Full of zeal the Normans surrounded some thousands who had pursued them and destroyed them in a moment, so that not a single one survived.

19. Emboldened by this, they launched an attack with greater determination on the main body of the army, which in spite of the heavy losses it had suffered seemed not to be diminished. The English fought confidently with all their might, striving particularly to prevent a gap being opened by their attackers. They were so tightly packed together that there was hardly room for the slain to fall. However paths were cut through them in several places by the weapons of the most valiant knights. Pressing home the attack were men of Maine, Frenchmen, Bretons, Aquitanians, above all Normans, whose valour was outstanding. A certain young Norman knight, Robert the son of Roger of Beaumont, nephew and heir of Hugh count of Meulan through Hugh's sister Adeline, while fighting that day in his first battle performed a praiseworthy deed, which deserves to be immortalized; charging with the battalion he commanded on the right wing, he laid the enemy low with the greatest audacity. We have not the means, and it is not our intention, to describe all the exploits of individuals as their merit deserves. The most eloquent writer who had seen that battle with his own eyes could scarcely have followed every detail. But now we hasten on to complete the praise of William the count so as to tell of the glory of William the king.

20. When the Normans and the troops allied to them saw that they could not conquer such a solidly massed enemy force without heavy loss, they wheeled round and deliberately feigned flight. They remembered how, a little while before, their flight had brought about the result they desired. There was

jubilation among the foreigners, who hoped for a great victory. Encouraging each other with joyful shouts, they heaped curses on our men and threatened to destroy them all forthwith. As before, some thousands of them dared to rush, almost as if they were winged, in pursuit of those they believed to be fleeing. The Normans, suddenly wheeling round their horses, checked and encircled them, and slaughtered them to the last man.

21. Having used this trick twice with the same result, they attacked the remainder with greater determination: up to now the enemy line had been bristling with weapons and most difficult to encircle. So a combat of an unusual kind began, with one side attacking in different ways and the other standing firmly as if fixed to the ground. The English grew weaker, and endured punishment as though confessing their guilt by their defeat. The Normans shot arrows, smote and pierced; the dead by falling seemed to move more than the living. It was not possible for the lightly wounded to escape, for they were crushed to death by the serried ranks of their companions. So fortune turned for William, hastening his triumph.

22. Those who took part in this battle were Eustace count of Boulogne, William son of Richard count of Évreux, Geoffrey son of Rotrou count of Mortagne, William fitz Osbern, Aimeri vicomte of Thouars, Walter Giffard, Hugh of Montfort, Ralph of Tosny, Hugh of Grandmesnil, William of Warenne, and many others of military distinction and great renown, whose names deserve to be remembered in the annals of history amongst the very greatest warriors. But William, their duke, so surpassed them in courage as well as in wisdom that he deserves to be placed above certain of the ancient generals of the Greeks and Romans, who are so much praised in their writings, and to be compared with others. He led his men nobly, checking flight, giving encouragement, courting danger, more often calling on them to follow than ordering them to go ahead. From this it is plain to see that his valour in the van opened the way for his followers and gave them courage. No small part of the enemy lost heart without being injured at the sight of this astounding and redoubtable mounted warrior. Three horses were killed under him and fell. Three times he sprang to the ground undaunted, and avenged without delay the loss of his steed. Here his speed, here his physical strength and courage could be seen. With his angry blade he tirelessly pierced shields, helmets, and hauberks; with his buckler he threw back many. Marvelling at seeing him fight on foot his knights, many of them smitten with wounds, took heart again. Some even, "weakened by loss of blood," leant on their shields and fought on courageously; others, incapable of more, encouraged their companions by word and gesture, to follow the duke without fear, so that victory should not slip through their hands. He himself helped and saved many of them.

Against Harold, who was such a man as poems liken to Hector or Turnus, William would have dared to fight in single combat no less than Achilles against Hector, or Aeneas against Turnus. Tydeus, when ambushed by fifty men, defended himself with a rock; William, his equal and in no way inferior in standing, single-handed did not fear a thousand. The authors of the *Thebaid* or the *Aeneid*, who in their books sing of great events and exaggerate them according to the law of poetry, could make an equally great and more worthy work by singing truthfully about the actions of this man. Indeed, if by the beauty of their style they could equal the grandeur of their subject matter, they would rank him among the gods. But our feeble prose will bring humbly to the notice of kings his piety in the worship of the true God, who alone is God from eternity to the end of the world and beyond, and will briefly and truthfully bring to a close this account of the battle which he bravely and justly won.

23. Towards the end of the day the English army realized that there was no hope of resisting the Normans any longer. They knew that they had been weakened by the loss of many troops; that the king himself and his brothers and not a few of the nobles of the kingdom had perished; that all who remained were almost at the end of their strength, and that they could hope for no relief. They saw that the Normans were not greatly weakened by the loss of those who had fallen and, seeming to have found new strength as they fought, were pressing on more eagerly than at first. They saw that the duke in his ferocity spared no opponent; and that nothing but victory could quench his ardour. So they turned to escape as quickly as possible by flight, some on horses they had seized, some on foot; some along roads, others through untrodden wastes. Some lay helplessly in their own blood, others who struggled up were too weak to escape. The passionate wish to escape death gave strength to some. Many left their corpses in deep woods, many who had collapsed on the routes blocked the way for those who came after. The Normans, though strangers to the district, pursued them relentlessly, slashing their guilty backs and putting the last touches to the victory. Even the hooves of the horses inflicted punishment on the dead as they galloped over their bodies.

24. However confidence returned to the fugitives when they found a good chance to renew battle, thanks to a broken rampart and labyrinth of ditches. For this people was by nature always ready to take up the sword, being descended from the ancient stock of Saxons, the fiercest of men. They would never have been driven back except by irresistible force. Recently they had easily defeated the king of the Norwegians, who was relying on a huge, warlike army. But when the duke at the head of the conquering banners saw that the troops had massed unexpectedly, although thinking them to be a newly-arrived relief force, he neither changed course nor halted. More terrible with only the stump of his lance than those who brandished long javelins, he raised his strong voice and ordered Count Eustace, who had turned tail with fifty knights and wished to sound the retreat, not to withdraw. But Eustace for his part, whispering

familiarly in the duke's ear, argued for a retreat and predicted his speedy death if he pressed forward. As he was uttering these words, Eustace was struck a resounding blow between the shoulders; its violence was immediately shown by blood streaming from his nose and mouth; and, half dead, he escaped with the help of his companions. The duke, utterly disdaining fear and dishonour, charged his enemies and laid them low. In that encounter some of the noblest Normans fell, for their valour was of no avail on such unfavourable ground.

25. So, after completing the victory, William returned to the battlefield and discovered the extent of the slaughter, surveying it not without pity, even though it had been inflicted on impious men, and even though it is just and glorious and praiseworthy to kill a tyrant. Far and wide the earth was covered with the flower of the English nobility and youth, drenched in blood. The king's two brothers were found very near to his body. He himself was recognized by certain marks, not by his face, for he had been despoiled of all signs of status. He was carried into the camp of the duke, who entrusted his burial to William surnamed Malet, not to his mother, though she offered his weight in gold for the body of her beloved son. For he knew it was not seemly to accept gold for such a transaction. He considered that it would be unworthy for him to be buried as his mother wished, when innumerable men lay unburied because of his overweening greed. It was said in jest that he should be placed as guardian of the shore and sea, which in his madness he had once occupied with his armies.

71. BATTLE OF HATTIN (1187)

Never during the 200 years that Western crusaders occupied at least part of the Holy Land did they face a leader more able to unite Islamic forces against them than the Kurdish general Saladin. Coming to power in Egypt in 1164, Saladin quickly consolidated his forces around the newly occupied Damascus, moving west into the crusader Kingdom of Jerusalem. He captured Lake Tiberias (the Sea of Galilee) and the town of Tiberias next to it. As the Islamic forces continued to gather under Saladin, the unity of the crusader states was beginning to show the strain of the varying ambitions of its leaders. One noble in particular, Reynald of Châtillon, had acted independently from other crusade leaders, ignoring treaties with the Muslims and attacking their trade caravans. Reynald's actions split the crusaders into two camps: moderates and hawks. While Saladin prepared his ever-growing Islamic army for war, the moderates argued for delay, believing that time would diminish Saladin's forces. The more zealous of the Franks, however, pressed to march out to meet him in battle, and it was this rash plan that was ultimately adopted. The armies met on 3 July 1187 in the dry, desolate valley under the Horns of Hattin. The battle was a crushing defeat for the resident crusader forces. Imad ad-Din (1125–1201), who gives an account of the battle below, was Saladin's secretary. Although rather florid in its style, his narrative of the battle includes many important details not found in the Christian sources.

Sources: trans. E.J. Costello, *Arab Historians of the Crusades*, ed. Francesco Gabrieli (Berkeley and Los Angeles: University of California Press, 1969), pp. 129–37.

Saladin surrounded [the fortified town of] Tiberias with his personal guard and his most faithful troops. He advanced the infantry and sappers ... and the artillery [trebuchets], surrounded the walls and began to demolish the houses, giving battle fiercely and not sparing the city in the attack. This was Thursday, and he was at the head of his troops. The sappers began to mine one of the towers. They demolished it, knocked it down, leapt onto it and took possession of it. Night fell, and while the dawn of victory was breaking for them, the night of woe was darkening for enemy. The citadel put up resistance and the [Frankish] countess [Eschiva] shut herself up there with her sons. When the count [that is, Raymond of Tripoli] heard that Tiberias had fallen and his princedom been taken he was seized with consternation and lost all his strength of purpose, putting himself completely in the hands of the [other] Franks. "From today onwards," he said, "not to act is no longer possible. We must at all costs drive the enemy back. Now that Tiberias is taken and the whole princedom with all my possessions, acquired or inherited, is lost, I cannot resign myself or recover from this reverse." The king [of Jerusalem] was his ally and offered no opposition, but consented to this without hypocrisy, with sincere and unmixed affection, in a friendly manner completely lacking in coldness. He gave him precise promises without having to be asked twice, and set out on the march with his army, his sight and his hearing, his dragons and demons, beasts and wolves, the followers of his error and the faction of his evil deeds. The earth trembled beneath their feet, the heavens were clouded with the dust thrown up by them. News came [to the Muslims] that the Franks had mounted and were on the move with the ranks of their steadfast faith, who leapt into the attack, drawn up for battle and flooding over the ground, creeping forward on the defensive, kindling the fire of war, responding to the cry of vengeance, running to reach their dwellings. This was Friday 24 Rabi' II [that is, July 3]. As soon as the news was verified, the sultan confirmed that his decision, based on his earlier judgment, was accurate, and rejoiced to hear that they were on the march: "If our objective is gained," he said, "our request will have been heard in full and our ambition will have been achieved. Thanks be to God, our good fortune will now be renewed, our swords sharp, our courage valiant, our victory swift. If they are really defeated, killed and captured, Tiberias and all Palestine will have no one left to defend them or to impede our conquest."

Thus he sought God's best [fortune] and set off, casting all delay aside. On Friday 24 Rabi' II the Franks were on the march toward Tiberias with all their forces, moving as fast as if they were always going downhill. Their hordes rolled on, their lions roared, their vultures flew above them, their cries rose up, the horizon was hidden by the clouds of them, their heads sought eagerly for those who were to strike them off. They looked like mountains on the march, like seas boiling over, wave upon wave with their crowding ranks, their seething approach—roads and mutilated barbarian warriors. The air stank, the light was dimmed, the desert was stunned, the plain dissolved, destiny hung over them, the Pleiades sent dust down upon them, the chargers' saddle-cloths brushed the ground and swept it, their hurrying hooves scored the earth. The knights clad in mail went with raised visors amid the swords, the hardened warriors and heroes of battle were loaded down with the apparel of war, and their number was complete. Ahead of them the sultan had drawn up his battalions and strengthened all his resolve for the fight. He set his army to face them and kept a watch on their vanguard in case they should charge; he cut off their access to water and filled in the wells, which caused them great hardship. He prevented their getting down to the water and set himself between them and their objective, keeping them at a distance. This was on a burning hot day, while they themselves were burning with wrath. The Dog Star was blazing with merciless heat that consumed their water supplies and offered no support against thirst.

Night separated the two sides and the cavalry barred both the roads. Islam passed the night face to face with unbelief, monotheism at war with trinitarianism, the way of righteousness looking down upon error, faith opposing polytheism. Meanwhile the several circles of hell prepared themselves and the several ranks of heaven congratulated themselves; Malik (the guardian of hell) waited and Ridwan (the guardian of paradise) rejoiced. Finally, when day dawned and the morning gleamed out, when dawn sent waves of light across the sky and the clangor of the trumpets startled the crow from the dust when the swords awoke in their sheaths and the lances flamed with eagerness: when the bows stirred and the fire glowed, when blades were unsheathed and prevarication ripped away, then the archers began to scorch with their burning shafts men destined for hell fire; the bows hummed and the bowstrings sang, the warriors' pliant lances danced, unveiling the brides of battle, the white blades appeared naked out of the sheath amid the throng, and the brown lances were pastured on entrails. The Franks hoped for a respite and their army in desperation sought for a way of escape. But at every way out they were barred, and tormented by the heat of war without being able to rest. Tortured by the thirst they charged, with no other water than the "water" of the blades they gripped. The fire of arrows burned and wounded them, the fierce grip of the bows seized tenaciously upon them and struck them dead. They were impotent, driven off, pushed to extremes and driven back, every charge thrown off and destroyed, every action or attack captured and put in chains. Not even an ant could have escaped, and they could not defend themselves by charging. They burned and glowed in a frenzied ferment. As the arrows struck them down those who had seemed like lions now seemed like hedgehogs. The arrows beat them down and opened great gaps in their ranks. They sought refuge on the hill of Hattin to protect them from the flood of defeat, and Hattin was surrounded by the flags of destruction. The sword-blades sucked away their lives and scattered them on the hillsides; the bows found their targets, the wild fates stripped them, disasters crushed them, destruction picked them out, they became death's target and fate's prey. When the count [Raymond of Tripoli] realized that they were defeated his anguish was clear to see. He gave up all effort and planned a way of escape. This was even before the main body of the army was roused and the embers were fanned, before the war was set alight and the flame burned. His band went off to find a way of escape and took the road across the wadi [that is, streambed], refusing to stop. He went off like a flash of lightning in his folly, before the leak became too big; he fled with a few followers and did not return to the attack. Thus he absented himself from the fight, seized by an unconquerable terror that forced him to flee. The fighting grew more violent as lance crossed lance and sword struck sword. The Franks were surrounded whichever way they turned and completely encircled. They began to pitch their tents and to rally their troops, setting up their pavilions on Hattin, while the gallant archers hammered away at their swords. But they were prevented from planting and raising their tents, and plucked from the roots and branches of life. They hoped to improve their position by dismounting from their horses, and they fought tenaciously, but the swords went through them as a torrent flows and our army surrounded them as hellfire surrounds the damned. Finally they resorted to saddling the ground, and their girth clasped the nipples of the plain.

The devil and his crew were taken, the king and his counts were captured, and the sultan sat to review his chief prisoners, who came forward stumbling in their fetters like drunken men. The grand master of the Templars was brought in his sins, and many of the Templars and Hospitallers with him. The king Guy and his brother Geoffrey were escorted in, with Hugh of Jubail, Humphrey, and Prince Arnat of al-Karak.... [Arnat, Reynald of Châtillon, was executed.]

This defeat of the enemy, this our victory occurred on a Saturday, and the humiliation proper to the men of Saturday [that is, the Jews] was inflicted on the men of Sunday [that is, the Christians], who had been lions and now were reduced to the level of miserable sheep. Of these thousands only a few individuals escaped, and of all those enemies only a few were saved. The plain was covered with prisoners and corpses, disclosed by the dust as it settled and victory became clear. The prisoners, with beating hearts, were bound in chains. The dead were scattered over the mountains and valleys, lying immobile on their sides. Hattin shrugged off their carcasses, and the perfume of victory was thick with the stench of them. I passed by them and saw the limbs of the fallen cast naked on the field of battle, scattered in pieces over the site of the encounter, lacerated and disjointed, with heads cracked open, throats split, spines broken, necks shattered, feet in pieces, noses mutilated, extremities torn off, members dismembered, parts shredded, eyes gouged out, stomachs disemboweled, hair colored with blood, the praecordium slashed, fingers sliced off, the thorax shattered, the ribs broken, the joints dislocated, the chests smashed, throats slit, bodies cut in half, arms pulverized, lips shriveled, foreheads pierced, forelocks dyed scarlet, breasts covered with blood, ribs pierced, elbows disjointed, bones broken, tunics torn off, faces lifeless, wounds gaping, skin flayed, fragments chopped off, hair lopped, backs skinless, bodies dismembered, teeth knocked out, blood spilt, life's last breath exhaled, necks lolling, joints slackened, pupils liquefied, heads hanging, livers crushed, ribs staved in, heads shattered, breasts flayed, spirits flown, their very ghosts crushed; like stones among stones, a lesson to the wise....

At the same time as the king was taken, the "true cross" was also captured, and the idolaters who were trying to defend it were routed. It was this cross, brought into position and raised on high, to which all Christians prostrated themselves and bowed their heads. Indeed, they maintain that it is made of the wood of the cross on which, they say, he whom they adore was hung, and so they venerate it and prostrate themselves before it. They had housed it in a casing of gold, adorned with pearls and gems, and kept it ready for the festival of the Passion, for the observance of their yearly ceremony. When the priests exposed it to view and the heads (of the bearers) bore it along all would run and cast themselves down around it, and no one was allowed to lag behind or hang back without forfeiting his liberty. Its capture was for them more important than the loss of the king and was the gravest blow that they sustained in that battle. The cross was a prize without equal, for it was the supreme object of their faith.... So when the great cross was taken great was the calamity that befell them, and the strength drained from their loins. Great was the number of the defeated, exalted the feelings of the victorious army. It seemed as if, once they knew of the capture of the cross, none of them would survive that day of ill-omen. They perished in death or imprisonment, and were overcome by force and violence. The sultan encamped on the plain of Tiberias like a lion in the desert or the moon in its full splendor.

72. BATTLE OF LAS NAVAS DE TOLOSA (1212)

In this 1212 letter, Blanche of Castile, the queen of France, writes to Blanche of Navarre, the countess of Champagne, about the recent battle of Las Navas de Tolosa. Both of these powerful women had reason to be interested in the Reconquista *of the Iberian peninsula: their fathers were two of the four Christian kings (the others being Aragon and Portugal) who had set aside their differences to regain lands lost to the Muslims in the eighth century.*

Source: trans. Joan Ferrante, "A Letter from Blanche of Castile, Queen of France (1212)," *Epistolae: Medieval Women's Latin Letters*, 2014, https://epistolae.ctl.columbia.edu/letter/705.html.

You should know that we had a messenger from Spain, who brought us letters about the war among the Christians in these words: "your nobility may be certain that there was a war between the kings, namely of Castile and Navarre and Aragon, against King Miramoraclim [Emir Muhammad-el-Nasir], on Monday, the 16th of July, and King Miramoraclim was shamefully defeated and fled six leagues/miles to the highly fortified castle which is called Gelien."

The outcome of the action was this: "As soon as the king of Navarre reached Calatrava, after Calatrava and all the fortifications around the port of Muredal, except the castles called Salvaterra and Dominar were taken, the king of Castile advised that they attack Salvaterra. To which the king of Navarre answered that it was very strong and the army might suffer from a lack of food, and could waste a lot of time in the siege, and it would be better to cross the port and enter the port of the Saracens and look for King Miramoraclim until they found him; and as the Lord might dispose, so they would do. The king of Aragon and the abbot agreed to this advice. Afterwards the king of Castile said it was enough that King Miramoraclim did not dare appear and he considered him conquered and that it would be sounder for them to return [to fighting] against the king of Santiago and remove him altogether. To which the king of Navarre answered that he would not come there except for a pilgrimage and in the sight of God, and that he would not bear arms against Christians, but only against Saracens. The king of Aragon and the abbot of Cîteaux agreed with this counsel.

They began, therefore to climb the port on the Thursday before the feast of Saints Justa and Rufina, and at the top of the mountain they found an enormous multitude of Saracens so they could not occupy the summit of the port. On the next day, Friday, all the Christians armed themselves and drove all the Saracens out of the port; but they could not cross it since the place was very narrow and very difficult to cross. The next day, Saturday, they had experienced guides who led the army through the back of the mountain to a less difficult crossing, and there they found the army of King Miramoraclim. On the following day, King Miramoraclim fixed his tent on a certain small mountain and ordered his lines of battle to war; but the Christians did not descend to them that day, since they were tired and had not yet arranged their lines of battle.

But on the following day, Monday, when the sun rose, Miramoraclim again arranged his lines of battle and the Christians similarly arranged theirs in this manner: in the first line was Didacus Lupi and Garcias Romanus and the abbot of Cîteaux, with 300 knights gathered from here and there; in the second line were all the bishops and all the clerics and all the religious orders, and Michael of Lusia. In the third were the kings thus: the king of Navarre had the right side, the king of Aragon the left, and the king of Castile was in the middle. The first line began to advance wondrously and the place was very rough and they could not reach them; and in the first encounter they killed about 40 Christian foot-soldiers. Then the king of Navarre moved a little to the right and climbed a small rather difficult mountain which the Saracens held and vigorously drove them back; and then all the Christians descended in one assault and immediately the Saracens turned tail and leaving a great multitude of Saracens on the field who were immediately slaughtered, the king of Miramoraclim fled with his army, as was said above, to Galien, and there was besieged. Nevertheless, a great number of the Saracen knights [cavalry] were captured in that flight. But of Christians no more than 30 knights fell, from the lower ranks. All the kings and dukes were safe, and the duke of Austria was not involved since he had not yet come.

73. BATTLE OF THE GOLDEN SPURS (1302)

The prosperity of Flemish towns at the beginning of the fourteenth century, built on the industrialization of cloth production, depended on the availability of English wool. Edward I had used this reason in 1297–98 to launch an attack on France through Flanders, although it stalled when the English king negotiated a marriage between his son, the future Edward II, and Isabella, daughter of King Philip IV the Fair of France. Philip imprisoned the count of Flanders, Guy de Dampierre, along with his eldest son, Robert of Béthune, for their support of the English. He also enacted stricter controls on Flemish economic sovereignty and forced garrisoning of French troops in the major towns. During the night of 18 May 1302 the townspeople of Bruges rose up and massacred the sleeping garrison, effecting a county-wide revolt. Joined by most of the other Flemish towns, the militia army that was formed surprisingly annihilated a French force of experienced soldiers outside of Courtrai at what would become known as the battle of Golden Spurs because of the large number of golden spurs—given only to knights by the king—that were collected from the battlefield and hung in Church of Our Lady in Courtrai. Although Ghent did not take part in the rebellion, a monk from that city has given us one of the most detailed accounts of the battle.

Source: trans. Hilda Johnstone, *Annales Gandenses: The Annals of Ghent* (Oxford: Clarendon Press, 1986), pp. 26–30.

About the beginning of June, Guy of Namur, the count's son [*sic*, second oldest], came to Bruges, and was welcomed most joyfully by the town and district and territory. Taking with him a sufficient army, he went on to Courtrai. There the town and territory of Courtrai and Oudenarde voluntarily surrendered to him, and the *leliaerts* [Flemish supporters of the French king] had all taken to flight. He besieged and assaulted the castle of Courtrai. He was a most doughty and popular knight. The Flemings friendly to his father grew as bold as lions through his presence and that of William [of Jülich, Guy of Dampierre's nephew]. The town of Ypres was also handed over to him, though the *leliaerts* remained in power there, and would have been unwilling to give up the town if they had not been afraid of him and of their own commonalty favourable to him. Being thus unwilling, they sent at their own expense and from their own commune only five foot and some crossbowmen for the attack on the castle of Courtrai.

The town of Ghent clung to the king, at the instigation and by the advice of the *leliaerts*, though almost all the commonalty favoured the count.

... So the king, by the advice of his barons and chamberlains (for that is what his intimate counsellors are called), gathered all the knighthood whom he could collect from France, Champagne, Normandy, Picardy and Poitou, and hired also a great number of knights skilled in warfare and of nobles outside his own realm, from the duchy and county of Lorraine and Brabant and Hainault. He assembled a very strong and numerous army, and put in command of it Robert, count of Artois, his own kinsman and the queen's uncle, strong, noble, courageous and from his youth practised in battles and expert in tournaments. He had been victorious in five or six mortal combats. About the end of June, count Robert set out with almost all the counts and barons of France capable of fighting as well as the army which the king had been able to raise, about ten thousand mounted men, besides such a host of crossbowmen and foot that I have not heard their number stated, and came to Lille. When Guy and William discovered this, through their scouts, and also that he intended to lead his army against Courtrai, to overthrow the Flemings and drive them away from the siege of the castle, if possible, as those of the king's party in the castle were provisioned for two months only, William left behind a force adequate for the siege of Cassel, and himself set out to his uncle Guy at Courtrai with a large army from western Flanders....

About the beginning of July, Robert moved from Lille, set out for Courtrai, and pitched his camp near that town, at a distance of about four or five furlongs. As the French entered Flemish-speaking Flanders, to show their ferocity and terrorise the Flemings they spared neither women nor children nor the sick, but slew all they could find. They even beheaded the images of the saints in the churches, as though they were alive, or chopped off their limbs. However, such doings did not terrorise the Flemings, but stimulated and provoked them to still greater indignation and rage and violent fighting.

When Guy and William heard of the approach of the enemies whom they hated so bitterly, they assembled their army with speed and rejoicing, about sixty thousand foot, strong and well armed [the actual numbers were probably closer to 8,000–10,400 Flemings and 8,000–8,500 French]. And they summoned all those faithful to them, who loved them, not only from the parts of Flanders those who were with them and had turned against the king, but also from Ghent, where about seven hundred well-armed men secretly left the town, and on this account were at once banished by the *leliaerts*. All those he had assembled were eager to come to blows with the French. In their whole army Guy and William had no more than about ten knights, of whom the most distinguished and experienced in warfare were Henry de Loncin from the duchy of Limburg, John de Renesse from the county of Zeeland, Gossuin of Goidenshoven from the duchy of Brabant, Dietrich of Hondschoote, Robert of Leewergem, Baldwin of Popperode of the county of Flanders. These, with Guy and William, drew up the Flemish army in order of battle and put heart into it. For three or four days there were individual assaults and combats between the two armies. But on a certain Wednesday, July 11, Guy and William found out through their scouts that all the French were making ready for battle in the morning, and did the same themselves, posting the men of Ypres to resist any of those in the castle who might wish to make a sally during the battle, and drawing up their army in a line both long and deep, about the hour of terce [9 a.m.], to await the enemy in the field.

About the hour of sext [noon], the French appeared in arms on the field. They had divided their whole army, both horse and foot, into nine lines of battle, but when they saw the Flemings drawn up in a single line, very long and deep, boldly ready for battle, they made three lines out of their own nine, placing one of them in the rear for protection and intending to fight with the other two. Battle was joined shortly before none [3 p.m.], with horrible crashing and warlike tumult, and with death for many. The fighting was fierce and cruel, but not prolonged, for God took pity on the Flemings, giving them speedy victory and put to confusion the French, who, as appeared clearly afterwards, had intended if victorious to do many cruel deeds in Flanders. When battle was joined, those in the castle, mindful of their friends, threw down fire from the castle, as they had done often before and had set alight many houses in Courtrai, and consumed one beautiful house by fire, to terrify the Flemings. Also both horse and foot came out from the castle, to attack the Flemings from the rear, but were forced ignominiously to return to it by the men of Ypres, who resisted them manfully and well. The count of St. Pol, who was in command of the third line, entrusted with the defence of the rear, though he saw his two half-brothers giving way with the [other] two lines, and in peril of death, did not go to their aid and succour, but most disgracefully taking to flight quitted the field. And so, by the disposition of God who orders all things, the art of war, the flower of knighthood, with horses and chargers of the finest, fell before weavers, fullers and the common folk and foot soldiers of Flanders, albeit strong, manly, well armed, courageous and under expert leaders. The beauty and strength of that great army was turned into a dung-pit, and the [glory] of the French made dung and worms. The Flemings, embittered by the cruelty the French had practised between Lille and Courtrai, spared neither the dying Frenchmen nor their horses, and slew them all cruelly, till they were completely assured of victory. An order had been proclaimed in their army by their leaders before the fight began that anyone who stole any valuable during the battle or kept as prisoner a noble, however great, should be straightway put to death by his own comrades. In the said battle, therefore, there perished that noble and victorious prince, Robert, count of Artois, with James his half-brother, already mentioned, to whose brewing all the evils then and later were mainly due; Godfrey, paternal uncle of John, duke of Brabant, with his only son, the lord of Vierzon (he, it is believed, because on the mother's side his nephew was of Flemish blood, would if the French had won have turned him out of his land, or slain him, and secured it from the king to hold himself); John, eldest son of the count of Hainault, called the Pitiless because of his cruelty; Pierre Flote, the crafty and powerful councillor of the king; the count of Aumâle; the count of Eu; the lord of Nesle, marshal, that is to say chief of the knighthood of France, with his brother Guy, a most valiant knight; and other barons and landed magnates, as noble, mighty and powerful as many counts of Germany, to the number of seventy-five. More than a thousand simple knights, many noble squires, and numbers of foot, fell there, and more than three thousand splendid chargers and valuable horses were stabbed during the battle. The total of those who were either killed in the battle or died of their wounds soon afterwards was as much as twenty thousand, and many more took to flight. The whole of the knightly force remaining to the king was not equivalent to the number there slain. After the victory the Flemings captured some nobles who had remained on the field, unable to flee because wounded. They were immensely enriched by booty and spoil taken from their enemies, and furnished and magnificently provided with weapons, tents and trappings of war.

... On the third day after the battle, the castle of Courtrai, where the garrison was running short of food and could not hope for rescue by the king, was surrendered to Guy on condition that, while John, castellan of Lens, who was in command there, and the other nobles, should remain prisoners, the humbler folk should be allowed free egress with their clothes and weapons.

Many of the Flemings engaged in the attack on the castles of Cassel and Courtrai were wounded, and some met their death, for the garrisons defended themselves most manfully. But in the actual battle of Courtrai, strange to say, barely a hundred were slain, though many were injured and wounded. During the battle Peter Coninck the weaver and many others, who previously little thought that such a thing could happen to them, were knighted. Many knights on the count's side who were in prison were exchanged for knights who had surrendered with the castle or were captured on the field after the battle, and returned to Flanders within two or three months.

74. BATTLE OF CRÉCY (1346)

Jean le Bel was born and raised in Liège, where his family was involved in civic and religious leadership. Jean was canon of Saint-Lambert when he came to the notice of the English queen Philippa of Hainaut and her husband, King Edward III, through Philippa's uncle, Jean de Hainaut, the lord of Beaumont, for whom he had performed some undisclosed service. This led to a close proximity to the king and queen. Jean came to admire Edward and traveled with him frequently, including on his Scottish campaign of 1327. He especially admired his military prowess, which he writes was one of the purposes for composing his chronicle. Most historians of the Hundred Years War have come to view Jean le Bel as a trustworthy, even if an extremely pro-English, chronicler. He was not with Edward on his Crécy campaign, but he clearly used the king and other eyewitnesses for his account of the battle. He continued to write his Chroniques *until 1361.*

Source: trans. Kelly DeVries, from Jean le Bel, *Chronique*, vol. 2, ed. Jules Viard and Eugène Déprez (Paris: Librairie Renouard, 1904), pp. 99–110.

Where is heard of the marvelous battle of Crécy where the great lords of France were defeated and captured.

You have well heard how King Philip [VI] came to Airaines after the king of England had left there. And he stayed, waiting for his troops coming after him. The next day he left and followed the English and everywhere found his lands burned and entirely devastated. He had gone for a long time before he was told that the English had crossed at Blanchetaque and killed the men there. It was very sad; there is no need to ask. He stopped and commanded that no part of his army should cross, it is said, if not by the bridge at Abbeville. So he went to Abbeville and stayed that day, so that his men might rest, and he made his crossing thus, that they would come to be ready the next day.

On the next day he departed from Abbeville with his standard displayed. Then it was beautiful to see his lords nobly mounted and armored, their standards blowing in the wind, and to know that the army was estimated at 20,000 men-at-arms on horse, armored in iron, and more than 100,000 men on foot, 12,000 both professional soldiers and Genoese. The king of England did not have more than 4,000 cavalry, 10,000 archers, and 10,000 Welsh and foot sergeants.

King Philip had ridden to reconnoiter the English, and he had sent some knights and squires to spy on them, because it was thought correctly that he was not far away. When he had gone three leagues [9 miles or 14 km], the riders returned, saying that the English were not more than four leagues [12 miles or 19 km] in front of them. Then the king commanded a knight who was very valiant and experienced in arms, and four others, whom he wished to advance and to go after the English and consider their composition. These valiant knights were very willing, and they returned to the king and recounted that from their standards he was a league to the English, and they stopped to wait for the others. Then they came to the king and told him that they had seen the English less than a league from there and had considered their composition, and they were arrayed in three divisions. So he asked his council what he was to do. The king took a certain monk knight, who was so valiant in arms, and he asked his advice. This knight, the Monk of Basel, told him that he was very nervous to go before the other lords, because they would not agree with him. He said to him: "Lord, your army is greatly spread out on the fields, so it will be a long time before they can all come together, because it has already passed Nones [3 p.m.]. I counsel you that your army make camp. Then tomorrow morning, after mass, you may array your divisions and go against your enemies in the name of God and St George, because I am certain that they will not leave, as they want to attack you. Therefore I advise you to do little."

This counsel pleased the king well and he was very willing, so it was decreed that all were to withdraw to their standards, because the English were arrayed so impressively. He wished to camp until the next day. Yet, none of the lords wished to turn back, and some who were in the front did not wish to return, because that act seemed to them to be dishonorable: instead, they held there without moving, so that others who were in the rear could not ride to the front. It was all because of pride and envy that they were destroyed, as they did not hold to the counsel of the valiant knight. Thus they rode out of pride and envy without order, the one in front of the other. They rode until they saw the English arrayed in three divisions, well ordered in the way they awaited them. Then it was a greater dishonor to retreat when they saw their enemy so near.

The masters of the professional soldiers, the crossbowmen, and the Genoese advanced their men and all went to the front of the divisions of the lords to take the first shot at the English, and they went so closely that they shot as many on their own side as on the other. All the professional soldiers and Genoese were defeated, and they were finished and wanted to flee; but the divisions of the great lords were so exalting one on top of the other for envy that they did not wait, not one of them, but they charged, all in chaos and entangled without any order, so that they closed in on the professional soldiers and Genoese between themselves and the English; because there was nothing those men could do, falling under the horses' hooves. And the other side's archers shot so marvelously that the horses, feeling the barbed arrows, which did marvels, did not want to advance: some rode against others as if deranged, others bucked dreadfully, others turned their backs to their enemies, despite their masters, because of the arrows that they felt, and others let their masters fall, because they were unable to do anything else. And the English lords standing on foot advanced and fell upon the men who were not able to deal with their horses.

In such a way the disaster for the French lasted all the way to midnight, because it was almost night when the battle began, as neither the king of France nor any of his company were able to arrive during the day for combat. So it happened that the king departed from there, his men remaining in the great duel, despite this and Sir Jean de Hainaut, who was responsible for guarding the king's body and his honor, and they rode so that night until they came to Labroye. There the king rested, profoundly defeated, and in the end, he went to Amiens to wait for his people, because he was delayed; and the remaining French, lords, knights, one and the other, who had remained behind fled as they were defeated. They did not know where to go, because the night was so endlessly black, so they knew neither town nor village, and they had not eaten all day. Thus they were by groups, three here, four there, as men isolated, and they did not know whether their masters or parents or brothers were killed or had escaped. Not one Christian had ever suffered such a great defeat as that which had occurred there to King Philip and his men. This happened in the year of grace 1346, the day following the Feast of St Bartholomew, on a Saturday at Vespers. It was fought near Crécy in Ponthieu. All that night the French did not know who had died, thus passing the night in such defeat as described.

What I have just described is truth, which was reported to me personally by my lord and friend, Jean de Hainaut (may God absolve him), and also 10 and 12 knights and companions of his household, who were in the press of the battle with the valiant and noble king of Bohemia, whose horses were killed beneath them. It was also reported in the same way by many English and German knights who were there on the other side.

Now I want to describe how the noble king of England had arrayed his divisions.

You should know that the brave king of England knew well on the Saturday at Vespers that King Philip was at Abbeville with all his great knights. So a large cheer was made, and he said to his men that each should kneel and pray to Our Lord that He might allow them to undertake the task with honor and joy, because this place was their rightful heritage, if he might defend it; and that he said that he would have to retreat any further, but, as King Philip wanted to come there to him, he would fight.

The next morning, he ordered his men to come from their tents and to arm themselves, and he made a large wagenberg [a field fortification of wagons] in front of the forest of all his army's wagons and carts, through which there was only a single opening, and he put all his horses inside the wagenberg. Then he arrayed his divisions splendidly. He gave the first to his son, the Prince of Wales [Edward the Black Prince], with 1,200 men-at-arms, 3,000 archers, and 3,000 Welsh, and he sent as guard the earl of Warwick, the earl of Stafford, the earl of Kent, and Sir Godfrey of Harcourt, along with many others who I do not know the number. Over the second division he put the earl of Northampton, the earl of Suffolk, and the bishop of Durham, with 1,200 men-at-arms and 3,000 archers. He retained the third division for himself, which ought to have been between the two, with 1,600 men-at-arms and 4,000 archers. All of these were known to be English or Welsh, because he had only 6 archers from Germany, one of whom was Sir Rasse Masures; I do not know the names of the others.

When the brave king had thus arrayed his divisions on a beautiful field, where there had been neither ditch nor pit, he went all around and laughingly admonished that each man endeavor to do what he ought to do. So sweetly did he pray and admonish them that a coward became a bold man. And he commanded that the bold ought not break from the rank, nor go after booty, nor despoil the dead or the living without his permission, because this was the task for each of them, each would come to have time to pillage; and if fortune turned against them, they would have no booty.

When he had thus arrayed them, he gave them all permission to drink and eat until the sound of the trumpet; after that they should have their meal in formation. Each loved him so, and doubted that any would disobey his commands.

At the hour of Nones, news came to the noble king that King Philip had come before him with all his army. Finally, Edward had the trumpet sound, and he immediately put each man in position. Thus they waited until the French came, and they did this so well that fortune turned toward them.

When the battle had begun and the night was falling, the king shouted the command that no one was to pursue the enemy, and that no one should despoil nor plunder the dead, until such a time that he gave permission to follow the flight when the bodies could be better recognized in the morning. He ordered everyone to go to their tents to rest without disarming and that all the lords should come to supper with the king; he commanded the marshals to set guards and watches over the army. One may well imagine with what joy the noble kings and all his barons and lords dined and passed the night, thanking God for their good fortune, that such a small company had held and defended the field against all the power of France.

The following morning there was a deep fog. In this a large number of English, with the permission of the king, went to the field to see if they might find any French regrouping. They found a large number of militia from the bonnes villes who had been sleeping in the woods, the ditches, and the hedges, and asking each other about the conflict and what might result, because they did not know what had occurred, nor where the king or the lords were. When they saw the English coming against them, they attacked because they thought that they were their men, and the English fell among them like lions among sheep, and they killed them at will. Another company of English ventured out, and they found another company of men before the battlefield wanting to hear news of their lords: some asked about their masters, some their parents, and some their companions. These English killed all they could find. Around the hour of Terce [9 a.m.], they returned to their tents just as the king and his lords had heard mass and they recounted their adventure. Then the king commanded Sir Reginald de Cobham, who was a very valiant knight, to take a herald who knew arms, and some other lords and heralds with them and go among the dead to write down all the dead knights they could recognize, and to carry all the princes and the great lords to one side, and on each of them to write their name. That Sir Reginald gave the order and it was done, and he found that there had been nine great princes dead, and around 1,200 knights, and at least 15,000 or 16,000 others, squires and Genoese and the rest, and he found only 300 English knights killed.

It is for this good reason that I account for you only the princes or high barons who were left dead there; accounting for the others would be endless. Thus, I commence with the most noble and most worthy: this was the valiant king [John] of Bohemia who, being entirely blind, wished to be among the first in the battle, and he commanded that his knights thus take him forward or be beheaded; that was how it was to be, so that he might strike an enemy with his sword.

The greatest prince after him was the count of Alençon, natural brother of the king of France.

After him was Count Louis of Blois, son of the natural sister of the king, then the count of Salm, then the count of Harcourt, the count of Auxerre, and the count of Sancerre. And it is said that not for a long time has one been able to say that so many princes were killed in one battle—not at Courtrai, not at Benevento, not anywhere else.

The following Sunday, the brave King Edward wandered on the field the entire day to see for himself that King Philip did not reassemble his men, but they did not return. So the valiant king and all his army departed from there, and they carried the bodies of their dead men to an abbey, which was close nearby.

75. BATTLE OF OTHÉE (1408)

The large and wealthy principality of Liège had been governed by a prince-bishop for almost 400 years before the appointment of Jean III of Bavaria, brother-in-law of John the Fearless, duke of Burgundy. Opposing Jean's harsh, tyrannical rule and fearful of losing their sovereignty to Burgundy, which had been expanding throughout the Low Countries during the previous decades, in 1307 the Liégeois rebelled. Outside of the village of Othée on 23 September 1408, the rebels and Burgundians battled. Although their numbers were equal, if not favoring the Liégeois, the experience, discipline and training of the Burgundians were easily able to defeat the rebels, who were mostly militia. In a letter to his brother, Antoine, duke of Brabant, John the Fearless describes why he did not need the Brabantese troops that Antoine had promised. As noted by John, gunpowder artillery was against his army in what is one of the first reports of its appearance in battle.

Source: Richard Vaughn, *John the Fearless: The Growth of Burgundian Power* (London: Longmans Green and Co., 1966), pp. 60–62.

To my dear and well-beloved brother, [Antoine] the duke of Brabant and Limbourg.

My dear and well-beloved brother, I have received your letters, which you sent me by the bearer of these, mentioning that you had heard that, by the grace of God, I had fought the Liégeois, and that, if I had let you know the day of the battle, you would very willingly have been present. Be pleased to know, dearest and well-beloved brother, that in what follows you shall learn how and in what manner things happened, and then you will realize that I was unable, at the appropriate moment, to let you know the day.

It is true, dearest and well-beloved brother, that [William of Bavaria], my brother-in-law of Hainault, and I entered the country of Liège last Thursday [20 September] with a numerous and excellent company of knights and squires, and we advanced by different routes across country to within a league of a town called Tongres in Hesbaye, where we arrived last Saturday evening; and there we received information from certain persons that on that very day the lord of Perwez and all the Liégeois in his company, had raised the siege which they had laid to Maastricht, in order to come and confront us. Because of this, my brother-in-law and I sent out some of our scouts on the Sunday morning [23 September 1408] to ascertain the truth, and these reported to us that they had definitely seen the Liégeois coming towards us in battle order and in vast numbers. So my brother-in-law and I arranged our forces in good order, joining them together in order to meet and oppose the aforesaid Liégeois.

When we had ridden forward about half a league, we saw them plainly, above and quite near the town of Tongres, and they saw us. At this point my brother-in-law and I, together with our people, dismounted in a fairly advantageous position, thinking that they would come and attack us there. We placed all our troops in a single mass in order to resist more effectively the shock and charge which the Liégeois were likely to give us; and we formed two wings of bowmen and men-at-arms. Soon, they approached us to within about three bowshots, concentrating somewhat towards the right, in the direction of the aforesaid town of Tongres, so that the men of that town, numbering some 10,000, could join them. There they stopped, drawn up in excellent order, and immediately opened fire on us with their cannon.

After we had waited a little and seen that they were not going to move, my brother-in-law and I, with the advice of the good captains and knights in our company, decided to advance in good order and attack the enemy where they were. [We also decided] that, to break up their array and throw them into confusion, we should need 400 mounted men-at-arms and 1,000 stalwart infantrymen to strike at their rear, while we engaged them [in frontal assault]; and we appointed the lords of Croy, of Heilly and of Rasse, your chamberlains and mine, to lead [this force], together with Enguerrand de Bournonville and Robin le Roux, my *écuyers d'écurie* [household squires].... One hour after midday we marched to attack [the enemy] in the name of God and of Our Lady, in handsome and excellent order, joining battle with them and attacking them in such a way that, with the grace and help of Our Lord, the day was ours. In truth, dearest and well-beloved brother, experienced people say that they have never seen men fight so well as they did; for the battle lasted nearly one and a half hours and, for at least half an hour, no one knew which way it would go. As far as can be ascertained from those who inspected the dead, the lord of Perwez, his son the rebel anti-bishop, another son of his, and a good 24,000 to 26,000 Liégeois, were killed. They were all, or nearly all, armed, and they had in their army 500 mounted men, and 100 archers from England.

It happened that, when the battle was almost over, the men of Tongres sallied forth in arms to come to the Liégeois' aid. They advanced to within three bow shots, but turned in flight when they saw how matters were going, and were forthwith closely pursued by the mounted men on our side, and many of them killed.

However, in this battle, we have lost at least 60 to 80 knights and squires, which saddens me a great deal; for these were not among the worst. God forgive them. And as to the number of Liégeois who may have been in the battle ... I have discovered for certain from some of their prisoners, taken in the battle, that they left the siege [of Maastricht] last Saturday morning [22 September] 40,000 strong, and went to Liège. There, some 8,000, whom the lord of Perwez considered to be unfit for battle, were left behind; [so] on the Sunday, the day of the battle, about 32,000 or more left Liège to advance towards us.

Moreover, my dear and well-beloved brother, be pleased to know that yesterday my brother-in-law of Liège [John of Bavaria] came handsomely accompanied to my brother-in-law of Holland and me. And today the towns of Liège, Huy, Dinant, Tongres and the other 'good towns' of the country have come to us to make submission, beseeching the said brother-in-law of Liège to have pity on them and pardon them. This he did, through the intervention of the aforesaid brother-in-law of Hainault and me, provided that they surrendered and handed over to him all the guilty persons—of whom there were still many—to do as he pleased with. Moreover, the said towns have asked pardon for everything they may have done in contempt of the said brother-in-law of Liège. All this has been arranged by my brother-in-law of Hainault and me; and to ensure that our decisions are obeyed, each town will give us whatever security we want.

Dear and beloved brother, may the Holy Spirit keep you.... Written in my army, in the fields near Tongres, the 25th day of September [1408]. Your brother, the duke of Burgundy....

76. BATTLE OF BARNET (1471)

By 1470 the dynastic struggle for the throne of England, the Wars of the Roses, had been raging off and on for 15 years, and two living men had worn the crown: the Lancastrian King Henry VI (the red rose) and the Yorkist King Edward IV (white rose). The changing allegiance of Richard Neville, the powerful earl of Warwick often called "the Kingmaker," from Henry to Edward had done much to bring tensions into open conflict at the beginning, but now Warwick's mind was changing again. With the backing of Louis XI, the king of France, Warwick led the forces that restored Henry to the throne and forced Edward to flee to the powerful duke of Burgundy, Charles the Bold. When the French king subsequently declared war on Burgundy, Charles sent Edward back to England at the head of an army the following year. Once more, Warwick found himself in arms, as he led the Lancastrian forces. The account below, from "Warkworth's" Chronicle, *describes Edward's swift gathering of Yorkist strength in London and his march to meet Warwick in fog and in confusion at Barnet, just north of the city, on 14 April 1471. When it was finished, Warwick was dead, and Henry VI was imprisoned in the Tower of London (where he would die under suspicious circumstances just over a month later). Though Edward IV would rule until his natural death in 1483, the Lancastrians won final victory in the war with the 1485 defeat of Richard III at Bosworth Field by Henry Tudor, who would rule as Henry VII.*

Source: John Allen Giles, *The Chronicles of the White Rose of York*, 2nd ed. (London: James Bohn, 1845), pp. 123–26; revised.

On the Wednesday next before Easter Day, King Henry VI, and the archbishop of York [George Neville] with him, rode about London, and desired the people to be true unto him. Every man said they would. Nevertheless, Christopher Urswick, recorder of London, and many aldermen, who had rule of the city, commanded all the people who were in arms, guarding the city and King Henry, to go home to dinner. And when dinnertime came, King Edward IV was let in. He went to the bishop of London's palace and there took King Henry and the archbishop of York and put them under guard, the Thursday next before Easter Day. The archbishop of Canterbury [Thomas Bourchier], the earl of Essex [Henry Bourchier], Lord Berners, and others who owed King Edward good will, both in London and in other places, gathered as many men as they could, thus strengthening Edward. So then he had 7,000 men and they refreshed themselves well there, on that day and Good Friday [12 April 1471]. And upon Easter Eve he went toward Barnet with his army and carried King Henry with him, for he had word that the earl of Warwick and the duke of Exeter [Henry Holland], the marquis of Montagu [John Neville], the earl of Oxford [John de Vere], and many other knights, squires, and commons—to the number of 20,000 men—were gathered together there to fight against King Edward. But it happened that he, with his army, entered into the town of Barnet before the earl of Warwick and his army. Warwick and his host lay outside the town all night, and each of them fired guns at the other all night long.

On Easter Day in the morning, 14 April, very early, each of them came upon the other. There was such a great mist that neither of them might see the other perfectly. There they fought, from 4 o'clock in the morning unto 10 o'clock of the forenoon. At various times the earl of Warwick's party had the victory and supposed that they had won the field. But it happened that the earl of Oxford's men had upon them their lord's livery, both in front and behind, which was a star with streams; this was much like King Edward's livery, which was the sun with streams. The mist was so thick that a man might not perfectly judge one thing from another, so the earl of Warwick's men shot and fought against the earl of Oxford's men, thinking and supposing that they were King Edward's men. And at once Oxford and his men cried "Treason! Treason!" and fled from the field with 800 men. The lord marquis of Montagu made an understanding with King Edward and put on King Edward's livery, but a man of the earl of Warwick saw this and fell upon him and killed him. When the earl of Warwick saw his brother dead, and the earl of Oxford fled, he leaped on horseback and fled to a wood by the field of Barnet, where there was no way out. One of King Edward's men spied him, came upon him, killed him, and despoiled him naked. Thus King Edward won the field.

There was slain from Warwick's party: the earl himself, the marquis of Montagu, Sir William Tyrell, knight, and many others. The duke of Exeter fought manfully there that day, and was greatly despoiled, wounded, and left naked for dead in the field; he lay there from 7 o'clock until 4 in the afternoon, when he was taken up and brought to a house by a man of his own. A leech was brought to him, and afterwards he found sanctuary at Westminster. Of King Edward's party was slain Lord Cromwell, son and heir to the earl of Essex; Lord Berners' son and heir, Sir Humphrey Bourchier; Lord Say, and many others to the number [of both parties] of 4,000 men.

II. At Sea

77. BATTLE OF NISA (1062)

Harald Hardrada was 15 years old when he fled from Norway after his half-brother Olaf was defeated at the battle of Stiklestad in 1030. He traveled to the lands of the Kievan Rus, and moved on to Constantinople, where he became the leader of the Varangian Guard. When the politics of the Byzantine Empire turned against him, he took the enormous fortune he had amassed and made his way back to the north. By 1047 he was the king of Norway and was making raids to press his claim to the throne of the Danes, as well. In 1062 King Sweyn II of Denmark agreed to meet at the mouth of the Nissan River, in modern-day Sweden. By the time Sweyn arrived on 9 August, Harald had already sent his non-professional forces away. Though facing hard odds, Harald employed a bold strategy to win the fierce naval battle that followed—though Sweyn's escape would force the Norwegian king to make peace just two years later.

Source: adapted and revised by Michael Livingston, from Snorri Sturluson, *The Heimskringla; or, Chronicle of the Kings of Norway*, trans. Samuel Laing (London: Longman, Brown, Green, and Longmans, 1844), pp. 55–65.

King Harald remained all winter at Nidaros [in 1062] and had a buss built out upon the strand. The ship was built of the same size as the Long Serpent [a legendary warship], and every part of her was finished with the greatest care. On the stem was a dragon-head, and on the stern a dragon-tail, and the sides of the bows of the ship were gilt. The vessel had thirty-five benches for rowers, and it was large for that size and remarkably handsome; the king insisted on the finest of everything belonging to the ship's equipment, both sails and rigging, anchors and cables. That winter King Harald sent a message south to King Sweyn of Denmark, that he should come northwards in spring; they should meet at the Gaut river and fight, and thus settle the division of the countries that the one who gained the victory should have both kingdoms.

King Harald during this winter called out a general levy of all the people of Norway, and assembled a great force towards spring. Then Harald had his great ship drawn down and put into the river Nid, and set up the dragon's head [making it the leading ship] on her....

When the Danes heard that the Northmen's army had come to the Gaut river, all who had the opportunity to do so ran away. The Northmen heard that the

Danish king had also called out his forces and lay in the south, partly at Fyen and partly around Seeland. When King Harald found that King Sweyn would not hold a meeting with him, or fight, according to what had been agreed upon between them, he took the same course as before—letting the bonde troops [the inexperienced levy] return home. He still had men for 150 ships, which he sailed south along Halland, where he ransacked all round. Then he brought his fleet to Lofufjord and laid waste to the country. A little afterward King Sweyn came upon them with all the Danish fleet, consisting of 300 ships. When the Northmen saw them King Harald ordered a general meeting of the fleet to be called by sound of trumpet; and many there said it was better to fly, as it was not now advisable to fight. The king replied, "Sooner shall all lie dead one upon another than fly." So says Stein Herdison:

With falcon eye, and courage bright,
Our king saw glory in the fight;
To fly, he saw, would ruin bring
On them and him—the folk and king.
"Hands up the arms to one and all!"
Cries out the king. "We'll win or fall!
Sooner than fly, heaped on each other
Each man shall fall across his brother!"

Then King Harald drew up his ships to attack, and brought forward his great dragon in the middle of his fleet. So says Thiodolf:

The brave king through his vessels' throng
His dragon war-ship moves along;
He runs her gaily to the front,
To meet the coming battle's brunt.

The ship was remarkably well equipped, and fully manned. So says Thiodolf:

The king had a chosen crew—
He told his brave lads to stand true.
The ring of shields seemed to enclose
The ship's deck from the boarding foes.
The dragon, on the Nis-river flood,
Beset with men, who thickly stood,
Shield touching shield, was something rare,
That seemed all force of man to dare.

Ulf, the marshal, laid his ship by the side of the king's and ordered his men to bring her well forward. Stein Herdison, who was himself in Ulf's ship, sings of it thus:

Our oars were stowed, our lances high,
As the ship moved swung in the sky.
The marshal Ulf went through our ranks,
Drawn up beside the rowers' banks:
The brave friend of our gallant king
Told us our ship well on to bring,
And fight like Norsemen in the cause—
Our Norsemen answered with huzzahs.

Hakon Ivarson lay outside on the other wing, and had many ships with him, all well equipped. At the extremity of the other side lay the Throndhjem chiefs, who also had a great and strong force.

Sweyn, the Danish king, also drew up his fleet, and he laid his ship forward in the center against King Harald's ship. Fin Arnason laid his ship next, and then the Danes laid their ships, according to their boldness and how well equipped they were. Then, on both sides, they bound the ships together all through the middle of the fleets, though very many ships remained loose because the fleets were so large. So each laid his ship forward according to his courage, and that was very unequal. Although the difference among the men was great, altogether there was a very great force on both sides. King Sweyn had six earls among the people following him. So says Stein Herdison:

Danger our chief would never shun,
With eight score ships he would not run:
The Danish fleet he would abide,
And give close battle side by side.
From Leire's coast the Danish king
Three hundred ocean steeds could bring,
And o'er the sea-weed plain in haste
Thought Harald's vessels would be chased.

As soon as King Harald was ready with his fleet, he orders the war-blast to sound, and the men to row forward to the attack. So says Stein Herdison:

Harald and Sweyn first met as foes,
Where the Nis in the ocean flows;
For Sweyn would not for peace entreat,

But, strong in ships, would Harald meet.
The Norsemen prove, with sword in hand,
That numbers cannot skill withstand.
Off Halland's coast the blood of Danes
The blue sea's calm smooth surface stains.

Soon the battle began, and became very sharp; both kings urging on their men. So says Stein Herdison:

Our king, his broad shield disregarding,
More keen for striking than for warding,
Now tells his lads their spears to throw,
Now shows them where to strike a blow.
From fleet to fleet so short the way,
That stones and arrows have full play;
And from the keen sword dropped the blood
Of short-lived seamen in the flood.

It was late in the day when the battle began, and it continued the whole night. King Harald shot for a long time with his bow. So says Thiodolf:

The Upland king was all the night
Speeding the arrows' deadly flight.
All in the dark his bow-string's twang
Was answered; for some white shield rang,
Or yelling shriek gave certain note
The shaft had pierced some ring-mail coat,
The foemen's shields and bulwarks bore
A Lapland arrow-scar or more.

Earl Hakon and his men did not make fast their ships in the fleet. Instead, they rowed against the Danish ships that were loose, and they slew the men of all the ships they came up with. When the Danes observed this each drew his ship out of the way of the earl, but he set upon those who were trying to escape, and they were nearly driven to flight. Then a boat came rowing to the earl's ship and hailed him and said that the other wing of King Harald's fleet was giving way and many of their people had fallen. The earl rowed there and gave so severe an assault that the Danes had to retreat before him. The earl went on in this way all the night, coming forward where he was most wanted, and wherever he came none could stand against him. Hakon rowed outside around the battle. Toward the end of the night the greatest part of the Danish fleet broke into flight, for then King Harald with his men boarded the vessel of King Sweyn. It was so completely cleared that all the crew fell in the ship, except those who sprang overboard. So says Arnor, the earls' skald:

> Brave Sweyn did not his vessel leave
> Without good cause, as I believe:
> Oft on his steel helm the sword-blade rang,
> Before into the sea he sprang.
> Upon the wave his vessel drives;
> All his brave crew had lost their lives.
> O'er dead courtmen into the sea
> The Jutland king had now to flee.

After King Sweyn's banner was cut down, and his ship cleared of its crew, his forces all took to flight, and some were killed. The ships that were bound together could not be cast loose, so the people who were in them sprang overboard. Some got to the other ships that were loose. All of King Sweyn's men who could get off rowed away, but a great many of them were slain. Where the king himself fought the ships were mostly bound together, and more than seventy of King Sweyn's vessels were left behind. So says Thiodolf:

> Sweyn's ships rode proudly o'er the deep,
> When, by a single sudden sweep,
> Full seventy sail, as we are told,
> Were seized by Norway's monarch bold.

King Harald rowed after the Danes and pursued them, but that was not easy, for the ships lay so thick together that they scarcely could move. Earl Fin Arnason would not flee; being also shortsighted, he was taken prisoner. So says Thiodolf:

> To the six Danish earls who came
> To aid his force, and raise his name,
> No mighty thanks King Sweyn is owing
> For mighty actions of their doing.
> Fin Arnason, in battle known,
> With a stout Norse heart of his own,
> Would not take flight his life to gain,
> And in the foremost ranks was ta'en.

Earl Hakon lay behind with his ships, while the king and the rest of the forces were pursuing the fugitives, for the earls' ships could not get forward on account of the ships that lay in the way before him. Then a man came rowing in a boat to the earl's ship and lay at the bulwarks. The man was stout and had on a white hat. He hailed the ship, "Where is the earl?"

The earl was in the fore-hold, stopping a man's blood. The earl cast a look at the man in the hat and asked what his name was. He answered, "Here is Vandrad: speak to me, earl."

The earl leaned over the ship's side to him. Then the man in the boat said, "Earl, I will accept my life from you, if you will give it."

Then the earl raised himself up, called two men who were friends dear to him, and said to them, "Go into the boat; bring Vandrad to the land. Take him to my friend Karl the bonde, and tell Karl, as a token that these words come from me, that he let Vandrad have the horse that I gave to him yesterday, and also his saddle, and his son to attend him."

Thereupon they went into the boat and took the oars in hand, while Vandrad steered. This took place just about daybreak, while the vessels were in movement, some rowing towards the land, some towards the sea, both small and great. Vandrad steered where he thought there was most room between the vessels; and when they came near to Norway's ships the earl's men gave their names and then they all allowed them to go where they pleased. Vandrad steered along the shore, and only set in towards the land when they had come past the crowd of ships. They went up to Karl the bonde's farm, and it was then beginning to be light. They went into the room where Karl had just put on his clothes. The earl's men told him their message and Karl said they must first take some food. He set a table before them and gave them water to wash with.

Then the housewife came into the room and said, "I wonder why we could get no peace or rest all night with the shouting and screaming."

Karl replied, "Did you not know that the kings were fighting all night?"

She asked who had the better of it.

Karl answered, "The Northmen gained."

"Then," said she, "our king will have taken flight."

"Nobody knows," says Karl, "whether he has fled or is fallen."

She said, "What a useless sort of king we have! He is both slow and frightened."

Then said Vandrad, "Frightened he is not; but he is not lucky."

Vandrad washed his hands, but when he took the towel he dried them right in the middle of the cloth. The housewife snatched the towel from him and said, "You've been taught little good! It is wasteful to wet the whole cloth at one time."

Vandrad replied, "I may yet come so far forward in the world as to be able to dry myself with the middle of the towel."

Thereupon Karl set a table before them and Vandrad sat down between them. They ate for a while and then went out. The horse was saddled and Karl's son ready to follow him with another horse. They rode away to the forest, and the earl's men returned to the boat, then rowed to the earl's ship and reported the success of their expedition.

King Harald and his men followed the fugitives only a short way, and rowed back to the place where the deserted ships lay. Then the battle-place was ransacked, and in King Sweyn's ship was found a heap of dead men. But the king's body was not found, although people believed for certain that he had fallen. Then King Harald had the greatest attention paid to his dead men, and had the wounds of the living bound up. The dead bodies of Sweyn's men were brought to the land, and he sent a message to the peasants to come and bury them. Then he let the booty be divided, which took up some time. The news came now that King Sweyn had come to Seeland, and that all who had escaped from the battle had joined him, along with many more, and that he had a great force.

Earl Fin Arnason was taken prisoner in the battle, as before related. When he was led before King Harald the king was very merry, and said, "Fin, we meet here now, and we met last in Norway. The Danish court has not stood very firmly by you; and it will be a troublesome business for Northmen to drag you, a blind old man, with them, and preserve your life."

The earl replied, "The Northmen find it very difficult now to conquer, and it is all the worse that you have the command of them."

Then said King Harald, "Will you accept life and safety, although you have not deserved it?"

The earl replied, "Not from you, you dog."

The king: "Will you, then, if your relation Magnus gives you quarter?"

Magnus, King Harald's son, was then steering the ship.

The earl replied, "Can the whelp rule over life and quarter?"

The king laughed, as if he found amusement in vexing him. "Will you accept your life, then, from your she-relation Thorer?"

The earl: "Is she here?"

"She is here," said the king.

Then Earl Fin broke out with the ugly expressions that since have been preserved, as a proof that he was so mad with rage that he could not govern his tongue:

"No wonder you have bit so strongly, if the mare was with you."

Earl Fin got life and quarter and the king kept him a while about him. But Fin was rather melancholy and obstinate in conversation. And King Harald said, "I see, Fin, that you do not live willingly in company with me and your relations. I will give you leave to go to your friend King Sweyn."

The earl said, "I accept the offer willingly, and the more gratefully the sooner I get away from here."

The king afterward let Earl Fin be landed and the traders going to Halland received him well. King Harald sailed from there to Norway with his fleet. He went first to Oslo, where he gave all his people leave to go home who wished to do so.

78. LANDING IN EGYPT (1249)

The Seventh Crusade, led by King Louis IX of France against the Egyptian Ayyubids, began with a victory at the city of Damietta on 6 June. In the following letter, Robert of Artois, brother of the king, reports the good news to their mother—Blanche of Castile, who was left regent of France in the king's absence. It would be almost the last good news to come from the crusade, which would end in extraordinary disaster: Robert dead, Louis captured, and nearly the whole crusading army destroyed (mostly imprisoned) in a series of massive, often blundering defeats. Robert's letter reveals not only the perils of the crusaders' voyage across the sea, but also the necessities of transferring them into a force on land.

Source: trans. Joan Ferrante, "A Letter from Robert of Artois (1249)," *Epistolae: Medieval Women's Latin Letters*, 2014, https://epistolae.ctl.columbia.edu/letter/733.html.

To his most excellent and dearest mother, Blanche, by the grace of God illustrious queen of France, count Robert of Artois her devoted son, greetings and the desire ready with filial love to do her will.

Since we know that you rejoice much in the prosperity of us and ours and the successes that occur to the Christian people, when you receive certain knowledge of them, your excellence should know that the dearest lord our brother king and the queen, [our] sister and we enjoy full health of body by the grace of God. Which we hope with fervent desire [is true] of you. Our dearest brother, the count of Anjou still has malaria, but less severe than usual.

And let your love know that our dearest lord, our brother, and the barons and pilgrims who spent the winter on Cyprus, reached the harbor of Limassol in their ships on the evening of the Ascension, so that they might make their way against the enemies of the Christian faith. Leaving the port, after many hardships of the sea and contrarieties of winds, with the Lord guiding them, they came at about noon on the Friday after the Trinity and anchored, gathering on that day in the ship of the lord king to consult about what they should do from then on, since they saw Damietta before them and the harbor fortified by a great multitude of Turks, horsemen and footsoldiers, and the mouth of the near river by a multitude of armed galleys.

In which council it was determined that on the next morning whoever could would come to land with the lord king. And your lordship should know that it was determined that on Saturday morning the Christian army, having left the great ships, would descend virilely armed into galleys and small ships. And trusting in the mercy of God and the help of the triumphal cross which the lord legate bore in the boat beside the lord king, happy and comforted by God, they removed towards the land against the enemy who were making many assaults with arrows and other things. But truly when those boats could not get to dry land for the excessive smoothness of the sea, the Christian army left them in the name of God and leaping into the sea reached dry land, the footsoldiers with their arms. And though a multitude of Turks defended the shore against the Christians, yet, with our Lord Jesus Christ favoring us, the Christian people won the shore with health and happiness and with great destruction of the Turks' horses and of certain people who were said to be of great name.

And when the Saracens returned to the city which was very strong because of the river as well as walls and strong towers around it, our almighty Lord "Who gives richly to all and not disproportionately" [cf. Ep.James 1:5], without the labor of men, on the next day, that is the octave of the Trinity, gave the city to the Christian people, with the infidel Saracens fleeing and leaving it. And this was done only by the gift of God and the generosity of the almighty Lord God. And you should know that those Saracens left that city fortified with great abundance of food and meat and machines and other goods of which a great part of the provisioning of said city remained. And from that part the army was quite satisfied.

Our Lord king, indeed, delayed there with his army, having his things taken from his ships. And we believed that the army should not leave until the river went down, because then it was said, he should occupy the land, since the Christian people incurred harm otherwise in other places. The countess of Anjou gave birth to a very elegant and well formed son in Cyprus, whom she gave over to be nursed there.

Dated at Jamas castle, in the year of the Lord 1249, in the month of June, on the eve of St. John the Baptist [29 August].

79. NAVAL WARFARE BETWEEN PISA AND GENOA (1284)

Venice ruled the east coast of Italy and the Adriatic and eastern Mediterranean seas that could be reached from it. But there were two medieval contenders for the west coast and the western Mediterranean, Genoa and Pisa. They frequently fought. Salimbene de Adam here details a single year of this conflict, 1284, and its consequences. The Pisans, losers, would not recover.

Source: trans. J.L. Baird, *The Chronicle of Salimbene de Adam*, Medieval and Renaissance Texts and Studies 40 (Binghamton, NY: Center for Medieval and Early Renaissance Studies, University Center at Binghamton, 1986), pp. 542–43.

The Fierce Sea Battle Between the Pisans and Genoese in this Year

In the year of the Lord 1284, the Pisans seeing all the evil inflicted on them by the Genoese and wishing to avenge themselves, built a large number of ships, galleys, and vessels on the river Arno, and then enacted a law that everybody between twenty and sixty years of age was required to go to war. And they sailed along the whole of the Genoese coast, destroying, burning, killing, capturing, and pillaging. Moreover, they sailed along the entire coastline from Genoa into Provence by the maritime cities of Noli, Albenga, Savona, and Ventimiglia, seeking out the Genoese. The Genoese, in the meantime, enacted the statute that no one between the age of eighteen and seventy was exempt from war. And so they went to sea, seeking out the Pisans. Finally, the two fleets met between Capo Corso and Gorgona, and they tied their ships together in the usual fashion of a naval battle. And there was such great slaughter on both sides at that place that the heavens appeared to weep in sympathy. Huge numbers were killed on both sides and many ships were sunk. And just as the Pisans appeared to be victorious, a large number of Genoese ships arrived and rushed upon the already exhausted Pisans. And another fierce battle was fought. Finally, seeing themselves overwhelmed, the Pisans surrendered. The Genoese then killed the wounded and imprisoned all the others. Yet neither side can boast of victory, for both sides suffered terribly. And so great was the weeping and crying in both Genoa and Pisa that the like was never heard "from the day of ... creation" [Ezechiel 28:15] in either of those cities until the present day. Who without weeping and great sadness can recount or even think about how these two noble cities, from which all Italians have received so much good, have mutually destroyed one another out of pride, ambition, and vainglory because the one sought to conquer the other, as if the sea were not sufficient for the two of them.

One should never take vengeance, however good the case,
If it makes matters worse and ends in disgrace.

A Sad Narrative of the Pisan Ladies Sorrowing for Their Beloved

Also in that year after the battle between the Pisans and the Genoans, many Pisan women—beautiful, noble, rich, and powerful ladies—went in groups of thirty and forty, walking on foot from Pisa to Genoa in order to inquire about and to visit the captives. For one had a husband there, another a son, brother, or other relative, men whom God [Psalms 105:46]: "gave unto mercies, in the sight of all those that had made them captives." And when they asked the jailers about the captives, they were told, "Yesterday thirty men died and today forty, and we threw them in the sea. It is the same every day with the Pisans." And when these ladies heard such things about their loved ones, and when they could not find them there, they fell prostrate out of their great fear and distress, and from pure anxiety and pain of heart they could scarcely breathe. Then on reviving they clawed their faces with their nails and tore their hair. And they wept aloud with great lamentation and "wept till they had no more tears" [1 Kings 30:4]. Then the Scripture in 1 Machabees 1 [:27–28] was fulfilled: "The beauty of the women was changed. Every bridegroom took up lamentation: and the bride that sat in the marriage bed, mourned." For needy and poor and hungry and wretched and distressed and sorrowful, the Pisans died in their prisons, because [Psalms 105:41–42]: "They that hated them had dominion over them. And their enemies afflicted them: and they were humbled under their hands," and they were not [Acts 5:41] "accounted worthy" to be buried "in the sepulchres of" their "fathers" [1 Machabees 2:70], but were denied burial altogether. Moreover, when these women returned home, they even found those whom they had left safe at home dead.

80. FIGHTING THE SARACENS AT SEA (1325–1332)

There were relatively few naval conflicts between the Islamic Middle East and North Africa and Christian Europe; at least, there were few recorded. Yet, numerous fleets sailed the Mediterranean, engaged in naval and piratical activities. Some of these are reported in the eyewitness chronicle of Ramon Muntaner, who was a leader of the so-called mercenary band the Catalan Company for several decades.

Source: trans. Lady Goodenough, *The Chronicle of Muntaner* (London: Hakluyt Society, 1920–21).

I will turn to speak a little of [Roger de Lauria's] brother-in-law Conrado Lansa, and tell of a fine thing which, by the favor of God and of the lord king Peter of Aragon [surnamed the Great, r. 1275–85], happened to him. It is the truth that the lord, King Peter, should come first, but I wish to tell and recount it to you now, for it may as well be done at once than later, and I will do it now, while I remember the affairs concerning those two *riches homens* [rich men]; and it is better to speak now of that deed performed by the said noble Conrado Lansa than further on. For a man, when he speaks the truth, can relate any deed in any part of the book. And perhaps I should have to speak of it in a place where it would disturb my narrative; and, besides, it is not a long story. And so I pray all to forgive me if in this place or in another, they find I tell them things before their proper time. Nevertheless, if they ask me for reasons, I shall give them such as will make them excuse me; but, whatever the reasons I give you, be sure that everything you will find written is the truth, and of this have no doubt whatever. So then, I wish to tell you the favor God did to that rich *hom* [man] Conrado Lansa.

The lord king of Aragon has of old a right to a tribute from [Muhammed IV] the king of Granada and from [Abu Tashufin I] the king of Tlemcen and from [Abu Bakr II] the king of Tunis. And because, for a long time, this tribute had not been sent to the lord king of Aragon, he had four galleys equipped at Valencia and he made the said noble Conrado commander of them. He went to the port of Tunis and to Bougie and all along the coast, sacking and destroying all the ports. He came to the sea of the king of Tlemcen, to an island called Habibas and he went there to get water. And as he came to that place to get water, ten armed Saracen galleys of [Muhammad bin Tughluq] the king of Morocco also came to that place to get water. And these ten Saracen galleys were the best equipped, and manned by better Saracens of any that ever were equipped and they had already done much injury to *lenys* [small vessels] which they had captured from Christians and they had many captives in their galleys, which was a great sin.

And when the galleys of Conrado Lansa saw the ten galleys coming, they left the place. And the Saracens, who saw them and had had news of them already, shouted in their Saracen language, "Aur, Aur" [nonsense words indicating that Muntaner did not understand the language] and they came towards the galleys of Conrado Lansa with great vigor. And the galleys of Conrado Lansa formed in a circle, and all four collected together and held council. And Conrado Lansa said to them, "You, my lords, know that the favor of God is with the lord king of Aragon and with all his subjects; and you know how many victories he has had over Saracens. You may well consider that the lord king of Aragon is present with us in these galleys, for you see here his standard, which represents his person, and as he is with you, so is the favor of God and he will help us and give us victory. And it would be a great disgrace for the said lord and for the city of Valencia to which we all belong, if, because of those dogs, we faced about, a thing no man of the lord king of Aragon has ever done. Therefore I pray you all that you remember the power of God and of Our Lady Saint Mary, and the Holy Catholic Faith, and the honor of the lord king and of the city of Valencia and of all the kingdom; and that, roped together as we are, we attack resolutely, and that, on this day, we do so much that we be spoken of forever. And, assuredly, we shall defeat them and be prosperous forever. However, you can all see that we have so much the advantage of them that we can retire if we like, and that they cannot force us to fight, if we do not wish to. And so, let everyone say what seems best to him, but as for me I have told you my opinion already. Again, I tell you and pray you and require you, in the name of the lord king of Aragon and of the city of Valencia, to attack them."

And all began to shout, "Let us attack them! Let us attack them! They will all be ours!" And with that they armed themselves well and the Saracens did the same. And when both sides were armed, Conrado with great strokes of the rowers, advanced towards the Saracens. Some of these told their commander that the galleys were coming towards them in order to surrender, and a great many Saracens were of this opinion, because there was a very accomplished knight amongst them and they did not think the Christians would be so mad as to wish to fight with them. But the Saracen admiral was a wise seaman and had been in many feats of arms and had had proof of what the Catalans are, and he shook his head and said, "Barons, your opinion is foolish; you do not know the people of the king of Aragon as I know them. Now be sure that they are preparing well and wisely to fight with us; and they come so ready to die that woe is to the mother's son who is awaiting them. Wherefore as they come prepared to vanquish or die, so put the same resolution into your hearts; for this will be the day in which, if we make not great endeavors, you will all die or be taken captive. Would to God I were a hundred miles away from them; but as things are as they are, I commend myself to God and Muhammad."

And with that, he ordered trumpets and *nakers* [small drums] to be sounded, and with great shouts they began a vehement attack. And the four galleys, most beautifully, and without shouts and words or any clamor, went to the attack in the midst of the ten galleys and there the battle was most grievous and hard, and it lasted from the morning until the hour of vespers [around 6 p.m.], and no one dared to eat or drink. But Our Lord the true God and his blessed mother, from whom come all favors, and the good luck of the lord king of Aragon, gave the victory to our men, in such manner that all the galleys were defeated and the men killed or taken. Blessed be the Lord who made it come to pass. And when they had won the battle and defeated and taken all the galleys, they delivered the Christian captives whom they found in them and gave to each of them as good a share of what God had enabled them to take as that of every man who had been in the battle. And so, with great honor and in great triumph, they returned to Valencia with the galleys which they brought there, and with many Saracen captives who had hidden below deck, of whom they had much profit.

81. BATTLE OF WINCHELSEA (1350)

The French navy had been nearly destroyed or captured at the battle of Sluys in 1340. But their allies, the Castilians, had escaped with most of their ships. These and others ships from Iberia continued to raid the English coastal towns and pirate English vessels. In 1350 King Edward III became determined to end these threats by outfitting and manning a fleet—the latter being difficult this close to the Black Death. Personally commanding the fleet, Edward caught and defeated the Spanish off the coast of Winchelsea. This account of the battle (known to the French as Les Espagnols sur Mer, *the Spaniards of the Sea) is by the contemporary chronicler Geoffrey le Baker, whose sources were among the English who fought in the battle.*

Source: trans. Trevor Russell Smith, from Geoffrey le Baker, *Chronicon*, ed. Edward Maunde Thompson (Oxford: Clarendon Press, 1889), pp. 109–11.

The following summer, a dispute arose between the sailors of England and of Spain, and the Spanish filled the English Channel with forty-four great, fierce ships. They sank ten English ships sailing from Aquitaine to England after they had been captured and plundered. Having thus avenged their previously suffered wrongs the Spanish put in at the harbor of Sluys in Flanders. When this was heard, the king, his vessel joined with fifty ships and small boats, prepared to catch the returning Spanish. He had with him the prince of Wales, the earls of Lancaster, Northampton, Warwick, Salisbury, Arundel, Huntingdon, Gloucester, and other barons, as well as men-at-arms, with their hand-chosen companions and archers.

And then on the feast of the beheading of St John [29 August], around the hour of vespers, the fleets clashed. The great Spanish wide-bellied transports stood above our light ships and vessels as castles over little houses. They made a dreadful advance against us, wounding us with stones flung from small turrets atop their masts, and sharply hurling javelins and shooting bolts. Nevertheless our men struggled hand-to-hand with spear and sword and bravely defended themselves with the fleet's arms. The dreadful encounter grew worse, many of its terrors beyond anything our men had experienced.

Finally our archers, with the longer range of their arrows, perforated the Spanish crossbowmen, who loosed their bolts to a shorter distance, and so drove them to cast aside their duty. Other Spanish, too, upon the sides of the transports and castles, struggling hand-to-hand with planks from the ships, prayed for protection. Aside from those throwing stones like lightning from towers, they pressed together to shelter all of themselves. They did not dare to expose their heads and shoulders, as was their accustomed habit, but raised only their hands, yet these too were not secure from the sharpness of our arrows. The Spanish did not now throw down stones, but released them to fall, to the destruction of their men rather than the ruin of ours. Then our men climbing up ladders fell upon their ships with zeal, cutting down with swords and hatchets those in their way. In a short time they emptied vessels full of Spanish, while filling them with English, until, in the darkness of the oppressive night that covered everything, they could not see the other twenty-seven Spanish ships.

There you could have seen ships painted with blood and brains, arrows fixed in masts, sails, beams, and castles, archers collecting arrows from the wounds of the dead and those fruitlessly praying, for the battle would be renewed on the following day. Our men anchored their ships, thinking on the desired fight, and knowing that there was much undone while something, killing, remained to be done. They care for the helpless wounded, throw the dead and dying Spanish down into the sea, restore themselves with food and slumber, and nevertheless commit a vigilant watch with armed forces.

After the silence of night, with dawn coming up, the English were prepared at new calls to war, rousing their men to arms by horns, trumpets, and pipes, but in vain. For under the full light of the rising sun, beholding the sea, they observed no signs of resistance. In fact the twenty-seven Spanish ships, fleeing at night with every effort, abandoned seventeen ships that had been stripped at night, and were painted with bloody, putrid gore and brains.

The king but reluctantly returned to England with triumph, yet with great peril prepared for him and his men. They brought back namely wounded heads wrapped in linen to hold them together, arms and legs perforated by bolts and spears, and teeth torn out, also noses cut off, lips cleaved, eyes plucked. Cheerful at the insignia of the glorious triumph and escape, the men mixed laughter with painful sorrows, and equally took pleasure in showing their cloaks stained by enemy blood. There the king promoted eighty inexperienced noble men-at-arms to knighthood. He grieved the hazards endured by one, namely Richard of Goldsborough, a knight, who, as it is said, sold his death at a dear price, or as it was seen by the Spanish, at too great a price.

III. In Siege

82. SIEGE OF JERUSALEM (614)

In 614 the Sasanian Persian (Iranian) Empire and the Byzantine Empire were at war, with the Holy Land caught in the struggle. Sasanian Persian Shah Khosrow II placed his general Shahrbaraz in control of the fight in this region, and he soon pushed the Byzantines back. In Jerusalem, Shahrbaraz appointed a Jewish council to lead the city, but not long after he moved on, the Christians in the city revolted against the council. According to a number of accounts, thousands of Jews were killed. Shahrbaraz took in those who fled and returned to besiege the city for roughly three weeks before it fell once more into his control. Those Christians who died or were deported were said—according to Christian sources like the Armenian writer Sebeos here excerpted—to have numbered in the tens of thousands.

Source: trans. Robert Bedrosian, Sebeos, *History* (http://www.attalus.org/armenian/seb8.htm), chap. 24; revised.

In that period Heraclius enthroned his son Constantine III, entrusting him to the Senate and to all the grandees of the palace. He confirmed him on the throne of his kingdom. Together with his brother Theodosius, Constantine assumed the military command, assembled a multitude of troops, and crossed into Asorestan by way of Antioch. A great battle took place in the area of Asia, and the blood of the generals coursed violently to the city of Antioch. The groupings and clashings were severe and the slaughter was great in the agitation. Both sides were worn and wearied in the fight. However, the Iranians grew stronger and pursued the fleeing Byzantines, receiving the victory, in addition to [the renown of] bravery. Yet another battle took place close to the defile leading to Cilicia. The Byzantines struck the Iranians in a front of 8,000 armed men. But they turned and fled. The Iranians grew stronger, went and took the city of Tarsus and all the inhabitants in the district of Cilicia.

Then the entire country of Palestine willingly submitted to the king of kings. The remnants of the Hebrew people especially rebelled from the Christians and, taking in hand their native zeal, wrought very damaging slaughters among the multitude of believers. Going [to the Iranians], [the Jews] united with them. At that time, the army of the king of Iran was stationed at Caesarea in Palestine. Their general was named Rhazmiozan [that is, Shahrbaraz]. He spoke with [the inhabitants of] Jerusalem so that they would submit voluntarily and be kept in peace and prosperity.

Now at first [the Jerusalemites] voluntarily submitted, offering the general and the princes very great gifts, and requesting that loyal *ostikans* be stationed with them to preserve the city. However, several months later the entire mob of the city's young braves united and killed the Iranian king's *ostikans*. Then they rebelled from his service. After this a battle took place among the inhabitants of the city of Jerusalem, Jew and Christian. The multitude of the Christians grew stronger, struck at and killed many of the Jews. The remainder of the Jews jumped from the walls, and went to the Iranian army. Then Shahrbaraz assembled his troops and went and encamped around Jerusalem and invested it, warring against it for 19 days. Digging beneath the foundations of the city, they destroyed the wall. On the 19th day [of the siege] which was the 27th day of June in the 25th year of the reign of Khosrow II [615], ten days after Easter, the Iranian forces took Jerusalem and putting their swords to work for three days they destroyed [almost] all the people in the city. Stationing themselves inside the city, they burned the place down. The troops were then ordered to count the corpses. The figure reached 57,000. 35,000 people were taken alive, among whom was a certain patriarch named Zakaria who was also custodian of the Cross. [The Iranians] sought for the life-bringing Cross and began to torment [the clerics], executing many clerics at that time. Finally [the clerics] pointed out the place where it was hidden. [The Iranians] took it into captivity and also melted all the city's silver and gold, which they took to the court of the king. Now regarding those who had been arrested, an order was issued by the king to have mercy on them, to build a city and to settle them there, establishing each person in his [former] profession. He commanded that the Jews be driven from the city, and the king's order was quickly implemented, with great urgency.

83. SIEGE OF PARIS (885–886)

After nearly a century of raiding along coasts and up rivers, Viking forces began to band together in larger fleets with more men to attack larger targets. Paris, a grand prize, was besieged twice, in 885–86 and 896. Abbo, a monk of Saint-Germain-des-Prés near Paris and an eyewitness to the sieges, wrote a Latin poem about these Norse assaults on Paris. The following excerpt is on the first siege.

Source: adapted by Kelly DeVries, from *A Source Book for Mediæval History: Documents Illustrative of European Life and Institutions from the German Invasions to the Renaissance*, ed. Frederic Austin Ogg (New York: American Book Company, 1908), pp. 168–71; revised by Paul Edward Dutton, *Carolingian Civilization: A Reader*, 2nd ed. (Peterborough: Broadview Press, 2004), pp. 514–16.

885. [The Northmen] came to Paris with 700 sailing ships, not counting those of smaller size which are commonly called barques. At one stretch the Seine was lined with the vessels for more than two leagues [about 3 miles or 4.8 km], so that one might ask in astonishment in what cavern the river had been swallowed up, for nothing was visible there, since ships covered that [river] as if with oak trees, elms, and alders. On the second day after the fleet of the Northmen arrived under the walls of the city, Siegfried, who was then king only in name but who was in command of the expedition, came to the dwelling of the illustrious bishop. He bowed his head and said: "Gauzelin, have compassion on yourself and on your flock. We beseech you to listen to us, in order that you may escape death. Allow us only the freedom of the city. We will do no harm and we will see to it that whatever belongs either to you or to Odo shall be strictly respected." Count Odo, who later became king, was then the defender of the city. The bishop replied to Siegfried, "Paris has been entrusted to us by the emperor Charles, who, after God, king and lord of the powerful, rules over almost all the world. He has put it in our care, not at all that the kingdom may be ruined by our misconduct, but that he may keep it and be assured of its peace. If, like us, you had been given the duty of defending these walls, and if you should have done that which you ask us to do, what treatment do you think you would deserve?" Siegfried replied, "I should deserve that my head be cut off and thrown to the dogs. Nevertheless, if you do not listen to my demand, on the morrow our siege machines will destroy you with poisoned arrows. You will be the prey of famine and of pestilence and these evils will renew themselves perpetually every year." So saying, he departed and gathered together his comrades.

In the morning the Northmen, boarding their ships, approached the tower and attacked it. [The tower blocked access to the city by the so-called Great Bridge, which connected the right bank of the Seine with the island on which the city was built, the Île de la Cité. The tower stood on the present site of the Chatelet.] They shook it with their engines and stormed it with arrows. The city resounded with clamor, the people were aroused, the bridges trembled. All came together to defend the tower. There Odo, his brother Robert, and Count Ragenar distinguished themselves for bravery; likewise the courageous Abbot Ebolus, the nephew of the bishop. A sharp arrow wounded the prelate, while at his side the young warrior Frederick was struck by a sword. Frederick died, but the old man, thanks to God, survived. For many this was their last moment of life, but they inflicted bitter blows on many of the enemy. At last the enemy withdrew, carrying off a vast number of Danish dead.

No longer did the tower appear as fine as it once did, but its conditions were still solid and it delighted a little in the windows that had been opened up to the sun. The people spent the night repairing the holes with boards. By the next day, on the old fortification had been erected a new tower of wood, a half higher than the former one. In the morning the sun and the Danes fell on the tower together. They engaged the [Parisians] in violent skirmishes. On every side arrows sped and blood flowed. With the arrows mingled the stones hurled by slings and war-machines; the air was filled with them. The tower which had been built during the night groaned under the strokes of the javelins; the city shook with the struggle, the people ran hither and thither, the bells jangled. The warriors rushed together to defend the tottering tower and to repel the fierce assault.

Among these warriors two, a count and an abbot [Ebolus], surpassed all the rest in courage. The former was the redoubtable Odo who never experienced defeat and who continually revived the spirits of the worn-out defenders. He ran along the ramparts and hurled back the enemy. On those who were secreting themselves so as to undermine the tower he poured oil, wax, and pitch, which, being mixed and heated, burned the Danes and tore off their scalps. Some of them died; others threw themselves into the river to escape the awful substance....

Meanwhile Paris was suffering not only from the sword outside but also from a pestilence within which brought death to many noblemen. Within the walls there was not ground in which to bury the dead.... Odo, the future king, was sent to Charles [the Fat], emperor of the Franks, to implore help for the stricken city.

One day Odo, powerful with his arms, suddenly appeared on Montmartre in splendor in the midst of three bands of warriors. The sun made his armor glisten and greeted him before it illuminated the country around. The Parisians saw their beloved chief at a distance, but the enemy, hoping to prevent his gaining entrance to the tower, crossed the Seine and took up their position on the bank. Nevertheless Odo, his horse at a gallop, got past the Northmen and reached the tower, whose gates Ebolus opened to him. The enemy pursued fiercely the comrades of the count who were trying to keep up with him and get refuge in the tower.... [The Danes were defeated in the attack.]

Now came Emperor Charles, surrounded by soldiers of all nations, even as the sky is adorned with resplendent stars. A great throng, speaking many languages, accompanied him. He established his camp at the foot of the heights of Montmartre, near the tower. He allowed the Northmen to have the country of Sens to plunder; and in the spring he gave them 700 pounds of silver on condition that by the month of March they leave France for their own kingdom. Then Charles returned [home].

84. SIEGE OF THESSALONIKI (904)

In 904 an Abbasid fleet commanded by a former Greek slave named Leo of Tripoli made an attempt on the Byzantine capital of Constantinople. Turned back, Leo shifted his attention to Thessaloniki, the second-largest city in the Byzantine Empire. Following a three-day siege, his forces took the city and sacked it. Among the citizens captured was John Kaminiates, who wrote the following account of the siege while in prison. Blame for the defeat, John writes, should be assigned to the poor condition of the city's fortifications (including sea-facing defenses) and the conflicting commands given by the city's authorities.

Source: trans. David Frendo and Athanasios Fotiou, *John Kaminiates: The Capture of Thessaloniki*, ed. David Frendo and Athanasios Fotiou (Perth: Australian Association for Byzantine Studies, 2000), pp. 41–63.

Chapter 23: While we were thus exerting ourselves in vain, someone arrived with the news that the ships of the barbarians were already nearing the neck of land described as the "Jetty." This occurred at daybreak on Sunday the 29th of July in the six thousand four hundred and twelfth year of the Creation of the World (AD 904). The report spread like wildfire through the city and there was turmoil, din and confusion on all sides, as people shouted out now one thing now another, trying to decide what to do about the immediate situation, and everybody armed himself as best he could and hastened to man the walls. And they were not yet properly deployed along the battlements, when the barbarian fleet appeared in view from the previously mentioned promontory, in full sail. And it so happened at the time that the ships were driven by a tailwind in such a way as to create the impression that they were not gliding over the surface of the water but floating through the air. It was, as has been remarked, the month of July, a time of year when the wind that blows across the Gulf (of Thessaloniki) is at its most sustained, blowing from the foothills of Mt. Olympus in Greece, and each summer day from daybreak to the ninth hour falling upon the city and causing a breeze. And so, with the wind abetting them in the first moments of daylight, the enemy swooped down from close by. First of all, they lowered the sails, having positioned themselves alongside the wall, and began to take careful note of the layout of the city. They did not, in fact, offer battle as soon as they had dropped anchor but left some time in order to probe our strength and the extent of our preparedness and to equip themselves for combat. They stood for a while filled with apprehension, unable to compare the spectacle that now confronted them with anything they had seen before: what they saw was a city of considerable dimensions with the entire course of its wall manned by great numbers of people. Consequently, they were even more dismayed and held back for a short time from giving battle. We, for our part, began to pluck up courage and in the short ensuing respite to restore our morale.

Chapter 24: While we were in this situation, the leader of the barbarian forces decided to patrol the entire section of the wall that is washed by the sea. He was a sinister and thoroughly evil person, who flaunted a style of behaviour singularly appropriate to the wild animal after which he was named and for whose ferocious ways and ungovernable temper he was more than a match. Assuredly, you yourself also know the man by reputation, a reputation which celebrates his wickedness with the claim that he has outshone all previous paragons of impiety by descending to such depths of madness as to gaze insatiably upon the spilling of human blood and to love nothing better than the slaughter of Christians. He too was once a Christian, was reborn in the saving grace of baptism and taught the precepts of our religion. But when he was taken prisoner by the barbarians, he embraced their impiety in exchange for the true piety of the faith and there is no way in which he more eagerly seeks to ingratiate himself with them than by making his deeds conform to his name and by taking a particular pride in flaunting the actions of a felon and a brigand. And so Leo [lion], this untamable beast, this felon, sailed around the wall gazing intently and searching out with studied malice a possible point from which to launch his attack. The other ships dropped anchor at a single point on the eastern shoreline and began to make their preparations. Our citizens also donned their armour, manned the battlements and braced themselves for the ensuing contest. And truly it was a contest—the great contest which had been so loudly proclaimed, not the mere trial of strength of a wrestler competing against his opponent for the applause of the spectators, not a contest that offers a material reward and holds out a fleeting moment of enjoyment for the winner or the simple stigma of defeat for the loser; what was at stake was whether so great a city would win the unparalleled distinction of surviving so great a danger or suffer the inconsolable grief of in some way succumbing to the fate that menaced her.

Chapter 25: But when that wild beast had surveyed the entire extent of the wall and had noticed that the entrance to the harbour was barred by an iron chain and obstructed by the sunken hulks of a number of ships, he decided to launch his attack just at those points which he perceived to be free of those blocks of stone which, lurking on the seabed where they had earlier been placed, impeded the access of his ships and where his fleet would not be under heavier fire from that part of the wall which had already been built up to some considerable height. He chose a location, in fact, where a great depth of sea water beat against a particularly low stretch of wall, made a careful note of his position, and then, returning to his men, gave the signal for battle. They swooped down with their ships towards those points which had been described to them, letting out harsh and savage cries and rowing furiously in the direction of the wall. And banging on rawhide drums, they raised a fearful din, and they tried with many other kinds of bluff to frighten the defenders on the battlements. But those who were manning the wall shouted back even louder and invoked the aid of the saving weapon of the cross against the enemy forces. And they did this to such an effect that the barbarians, at the sound of so many people uttering a cry more fearsome than any they had previously heard, were dazed for a while and did not expect to achieve anything. Estimating the numbers of the citizens from the loudness of their shouts, they concluded that it would be no easy matter to enter the fray against such odds and to sack so great a city, the like of which they had never seen. Nevertheless, in order not to create the impression of having lost their nerve at the start of their offensive, they advanced neither fearlessly, nor with the rage which they later displayed, but with a certain blend of frenzy and fear, protecting themselves against their opponents by means of a barrage of missiles. Then their approach became more reckless and they strove to bring the fighting nearer, rousing themselves to fury like barking dogs and thoroughly enraged by the weapons that were hurled down at them from the wall. The citizens, in fact, were anything but remiss in their use of archery, and used it to great and conspicuous effect by stationing all the Sklavenes [a southern Slavic people] gathered from the neighbouring regions at those points from which it was easiest to shoot accurately and where there was nothing to deflect the momentum of their missiles.

Chapter 26: But while both parties were shooting and being shot at, and neither side was gaining the upper hand, a detachment of barbarians, consisting no doubt of individuals bolder and more daring than the rest, leaped overboard. They took with them a wooden ladder, which they propelled through the water and with which they attempted to scale the wall, paying no heed to the weapons discharged against them from that quarter. In fact, they kept their bodies underwater until they got close up and swam in holding their shields over their heads. Once they got near, however, left without the protection afforded by the water and using their shields to cover their heads, they struggled manfully against a rain of missiles. Then, rapidly drawing up the ladder against the rampart, they tried to scale the wall. But death forestalled their plan and before they could form a clear idea of how to carry out their scheme they lost their lives. No sooner, in fact, had their feet touched the rungs of the ladder than a volley of stones as thick as hail was unleashed against them, toppling them off and sending them headlong to a watery grave. Whereupon the ships all drew back quickly, not daring for the time being to venture anything further of the kind. They resorted, instead, to discharging from a distance a hail of missiles that darkened the air, but they too came equally under fire from well-aimed shafts that rarely missed their mark and from shot from the stone-throwing engines, the mere sound of which as it whistled through the air struck terror into the hearts of the barbarians.

Chapter 27: Already Niketas, who has been mentioned before, the one who had been sent by the emperor, was hurrying up and down the entire length of the wall, encouraging the people in the following words: "Men of Thessaloniki, I held a different opinion of you before this moment and would not have considered you to be so gallant and daring in action, since you had neither been put to the test nor had you proved yourselves in this sphere in the past. But now the present crisis has afforded an occasion for entertaining high hopes of you. I see that you all have strong bodies and stout hearts, that you are wholly committed to the present action, that you scorn the enemy and that you gallantly brush aside their ruses. You are quite right to do so. For the struggle concerns you yourselves, men of substance and of principle, and it concerns the rest of the city, whose title to fame has no serious contender. If you prove superior to the present peril you will become a fitting object of praise in the estimation of all men. But should you suffer some reverse and succumb to the threats of the barbarians, there will be nothing to which one can liken the extent of your misfortune and the depth of your shame. Therefore, stand your ground courageously and endeavour to secure victory for your native city and for yourselves and do not turn and flee from the enemy, lest, having for the sake of one small moment of weakness placed yourselves in such terrible danger, you leave behind you a novel tale for posterity to tell." With these fighting words he encouraged the people and went the rounds, instilling no small degree of confidence into the hearts of all. And the *strategos* [Leo Chitzilakes], as though oblivious of his own affliction, though it was grievous (resulting as it did from the fall that we related earlier) and unbearably painful, also went around, mounted on a mule, not sitting astride it but sidesaddle, to the extent that the pains in his shattered limbs permitted. He posted the more stalwart members of the imperial guard at certain vital points along the wall, so that for their part they might also spur on those near them to imitate their actions, and thus dispose them to battle.

Chapter 28: The barbarians attacked not once but several times in the course of that day, but they suffered more casualties than before and withdrew. At a preconcerted signal they suspended operations at sea, retired with their ships and dropped anchor beside a stretch of coast to the east of the city. Then they disembarked and began to shoot at those who were positioned on the high section of wall where the so called "Rome Gate" stands, close to the sea. They fought there until late into the night and then, apparently fatigued by their exertions, rested on board their ships; though perhaps they were exercising their minds how best to attack us on the following day and were intent on preparing a further series of treacherous and deceitful moves. No sooner, therefore, had we paused a moment from the heat of battle than we were thrown into a further state of anxiety over the level of vigilance maintained by the troops manning the fortifications that ringed the city and the suspicious movements of the barbarians, movements which might be the prelude to a successful ambush carried out under cover of darkness that would allow them to penetrate our defences undetected and thus encompass our destruction. They are in fact extremely clever in this area, and once they have decided to act, they act decisively. Moreover, they are ready to brave any danger as long as they can make a start of putting their plans into action. And even if their plans miscarry, they consider it a glorious achievement to struggle boldly to accomplish what for the time being proves incapable of fulfilment. Accordingly, we stayed awake all that night, even though we had every reason to be proud of our exploits to date. In fact we had displayed a degree of raw courage that had astonished even the leader of the barbarians, who subsequently made a point of learning the reason why we had resisted each attack so valiantly and of ascertaining how things had turned out to be the reverse of what he had heard about us, so that his own expectations had been completely overturned.

Chapter 29: But when daybreak came and announced the second day of fighting, the *strategoi* [Leo Chitzilakes and Niketas] once more went to great lengths to put us on our mettle and prepare us for action. As the sun's rays spread daylight over the air, the barbarians disembarked and launched a further attack against the wall. They deployed, distributing themselves along certain points in battle formation. And concentrating their greatest numbers on the openings in the wall where the gates stood, they brought the full weight of their weapons to bear against us. Some used bows and arrows, others the handmade thunder of stones. Others applied themselves to stone-throwing engines and sent giant hailstones of rock hurtling through the air. Death threatened us in many shapes, and since it came from all directions, it lent a further dimension of terror to the experience of those who happened to be nearby. Against the already-mentioned gate alone they placed seven stone-throwing engines heavily protected on all sides, which they had previously equipped specially for this purpose during their progress by way of Thasos.

In front of these they brought up wooden ladders, which they placed against the wall and tried to climb up, providing themselves with cover by means of a barrage of stones from the stone-throwing engines, whose relentless fire made it impossible for anyone to venture forth with impunity on to the wall. And already they had attached a ladder to the battlements of the outwork and their plan would have been realized, had not a heavenly power given certain daring men the strength to leap down on to the spot. They wounded the barbarians with their spears and sent them pitching backwards together with the ladder. When they saw that this strategem too had failed, they fled and even left the ladder behind. We were so far emboldened as to mock them and to hurl missiles at them and stones from the stone-throwing engines even more eagerly than on the day before. And we no longer allowed them to get anywhere near the wall for even a short time, even though they were kindled to greater fury and sharpened their tusks like wild boars and would have torn us up alive with them, had it been possible. How terrifying it was to hear them raving like maniacs against us! What towering fits of anger they displayed, when they gnashed their teeth furiously and their demonic nature was revealed by the way they continually foamed at the mouth! Nor would they take any food throughout the entire course of that day but were insatiable for battle in spite of the tremendous heat. Indeed they were not even vaguely aware of the fact that their own bodies were broken with fatigue and scorched by the sun which was beating down on their heads. Their one preoccupation was either to sack the city and vent their rage upon us or, in the event of failure, to despair of life and to dispatch themselves with their own weapons. For once the wrath of the barbarians has been kindled, it is borne along by an unreasoning impulse, and will not desist until it witnesses the shedding of its own or its opponent's blood.

Chapter 30: But since it was highly dangerous for them to approach the wall, they relied exclusively on missiles and on stone-throwing engines. Drawing themselves up in rows, they took their stand some distance away yet near enough for their shots to fall upon the city with undiminished force. Protecting themselves with their shields and throwing their entire being into the struggle, they stood like statues with bodies of bronze or some other hard material and displayed limitless qualities of endurance and a fighting spirit that defied description. And in fact, when the sun was in its noonday course, when more than any other time of day it heats the air up like a furnace, they kindled their inborn fury with that last extreme of heat and goading their irrational frenzy still further with the stimulus of despair, they threw all their energies into a different (and particularly deadly) kind of siege. There were four gates in the wall on the east side of the city. Two of these, the previously mentioned Rome Gate, and the so-called Kassandreiotic Gate, they planned to burn down. The idea was that, if they could penetrate the outwork when the outer gates were burnt down and creep up to the high wall, they could wreck the inner gates without having anything to fear and pen everyone up in the city by posting expert archers opposite the wall to shoot their arrows continually and prevent anyone inside from venturing out.

Chapter 31: They set about their cunning plan in the following way: They found carts on which they placed upside down very small boats of the kind our fishermen use to fish with, adding a great quantity of firewood and a pile of brushwood. Then they sprinkled it all with pitch and sulphur, put their shoulders to the carts, set their wheels in motion and guided them with their hands until they reached the gates. Then they lit the wood from underneath and covering themselves with their shields, went back to the archers, having carried out their plan unnoticed. The fire took hold of the wood, feeding its flame until it flared up and caused the outer surface of the gates, which were iron-plated, to turn white-hot. Then the white heat, spreading inwards, reduced the gates to a sheet of flame, so that in a short time they collapsed, which threw everyone into a state of abject fear. No sooner was the news reported throughout the city that the gates had been burnt down than the effect was as though everyone had been stabbed through the heart; such was the state of terror and dejection to which people were reduced, as the colour drained from their cheeks, and as they abandoned abruptly every confident expectation. And those who a short while ago had been leaping down from the walls and keeping the enemy at bay and exhorting others to join in the fray were showing themselves in actual fact to be feebler than hares. The mere fact that that cunning expedient had succeeded gave more than a hint to everyone of what might be the end. Nevertheless, now that the outer gates had been destroyed by fire, we quickly protected the inner ones with a new wall. And we put water in containers on the battlements and kept a close watch in case the enemy should by any chance launch an attack against these gates too, so that when they tried to cause further damage, we might have some means of contending with the flames and preserving the gates from their treacherous designs. When they realized this, however, they no longer resorted to these particular evil tactics. Yet by resorting to other tactics still more cunning and more violent, they were destined to bring about our destruction by a means so effective and so far surpassing all contrivance that it was henceforth in no wise possible to stave it off. They employed this pause in their incendiarism by shooting at us with stone-throwers and with bows during the rest of the day until darkness succeeded daylight and put an obligatory stop to their exertions.

Chapter 32: Then, when they had stopped fighting, they went aboard their ships and after a brief spell of inaction, they began to carry out the plan of attack they had cunningly contrived beforehand. The plan involved a peculiar kind of gamble. If, thanks to it, they should be able to sack the city, they would have an easy success since there is no more effective siege tactic in existence, especially when the offensive is conducted from the water with no intervening dry land to cramp one's style. But if, along with their previous ventures, this too were to fail, they would first dispatch with their weapons those who had put the idea into their heads and had made them sail so far to no purpose, and then would return home. Having agreed, therefore, upon this plan, they began early in the night to put into effect their complicated scheme. Lighting lamps everywhere, they coupled the ships together in adjacent pairs and lashed their sides together with stout cables and iron chains so that they would not easily drift apart. Then they hoisted by means of the rigging at the fore the pieces of wood that stand up in the middle, which sailors call masts, and attaching by their handles to these the steering-paddles of each ship, they slung them high up in the air across the ropes leading to the prow so that their blades projected beyond the side of the ship. The result was a remarkable and novel contraption. For when the steering paddles had been suspended aloft by their handles in the manner described, they placed long strips of wood over them in rows, one next to the other, flooring in by this ingenious method the intervening space. They then fenced in the edges on all sides with boards, and secured the ends of the steering-paddle handles by making them fast to very strong cables at the stern end of the ships. In this manner they devised towers that were more effective than those surmounting walls on dry land. In them they posted armed barbarians, an elite force mounted aloft on account of their physical strength and natural daring and destined to deal us the coup de grace. They ordered some to shoot arrows, others to fling large stones (big enough to fill a man's hand) at those manning the inner circuit of the fortification. Others were equipped with fire (it too artificially contrived) which had been prepared in advance in earthenware vessels and which they were instructed to hurl at those advancing to confront them. All these expedients were effective and appropriate because they no longer had to operate on land but, thanks to the devilish invention already described, had been placed on a higher level than the structure of the fortification and they were thus provided with a useful vantage point for the accomplishment of their evil designs.

Chapter 33: But when on that same night these impious men had brought all their preparations into effect and no detail of what was being done escaped our notice because, as has been pointed out, they had plentiful illumination and the beach on which they had forged ahead with their plans was nearby, all of us were overcome by fear and consternation, not knowing how to preserve our safety for the future. One could see that the entire population was in a state of utter confusion and helplessness, unable to make up their minds from one moment to the next, and that their very lives were in jeopardy. There was indeed no concern to ward off impending disaster, only a morbid obsession with the question of how soon and how painfully death would occur. Flight was no longer an available or a safe option with the barbarians occupying positions all around the wall and keeping a close watch on the gates. Yet the danger that met the eye made waiting out of the question. Abandoning all hope of safety, they walked as though dazed up and down the wall, completely overwhelmed by the magnitude of their misfortune. But some, in whose hearts the flame of courage had not been entirely extinguished, decided while waiting for the enemy to make some preparations to defend the wall and repel their advance. These consisted of pitch, firebrands, quicklime and other flammable substances got ready in earthenware vessels for possible use against ships riding at anchor, the idea being to hurl these objects in their midst and put them out of action.

Chapter 34: Nevertheless, these were the actions and decisions of bewildered men. Already the light of day was dissolving the darkness of night, when to and behold! The ships, distributed at several points according to their equipment, crashed against the wall, presenting to the eyes of all a novel and extraordinary spectacle. Each pair of ships brought along its own ingeniously constructed wooden turret, which hugely overtopped the structure of the fortification and held aloft its freight of barbarians leaping up like frenzied bulls and threatening everybody with destruction. Whereupon, all that part of the population of the city that had come to think nothing of death, since it was both inevitable and staring them, so to speak, in the face, threw themselves unreservedly into the struggle. Making of the moment of maximum danger an occasion for displaying their courage, they stood their ground and fought like heroes; every man did his utmost. In fact, they did not allow the ships to get anywhere near, but by showering them with missiles and firebrands, they prevented them from approaching the wall and putting their plans into effect. But those who were smitten with cowardice and in their utter helplessness lacked the strength to even consider the experience of misfortune let themselves down gradually from the wall and fled to the mountainous part of the city, giving further encouragement thereby to the enemy. When, in fact, the latter saw that the structure of the wall was in a more serious state of disrepair in one place than anywhere else (it was the spot where we had earlier erected wooden breastworks), and noticed also that the sea was deeper just at that point, they propelled in that direction one of the pairs of ships that had been lashed together, rowing gently until they got near and had brought the bows of the ships right up to the battlement. Then, when the men on the wooden fortifications tried to hurl stones at them, the barbarians who were standing on top of the contraptions previously described uttered a loud and raucous cry, let fly with huge stones (which were not just big enough to fill a man's hand this time but were absolutely enormous) whose impact none could withstand, blew fire by means of air through tubes, hurled other receptacles also filled with fire into the fortifications and struck such terror into the hearts of the defenders that they leaped down swiftly and took to their heels, leaving the entire stretch of wall deserted. When the enemy saw that they had achieved their end (the defenders had all fallen to earth like leaves in the wind, not alighting by means of ladders but crashing down in terror) they sent against the fortifications a particularly daring barbarian with the complexion of an Ethiopian, who was apparently more frenzied than the others. He had a sword in his hand, which he brandished as he leaped down from the wall. Then he waited for the crowd to surge forward, trying to discover whether they had made off in feigned or in genuine flight. For they suspected that the inhabitants might have laid some hidden ambush for them in the streets, in order to waylay them once they had split up into separate groups.

Consequently, they were reluctant to enter the city, and set about their task without first taking precautions. But then (it was the third hour of the day) the glint of swords brandished by barbarian hands flashed like lightning through the air and revealed at every point the entry of the enemy. Beholding that disaster had well and truly struck, people all began to mill about in different directions, herded together by death, which loomed over them and left no further loophole for escape.

Chapter 35: Then, when the barbarians saw that the entire wall had been cleared and that the mass desertion of its defenders now guaranteed their safety, they sallied forth eagerly from the ships, leaped down on to the battlements and set fire to the gates, thus signalling to the other ships that their mission had been accomplished. These too hove swiftly into sight and dispatched against the city their contingents of barbarians, naked except for a small loincloth, and armed with swords. Once these barbarians were inside, they slew all those whom they found writhing about on the ground in the vicinity of the wall, regardless of whether they found them prostrated and paralysed with fear and so unable to move or languishing without any hope of flight owing to the injuries they had sustained during their earlier falls. After that they split up, and moved down the main thoroughfares.

85. FIGHT AT FINNESBURH (c. 1000)

There are two surviving accounts in Old English of the so-called Fight at Finnesburh: one told at Hrothgar's court in Beowulf *and the fragmentary poem provided here. Despite differences in detail, the poems share the same story of a Danish prince named Hnæf, who for five days is besieged in a stronghold with 60 of his retainers before succumbing to his wounds. The poet's striking account of this story is a stunning presentation of both a warrior ethos and a local siege.*

Source: trans. Michael Livingston, from *Anglo-Saxon Minor Poems*, in *Anglo-Saxon Poetic Records: A Collective Edition*, vol. 6, ed. George Philip Krapp and Elliot Van Kirk Dobbie (New York: Columbia University Press, 1942), pp. 3–4.

"... the gables burning?"
Hnæf then answered, that battle-young king:
"No eastern dawn is that, nor a dragon on the wing,
Nor does this hall's horned-roof burn.
But now battle begins: the startled birds mourn,
The wan-wolves howl, the war-wood resounds,
The shield answers shaft. Now shines the moon
Wandering under clouds. Now woe-deeds come,
Which these people's hate makes to happen.
Awaken yourself, my warriors now,
Heft your linden shields. Take courage to heart,
Fight in the front, be fierce in spirit!"
Up rose many a gold-laden thane, girded with his sword.
Charging to the door, a duo of champions,
Sigeferth and Eaha, who eased out their swords,
While at the other door, Ordlaf and Guthlaf
And Hengest himself advanced just behind.
Then did Garulf urge Guthere,
Who had a fine life, not at the forefront to be,
At the doors of the hall in armor not to haste,
Since one wound with hate wanted to waste it away.
But he asked of them all, without hiding aught,
Who was worthy-hearted who there held the doors.
"Sigeferth is my name!" he said, "I am a Sedgean man,
An adventurer renowned. I have seen rough fortunes,
Fought in fierce battles. To you is doom fated,
The end by this hand that you will endure.
Then sounded in the hall a havoc of slaughter,
The hard-leathered boards in the hands of the bold
And the boar-helms both burst; the walls of the fortress boomed.
Until in the battle Garulf breathed his last:
The first-most to fall of the hosts in that hall,
Guthlaf's strong son, surrounded by many
Of the remains of the brave. The raven hovered
Swarthy and shimmering-dark. Sword-light danced

As if all of Finnesburh were washed in flames.
I have never heard it said that more heroically in strife
Did sixty bold warriors ever bear themselves better,
Nor for sweet mead make finer repayment,
Than his retainers regave to Hnæf.
They fought for five days, and not one of them fell,
Those troop-companions, but they held the doors.
Then the hero was wounded, went the way of all flesh,
He said that his byrnie was broken asunder,
His war-garb useless, his helmet pierced.
Then promptly one asked him, that protector of the people,
How well the warriors their wounds endured
Or whether any of the young men ...

86. SIEGE OF JERUSALEM: WOOD AND WAR (1099)

Dumb luck plays a role in any engagement, no matter how well planned. In some cases, as in the story here told, from the Deeds of Tancred, *written by a likely eyewitness of the First Crusade about one of its most dynamic leaders, dumb luck can turn the tide of a war. Victory in the First Crusade has always been attributed to the tenacity of the men who persisted for three years through the deprivations, sickness, battles, and sieges until about only one-fourth of those who had set out arrived at Jerusalem. Facing the mighty walls of the city, the crusaders despaired of success because of a lack of wood for the building of siege machines—until Tancred, driven by dysentery to find a place to relieve himself out of sight from his troops, found some. Thinking that God had indeed worked in mysterious ways, this "miracle" wood was at once put to use in taking the city. The story of that siege is told here by Raymond of Aguilers, a chaplain in the service of the crusading count of Toulouse. Raymond's chronicle is a gruesome one, particularly so in its account of the massacres that befell many of Jerusalem's citizens when its walls were finally breached on 15 June.*

Source: trans. Michael Livingston, from Radulphus Cadomensis, *Gesta Tancredi in expeditione Hierosolymitana*, ed. J.-P. Migne, Patrologiae Latina 155 (Paris, 1844–55), p. 566; trans. A.C. Krey, Raymond of Aguilers, *The First Crusade: The Accounts of Eye-Witnesses and Participants* (Princeton, NJ: Princeton University Press, 1921), pp. 257–62.

From the *Gesta Tancredi*

Siege-timber, which had been sought in vain, was discovered as if by an act of God.

Meanwhile the leaders consulted together and determined to find and gather wood from everywhere, through the hiding places, on the roads and off the roads, and not one of them was to be spared this duty. What was decided was quickly implemented. Yet while the others labored in vain, Tancred was not deprived of what he sought. What I will say is a kind of miracle, and you, if you contemplate it, cannot deny that it is a heavenly act.

Tancred was tormented by a serious case of dysentery, yet he did not spare himself from his part in the riding. Scarcely able to sit on his horse, however, the illness frequently forced him to get down, to slink away, to search for a hidden spot. Having been assaulted in this way many times, weary from the journey, he had decided to give up his task and return to his companions empty-handed when the usual ailment struck, beginning to bear down on him. He withdrew and got down, dismounting with the intention of not being seen by his men. Looking around, however, he recognized he'd hardly gone far enough. So he searched even further away for a hidden spot, but once again everywhere he looked there were people wandering around, and so it was the third time and the fourth time that he moved. At last, after walking far away, he found solitude beneath a hollowed-out cliff, enclosed around by bristling trees. Father! Who but God brings water from the rock, causes an ass to speak, creates everything from nothing? He cured this army from one soldier's dismaying trauma, He made strength from weakness, He crafted an antidote more precious than any metal from a vile wound. For while laboring, his strength being expelled, Tancred recognized four lengths of wood standing just there against the opposite, back wall of the cave-like place—which were more useful than anything anyone could have proposed for the assigned labor since, it is said, these lengths of wood were from the labors of the king of Egypt in his siege of Jerusalem. As soon as he saw them, his joy was so great that he believed neither it nor his eyes. He rose up and went forward, touching and examining them.

At once, "Hey! Hey! Companions! Here! Hurry here!" he exclaimed. "Here! Here!" he shouted more loudly. "God has given even more than we desired! We searched for unhewn timber; we discovered it already finished." Being called, his companions appeared at once. Those who were moaning were now rejoicing, and Tancred hurried to send word to console the groaning army. As the joy spread through the people, voices of gladness and exultation arose in the tents of the Franks, and the sound came forth as if they were singing litanies.

From Raymond of Aguilers

The duke [Godfrey of Bouillon] and the counts of Normandy and Flanders placed Gaston of Beert in charge of the workmen who constructed machines. They built mantlets and towers with which to attack the wall. The direction of this work was assigned to Gaston by the princes because he was a most noble lord, respected by all for his skill and reputation. He very cleverly hastened matters by dividing the work. The princes busied themselves with obtaining and bringing the material, while Gaston supervised the work of construction. Likewise, Count Raymond made William Ricau superintendent of the work on Mount Zion and placed the bishop of Albara in charge of the Saracens and others who brought in the timber. The count's men had taken many Saracen castles and villages and forced the Saracens to work, as though they were their serfs. Thus for the construction of machines at Jerusalem fifty or sixty men carried on their shoulders a great beam that could not have been dragged by four pair of oxen. What more shall I say? All worked with a singleness of purpose, no one was slothful, and no hands were idle. All worked without wages, except the artisans, who were paid from a collection taken from the people. However, Count Raymond paid his workmen from his own treasury. Surely the hand of the Lord was with us and aided those who were working!

When our efforts were ended and the machines completed, the princes held a council and announced: "Let all prepare themselves for a battle on Thursday; in the meantime, let us pray, fast, and give alms. Hand over your animals and your boys to the artisans and carpenters, that they may bring in beams, poles, stakes, and branches to make mantlets. Two knights should make one mantlet and one scaling ladder. Do not hesitate to work for the Lord, for your labors will soon be ended." This was willingly done by all. Then it was decided what part of the city each leader should attack and where his machines should be located.

Meanwhile, the Saracens in the city, noting the great number of machines that we had constructed, strengthened the weaker parts of the wall, so that it seemed that they could be taken only by the most desperate efforts. Because the Saracens had made so many and such strong fortifications to oppose our machines, the duke, the count of Flanders, and the count of Normandy spent the night before the day set for the attack moving their machines, mantlets, and platforms to that side of the city which is between the church of St. Stephen and the valley of Josaphat. You who read this must not think that this was a light undertaking, for the machines were carried in parts almost a mile to the place where they were to be set up. When morning came and the Saracens saw that all the machinery and tents had been moved during the night, they were amazed. Not only the Saracens were astonished, but our people as well, for they recognized that the hand of the Lord was with us. The change was made because the new point chosen for attack was more level, and thus suitable for moving the machines up to the walls, which cannot be done unless the ground is level; and also because that part of the city seemed to be weaker, having remained unfortified, as it was some distance from our camp. This part of the city is on the north.

Count Raymond and his men worked equally hard on Mount Zion, but they had much assistance from William Embriaco and the Genoese sailors, who, although they had lost their ships at Joppa, as we have already related, had been able, nevertheless, to save ropes, mallets, spikes, axes, and hatchets, which were very necessary to us. But why delay the story? The appointed day arrived and the attack began. However, I want to say this first, that, according to our estimate and that of many others, there were 60,000 fighting men within the city, not counting the women and those unable to bear arms, and there were not many of these. At the most we did not have more than twelve thousand able to bear arms, for there were many poor people and many sick. There were twelve or thirteen hundred knights in our army, as I reckon it, not more. I say this that you may realize that nothing, whether great or small, which is undertaken in the name of the Lord can fail, as the following pages show.

Our men began to undermine the towers and walls. From every side stones were hurled from the tormenti and the petrariae [that is, catapults], and so many arrows that they fell like hail. The servants of God bore this patiently, sustained by the premises of their faith, whether they should be killed or should presently prevail over their enemies. The battle showed no indication of victory, but when the machines were drawn nearer to the walls, they hurled not only stones and arrows, but also burning wood and straw. The wood was dipped in pitch, wax, and sulfur; then straw [was] fastened on by an iron band, and, when lighted, these firebrands were shot from the machines. [They were] all bound together by an iron band, I say, so that wherever they fell, the whole mass held together and continued to burn. Such missiles, burning as they shot upward, could not be resisted by swords or by high walls; it was not even possible for the defenders to find safety down behind the walls. Thus the fight continued from the rising to the setting sun in such splendid fashion that it is difficult to believe anything more glorious was ever done. Then we called on almighty God, our leader and guide, confident in his mercy. Night brought fear to both sides. The Saracens feared that we would take the city during the night or on the next day, for the outer works were broken through and the ditch was filled, so that it was possible to make an entrance through the wall very quickly. On our part, we feared only that the Saracens would set fire to the machines that were moved close to the walls, and thus improve their situation. So on both sides it was a night of watchfulness, labor, and sleepless caution: on one side, most certain hope, on the other doubtful fear. We gladly labored to capture the city for the glory of God; they less willingly strove to resist our efforts for the sake of the laws of Mohammed. It is hard to believe how great were the efforts made on both sides during the night.

When the morning came, our men eagerly rushed to the walls and dragged the machines forward, but the Saracens had constructed so many machines that for each one of ours they now had nine or ten. Thus they greatly interfered, with our efforts. This was the ninth day, on which the priest had said that we would capture the city. But why do I delay so long? Our machines were now shaken apart by the blows of many stones, and our men lagged because they were very weary. However, there remained the mercy of the Lord which is never overcome nor conquered, but is always a source of support in times of adversity. One incident must not be omitted. Two women tried to bewitch one of the hurling machines, but a stone struck and crushed them, as well as three slaves, so that their lives were extinguished and the evil incantations averted.

By noon our men were greatly discouraged. They were weary and at the end of their resources. There were still many of the enemy opposing each one of our men; the walls were very high and strong, and the great resources and skill that the enemy exhibited in repairing their defenses seemed too great for us to overcome. But, while we hesitated, irresolute, and the enemy exulted in our discomfiture, the healing mercy of God inspired us and turned our sorrow into joy, for the Lord did not forsake us. While a council was being held to decide whether or not our machines should be withdrawn, for some were burned and the rest badly shaken to pieces, a knight on the Mount of Olives began to wave his shield to those who were with the count and others, signaling them to advance. Who this knight was we have been unable to find out. At this signal our men began to take heart, and some began to batter down the wall, while others began to ascend by means of scaling ladders and ropes. Our archers shot burning firebrands, and in this way checked the attack that the Saracens were making upon the wooden towers of the duke and the two counts. These firebrands, moreover, were wrapped in cotton. This shower of fire drove the defenders from the walls. Then the count quickly released the long drawbridge which had protected the side of the wooden tower next to the wall, and it swung down from the top, being fastened to the middle of the tower, making a bridge over which the men began to enter Jerusalem bravely and fearlessly. Among those who entered first were Tancred and the duke of Lorraine, and the amount of blood that they shed on that day is incredible. All ascended after them, and the Saracens now began to suffer.

Strange to relate, however, at this very time when the city was practically captured by the Franks, the Saracens were still fighting on the other side, where the count was attacking the wall as though the city should never be captured. But now that our men had possession of the walls and towers, wonderful sights were to be seen. Some of our men (and this was more merciful) cut off the heads of their enemies; others shot them with arrows, so that they fell from the towers; others tortured them longer by casting them into the flames. Piles of heads, hands, and feet were to be seen in the streets of the city. It was necessary to pick one's way over the bodies of men and horses. But these were small matters compared to what happened at the Temple of Solomon, a place where religious services are ordinarily chanted. What happened there? If I tell the truth, it will exceed your powers of belief. So let it suffice to say this much, at least, that in the Temple and porch of Solomon, men rode in blood up to their knees and bridle reins. Indeed, it was a just and splendid judgment of God that this place should be filled with the blood of the unbelievers, since it had suffered so long from their blasphemies. The city was filled with corpses and blood. Some of the enemy took refuge in the Tower of David, and, petitioning Count Raymond for protection, surrendered the Tower into his hands.

Now that the city was taken, it was well worth all our previous labors and hardships to see the devotion of the pilgrims at the Holy Sepulcher. How they rejoiced and exulted and sang a new song to the Lord! For their hearts offered prayers of praise to God, victorious and triumphant, which cannot be told in words. A new day, new joy, new and perpetual gladness, the consummation of our labor and devotion, drew forth from all new words and new songs. This day, I say, will be famous in all future ages, for it turned our labors and sorrows into joy and exultation; this day, I say, marks the justification of all Christianity, the humiliation of paganism, and the renewal of our faith. "This is the day which the Lord hath made, let us rejoice and be glad in it," for on this day the Lord revealed himself to his people and blessed them.

On this day, the Ides of July [that is, 15 July], Lord Adhemar, bishop of Puy [who had died at Antioch], was seen in the city by many people. Many also testified that he was the first to scale the wall, and that he summoned the knights and people to follow him. On this day, moreover, the apostles were cast forth from Jerusalem and scattered over the whole world. On this same day, the children of the apostles regained the city and fatherland for God and the fathers. This day, the Ides of July, shall be celebrated to the praise and glory of the name of God, who, answering the prayers of his church, gave in trust and benediction to his children the city and fatherland which he had promised to the fathers. On this day we chanted the office of the resurrection, since on that day he, who by his virtue arose from the dead, revived us through his grace. So much is to be said of this.

87. SIEGE OF LISBON (1147)

In 1147 a fleet left England containing soldiers from England, Flanders, Boulogne, the northern Holy Roman Empire and Scandinavia, intending to sail to the Holy Land for the Second Crusade. En route, these crusaders stopped for supplies in Portugal, where Pope Eugenius III—at the instigation of King Alfonso VII of Leon and Castile—had equated the Spanish Reconquista with the crusading effort. While there, the Christian crusaders met with King Alfonso I of Portugal, who convinced them to aid him in seizing the city of Lisbon from the Moors. What follows is an excerpt from an anonymous account of what followed: a 17-week siege that ended with the widespread looting of the city and the murder and rape of thousands of civilians inside.

Sources: sections 1, 3, and 5: trans. Charles Wendell David, *The Conquest of Lisbon: De Expugnatione Lyxboniensi* (New York: Columbia University Press, 2001), pp. 53–59, 101–05, 137–39; sections 2, 4, and 6: trans. James A. Brundage, *The Crusades: A Documentary Survey* (Milwaukee, WI: Marquette University Press, 1962), pp. 97–98, 100–03.

[1.] To begin, then, men of diverse nations, customs, and speech assembled in the port of Dartmouth [on the south coast of England] in about one hundred and sixty-four vessels. The whole expedition was divided into three parts. Under Count Arnold of Aerschot, nephew of Duke Godfrey [of Lower Lotharingia] were the forces from the territories of the [Holy] Roman Empire; under Christian of Ghistelles, the Flemings and the men of Boulogne. All the others were under four constables: the ships of Norfolk and Suffolk under Hervey de Glanvill, those of Kent under Simon of Dover, those of London under Andrew, and all the rest under Saher of Archelle ...

[2.] The city of Lisbon at the time of our arrival consisted of sixty thousand families paying taxes ... The city was populous beyond belief, for, as we learned from its alcayde, or governor, after the capture of the city, it had one hundred fifty-four thousand men, not counting women and children.... The reason for such a dense population was that there was no established religion there. Each man was a law unto himself. As a result the basest element from every part of the world had gathered there, like the bilge water of a ship, a breeding ground for every kind of lust and impurity....

[3. King Alfonso now asked the crusaders to delay going to Jerusalem and to help him capture Lisbon.] To frame a reply to this we all assembled in council ... [where] William Viel, yet breathing out threatenings and piratical slaughter, and his brother Ralph and almost all the men of Southampton and Hastings, together with those who had come to besiege Lisbon five years before this, all with one voice declared that they took the king's promise [of rewards and plunder] to be nothing but treachery; and, bringing up many points against it which were either false or, if in any respect true, to be imputed to their own foolishness rather than the king's baseness, or things which were even more obvious, [they said] that they were unwilling to bear the expense of a long labor in the siege. Moreover, it would be more profitable if they should sail quickly past the coast of Spain and then extort much easy money from the merchant vessels of Africa and Spain. And, besides, they recalled that the wind at that season was very favorable for voyagers to Jerusalem. And they said that they would not wait for anyone, if only they should have eight or ten ships associated with them, and many other similar things which depend upon the turn of fate rather than upon virtue. But the greater part of our force, setting aside every objection, agreed to remain....

[4. After an unsuccessful attempt to persuade the Muslims to surrender the city, the crusaders besieged Lisbon.] The Moors, meanwhile, made frequent sorties against our men by day because they held three gates against us. With two of these gates on the side of the city and one on the sea, they had an easy way to get in and out. On the other hand, it was difficult for our men to organize themselves. The sorties caused casualties on both sides, but theirs were always greater than ours. While we kept watch, meanwhile, under their walls through the days and nights, they heaped derision and many insults upon us.... They also continuously attacked blessed Mary, the mother of God, with insults and with vile and abusive words, which infuriated us. They said that we venerated the son of a poor woman with a worship equal to that due to God, for we held that he was a God and the Son of God, when it is apparent that there is only one God who began all things that have begun and that he has no one coeval with him and no partaker in his divinity.... They attacked us with these and similar calumnies. They showed to us, moreover, with much derision the symbol of the cross. They spat upon it and wiped the feces from their posteriors with it. At last they urinated on it, as on some despicable thing, and threw our cross at us....

[5. Meanwhile,] the men of Cologne five times began to dig mines for the purpose of overturning the [city] wall and were as many times overwhelmed. Hence our forces again had cause for deep discouragement, and, murmuring much among themselves, they were making such complaints as that they might have been better employed elsewhere, when, after some days, there came to us by the determination of divine mercy no small consolation.

For in the evening ten Moors entered a skiff beneath the wall and rowed away in the direction of the castle of Palmela. But our men pursued them so closely that they abandoned the skiff in desperation, and everything they were carrying in it. Letters were found in it, directed to several parties and written in the Arabic language. An example of one, as I got it from an interpreter, is as follows:

> To Abu Muhammed, king of Evora, [from] the unfortunate people of Lisbon: may he maintain his kingdom in safety. What great and terrible and unexpected disasters have come upon us, the desolate ruin of our city and the great effusion of noble blood—memorials, alas, of our everlasting grief—proclaim. Already the second moon has almost passed since the fleet of the Franks, which has been borne hither to our borders with the aid of heaven and earth and sea, has kept us shut within the circuit of this close-drawn wall. And what is to be hoped for amid this sum of woes is more than doubtful, except only to look for succor by means of ransom. But with our cooperation we doubt not that you will liberate the city and the country from the barbarians. For they are not so very numerous or warlike, as their tower and engines which we have burned with force and arms bear witness. Otherwise, let your prudence beware, for the same outcome of events and evils awaits you.

And the other letters besought the same things from parents and other relatives and friends, and from debtors; and ... also gave information concerning their supply of bread and other foodstuffs. When our men learned of these things, their spirits were greatly encouraged to continue the attack against the enemy for some days longer. After a short time the corpse of a man who had been drowned was found beneath our ships; and on an arm a letter was tied, of which the tenor was as follows:

> The king of Evora to the men of Lisbon.... Having long since entered into a truce with the king of the Portuguese, I cannot break faith and wage war upon him and his people. For the rest, take heed in good time. Buy safety with your money, lest that prove a cause of your hurt which ought to be a cause of your well-being. Farewell. Give something worthwhile to this our messenger.

So, finally, as the Moors' last hope of relief was destroyed, our men kept watch the more vigilantly ... [and the siege continued until the Moors agreed to surrender].

[6.] When these matters had been agreed upon by both sides, the arrangements which the Moors had proposed on the previous day for the delivery of the city, were accepted. It was decided among us that one hundred and forty of our armed men and one hundred and sixty of the Flemish and the Cologne contingents should enter the city before everyone else and peacefully take over the fortifications of the upper fortress so that the enemy might bring all of their money and possessions there and give a guarantee by swearing before our men. When all these things had been collected, the city was then to be searched by our men. If any further possessions were found, the man in whose house they were discovered was to pay for it with his head. When everyone had thus been despoiled, they were to be let go in peace outside of the city. When the gates had been opened and those who were chosen were allowed to enter, the men of Cologne and the Flemings thought up a sly method of deceiving us: they requested our men to allow them to enter first for the sake of their honor. When they had received permission and got a chance to enter first, they slipped in more than two hundred of their men, in addition to those who had been selected. These were also in addition to others who had already slipped through the ruined places in the walls which lay open to them, while none of our men, except those selected, had presumed to enter.

The archbishop and the other bishops went in front of us with the Lord's cross and then our leaders entered together with the king and those who had been selected. How everyone rejoiced! What special glory for all! What great joy and what a great abundance there was of pious tears when, to the praise and honor of God and of the most Holy Virgin Mary the saving cross was placed atop the highest tower to be seen by all as a symbol of the city's subjection, while the Archbishop and bishops, together with the clergy and everyone, intoned with wonderful rejoicing the *Te Deum laudamus* and the *Asperges me*, together with devout prayers.

The king, meanwhile, went around the strong walls of the fortress on foot. The men of Cologne and the Flemings, when they saw in the city so many spurs to their greed, did not observe their oaths or their religious guarantees. They ran hither and yon. They plundered. They broke down doors. They rummaged through the interior of every house. They drove the citizens away and harassed them improperly and unjustly. They destroyed clothes and utensils. They treated virgins shamefully. They acted as if right and wrong were the same. They secretly took away everything which should have been common property. They even cut the throat of the elderly Bishop of the city, slaying him against all right and justice.... The Normans and the English, however, for whom faith and religion were of the greatest importance, contemplating what such actions might lead to, remained quietly in their assigned position preferring to stay their hands from looting rather than to violate the obligations of their faith and their oathbound association.... Finally [the men of Cologne and the Flemings] came to themselves and besought our men with earnest prayers that we should occupy the remaining sections of the city together with them so that, after the loot had been divided, all the injuries and thefts might be discussed peacefully and they would be prepared to make amends for the evils they had presumed to commit. The enemy, when they had been despoiled in the city, left the town through three gates continuously from Saturday morning until the following Wednesday. There was such a multitude of people that it seemed as if all of Spain were mingled in the crowd....

88. SIEGE OF ORLÉANS (1429)

The city of Orléans had been under English siege for nearly seven months before Joan of Arc arrived on 29 April 1429. At the beginning of the siege, the Orléanais had destroyed the bridge across the Loire River, leaving the besiegers the fortified bridgehead, the Tourelles, but no access to an easy attack on the city walls. The English decided to "wait out" the Orléanais, which was difficult to do as they did not have sufficient numbers to surround the city. These were gathered into several strategically located earth and wood fortifications, known as boulevards (including one in front of the Tourelles), although they were unable to keep the city from being supplied. Eventually a large French relief army arrived, but its leader, Jean, the Bastard of Orléans, refused to risk the high casualties that would certainly result from an attack of the boulevards or the Tourelles. This all changed with the arrival of Joan of Arc, as recorded in this Journal *written from within the besieged city. Prior portions of Joan's story were subsequently added back into what had been a daily account, providing an early biography of the girl who would be called the Maid.*

Source: trans. Kelly DeVries, from *Journal du siège d'Orleans, 1428–1429*, ed. Paul Charpentier and Charles Cussard (Orléans, France: Libraire R. Houzé, 1896), pp. 34, 44, 46, 57, 62, 74–91.

Around this day [8 February 1429?] there was a young maid named Jehanne [Joan], a native of a village in Bar, called Domrémy, near to one called Gras, in the seigneury of Vaucouleur. Which for some time had kept a garden at the house of her father and mother and at other times had done some sewing and making thread, Our Lord appeared to her many times in visions, during which he commanded her to go and relieve the siege of Orléans, and to crown the king at Rheims, because He was with her and would provide the divine aid and force of arms to accomplish this enterprise. Because of this she went to Sir Robert de Baudricourt, the captain of Vaucouleurs. She recounted her vision, pleading with him and requesting that for the very great good and profit of the king and kingdom that she wished to dress in men's clothes, mount a horse, and go before the king, just as God had commanded her to do. But for several days after, he did not wish to believe her but began to mock her, reputing her vision to be fantasy and crazy imaginations, that unless the people wished to commit a carnal sin, they restrain her. Because of this everyone then, and afterwards, feared her return: that they looked at her, they might be chilled with lust....

Also around this day [13 February?], it happened that Joan the Maid, by divine grace, said to Sir Robert de Baudricourt that the king had suffered great damage to Orléans, and would suffer even more, were she not taken to him. To this Baudricourt, who had already heard it, now found it very wise and true, persisting in [agreeing with] her initial requests, that she be clothed in men's clothing, as she required. And to lead her along the perilous route he placed two gentlemen of Champagne, the one named Jehan de Metz, and the other Bertrand de Polongy[?], who were well thought of. But she assured them that no harm would come to them if they traveled with her, and two of her brothers, to go to the king, who was in Chinon....

Around this day [6 March] Joan the Maid and those who had led her arrived at Chinon, marveling strongly at how they had arrived safely, considering the perilous roads that they had taken, the dangerous and large rivers which they had crossed, and the long journey which they had agreed to make. Along it they had passed by several English-held towns and villages, none of which were French, as well as bandits and looters. For which our Lord was praised for the grace he had done, as the Maid had promised them before. And they let the king know of this, as before this time he had been told many times in Council that it would be better if he retired to the Dauphiné, to be protected with the lands of Lyon, Languedoc and Auvergne. At least he would be saved, although the English would gain Orléans. But all was changed, for he sent for the two gentlemen to be presented before his Great Council and interrogated about the person and status [*faict et estat*] of the Maid, who told them the truth. This was put to the Council and it was decided that they talk to the king. In fact, they spoke to him, gave him reverence, told him that they knew how many of his people knew him to be king and who did not; he should make a grand appearance, because she had never seen him. So she said many beautiful words to him, that God had sent her to give him aid and succor, so that he may protect his people. By the divine grace and strength of arms, she would raise the siege of Orléans, then take him to be crowned in Rheims, as God had commanded her. She wished the English return to their land and to leave his kingdom which had been lost to him in peace; and if they did not go, she would strike them down. These words, thus said by her, caused the king to take her into his lodgings. He assembled his Great Council, where there were many prelates, knights, squires and generals, with some doctors in theology, in [secular] law and in canon law. They advised him to have her interrogated by the doctors, in order to be certain for himself that she could, with evidence and reason [*évidente raison*] could accomplish what she said. And the doctors found her to have such an honest countenance, so wise in her words, that their conclusion was that they held her in the highest regard [*très grant compte*]. Because of this; and also because he found she truly knew the day and hour of the battle of the Herrings [12 February]—it was found in the letters of Baudricourt that he had written the hour that she had said, while she was still in Vaucouleurs; and because she had told the king a secret, in the presence of his confessor and a few of his closest [secret] councilors, something that he had done, which astounded him, because it was only known by God and him, he concluded that she would be taken honorably to Poitiers, so that she might be interrogated again and her persistence known, as well as to find funds to pay for men, victuals and artillery to be taken to relieve Orléans. That she saw herself to have divine grace, because she was in the middle of her journey, she said to many: "In the name of God, I see well that I will have a good result at Poitiers, where I am being taken, as God aids me, traveling there on behalf of God!" This was the way she spoke.

When she was in Poitiers, where she was in front of the Parliament of the king, many doctors and other people of great status interrogated her separately, to whom she responded very well. And especially a young Jacobin doctor said to her that if God wished the English to leave they would not need weapons. To which she responded that she only wanted a few men to fight, and God would give them victory. This response, with many others that she had made, and the firmness of her earlier promises, everyone concluded that the king ought to trust her, and to send supplies and men with her to Orléans, which he did. She was well armed and given a good horse. And the king ordered that she carry a banner, on which she wanted to have painted with the majestic words *IHESUS MARIA*. The king wished to give her a good sword. She thanked him but she would be pleased if he sent to acquire one, which had five crosses drawn across its crossguard, which was at Sainte-Catherine-du-Fierbois. The king marveled at this and asked if she had seen this. To this she responded, no, however she knew that it was there. The king sent for it, and this sword was found with others, which had been given there over time. And it was carried to the king, who had it cleaned and sheathed honorably. And he commanded that a very valiant and wise gentleman, named Jehan d'Aulon, accompany her; and as her page, to serve her honorably, he commanded another gentleman named Louis de Coutes. These things were all said and done in this chapter house [where the meetings had taken place], but for brevity, I have combined them altogether....

... on the same day that the English commenced to build a bastille, which they fortified [10 March], as a site to besiege Orléans. To relieve this Joan the Maid was sent to the fields accompanied by a large number of lords, squires and men-at-arms, together with victuals and artillery. They had taken leave of the king, who had expressly commanded the lords and men-at-arms that they obey her as they would him. And they did so....

That same day in March [26], the Maid was at Blois, where she had gone, together with part of her company, who had already arrived. She sent a herald to go before the English lords and captains at Orléans, to whom she had written a letter that she had dictated. And it had at its top, as its principle title, *Iesus Maria*, and it began after a break as such:

[For the letter to the English, see doc. 66.]

When the English lords and captains came together and heard the letter, they marveled, and also despised the Maid; they used vulgar words, especially calling her wench and cow. They threatened to burn her, they retained the herald, who carried the letter, mocking what she had written....

On their side, the Maid and the other lords and captains who were with her knew how the English despised and mocked her and her letter, that they had retained the herald who had delivered it to them. Because of this they decided to march with all their soldiers, victuals and artillery, passing by Sauloigne, as the greatest power of the English was on the side of the Beausse. None of this was told to the Maid, however, as she wanted to go and pass in front of them by force of arms. For this she ordered that all of her soldiers confess, and to leave all their women and possessions behind. And then they went, making their way to a village named Chécy, where they spent the following night.

The following Friday, 29th day of the month [April], inviolable news came to Orléans that the king had sent by way of Sauloigne victuals, powder, cannons and other war materiel, to be brought there by the Maid, who came because Our Lord told her to resupply and comfort the city, to raise the siege. This did comfort those of Orléans greatly. And because it was said that the English would endeavor to stop these victuals, it was ordered that everyone be armed and be placed around the city; and it was done.

On this day fifty infantry, armed with staff weapons [*guisarmes*] and other weapons. They came from the land of Gastinois, where they had been in garrison.

That same day there was a large skirmish, because the French wanted to give place and time for the victuals that were being brought to them to enter. And to distract the English, they sallied in great strength, rushing to skirmish at Saint-Loup of Orléans. As soon as they did this there were many killed, wounded and taken prisoner on both sides, although the French did carry one of the English standards into the city. And during this skirmish the victuals and artillery which the Maid had brought from Chécy, entered into the city. She had been escorted from the village by the Bastard of Orléans [later Jean, lord of Dunois, then commanding the relief forces outside of Orléans], and other knights, squires and soldiers. All in Orléans were very joyous at her arrival; they had great reverence for her, and held her dear. So had she for them. It was decided by them all that she not enter into Orléans until the night, to avoid the tumult of the people, and that Marshal [Gilles de] Rais and Sir Ambroise de Loré, who had been commanded by the king to lead her there, should return to Blois where there were many French lords and soldiers. And it was done. Thus around the eighth hour in the evening, despite all the English who tried to prevent her from doing so, she, entirely armed and mounted on a white horse, with her standard—also white, with two angels, each holding a fleur-de-lys in their hands, the pennon painted, in the manner of an Annunciation, with the image of Our Lady presenting a lily to an Angel—carried before her.

Thus, she entered into Orléans, with the Bastard of Orléans on her left, very richly armed and mounted. After them came many other nobles and valiant lords, squires, captains, and soldiers, besides some of the garrison and other citizens of Orléans, who had gone to meet her. From another part of the city came other soldiers and citizens of Orléans, carrying a large number of torches, filled with joy just as if they had seen God descend among them. And not without cause, for they had much worry, labor and pain, and, what was worse, they doubted that they would be saved, with all people and possessions lost. But they all—men, women and children—felt comforted, that the siege would be raised by divine virtue that was said to be in this simple Maid, whom they regarded with much affection. And there was a great many who pressed to touch her, or the horse on which she rode, so that those carrying torches came so close to the pennon of her standard that it caught on fire. Because of this she spurred her horse and turned it gently toward the pennon that she extinguished the fire, as if she had long fought in wars. This the men-at-arms held as a great miracle, and the citizens as well. They accompanied her throughout the city, holding her very dear, and that is was a very great honor to lead her all the way to the Regnart Gate, and the house of Jacquet Boucher, the treasurer of the duke of Orléans, where she was received with very great joy, with her two brothers, two gentlemen and a valet, who had come with her from the land of Bar....

[The next day] as night approached the Maid sent two heralds to the English army and demanded that they return the herald who had taken her letter from Blois. At the same time the Bastard of Orléans demanded that, were he not returned, he would brutally kill all the English prisoners in Orléans, as well as any English lord who were there to procure the ransom of others. Because of this the English generals returned all the heralds and messengers of the Maid, telling them that they would burn and cause her to die by fire, and that she was nothing more than a wench, and should return to the cows. Then she was very angry, and when night came she went to the boulevard at Belle Croix, on the bridge, and she spoke to Glasdale and other English in the Tourelles. She told them on behalf of God that the English ought to surrender to save all their lives. But Glasdale and those on his side responded with villainy, insulting her and calling her coward, as before, crying very loudly that they would kill her by fire were they to catch her. At this she was incredibly angry and responded that they lied; and saying this she retired into the city.

The Sunday afterwards, which was the first day of May, of 1429, the Bastard of Orléans departed from the city to go to Blois to [Charles of Bourbon, the duke] of Clermont, the Marshal [Jean de Brosse, lord] of Sainte-Sèvere, the lord [Gilles] of Rais, and many other knights, squires and soldiers. That day also Joan of Arc also rode from the city accompanied by many knights and squires, because those of Orléans had such a desire to see her that they destroyed everything to the front of the house where she stayed. To be able to see her was why so many important people crowded the roads of the city as she passed through, which made it difficult to travel: the people were not satisfied to just see her. Many thought it was a great miracle that she would able to hold onto her horse as nobly as she did. In fact, she also held herself nobly in all ways, as if she knew how to be a man-at-arms, trained in warfare from adolescence.

That same day the Maid spoke to the English near the Cross of Morin, and there said that they each should surrender to save their lives, and for God to return to England, or she would not treat them well. But they responded with similar villainies as had been said at the Tourelles previously. After this she returned to Orléans.

On Monday, May 2, the Maid left Orléans on her horse and rode through the fields to visit the boulevards of the English army, after which the people gathered in a very great mob, taking very great pleasure in seeing and being around her. And when she had seen and reconnoitered the English fortifications, she returned to the Church of the Holy Cross of Orléans in the city, where she heard vespers.

On Wednesday, May 4, the Maid rode into the fields acommpanied by [Archambaud] the Lord of Villars and Sir Florent d'Iliers, [Étienne de Vignolles, called] La Hire, Alain Giron, Jamet de Tilloy and many other squires and soldiers, numbering in all around 500. She went to the Bastard of Orléans, Marshal of Rais, Marshal of Sainte-Sévère, [Jean de La Haye] the baron of Coutonces, and many other squires and solders armed with staff weapons and lead mallets, who were bringing victuals sent to Orléans from Bourges, Angiers, Tours and Blois. These were received with very great joy in the city, into which they entered passing by the boulevard of the English, who were unable to sally out against them, but defended themselves strongly.

That same day, after midday, the Maid and the Bastard of Orléans departed from the city, taking with them a large number of nobles and around 500 soldiers, and they attacked the boulevard of Saint-Loup, where they found very strong resistance by the English, who had fortified it well and defended it very valiantly for three hours, enduring very harsh assaults. Although by the end the French took it by force, killing 114 English and capturing and returning into the city with 40 prisoners. Before doing so, however, they dismantled, burned and destroyed the entire boulevard, which caused great wrath, despair and displeasure among the English. Some English soldiers from the boulevard of Saint-Pouër sallied out in great power during this assault, wishing to aid their fellow-soldiers. When the Orléanais saw this they rang the bell in the belfry twice, to which the Marshal of Sainte-Sévère, [Louis Malet] lord de Graville, [Jean de la Haye] baron of Coulonces and many other knights and squires, soldiers and citizens, in total 600 soldiers, rushed hastily from Orléans and took to the battlefield in very good order and fought against the English. But when they saw the way that the French had sallied out and ordered for battle, these English soldiers abandoned their enterprise of aiding their companions and returned sadly to their boulevard, which they did in great haste. Despite this they had to retreat to their boulevard more and more. Yet, in the end the French captured it, as is said.

The Friday afterwards, which was the Ascension of Our Lord, the Maid, the Bastard of Orléans, the Marshals of Sainte-Sévère and of Rais, the lord of Graville, the baron of Coulonces, the lord of Villars, [Poton] the lord of Xaintrailles, [Raoul] the lord of Gaucourt, La Hire, [Raimond Arnaud] the lord of Corraze, Sir Denis de Chailly, Thibault [d'Armagnac, called] de Termes, Jamet de Tilloy and a Scottish captain, named [Sir Hugh] Kennedy, and other captains and leaders of war, and also the bourgeois of Orléans held a council, to discuss and decide what to do against the English who were laying siege. It was concluded that an assault would be made on the Tourelles and the boulevards at the end of the bridge, where the English had marvelously fortified the defensible places and a large number of men well experienced in war. For this the captains were commanded to be prepared on the next morning, ready to make attacks on all the places. This command was well obeyed, because during the night a great diligence was taken that all would be completely prepared for the morning, when announced by the Maid.

They left from Orléans: before the company was the Bastard of Orléans, the Marshals of Sainte-Sévère and Rais, the lord of Graville, Sir Florent d'Iliers, La Hire and many other knights and squires, around 4000 soldiers. They crossed the Loire River, between Saint-Loup and the New Tower. First they captured Saint-Jean-de-Blanc, which the English had captured and fortified. And afterwards they retreated to a small island, which was to the right of Saint-Aignan. The English sallied out in great strength, giving a large shout, and charging at them very strongly and closely. But the Maid and La Hire, and some of their men, joined together and struck them with such great strength and power against the English whom they forced to recoil all the way to their boulevard and the Tourelles. The whole army then delivered such an assault on the boulevard and the rampart that had previously been fortified by the English at the site where the Augustinian Church had been, that it was taken by force, delivering a large number of prisoners to the French, and killing many English who were there and had defended it very strongly. On both sides impressive feats of arms. The following night the French laid siege to the Tourelles and the boulevard around it. All night the Orlèanais made a great effort to carry bread, wine and other victuals to the besieging soldiers.

Early in the morning on the day afterwards, which was Saturday, May 6, the French attacked the Tourelles and the boulevard, while the English were fortifying it. It was a very marvelous assault, during which many impressive feats of arms, by both the attackers and the defenders, because there were a large number of strong soldiers, and abundantly filled with defensive equipment. They used these well. For although the French placed their many ladders in very many places, attacking very valiantly and strongly the very highest of their fortifications in the front; they were so strong that they seemed to be immortal. They were rebuffed many times and thrown from the top to the ground, sometimes by cannons and other shot, sometimes by axes, spears, staff weapons, lead mallets, and even by hands, such that many French were killed and wounded. Among the wounded was the Maid, pierced by an arrow between her shoulder and neck, so deeply that it passed through. All the attackers were very saddened and distraught, especially the Bastard of Orléans and other captains who had come before her and said that they should leave the assault until the following day. But she comforted them with good and encouraging words, exhorting them to maintain their bravery. Not believing her, they abandoned the assault and retreated to the rear. They also brought their artillery back until the next day. At this she was very distraught and said to them: "In the name of God, you will be in [the Tourelles] very shortly, do not doubt it, and the English will have no more strength against you. Rest for a short time, drink and eat." They did this: it was a miracle that they obeyed her. And after they had done so, she said to them, "On behalf of God return to the assault, because without doubt the English will have no more strength defend themselves and the Tourelles and the boulevard will be captured."

Having said this, she left her standard and went on her horse away to a place where she could pray to Our Lord. She said to a young noble near her: "Tell me when the end of my standard is placed on the boulevard." A short time later he said: "Joan, the end has touched!" And she responded to him: "All is yours; enter!" These words were afterwards understood to be a prophecy, because when the valiant leaders and men-at-arms who remained in Orléans saw that she wished to attack again, some of them rushed from the city over the bridge. Because many arches were broken, they brought a carpenter and carried gutters and ladders, from which they made planks. Seeing that these were not long enough to carry them across two broken arches, they joined one small piece of wood to one of the long gutters, and this made it so that they could. The first to cross was a very valiant knight of the Order of Rhodes, called that of Saint John of Jerusalem [the Hospitallers] named Brother Nicole de Giresme, with many others following his example. This was said to be a great miracle of Our Lord: otherwise how could the long and narrow gutter, so high in the air, have held without any support.

Those who crossed over joined with their other companions in an assault which lasted only a short time afterwards, because as soon as they began again, the English lost their strength and power to resist any longer. They tried to enter the boulevard next to the Tourelles. Although a few were able to save themselves, 400 or 500 soldiers were killed or drowned, except for some who were taken prisoner; none were great lords. William Glasdale, [Guillaume] the lord of Molins, [Richard] lord of Pommins, [Thomas Gifford] the bailli of Nantes and many other knight bannerets and English nobles were drowned because when they had tried to save themselves the bridge collapsed underneath them. This was a great embarrassment to the English army and did great harm to the French who wished to gain great wealth from their ransoms. However, there was great happiness, and they praised Our Lord for this good victory when he had given them. They certainly ought to have done this, because it was this assault, which had lasted from morning all the way until the sun set, that was very well fought both by attackers and defenders. It was one of the greatest feats of arms that had been done for a long time before. It was also seen as a miracle of Our Lord, at the request of Saint-Aignan and Saint-Euvertre, formerly bishops and patrons of Orléans, so it appeared according to common opinion, and also to the people who were brought as prisoners into the city. One certified that for him and for the other English in the Tourelles and the boulevard it seemed that those when they attacked there were so many that it was a miracle, as if the whole world had assembled against them. On behalf of the victory all the clergy and people of Orléans sang Te Deum laudamus with great devotion, and all the bells of the city were rung, giving thanks very humbly to Our Lord and the two saint-confessors for their glorious divine comfort. There was much joy in all parts, giving marvelous praises to their valiant defenders, and especially above all to Joan the Maid. She spent the night on the battlefield, together with the lords, captains and men-at-arms, both to protect the Tourelles which had been valiantly conquered and to learn if the English on the side of Saint-Laurent [northwest of them] might wish to aid or avenge their companions; but they wished no such thing.

Thus the next morning, Sunday, May 7, 1429, they left their fortifications, as did the English in Saint-Pouër and elsewhere, and they raised their siege, placing themselves in battle array. At this the Maid, the Marshals of Sainte-Sévère and Rais, the lord of Graville, the baron of Coulonces, Sir Florens d'Illiers, the lord of Corraze, the lord of Xantrailles, La Hire, Alain Giron, Jamet du Tilloy and many other valiant soldiers and militia sallied out of Orlèans in great power, and they arrayed themselves in battle order. At this point they were very near to each other, for the space of an entire hour without contact. The French endured this with great difficulty, obeyed the will of the Maid, who had commanded and ordered since the beginning, on account of the love and honor of the holy day of Sunday, they would not begin the battle nor attack the English. But if the English were to attack them, they could defend themselves strongly and bravely, for the English had no power, and they would be the masters of the battlefield. The hour passed and the English left and they traveled in good ranks and order to Meung-sur-Loire. They raised the siege and all left. They had been before Orléans from October 12, 1428, all the way to this day.

89. SIEGE OF CONSTANTINOPLE (1453)

The historical impact of the fall of Constantinople—for over a thousand years the capital of the Eastern Roman/Byzantine Empire and one of richest cities in the world—can hardly be overstated. Indeed, for many historians, its conquest on 29 May 1453, after a 53-day siege by the Ottoman armies of Sultan Mehmed II, only 21 years old at the time, marks the chronological end of the Middle Ages. What it represented, of course, depended largely on one's point of view. For the Byzantines it was a tragic defeat that effectively ended a once-glorious Roman Empire. For the Ottomans it was a powerful triumph that opened the gate toward further successes in the kingdoms of Europe; Mehmed would make it his capital. Beyond the political, social, and religious aspects of the event, the fall of Constantinople holds enormous significance in terms of military history: its mighty walls, which had withstood the tests of centuries, had been breached by the power of gunpowder artillery, which would play an increasingly important role in warfare. The account of the fall provided here comes from Hermodoros Michael Kritovoulos, a Greek politician who, while lamenting the loss for Christendom, nevertheless held Mehmed in high esteem as "the Conqueror."

Source: trans. Charles T. Riggs, Kritovoulos, *History of Mehmed the Conqueror* (Princeton, NJ: Princeton University Press, 1954), pp. 41–52, 55–77.

Review of the Whole Army, and the Assignment of the Parts of the City on Landward and Seaward Sides to the Generals by the Sultan

117. After this, he reviewed the whole army and gave to the governors and cavalry captains and generals of divisions and chiefs of battalions, to each his orders, assigning the stations where they must guard and fight and giving them directions what to do. And he divided the whole City into parts, the land-walls and the sea-walls. To Zaganos and his men with certain others of the captains, he entrusted the siege of Galata and the region all around it, with the Horn and the entire harbor, going as far as what is called the "Wooden Gate" of the City. He ordered him to make a bridge across that part of the Horn, from Ceramica [the brick-kilns] to the other side. Opposite them was the wall of the City. He knew that by sending the heavy infantry and the bowmen across this bridge, he could attack the City from every point, and so would make the siege complete.

118. To Karaja, the Governor of Europe, and to others of the generals, he committed the section from the Wooden Gate going up toward the Palace of Porphyrogenitus and extending to what is known as the Gate of Charisus; and he gave him some of the cannon, accompanied by the founders who had cast them, to bombard the wall at that point, if perchance it might be weak and vulnerable and he might knock it down.

119. And he assigned to Ishak, the Governor of Asia at that time, and to Mahmud, the Count of that region, brave men and men of remarkable experience and daring in battle, the section from Myriandrion to the Golden Gate and the sea at that point.

120. The Sultan himself, with the two Pashas, Halil and Karaja, took over the middle of the City and of the land-wall, where he certainly expected there would be the most of the fighting. He had with him the whole imperial guard,

by which I mean the best of the infantry and the bowmen and the aides-de-camp and the rest of his personal forces, which were the finest in the army.

121. When he had thus deployed his land forces, and had secured the wall in every section by means of them, and had hemmed it in with his army, he entrusted the fighting by sea to Baltaoglou, a brave man, experienced in all sorts of maritime enterprises, and a skilled commander, whom he appointed Admiral of the whole fleet, and of all the shore, both Asiatic and European. He was the governor of Gallipoli. This man blockaded the entire sea-wall with his ships, from the Golden Gate at the corner as far as the Neorion region of Galata, a distance of just about forty-three stadia. The blockade included the chain and the fighting-ships and galleons anchored by it.

122. It was at this chain that he attacked daily, and he pushed the fighting, being desirous of forcing an entrance into the harbor, so that he might carry the battle to the whole of the wall along the Horn.

123. The entire circuit of the City as besieged by the army by land and sea, carefully calculated, was about 126 stadia; of this, only the wall along the Horn, inside the chain, was unguarded—35 stadia; all the rest was defended.

124. Having done all this, the Sultan summoned the cannon-makers and spoke to them about the cannon and the walls, and about how the wall could most easily be demolished. They assured him it would be easy to demolish it if, in addition to the guns they already had (for they already had some others, made earlier), they should construct one more, which, they believed, would be strong enough to batter down and destroy the wall. For this, heavy expense was needed, to purchase both a large amount of brass and many other materials.

Statement as to the Construction of the Cannon, and as to Its Shape and Power

125. No sooner said than done. The Sultan immediately provided them in abundance with everything they needed, and so they constructed the cannon, a thing most fearsome to see and altogether unbelievable and hard to accept when one hears about it. I shall describe its construction, its appearance, and its power, as it really was.

126. Clay was mixed for many days, so as to make it very workable, made of the lightest, cleanest and finest earth. It was thoroughly mixed together and mingled with linen, hemp, and other such things combined and worked in, after having been chopped up fine, so as to form one body, continuous and inseparable.

127. Of this, a round model was constructed like a pipe, oblong, to be the core. The length of this was forty spans. Of this the forward half, for the

reception of the stone cannonball, was of twelve spans as the circle and circumference of its thickness; while the hinder half, or tail, for the reception of the substance called "fodder" was of four spans or slightly more, as the circumference of its thickness, in proportion, I believe, to the whole.

128. There was also another, an outer casing, made to receive this, altogether hollow, and like a scabbard, but wider, so as to fit over the core and leave some space between. And the space between the core and the casing, uniform throughout the whole length, was of one span, or a little more. It was to receive the bronze poured out from the crucible to form the body of the cannon. And this outer mold was made of the same clay, but was completely bound around and protected by iron and wood and earth and stones built up and reinforced from outside, so that the great weight of the bronze bearing down within, might not break it apart or spoil the form of the cannon.

129. Two furnaces were then built, very near to the mold, ready for the foundry, very strong and reliable, made on the inside with burnt brick and of clay well worked and hardened, and on the outside completely strengthened with immense stones, lime, and everything else suitable for this purpose.

130. Of bronze and tin an amount of great value and of great weight was cast into the foundries—in fact, 1500 talents, as was reported. Besides, a great quantity of charcoal and of tree-trunks was heaped up on the outside of the crucibles, above and below and all around, to such a depth as to hide the furnaces, all but their mouths.

131. Around them were bellows blowing violently and continuously, setting fire to the whole mass for three whole days and as many nights, until the bronze was entirely melted and dissolved, becoming liquid and fluid.

132. Then, when the mouths were opened, the bronze poured out through the conduits into the mold until the whole receptacle was completely full, and it covered the inner core entirely, and overflowed this by a cubit in height; and thus was the cannon completed. After that, when the bronze had cooled off and become cold, it was cleared of both the inner core and the outer casing, and being smoothed and polished by scrapers, it shone altogether. Such was the construction and the form of the cannon.

133. And now I will speak of its method of working. First, what is called "fodder" [powder] was put in, filling up tightly the rear compartment and cavity of the machine up to the opening of the second compartment which was to receive the stone cannonball. Then there was put in a huge rod of strongest wood, and this, pounded hard by iron bars, pressed down on the material inside, closing in and packing down the powder so completely that, whatever happened, nothing could force it out in any way except by an explosion.

134. Then they brought the stone also, pushing it in until they used the rod and fitted the stone in snugly on all sides.

135. After this, having pointed the cannon toward whatever it was intended to hit, and having leveled it by certain technical means and calculations toward the target, they brought up great beams of wood and laid them underneath and fitted them carefully. On these they placed immense stones, weighting it down and making it secure above and below and behind and everywhere, lest by the force of the velocity and by the shock of the movement of its own emplacement, it should be displaced and shoot wide of its mark.

136. Then they set fire to it through the short hole behind, igniting the powder. And when this took fire, quicker than it takes to say it, there was a fearful roar first, and a shaking of the earth beneath and for a long way off, and a noise such as never was heard before. Then, with an astounding thunder and a frightful crashing and a flame that lit up all the surroundings and then left them black, the rod, forced out from within by a dry hot blast of air, violently set in motion the stone as it came out. And the stone, borne with tremendous force and velocity, hit the wall, which it immediately shook and knocked down, and was itself broken into many fragments and scattered, hurling the pieces everywhere and killing those who happened to be nearby.

137. Sometimes it demolished a whole section, and sometimes a half-section, and sometimes a larger or smaller section of a tower or turret or battlement. And there was no part of the wall strong enough or resistant enough or thick enough to be able to withstand it, or to wholly resist such force and such a blow of the stone cannonball.

138. Such was the unbelievable and inconceivable nature of the power of this implement. Such a thing, the ancients, whether kings or generals, neither had nor knew about. Had they possessed it, nothing could have withstood them at all, nor stood up against them in their sieges; nor would it have been difficult for them to topple over and destroy walls. Even the best fortified of them would have offered no obstacle. They built walls, and dug entrenchments, and mined under the earth, and did all sorts of other things so as to secure possession of cities and capture forts, but all these would have surrendered quicker than it takes to tell it, if shattered and overthrown by these machines. But they had none.

139. This is a new invention of the Germans or Kelts, about a hundred fifty years ago or a little more—a very wise and ingenious invention. Especially the composition and formation of "fodder," which is a combination of the very warmest and driest forms of nitre, sulphur, carbon, and herbs, making a dry and warm gas, which, being enclosed in the impervious, strong, compact body of the bronze and not having any other exit of any sort anywhere except this one, is impelled by the explosion and force from within and gives so great and powerful a force to the stone ball. But it also frequently causes the bursting of the bronze as well. Now no ancient name is found for this machine, unless someone may speak of it as the battering-ram or the propeller. But in common

language everybody today calls it an apparatus. Such are the details about the cannon, as far as we have been able to learn from those who could inform us.

140. Sultan Mehmed, since the makers of the cannon had completed them successfully, ordered them to bring the cannon near the walls. Over against the Middle Wall where he had his camp, and where his tent was, he ordered them to set up three of them, chosen as the largest and most powerful, and to bombard and shake the wall at that point. He ordered the others to be brought up against portions of the wall here and there, choosing the most vulnerable and weakest parts of the walls. For he judged it best to attack the wall at many points, so that, after he had begun the battle in several places, the capture of it would prove easier and more facile for him, as indeed it turned out to be.

141. And the cannon, on being brought up to the wall, shook it to pieces and toppled it down as they were expected to.

142. Then the Sultan filled up the moat in front of the cannon, bringing up stones and wood and earth and collecting every other sort of material so that when the wall was battered down and had fallen, the way should be easier for the heavy infantry, and their approach and attack facilitated. And he ordered the sappers to dig underneath the wall, and to dig subterranean galleries in toward the City, so that the heavy infantry might get in secretly by night through these. This work also went forward, but later he deemed this superfluous and a useless expenditure, since the cannon were accomplishing everything ...

147. Now the Romans [Byzantines] and Giustinianni, seeing the City wall so severely battered and damaged by the guns, both within and without, extended great beams from above the wall, and let down bales of wool on ropes, and placed with them other similar things so as to break the force of the stone balls as much as possible and lighten the effect.

148. But since this proved of use only a short time and accomplished nothing worth mentioning inasmuch as the cannon were piercing and scattering everything and demolishing the wall—for already a large part of the lesser outer wall had fallen and also two towers and a turret of the main wall—they devised another thing. They brought up huge stakes and made a palisade along the damaged part of the wall—that is, on its outer side—fastening the stakes securely together. In addition they brought a quantity of all kinds of stones and wood, bundles of brushwood and branches and reeds and many other bushes of all sorts, putting them together in bundles and so raising the stockade higher. There were also screens, made of skins and hides, put over the wood of the palisade so that it should not be injured by the firebrand arrows. They thus had a fine shelter against the enemy, and a strengthening of the palisade from within, which was in place of a wall. Moreover the stone ball, hurled with great force, fell and was buried in the soft and yielding earth, and did not make a breach by striking against hard and unyielding materials.

149. On the top of the palisade and of the earthworks were placed rows of wooden containers filled with earth, to act as breastworks for the fighters in the forefront and as a protection so that they should not be hit by the arrows.

First Assault Attempted by the Sultan against the Wall, and Its Failure

150. When Sultan Mehmed returned from the fortresses, he believed he could after a few days try an assault on the City at the points where the wall had been broken through. Therefore, taking the heavy infantry and the bowmen and javelin-men and all the imperial foot-guards, he made a vigorous attack on the wall. The moat was already filled up, so the foot-soldiers, with shout and battle cry, quickly crossed it and assaulted the wall. First they tried to set fire to the gate, so as to burn the stockade and spread confusion and panic among their opponents in the fight.

151. But since this did not succeed as they had hoped, because the men who were stationed at the top of the stockade fought finely and put out the fire, they changed to another plan. Fastening hooks on the ends of their spears, they pulled down from above the wooden containers and thus stripped the defenders of their shelter. These containers had served them like the crenellations of a wall, but now the archers and slingers and javelin-hurlers could easily attack the undefended enemy. Others brought ladders and put them up against the wall and tried to climb up them while the cannon fired stones frequently against the defenders and did considerable damage.

152. Giustinianni and his men (for they and a considerable number of the Romans also, had been detailed to the damaged part of the wall), since they were fully armored, sustained no injury from the arrows or other missiles. Instead, they stoutly resisted, fighting bravely and using every measure to withstand and frustrate whatever their opponents did. At last the Romans and Giustinianni prevailed and repulsed them, though not without difficulty, and drove them from the wall, wounding many of them and killing not a few.

153. Other attacks were made daily, here and there, on the wall, especially where it had been demolished. During these attacks the defenders in the City were by no means worsted, but fought vigorously and resisted bravely.

154. Baltaoglou ... sailed to the harbor where the other galleys were drawn up. On the second or third day he received an order from the Sultan to make careful preparation and collect his ships and join battle with the galleons and galleys that were guarding the mouth of the harbor and the chain, so as to force an entrance if he could. The Sultan had determined by all means to get the harbor and the Horn under his control so that he might attack the City from all sides, by land and by sea, for he thought (as was true) that if he could make an opening in the sea-wall as well, the capture of the City would be easier for

him, since the defenders were insufficient for the entire circuit, they being few and the circuit great.

Attack of Baltaoglou against the Vessels at the Entrance to the Harbor, and at the Chain; the Great Sea-battle

155. Having put all the ships in good condition and fully armed them, and the fighting men with them, Baltaoglou attacked the galleons and the chain with great force, fury, and vigor, and with shouts and battle cries. And first, having slowed down the ships, when they were about a bowshot from the enemy, they attacked from afar, firing on them and being fired upon with arrows and with great stone balls from the guns. Then he furiously attacked the center of the fleet. Of the heavy infantry on the decks, some carried fire in their hands with the purpose of setting fire to the ships. Others hurled flaming arrows, while others tried to cut the ropes of the anchors, and still others attempted to board the ships, climbing up by grappling-hooks and ladders. Others with javelins and pikes and long spears attacked the defenders. Their attack and their zeal for the task were very great.

156. Now those on the large galleons had already been prepared for such attack by the Grand Duke, who had been placed in command over the ships as well as of the sea-walls of the City; so, fighting from a higher position, and hurling down on the attackers stones, javelins, spears and pikes, especially from the crowsnests at the top of the masts, they succeeded in wounding many, and killed not a few. Furthermore they brought great jars of water to put out the fires, and heavy stones which they let fall, tied by ropes, and thus did a great deal of damage.

157. There was the greatest zeal on both sides, and energy too, the attackers determined to prevail and to force their way in while the defenders were bound to fight their best to guard the harbor and the ships and drive off the enemy. At last the crews of the galleons, fighting magnificently, turned the flank of the attackers and drove them off, having proved themselves valiant men to the very end.

The Invention of Another and Newer Sort of Cannon

158. Sultan Mehmed, seeing that he had been repulsed in this attack, set himself to discover another sort of machine. Hence, calling the makers of the cannon, he demanded of them whether it was not possible to fire cannon-balls at the galleons fighting at the entrance to the harbor, and sink them there. They replied that they were unable to do this, especially because the walls of Galata were in the way at every point. He then showed them another way to do this by a new

form of cannon. For, he said, if they were willing, it was possible to construct a different sort of gun with a slightly changed design that could fire the stone to a great height, so that when it came down it would hit the ships amidships and sink them. He said that they must first aim it and level it, getting the measures by mathematical calculation, and then fire on the galleons. Thus he explained to them his plan.

159. When they had reasoned out the scheme, they decided it was possible. So they constructed a cannon of this type, as designed by the Sultan, and after a careful survey of the land, they placed it a little beyond the point of Galata on a slight elevation opposite the galleons. Then having aimed it with care, and after leveling it by a special design, they fired it by applying a live coal to it. It shot the stone up to a great height, but as this first stone descended, it missed the ships, falling into the sea quite near them. However, when they had immediately corrected the error by changing the aim a little, they fired again, and this stone went to an immense height and came down with tremendous crash and velocity, striking the galleon in the center. It immediately crushed it completely and sank it in the depths, killing some of those on board immediately and drowning others. The very few who were not killed swam with difficulty to the other galleons and galleys nearby.

160. This unexpected event frightened all those in the City, and threw them into the greatest terror and anguish. Nonetheless, since this was the only possible safe step, the rest of the galleons and galleys were retired a short distance to a safer place, and a guard was set. Thus they suffered no further injury from the cannon-balls, but strongly guarded the harbor and the Horn.

...

A Surprising Plan and Decision

172. Sultan Mehmed considered it necessary in preparation for his next move to get possession of the harbor and open the Horn for his own ships to sail in. So, since every effort and device of his had failed to force the entrance, he made a wise decision, and one worthy of his intellect and power. It succeeded in accomplishing his purpose and in putting an end to all uncertainties.

173. He ordered the commanders of the vessels to construct as quickly as possible glideways leading from the outer sea to the inner sea, that is, from the harbor to the Horn, near the place called Diplokion, and to cover them with beams. This road, measured from sea to sea, is just about eight stadia. It is very steep for more than half the way, until you reach the summit of the hill, and from there again it descends to the inner sea of the Horn. And as the glideways were completed sooner than expected, because of the large number of workers, he brought up the ships and placed large cradles under them, with stays against

each of their sides to hold them up. And having under-girded them well with ropes, he fastened long cables to the corners and gave them to the soldiers to drag, some of them by hand, and others by certain machines and capstans.

174. So the ships were dragged along very swiftly. And their crews, as they followed them, rejoiced at the event and boasted of it. Then they manned the ships on the land as if they were on the sea. Some of them hoisted the sails with a shout, as if they were setting sail, and the breeze caught the sails and bellied them out. Others seated themselves on the benches, holding the oars in their hands and moving them as if rowing. And the commanders, running along by the sockets of the masts with whistlings and shouting, and with their whips beating the oarsmen or the benches, ordered them to row. The ships, borne along over the land as if on the sea, were some of them being pulled up the ascent to the top of the hill while others were being hauled down the slope into the harbor, lowering the sails with shouting and great noise.

175. It was a strange spectacle, and unbelievable in the telling except to those who actually did see it—the sight of ships borne along on the mainland as if sailing on the sea, with their crews and their sails and all their equipment. I believe this was a much greater feat than the cutting of a canal across at Athos by Xerxes, and much stranger to see and to hear about. Furthermore, this event of but yesterday, before our very eyes, makes it easier to believe that the other also actually happened, for without this one, the other would have seemed a myth and sounded like idle talk.

176. Thus, then, there was assembled in the bay called Cold Waters, a little beyond Galata, a respectable fleet of some sixty-seven vessels. They were moored there.

177. The Romans, when they saw such an unheard-of thing actually happen, and warships lying at anchor in the Horn—which they never would have suspected—were astounded at the impossibility of the spectacle, and were overcome by the greatest consternation and perplexity. They did not know what to do now, but were in despair. In fact they had left unguarded the walls along the Horn for a distance of about thirty stadia, and even so they did not have enough men for the rest of the walls, either for defense or for attack, whether citizens or men from elsewhere. Instead, two or even three battlements had but a single defender.

178. And now, when this sea-wall also became open to attack and had to be guarded, they were compelled to strip the other battlements and bring men there. This constituted a manifest danger, since the defenders were taken away from the rest of the wall while those remaining were not enough to guard it, being so few.

179. Not only was there this difficulty, but, the bridge being completed, heavy infantry and bowmen could cross against the wall. Hence that part also

had to be guarded. And the ships near the mouth of the harbor and at the chain, galleons and galleys alike, as well as the other ships in the harbor had the greater need to be on guard since now they were subject to attack from within as well as from outside. Therefore in many directions they appeared to have, and actually had, difficulties. Still, they did not neglect anything that could be done.

180. Giustinianni removed one of his galleons from the mouth of the harbor plus three of the Italian galleys, and took them against the end of the gulf where the Sultan's ships were anchored. There he anchored so as to fight from them and prevent the [Ottoman] warships from going out anywhere in the gulf or being able to do any harm to the harbor or its shipping. This he thought was the best plan as a counter-measure. But it was only a temporary expedient.

181. For Sultan Mehmed, seeing this, made the following counter-moves: He ordered the cannon-makers to transfer the cannon secretly by night and place them near the shore, opposite to where the ships and the galleon were moored, and fire stones at them. This they did with great speed, and they hit one of the galleys in the middle and sank it with all on board, excepting a very few who swam to the other galleys. Then the crews quickly moved the ships away a good distance, and anchored there. If this had not been done quickly, the other galleys also would have been sunk, with their crews, as well as the galleon, for they seemed to have had no sense at all of their danger. They were thus very near to destruction, for the cannon were ready to fire the stone balls at them.

182. But when this failed, the Romans had nothing else they could do. They simply fired at the ships from the walls with catapults and javelins and prevented them from moving about. And from the galleys at the mouth of the harbor some attacked them every day and chased them back and prevented their injuring anything in the harbor. And they often pursued them till near the land, toward their own men. Then these ships would again turn and attack the galleys, and men would follow on foot, firing and being fired on, and so they had long-range exchanges daily.

Of Some Marvels

183. During those same days there occurred the following divine signs and portents of the terrors that were very soon to come to the city. Three or four days before the battle, when all the people in the City were holding a religious procession, men and women together, and marching around with the Icon of the Mother of God, this latter slipped suddenly from the hands of its bearers without any cause or power being apparent, and fell flat on the ground. And when everybody shouted immediately, and rushed to raise up the icon, it sank down as if weighted with lead, and as if fastened to the ground, and became well-nigh impossible to raise. And so it continued for a considerable time, until,

by a great effort and much shouting and prayers by all, the priests and its bearers barely managed to raise it up and place it on the shoulders of the men.

184. This strange occurrence filled everyone with much terror and very great agony and fear, for they thought this fall was no good omen—as was quite true. Later, when they had gone on but a short distance, immediately after that, at high noon, there was much thunder and lightning with clouds, and a violent rain with severe hail followed, so that they could neither stand against it nor make any progress. The priests and the bearers of the icon and the crowds that followed were depressed and hindered by the force of the waters that flowed down and by the might of the hail. Many of the children following were in danger of being carried away and drowned by the violent and powerful rush of water, had not some men quickly seized them and with some difficulty dragged them out of the flood. Such was the unheard-of and unprecedented violence of that storm and hail which certainly foreshadowed the imminent loss of all, and that, like a torrent of fiercest waters, it would carry away and annihilate everything.

Still Another Portent

185. Such, then, were the events of the first day. On the next day in the morning a dense fog covered the whole city, lasting from early morning till evening. This evidently indicated the departure of the Divine Presence, and its leaving the City in total abandonment and desertion, for the Divinity conceals itself in cloud and appears and again disappears. So then, this happened thus and let no one disbelieve, for there were many witnesses of these things, observers who were both visitors and dwellers in the City.

186. For Sultan Mehmed, then, all went well. There was as yet no hindrance, for both the inner wall and the outer one had been wrecked to the ground by the cannon; the whole moat was filled up; the Horn and all the wall along its shores had been opened up for battle by brilliant tactics; and the siege was complete all around the City, with ladders, wooden towers, and all the rest well prepared. And the siege had lasted quite a while, for nearly fifty days had passed. But there was fear lest something might happen, or that help might appear by sea from somewhere. The Sultan had already heard that a convoy of ships had arrived in Chios, so he knew he had better not delay any longer or wait further, but should join battle quickly and try to capture the City with all speed and with all his force, by an attack by land and sea, and make this greatest and final attempt on it.

187. So he called together all the high officers and those in his entourage, namely: the governors, generals, cavalry officers, majors and captains, the captains over a thousand, over a hundred, and over fifty, and the sub-officers of his soldiers and the cavalry of his body-guard; also besides these, the captains of

the heavy transports and of the galleys, and the Admiral of the whole fleet; and he made the following speech.

Second Address of the Sultan, Calling upon All to Fight Bravely, and Promising Them that They Would Be Rewarded with Goods and Many Other Fine Things, If They Fought Well

188. "My friends and my comrades in the present struggle! I have called you together here, not because I would accuse you of any laziness or carelessness in this business, nor try to make you more eager in the present struggle. For a long time past I have noted some of you showing such zeal and earnestness for the work that you would willingly undergo everything necessary rather than leave here without accomplishing it, and others of you not only zealous themselves but even inciting the rest with all their might to redouble their efforts.

189. "So it is not for this that I have called you together, but simply in order to remind you, first of all, that whatever you have at present you have attained, not by sloth and carelessness, but by hard work and with great struggles and dangers together with us, and these things are yours as the rewards of your own valor and manliness rather than as gifts of fortune. And secondly, as to the rewards now put before you here, I wish to show you how many and how great they are and what great glory and honor accompany the winning. And I also wish that you may know well how to carry on the struggle for the very highest rewards.

190. "First, then, there is great wealth of all sorts in this city, some in the royal palaces and some in the houses of the mighty, some in the homes of the common people and still other, finer and more abundant, laid up in the churches as votive offerings and treasures of all sorts, constructed of gold and silver and precious stones and costly pearls. Also there is countless wealth of magnificent furniture, without reckoning all the other articles and furnishings of the houses. Of all these, you will be the masters!

191. "Then too, there are very many noble and distinguished men, some of whom will be your slaves, and the rest will be put up for sale; also very many and very beautiful women, young and good-looking, and virgins lovely for marriage, noble, and of noble families, and even till now unseen by masculine eyes, some of them, evidently intended for the weddings of great men. Of these, some will be wives for you, while others will do for servants, and others you can sell. So you will gain in many ways, in enjoyment, and service, and wealth.

192. "And you will have boys, too, very many and very beautiful and of noble families.

193. "Further, you will enjoy the beauty of the churches and public buildings and splendid houses and gardens, and many such things, suited to look at and enjoy and take pleasure in and profit by. But I must not waste time listing all

these. A great and populous city, the capital of the ancient Romans, which has attained the very pinnacle of good fortune and luck and glory, being indeed the head of the whole inhabited globe—I give it now to you for spoil and plunder—unlimited wealth, men, women, children, all the other adornments and arrangements. All these you will enjoy as if at a brilliant banquet, and will be happy with them yourselves and will leave very great wealth to your children.

194. "And the greatest of all is this, that you will capture a city whose renown has gone out to all parts of the world. It is evident that to whatever extent the leadership and glory of this city has spread, to a like extent the renown of your valor and bravery will spread for having captured by assault a city such as this. But think: what deed more brilliant, what greater enjoyment, or what inheritance of wealth better than that presented to you, along with honor and glory!

195. "And, best of all, we shall demolish a city that has been hostile to us from the beginning and is constantly growing at our expense and in every way plotting against our rule. So for the future we shall be sure of guarding our present belongings and shall live in complete and assured peace, after getting rid of our neighboring enemies. We shall also open the way to further conquest.

196. "You must never imagine that, although this is all true, the City is impregnable or its wall hard to approach and difficult to pierce, or that very great danger awaits those who attack it, as if it were not easily to be taken. Lo, as you can see, the moat has all been filled up and the land-wall at three points has been so broken down that not only heavy and light infantry like yourselves, but even the horses and heavily armed cavalry can easily penetrate it. Thus I do not offer you an impregnable wall, but a wide plain fit for cavalry for you to cross with your weapons.

197. "And what should I say about our opponents? There are very few of them, and most of these are unarmed and inexperienced in war. For, as I have learned from deserters, they say that there are but two or three men defending a tower, and as many more in the space between towers. Thus it happens that a single man has to fight and defend three or four battlements, and he, too, either altogether unarmed or badly armed.

198. "How then can they do anything against such a multitude as we are? And especially since we are fighting by relays, and new troops are constantly coming into the fray, so that our men have time to indulge in sleep and food and to rest themselves, while they on the other hand fight continuously, without intermission, and desperately, and have no time to snatch sleep or food or drink or rest, since we are attacking in battle and forcing the fighting. Now we shall no longer merely use skirmishes and sallies, or simple attacks and feints, as we did at first—and as they anticipate—but once we have begun to fight, the battle will be continuous and uninterrupted, night and day, without any rest or armistice until all is up with them. Therefore I think these men, under the

constraint of continuous fighting and of distress and starvation and sleeplessness, will easily yield to us.

199. "And as for such Italians as are stationed on the ruined wall, if any think these are seasoned veterans able to defend themselves against the attackers, as though they were well armed and experienced in battle, especially behind fortifications, I, at least, believe the opinion of such persons altogether incredible and mistaken.

200. "In the first place, being intelligent men, they will not be willing to fight on behalf of the goods of others, or suffer and expose themselves to evident risks when they have nothing to gain for themselves. And besides, they are a motley crew, coming from here and there and thinking simply of getting something and going back home in safety, not of dying in battle. For the present they do actually bear it and keep on, because we have been bombarding and attacking only at intervals, and they think that in future also we will go at it as if in child's play.

201. "But when they see the battle rolling in on them, and brilliantly and relentlessly pressed on every side, and death imminent before their eyes, then I am perfectly sure they will not hesitate at all, but will throw away their weapons, turn their backs, and flee, and never turn around. And there will be nothing to deter them or give them courage at all.

202. "But even if by some means they should stand firm, so be it! We will still easily put them to flight by our might and experience and daring. Thus even in that case I do not in the least think we have any good reason at all for worry. All things go to show that victory is on our side, and that we shall capture the City. As you see, it is entirely surrounded, as if in a net, by land and sea; and it cannot finally escape our arms and our grasp.

203. "Then be brave yourselves and urge all the men under you to follow you bravely, and to use all zeal and diligence in the task, in the belief that there are three elements in good fighting: the will to fight, a realization of what is and is not honorable, and obedience to authority. Know that this obedience involves each keeping his own position and going to the attack quietly and in good order so that one can quickly hear the commands given and pass them on to the rest: when they must advance silently, to be silent, when they must shout and yell, to do so with fearsome yells. For while many of these things are wise in every sort of fighting, they are not the least so in battles at the walls. As for the rest, order them all to do everything well and in good order and discipline.

204. "So then, fight bravely and worthily of yourselves and of those who have fought before you; and do not weaken, for you see how much hangs on this struggle, and do not allow any of your men to do so either. I myself will be in the van of the attack [applause by all the gathering]. Yes, I myself will lead the attack, and will be fighting by your side and will watch to see what each one of you does.

205. "Go back, then, each one to his post and his tent, have your supper and rest yourselves. Give like orders to the men in your commands. Then be up early and get your divisions in good order and well arranged, paying no attention to anything outside and listening to no one else. And let the ranks keep silent. But when you hear the battle-cry and see the signal, then get to your jobs!

Position and Orders Given the Generals

206. "You, then, Hamza, sail with your ships along the sea-walls, have some of the ships lie to within shooting range, and order the archers and those who have crossbows in their hands, and muskets, to fire from the decks against the battlements so continuously that no one may lean out at all, nor have a chance to attack in the battle. And run some of the ships aground, if it seems advantageous, by the wall. Then have the men in charge bring out the ladders, and let the infantry try to scale the wall. So fight bravely and show yourself to be a hero.

207. "And you yourself, Zaganos, cross the bridge quickly and attack the Golden Horn wall very vigorously. Take with you the ships inside the harbor, which are assigned to you for this purpose, and be a hero!

208. "Now too you, Karaja, take your men and cross the moat and attack the ruined part of the wall just in front of you. Stoutly hurling back the defenders, try to scale the wall, struggling manfully, like a hero.

209. "And you also, Ishak and Mahmud, cross the moat safely with your own divisions and try to scale the wall with ladders. Have the archers and cannoneers and musketeers shoot incessantly at those on the battlements, so that they may be the least possible hindrance to your attack.

210. "Lastly you, Halil and Saraja, have your troops close ranks on both sides and fight. When you see me struggling and trying to climb up the ruined parts of the wall and forcing the Italians back and opening access for my men into the City, do your utmost on both sides to check those drawn up opposite you, attacking them strongly, so that being given no respite by you they may be less able to pay attention to us, and wholly unable to help those hard pressed by us.

211. "So much for the present. I myself will take care of all the rest. Therefore go back now to your tents and to your troops, and good luck to you! Eat, and drink, and rest."

212. Having said this much, he dismissed the assembly. Each man went to his own troops and tents, and the Sultan himself, after his evening meal, went to rest.

213. Rising at dawn, he first called the gunners and ordered them to make the guns ready and aim them at the wrecked parts of the wall, so that when the time came they might fire on the defenders there.

214. Afterward he summoned the cavalry and infantry of his guard—I mean the heavy infantry and shield-bearers and archers and all the royal guard—and grouped them effectively by bands, masses, groups, and companies, by thousands and sometimes in larger numbers. He ordered them to fight in shifts, when their turns came. Some were to fight and do battle while others took food and sleep and rested so that they might be refreshed and renewed for the struggle. Then those should replace the others, and that thus, with one division constantly succeeding another and with periods of rest, the battle should go on incessantly and continuously, so as to allow their opponents no respite or relaxation in the fight. He also appointed a place for each, and a time and a regular order, and commanded them how and where and when to make their best effort.

215. Then the Sultan mounted his horse and went around to all the other divisions, reviewing them and giving his orders to all in general and each in particular. He encouraged them and stirred them up for the battle, especially the officers of the troops, calling each one by name. Then, having passed along the entire army, along the wall from sea to sea, and having given the necessary orders and encouraged and incited all for the fight, and having urged them to play the man, he ordered them to have their food and rest until the battle-cry should be given and they should see the signal. And after doing all this, he went back to his tent, had his meal, and rested.

216. Now the Romans, seeing the army so quiet and more tranquil than usual, marveled at the fact and ventured on various explanations and guesses. Some—not judging it aright—thought this was a preparation for withdrawal. Others—and this proved correct—believed that it was a preparation for battle and an alert, things which they had been expecting in the near future. So they passed the word along and then went in silence to their own divisions and made all sorts of preparations.

217. The hour was already advanced, the day was declining and near evening, and the sun was at the Ottomans' backs but shining in the faces of their enemies. This was just as the Sultan had wished; accordingly he gave the order first for the trumpets to sound the battle-signal, and their instruments, the pipes and flutes and cymbals too, as loud as they could. All the trumpets of the other divisions, with the other instruments in turn, sounded all together, a great and fearsome sound. Everything shook and quivered at the noise. After that, the standards were displayed.

218. To begin, the archers and slingers and those in charge of the cannon and the muskets, in accord with the commands given them, advanced against the wall slowly and gradually. When they got within bowshot, they halted to fight. And first they exchanged fire with the heavier weapons, with arrows from the archers, stones from the slingers, and iron and leaden balls from the cannon and muskets. Then, as they closed with battleaxes and javelins and spears, hurling

them at each other and being hurled at pitilessly in rage and fierce anger. On both sides there was loud shouting and blasphemy and cursing. Many on each side were wounded, and not a few died. This kept up till sunset, a space of about two or three hours.

219. Then, with fine insight, the Sultan summoned the shield-bearers, heavy infantry and other troops and said: "Go to it, friends and children mine! It is time now to show yourselves good fighters!" They immediately crossed the moat, with shouts and fearful yells, and attacked the outer wall. All of it, however, had been demolished by the cannon. There were only, stockades of great beams instead of a wall, and bundles of vine-branches, and jars full of earth. At that point a fierce battle ensued close in and with the weapons of hand-to-hand fighting. The heavy infantry and shield-bearers fought to overcome the defenders and get over the stockade, while the Romans and Italians tried to fight these off and to guard the stockade. At times the infantry did get over the wall and the stockade, pressing forward bravely and unhesitatingly. And at times they were stoutly forced back and driven off.

220. The Sultan followed them up, as they struggled bravely, and encouraged them. He ordered those in charge of the cannon to put the match to the cannon. And these, being set off, fired their stone balls against the defenders and worked no little destruction on both sides, among those in the near vicinity.

221. So, then, the two sides struggled and fought bravely and vigorously. Most of the night passed, and the Romans were successful and prevailed not a little. Also, Giustinianni and his men kept their positions stubbornly, and guarded the stockade and defended themselves bravely against the aggressors.

222. And the other generals and officers with their own troops, and particularly the admiral of the fleet, also attacked the wall by land and sea and fought vigorously. The archers shot arrows from their bows, others fired cannon, and others brought up ladders and bridges and wooden towers and all sorts of machines to the walls. Some of them tried to climb up the wall by main force, especially where Zaganos and Karaja were in command.

223. Zaganos had crossed the bridge in safety, and brought ladders and bridges up to the wall. He then tried to force the heavy infantry to climb up, leaving with him the archers and musketeers from the ships inside the harbor. These fired from the decks fiercely, attacking the left flank of those who were on the fortifications as the ships sailed by.

224. Karaja crossed the moat and bravely attacked, attempting to get through inside the demolished wall.

225. But the Romans on their part met them stubbornly and repulsed them brilliantly. They fought bravely and proved superior to the Ottomans in battle. Indeed they showed that they were heroes, for not a one of all the things that occurred could deter them: neither the hunger attacking them, nor sleeplessness,

nor continuous and ceaseless fighting, nor wounds and slaughter, nor the death of relatives before their very eyes, nor any of the other fearful things could make them give in, or diminish their previous zeal and determination. They valiantly kept on resisting as before, through everything, until evil and pitiless fortune betrayed them.

226. Sultan Mehmed saw that the attacking divisions were very much worn out by the battle and had not made any progress worth mentioning, and that the Romans and Italians were not only fighting stoutly but were prevailing in the battle. He was very indignant at this, considering that it ought not to be endured any longer. Immediately he brought up the divisions which he had been reserving for later on, men who were extremely well armed, daring and brave, and far in advance of the rest in experience and valor. They were the elite of the army: heavy infantry, bowmen, and lancers, and his own bodyguard, and along with them those of the division called Yenitsari [Janissaries].

227. Calling to them and urging them to prove themselves now as heroes, he led the attack against the wall, himself at the head until they reached the moat. There he ordered the bowmen, slingers, and musketeers to stand at a distance and fire to the right, against the defenders on the palisade and on the battered wall. They were to keep up so heavy a fire that those defenders would be unable to fight, or to expose themselves because of the cloud of arrows and other projectiles falling like snowflakes.

228. To all the rest, the heavy infantry and the shield-bearers, the Sultan gave orders to cross the moat swiftly and attack the palisade. With a loud and terrifying war-cry and with fierce impetuosity and wrath, they advanced as if mad. Being young and strong and full of daring, and especially because they were fighting in the Sultan's presence, their valor exceeded every expectation. They attacked the palisade and fought bravely without any hesitation. Needing no further orders, they knocked down the turrets which had been built out in front, broke the yardarms, scattered the materials that had been gathered, and forced the defenders back inside the palisade.

229. Giustinianni with his men, and the Romans in that section fought bravely with lances, axes, pikes, javelins, and other weapons of offense. It was a hand-to-hand encounter, and they stopped the attackers and prevented them from getting inside the palisade. There was much shouting on both sides—the mingled sounds of blasphemy, insults, threats, attackers, defenders, shooters, those shot at, killers and dying, of those who in anger and wrath did all sorts of terrible things. And it was a sight to see there: a hard fight going on hand-to-hand with great determination and for the greatest rewards, heroes fighting valiantly, the one party struggling with all their might to force back the defenders, get possession of the wall, enter the City, and fall upon the children and women and the treasures, the other party bravely agonizing to drive them

off and guard their possessions, even if they were not to succeed in prevailing and in keeping them.

230. Instead, the hapless Romans were destined finally to be brought under the yoke of servitude and to suffer its horrors although they battled bravely, and though they lacked nothing of willingness and daring in the contest, Giustinianni received a mortal wound in the breast from an arrow fired by a crossbow. It passed clear through his breastplate, and he fell where he was and was carried to his tent in a hopeless condition. All who were with him were scattered, being upset by their loss. They abandoned the palisade and wall where they had been fighting, and thought of only one thing—how they could carry him on to the galleons and get away safe themselves.

231. But the Emperor Constantine besought them earnestly, and made promises to them if they would wait a little while, till the fighting should subside. They would not consent, however, but taking up their leader and all their armor, they boarded the galleons in haste and with all speed, giving no consideration to the other defenders.

232. The Emperor Constantine forbade the others to follow. Then, though he had no idea what to do next—for he had no other reserves to fill the places thus left vacant, the ranks of those who had so suddenly deserted, and meantime the battle raged fiercely and all had to see to their own ranks and places and fight there—still, with his remaining Romans and his bodyguard, which was so few as to be easily counted, he took his stand in front of the palisade and fought bravely.

233. Sultan Mehmed, who happened to be fighting quite nearby, saw that the palisade and the other part of the wall that had been destroyed were now empty of men and deserted by the defenders. He noted that men were slipping away secretly and that those who remained were fighting feebly because they were so few. Realizing from this that the defenders had fled and that the wall was deserted, he shouted out: "Friends, we have the City! We have it! They are already fleeing from us! They can't stand it any longer! The wall is bare of defenders! It needs just a little more effort and the City is taken! Don't weaken, but on with the work with all your might, and be men and I am with you!"

Capture of the City

234. So saying, he led them himself. And they, with a shout on the run and with a fearsome yell, went on ahead of the Sultan, pressing on up to the palisade. After a long and bitter struggle they hurled back the Romans from there and climbed by force up the palisade. They dashed some of their foe down into the ditch between the great wall and the palisade, which was deep and hard to get out of, and they killed them there. The rest they drove back to the gate.

Death of Emperor Constantine

235. He had opened this gate in the great wall, so as to go easily over to the palisade. Now there was a great struggle there and great slaughter among those stationed there, for they were attacked by the heavy infantry and not a few others in irregular formation, who had been attracted from many points by the shouting. There the Emperor Constantine, with all who were with him, fell in gallant combat.

236. The heavy infantry were already streaming through the little gate into the City, and others had rushed in through the breach in the great wall. Then all the rest of the army, with a rush and a roar, poured in brilliantly and scattered all over the City. And the Sultan stood before the great wall, where the standard also was and the ensigns, and watched the proceedings. The day was already breaking.

Great Rush, and Many Killed

237. Then a great slaughter occurred of those who happened to be there: some of them were on the streets, for they had already left the houses and were running toward the tumult when they fell unexpectedly on the swords of the soldiers; others were in their own homes and fell victims to the violence' of the Janissaries and other soldiers, without any rhyme or reason; others were resisting, relying on their own courage; still, others were fleeing to the churches and making supplication—men, women, and children, everyone, for there was no quarter given.

238. The soldiers fell on them with anger and great wrath. For one thing, they were actuated by the hardships of the siege. For another, some foolish people had hurled taunts and curses at them from the battlements all through the siege. Now, in general they killed so as to frighten all the City, and to terrorize and enslave all by the slaughter.

Plunder of the City

239. When they had had enough of murder, and the City was reduced to slavery, some of the troops turned to the mansions of the mighty, by bands and companies and divisions, for plunder and spoil. Others went to the robbing of churches, and others dispersed to the simple homes of the common people, stealing, robbing, plundering, killing, insulting, taking and enslaving men, women, and children, old and young, priests, monks—in short, every age and class.

Here, Too, a Sad Tragedy

240. There was a further sight, terrible and pitiful beyond all tragedies: young and chaste women of noble birth and well to do, accustomed to remain at

home and who had hardly ever left their own premises, and handsome and lovely maidens of splendid and renowned families, till then unsullied by male eyes—some of these were dragged by force from their chambers and hauled off pitilessly and dishonorably.

241. Other women, sleeping in their beds, had to endure nightmares. Men with swords, their hands bloodstained with murder, breathing out rage, speaking out murder indiscriminate, flushed with all the worst things—this crowd, made up of men from every race and nation, brought together by chance, like wild and ferocious beasts, leaped into the houses, driving them out mercilessly, dragging, rending, forcing, hauling them disgracefully into the public highways, insulting them and doing every evil thing.

242. They say that many of the maidens, even at the mere unaccustomed sight and sound of these men, were terror-stricken and came near losing their very lives. And there were also honorable old men who were dragged by their white hair, and some of them beaten unmercifully. And well-born and beautiful young boys were carried off.

243. There were priests who were driven along, and consecrated virgins who were honorable and wholly unsullied, devoted to God alone and living for Him to whom they had consecrated themselves. Some of these were forced out of their cells and driven off, and others dragged out of the churches where they had taken refuge and driven off with insult and dishonor, their cheeks scratched, amid wailing and lamentation and bitter tears. Tender children were snatched pitilessly from their mothers, young brides separated ruthlessly from their newly-married husbands. And ten thousand other terrible deeds were done.

Plundering and Robbing of the Churches

244. And the desecrating and plundering and robbing of the churches—how can one describe it in words? Some things they threw in dishonor on the ground—icons and reliquaries and other objects from the churches. The crowd snatched some of these, and some were given over to the fire while others were torn to shreds and scattered at the crossroads. The last resting-places of the blessed men of old were opened, and their remains were taken out and disgracefully torn to pieces, even to shreds, and made the sport of the wind while others were thrown on the streets.

245. Chalices and goblets and vessels to hold the holy sacrifice, some of them were used for drinking and carousing, and others were broken up or melted down and sold. Holy vessels and costly robes richly embroidered with much gold or brilliant with precious stones and pearls were some of them given to the most wicked men for no good use, while others were consigned to the fire and melted down for the gold.

246. And holy and divine books, and others mainly of profane literature and philosophy, were either given to the flames or dishonorably trampled under foot. Many of them were sold for two or three pieces of money, and sometimes for pennies only, not for gain so much as in contempt. Holy altars were torn from their foundations and overthrown. The walls of sanctuaries and cloisters were explored, and the holy places of the shrines were dug into and overthrown in the search for gold. Many other such things they dared to do.

247. Those unfortunate Romans who had been assigned to other parts of the wall and were fighting there, on land and by the sea, supposed that the City was still safe and had not suffered reverses, and that their women and children were free—for they had no knowledge at all of what had happened. They kept on fighting lustily, powerfully resisting the attackers and brilliantly driving off those who were trying to scale the walls. But when they saw the enemy in their rear, attacking them from inside the City, and saw women and children being led away captives and shamefully treated, some were overwhelmed with hopelessness and threw themselves with their weapons over the wall and were killed, while others in utter despair dropped their weapons from hands already paralyzed, and surrendered to the enemy without a struggle, to be treated as the enemy chose.

Death of Orhan

248. Orhan, the uncle of the Sultan, of the Ottoman family, happened to be present there at the time and fighting on the wall with them [the Byzantines], for the Emperor Constantine had him in the City and was treating him with much respect and honor because of his hopes. Orhan had been a fugitive for a long time through fear of his brother who had tried to kill him. When he saw that the City was captured, he sought to save himself. At first he thought he would run away secretly, as if he were one of the army, because of his uniform and of his correct pronunciation [of Greek]. But as soon as he saw he was recognized and being pursued, he threw himself immediately from the wall and died. And the soldiers rushed up, cut off his head, and took it to the Sultan, for he had wished to see him quickly, dead or alive.

249. At this same time Hamza, Admiral of the fleet, when he saw the City already taken and the heavy infantry plundering it, quickly sailed up to the chain, cut it, and got inside the harbor. And of all the Roman ships which he found (for the Italian galleys and galleons had immediately put on all sail and made for the open sea), he sank some on the spot, and others he captured with all hands and ran them aground at what is called the Imperial Gate. When he found this still shut, he broke open the locks and bars and knocked down the gates.

250. Entering the City with his marines, he found there many of the Romans gathered and making a brave stand. The [Ottoman] land forces had not yet

reached that point, as they were plundering the rest of the City. Encountering these, he overcame them and killed them all, so that much blood flowed out of the gates. At that juncture the land army also arrived.

251. In the same way, the sea army streamed in victoriously through the other shore gates, smashing them and throwing them down. Thus the whole naval force, scattering through the whole City, turned to plunder, robbing everything in their way, and falling on it like a fire or a whirlwind, burning and annihilating everything, or like a torrent sweeping away and destroying all things. For they hunted out everything, more carefully than Datis is said to have done in Eretria. Churches, holy places, old treasuries, tombs, underground galleries, cisterns and hiding-places, caves and crannies were burst into. And they searched every other hidden place, dragging out into the light anybody or anything they found hidden.

252. Going into the largest church, that of the Holy Wisdom [Sancta Sophia], they found there a great crowd of men, women, and children taking refuge and calling upon God. Those they caught as in a net, and took them all in a body and carried them captives, some to the galleys and some to the camp.

Surrender of Galata to the Sultan

253. Upon this, the men of Galata, seeing the City already captured and plundered, immediately surrendered en masse to the Sultan so as to suffer no ills. They opened their gates to admit Zaganos and his troops, and these did them no harm.

254. The entire army, the land force and the marine, poured into the City from daybreak and even from early dawn until the evening. They robbed and plundered it, carrying all the booty into the camp and into the ships. But some, like thieves, stole some of the booty and secretly went out of the gates and off to their abodes. Thus the whole City was emptied and deserted, despoiled and blackened as if by fire. One might easily disbelieve that it had ever had in it a human dwelling or the wealth or properties of a city or any furnishing or ornament of a household. And this was true although the City had been so magnificent and grand. There were left only ruined homes, so badly ruined as to cause great fear to all who saw them.

Number of Romans Who Died in the Struggle, and of the Prisoners Taken

255. There died, of Romans and of foreigners, as was reported, in all the fighting and in the capture itself, all told, men, women, and children, well-nigh four thousand, and a little more than fifty thousand were taken prisoners, including about five hundred from the whole army.

Entry of the Sultan into the City, and His Seeing of It All, and His Grief

256. After this the Sultan entered the City and looked about to see its great size, its situation, its grandeur and beauty, its teeming population, its loveliness, and the costliness of its churches and public buildings and of the private houses and community houses and of those of the officials. He also saw the setting of the harbor and of the arsenals, and how skillfully and ingeniously they had everything arranged in the City—in a word, all the construction and adornment of it. When he saw what a large number had been killed, and the ruin of the buildings, and the wholesale ruin and destruction of the City, he was filled with compassion and repented not a little at the destruction and plundering. Tears fell from his eyes as he groaned deeply and passionately: "What a city we have given over to plunder and destruction!"

Sympathy

257. Thus he suffered in spirit. And indeed this was a great blow to us, in this one city, a disaster the like of which had occurred in no one of the great renowned cities of history, whether one speaks of the size of the captured City or of the bitterness and harshness of the deed. And no less did it astound all others than it did those who went through it and suffered, through the unreasonable and unusual character of the event and through the overwhelming and unheard-of horror of it.

90. SIEGE OF RHODES (1480)

Mehmed II gained his nickname "the Conqueror" by capturing Constantinople in 1453. But following this the sultan had more defeats against large targets than victory. In 1456 he was personally turned back from Belgrade by János Hunyadi, the town's citizens, and a motley crew of "peasant" crusaders led by a 70-year-old saint, Giovanni da Capistrano. And at Rhodes in 1480, with the sultan ailing in Constantinople (he would die the next year), the Ottoman Turkish army faced a formidable foe in the Knights Hospitaller who had held the island since 1306. The "official" account of the siege, Obsidionis Rhodiae urbis descriptio, *by Guillaume Caoursin, the Hospitallers' secretarius, was printed the year of the siege, and was quickly disseminated and widely read. But it is the letters sent by Pierre d'Aubusson, grand master of the Hospitallers, to Emperor Frederick III and Pope Sixtus IV announcing the victory that most poignantly recount a defense d'Aubusson prepared for, led, fought in, and was wounded at—several times in fact. Nowhere does d'Aubusson trumpet his own leadership or feats of bravery, although from Caoursin's account we know he could have. The Church recognized these, however, naming him*

Cardinal of All Asia in 1489. The letters are the same with only the addresses at their beginning altered slightly.

Source: trans. Kelly DeVries, from Pierre d'Aubusson, "Letter to Emperor Frederick III," in *Scriptorum rerum germanicarum*, vol. 2. (Berlin, 1602), pp. 306–09.

The master of the militia of Rhodes, having been preserved in their own city by a brilliant victory against the Turks, to Emperor Frederick III.

Most invincible and serene prince. It does not seem unusual that we should tell your majesty what happened during the siege of the city of Rhodes, with the Turks attacking and us defending, when that day of battle has ended in the glorious honor of the name of Christ. And we do not doubt that your imperial majesty will gain no small pleasure from this victory. The Turks had set up their camp around the city and diligently explored places to attack. They then began to shake and destroy the city on all parts with their bombards, and they soon showed us what they planned to do: by surrounding the city with bombards and mortars, to smash nine towers and boulevards, and strike and demolish the palace of the grand master. However, it seemed to be most opportune for them to fight and attack three sides of the city; and, in particular, it seemed the most promising to attack the tower on the mole of St. Nicholas, to complete their task, as they deemed this would place the city most easily under their control.

This fortification is located on the very end of the mole, which projects out into the sea to the north, as far as the port extends, and it aids sailors who can easily hold to it or sail from it, whatever they wish. On the west is the Oratory of St. Anthony, around 200 paces [meters] from the tower, with the sea in between. Having seen the advantage of such a location, the enemy eagerly did everything to bring it into their possession. At St. Anthony's they set up three huge bronze bombards, the size and power of which were incredible, and these fired stone balls nine palms in circumference [a caliber of approximately 70 cm or 27.5 inches] and aimed them at the tower. Indeed, it is wonderful to relate, most sad to see, that of this celebrated work, which seemed to have been most strong, a greater amount of the tower was destroyed, knocked down, and ruined after being hit daily by 300 stone balls. The enemy seeing this rejoiced in the destruction, filling the air with their shouts; however, these soon turned into sorrow. For we, worrying about the safety of the tower, seeing it a great and terrible ruin, ordered that the fortification be propped up. But it seemed too little, after such a great destruction. Instead, we decided not to rebuild the tower but to defend the mole of St. Nicholas. Therefore, with all vigilance, care and genius, and nearly a thousand laborers working day and night, the entire time digging a very deep ditch, and building a wooden fortification at the end of the mole with the tower in the middle, also on the foundations of the tower, we made the mole impregnable at no small cost. Then we placed a garrison of our most powerful soldiers in the ruins of the mole, within the fortifications and defences we had built. We also placed other garrisons of infantry to the west and east of the end of the mole. For there the wall ends and the sea is shallow, which is why it was necessary to watch and defend it, so that the Turks should not cross there, and attack us in the rear. On the walls of the city we ordered bombards to be placed, which would fire on them during an attack. And we prepared fire-pots to throw onto ships.

Encouraged by the ruins of the towers, twice the Turks attacked the tower. First, when they thought it easy to take, they attacked the tower with only a moderate force at dawn before the beginning of day, with *triremes* [war galleys] prepared for that purpose, and they fought. But our men, intent on the defence of the place, were constantly on watch. Thus victory eluded the enemy. And in this battle nearly 700 Turks were killed, as was indicated by deserters. Several days after the first repulse, they attacked the tower by sea with powerful and ingenious skill, and they shook the repairs and fortifications with bombard shot, and some were crushed. However, we rebuilt what had been destroyed with the greatest of speed.

The specially built war-galleys were completely armed, and ingeniously outfitted for battle. And there were also added certain heavy vessels (called *parendarias* in the vernacular) on which there were bombards and stones, that they might be set up on the tower and mole, which they believed they would capture, to engage, destroy and attack the city. They prepared certain *cymbas* (small, flat-bottom boats), from which some very energetic Turks easily landed on the mole and they built a bridge of marvelous skill, over which they could cross from St. Anthony's to the tower on the mole. But we, suspecting after the first attack what might occur, had worked fully day and night with all our strength and genius, had rebuilt walls and added fortifications. We had spared no serious expense, for we judged that there depended the safety of the city. Therefore, in the middle of the night on the thirteenth kalends of July [20 June], burning with a very fierce ardor, the Turks approached the tower with utmost silence and attacked on all sides with great impetus. But our ears were open, and we were not asleep. When the enemy was discovered, our guns fired their stones, our soldiers girded their swords, and crossbows and slings shot their projectiles from the tower and mole at the enemy. A great battle was fought from the middle of night all the way until the hour of ten. Many Turks, who landed onto the mole from the *cymbas* and *triremes* were butchered. The floating bridge, loaded with Turks, was broken by our gunfire, with those Turks on top drowned. Four of the *triremes* loaded with bombards and stones, and the sailors on them, were destroyed by the stones fired from our guns, and they were sunk. Ships were set on fire, which compelled them to retreat. The Turks who had landed on the mole were killed. Important men who led the Turks were killed in this battle; they were mourned by the army.

Some deserters who joined us after the battle confirmed that the Turks had suffered a great defeat, and that more than 2,500 had been killed.

When the Turks had lost hope of capturing the tower, they turned their labor, skill, strength, and every thought to attacking the city. Although the entire city was shaken and breached by their guns, with scarcely the original shape of the city remaining, they intended to attack most strongly that part of the walls looking to the east where the Jewish houses were enclosed, against that part leading to the tower of Italy. Therefore, they set up eight very large bombards to aim and shoot at the walls, firing stones of nine palms [around 70 centimeters] in circumference, which constantly hit the walls day and night. Also, the bombards and mortars placed around the city likewise fired stones, which fire likewise increased the terror and anguish. To avoid the mortar fire, we relocated the infirm, aged and women under arches, in niches and in many places within the city, with the result that few of them were killed by gunfire. They also set up other guns firing fire-arrows, and ballistae and catapults shot burning arrows which set fire to the buildings. For the care of the city we chose men experienced in doing so who extinguished with great care the flames caused by the arrows. Because of these preparations, the Rhodians were saved from many disasters. These impious ones attempted to approach the walls ingeniously hidden, digging intricate ditches, which they partly covered with wood and earth so that they approached the moat of the city under cover. They built defences in many places from which they shot arrows continually, and they harassed and fatigued us with couleuvrines, serpentines, and bombards. And they also thought it would help to fill that part of the moat near to the fortification that had been added to the wall [a *faussebraye* added by Pierre d'Aubusson shortly before the siege to strengthen the corner of the wall]. The tenacious enemy did not cease to collect stones and secretly throw them into the ditch, so that part of the moat might be filled up until it equalled the *faussebraye* and formed a pathway in the shape of a back, from which they could more easily enter the walls of the city. We, however, seeing their attempt, watched over the safety of the city, and throughout the town and castle repaired and armed fortifications and made ditches very diligently. The Turks, seeing this, turned in despair to the walls of the Jewish Quarter and elsewhere; and we made very strong defences and repairs across the breach caused by the Turks, fixing stakes of green wood into the ground, and covered them with roots and branches interlaced which, clinging together most tenaciously and firmly, withstood the power of their gunfire, and protected the breach so that the collapsed wall might prevent an easy descent into the city. And we filled our earthen defences with stakes and brushwood which protected our men and would be an obstacle to the Turks climbing up. We also prepared artificial fire and other incendiaries which might prove useful in repelling the attack of the Turks. Also, it was thought to empty that part of the moat which the Turks had filled with stones. But as that could not be done openly, we secretly made for ourselves an exit beneath the stones, and in secret brought them into the town. The Turks nearest the moat thought that the heap of stones had diminished and that their opportunity for an attack was lessening, unless they rapidly carried it out.

We performed these labors for 38 days; during that time around 3,500 huge stones were fired into the walls and the city. The Turks, seeing that the chance of their attacking the city was being taken away from them, accelerated making their preparations. And the day and night prior to the attack, even on the morning before the assault, the eight bombards aimed at the walls mentioned above fired huge stones battering the repairs made to the breach. The sentries, guards and those stationed on the walls were for the greater part killed, so that it was only with difficulty that one could climb the wall, unless hidden by the greatest stealth.

At the sound of a small bell the Turks descended and then ascended [into and out of the moat]. Nor was there time for us to repair the fortifications, since the bombard shot increased, so that in a short time around 300 stones had been fired. Once the bombard fire had ended, the Turks, at the signal of a shot from a mortar, which they had placed there the previous day, attacked quickly and with a great charge on the seventh kalends of August [26 July]. Their ascent up the walls was easy (as we said), more easily than we could climb up our ladders. At the highest places on our walls, having eradicated our soldiers who were stationed there (who were unable to resist that first attack), before our reinforcements could climb the ladders, the Turks placed their banners. The same thing was accomplished at the tower of Italy, the top also captured. The alarm was sounded everywhere, and vigorous hand-to-hand fighting began, fought with great strength. Suddenly, our men faced the enemy, on the right and left of the walls, fought them in the highest places, causing great confusion and preventing them from moving from the wall. On the four ladders there that they had placed to climb down into the Jewish Quarter, one broken by our order, we climbed up to the enemy, opposing them, and we protected and defended the place.

There were 2,000 very well armed Turks on top of the walls, crowded together with us and fighting hand-to-hand, who struggled by force of arms to drive us away. But by the persistence of the firm valor of our soldiers, we held on. Following those Turks who were already on the walls, was a huge number of Turks from their camp who filled the breach, the wall and the moat, so that it was impossible to see the ground. Deserters stated that 4,000 Turks had made the assault. Our men drove about 300 of the enemy who were on the walls into the Jewish Quarter, where they were killed to a man. In this conflict we raised the standard bearing the image of our most sacred Lord Jesus Christ, and that of our Religion [the Hospitallers], in the presence of the enemy. The battle was fought with great ferocity for two hours. Finally, the Turks, pressed, fatigued, terrified and wounded, turned their backs, and took to flight with such great haste that they became an impediment to one another, and added to their destruction. In the fight there fell about 3,500 Turks, whose corpses were found inside the city and upon the walls, in the moat, among the enemy's fortifications and in the sea, and which afterwards were burnt to prevent disease. The spoils of their corpses were taken by our men, who, following the fleeing Turks all the way to their camp on the plain, killed them vigorously and afterwards returned unharmed. In the battle many of our soldiers and officers were killed in the crowded midst of the enemy soldiers. We and our soldiers received many wounds. But, thanks to God, with a strong garrison placed on the walls, we returned home. Nor would it have happened without divine aid to avert such a calamity. For God (we do not doubt) sent aid from heaven, so that poor devout Christians might not be infected with Mohammed's filth. Hoping that they would capture the city, Turkish women had prepared ropes to bind the captives, and a large number of stakes to impale the living. For they decreed that all humans, men and women, above ten years of age were to be impaled, and those under ten led into captivity, compelling them to renounce their faith. And all possessions were made booty, the city reserved for the governing by the Turks. But frustrated in their nefarious hopes, they were killed like cattle. During these battles, with attacks made on different days, we prohibited their approaches, cleared out their ditches and defended what the city needed to be defended. Even the firing of guns into their army and places where they were (as Turkish deserters divulged) killed nine thousand. A large number were wounded, including several captains; both the *Germanus Balse* [who d'Aubusson is referring to is unknown; the second word might be a derivation of *pasha*] and a son-in-law of the sultan were killed. The fighting ended, the Turks having retreated from their siege-works to their camp, a short distance, where they loaded their possessions, equipment and guns on cargo ships, and, taking several days, transported them to Lycia. They took their treasury from the shores of Rhodes to an ancient city on the mainland. Thus conquered they retreated in ignominy.

May the Omnipotent God happily keep your imperial majesty in our prayers!

Given at Rhodes, 13 September, in the year of the Incarnation of our Redeemer 1480.

Your imperial majesty's humble servant,

Pierre d'Aubusson, master and consul of the Hospital of Jerusalem

E. FEATS OF BRAVERY

91. BATTLE OF MALDON (991)

The battle of Maldon, fought on 10 or 11 August 991, was a defeat for the men of Essex and their commander, Brythnoth, who had marched out from Maldon to meet a band

of Vikings who were preparing to attack the town. Sometime afterward, an anonymous poet penned a now fragmentary poem, The Battle of Maldon, *that tells of Brythnoth's fall and the subsequent last stand of his remaining retainers. In this final stage of the battle, excerpted here, the poet captures both the fury of such engagements and the spirit of determination that drew men into them.*

Source: trans. Michael Livingston, from *The Anglo-Saxon Minor Poems*, in *Anglo-Saxon Poetic Records: A Collective Edition*, vol. 6, ed. George Philip Krapp and Elliot Van Kirk Dobbie (New York: Columbia University Press, 1942), pp. 7–16.

Then they went forth, fears reckoned for naught.
The household's retainers harshly began to fight,
powerful spear-bearers, and they prayed God
that they might avenge their lord-friend,
and on their foes make full slaughter-work.
Them did the hostage eagerly start to help;
he was a Northumbrian, of a hard people:
Ecglaf's child, Æscferth was his name.
He winced not from war-play,
but shot his arrows again and again.
Some he shot into shields, some he shot into men;
ever at intervals he inflicted wounds
while weapons he could wield.
Still in the front stood Edward the Tall,
ready and alert, and vaunted aloud,
that he would not flee a single foot of land,
or bend at all back when his better lay dead.
He broke the board-wall, battled with those warriors,
until for his wealth-giver on those wide-farers
he had worthily worked. Then he lay with the slain.
So also did Æthelric, noble companion,
eager and raring to go, he raged earnestly.
Sigeberht's brother, and so many others,
cleft curved shields, keenly defended them.
Shield borders burst, and the byrnie sang
a song of horrors. Then Offa at battle
struck the sea-farer, that he fell down on earth,
and there Gadd's kinsman did seek the ground.
Fast in the heat of it Offa was hewn down,
yet he had performed what he had promised,
as he had vowed before to his ring-giver
that both of them should ride into the burg:

home in full health or here fallen in the fight,
on the place of slaughter succumbing to wounds.
He lay like a thane, near to his lord.
Splintering was the wood. The sea-foes waded up,
spurred with war-rage. Spear often pierced
a fated man's life-house. Forth went Wistan,
Thurstan's son, thrashed against those men.
He was in that throng the bane of three of them,
before Wighelm's son lay slain with him.
There was a stiff press; they stood proud,
firm in the struggle. Fighters struck down,
succumbing to wounds. The slain fell on earth.
Oswold and Eadwold, all the while,
both those brothers, emboldened the men,
their dear kinsmen bade with cries
that in this time of need they should endure,
without wavering use their weapons.
Byrhtwold spoke, hefted his board—
he was an old retainer— rattled his ash-spear;
full of courage he coached the men:
"Will must be the harder, heart the bolder,
our spirit the greater, while our strength lessens.
Here lies our lord all hewn down,
a good man on the gravel. He will ever regret it,
who from this war-play wants now to turn.
I am old in this life: I will not go away,
but I will put myself beside my lord.
By such a beloved man, I believe I will lie."

92. GATHERING BOLTS AT TOURNAI (1340)

Bravado and braggadocio went hand in hand with chivalry and soldiering in the Middle Ages. Young men often promised feats of arms to their companions, and especially ladies, whom they wished to impress. Embellished or not, this account of a London squire at the siege of Tournai in 1340, found in the late-fourteenth-century Chronique des Pays-Bas, de France, d'Angleterre et de Tournai [Chronicle of the Low Countries, France, England and Tournai], *captures the spirit—and fate—of one such young man, forced to action by the boredom of a prolonged siege.*

Source: trans. Kelly DeVries, from *Chronique des Pays-Bas, de France, d'Angleterre et de Tournai,* in *Corpus chronicorum Flandriae III,* ed. J.J. de Smet (Brussels: Commission royale d'histoire, 1856), p. 154.

A squire of London said that he had promised his beloved lady that, as King Edward [III] besieged a town in France, he would take a quarrel from each tower or die in the process; which act he would do for her. There [at Tournai] he armed himself and mounted a horse. He took along a helmet and a coat of mail, and he proceeded to ride to the gate of St-Fontaine. Afterward, he went from tower to tower, to the gate of Bourdeil, where he passed the Scheldt river at Marvis, and passed it again at Caufours, until he had come to the gate at Blengenoisse. There was at that gate a crossbowman who had seen him and had shot a mounted crossbow into his [the squire's] body; afterward [the crossbowman] was killed. But so blessed was he [the squire] that he finished his journey all the way back to the gate of St-Fontaine from where he had begun. After this, he went to the tent of King Edward. There he drew the quarrel from his body and died. All the lords sorrowed greatly. Later they sent the quarrel by which he was killed to his beloved lady and told her the story of his death.

93. ARCHER-WOMAN OF KARIA (1341)

This brief passage, from an obscure manuscript in the Mediceo-Laurentian Library in Florence, is the single reference to a woman known by the single name, Makouraino, whose heroic military activities protected her village from pirate raids. The author of the passage is unknown; it was found stuck in between the writings of the Byzantine monastic theologian Maximos Planoudis, a poem on meter, and the works of the late antique Greek rhetorician Libanius. The story's obscurity emphasizes the ways that women can be largely pushed from the historical record despite being an inevitable (and, as here, powerful) force in military engagements.

Source: trans. George T. Dennis, "Woman Repels Pirates: Note in a Florentine Manuscript," *Byzantine and Modern Greek Studies* 23 (1999): 256–57.

In the part of Karia just opposite Chios, it is reported that, in our own day, a mature woman, with some facial hair, named Makouraino, married and with children, displayed her valor and leadership when the occasion presented itself. What she did was no less than what a man would do, indeed what the bravest men would do. For her ability to stretch tight and stiff bows was awesome. It is said that, by herself, she stood up to two pirate ships and drove them from the shore by shooting arrows at them. In the year 1341.

94. THE MAID OF ORLÉANS (1429–1431)

News of Joan of Arc's appearance and victory at Orléans in May 1429 (doc. 88) spread quickly throughout France. As can be seen in this diary kept in Paris, however, not all of the French welcomed her involvement in the war. Many, like this anonymous author from the merchant or guild class, preferred Anglo-Burgundian rule to that of the Valois royal dynasty.

Source: trans. Janet Shirley, *A Parisian Journal, 1405–1449* (Oxford: Clarendon Press, 1968), pp. 233–34, 240–42, 249, 253–54, 260–65.

[1429]

There was at this time a Maid, as they called her, in the Loire country who claimed to be able to foretell the future and who used to say "Such a thing will certainly happen." She was altogether opposed to the Regent of France and his supporters. And it was said that in spite of all the forces in front of Orléans she made her way into the city, bringing in large numbers of Armagnacs [supporters of the dauphin, Charles, as king] and a good supply of provisions, and that none of the army made any move to stop her, although they could see them going by about one or two bowshots away from them and although they needed food so desperately that one man could well have eaten three *blancs*' worth of bread at one meal. Other things were said of her too, by those who loved the Armagnacs better than the Burgundians or the Regent of France, such as that, when she was very small and looked after the sheep, birds would eat bread in her lap as if they were tame. *In veritate appocrisium est* [in truth that is a lie]. The Armagnacs now raised the siege and forced the English to retreat from before Orléans. [But they went, it is said, to Vendôme and took that.] This Maid went everywhere with the Armagnacs, wearing armour and carrying her banner, which bore the one word, "Jesus." It was said that she told an English commander to leave the siege with all his men or they would all come to grief and shame. He answered her abusively, calling her bitch and tart; she told him that in spite of them all they would very soon all be gone but that he would not see it and that many of his men would be killed. And so it happened, for he was drowned the day before the slaughter....

On the eve of Our Lady Day in September [September 6] the Armagnacs approached to attack the walls of Paris. They hoped to take the city by assault, but little did they gain there except sorrow, suffering, and disgrace. Many of them were maimed for the rest of their lives, men who before the attack had been strong and healthy—but a fool will never believe anything till he has tried it. I say this because of these men who were so unfortunate, so full of foolish trust, that they relied upon the advice of a creature in the form of a woman, whom they called the Maid—what it was, God only knows—and unanimously agreed to attack Paris on the actual day of Our Lady's holy nativity. They assembled, a good twelve thousand or more of them, and came up, their Maid with them, at about the time of high mass, between eleven and twelve, with a large number of carts, wagons, and horses, all laden with huge trebly-roped faggots of wood with which to fill up the moats. They mounted a fierce assault between the Portes St. Honoré and St. Denis and as they fought they shouted abuse and hard words at the city's defenders. Their Maid was there with her standard on the bank above the moat, and she said to the Parisians, "Surrender to us quickly, in Jesus' name! If you don't surrender before nightfall we shall come in by force whether you like it or not and you will all be killed." "Shall we, you bloody tart?" said a crossbowman, and shot at her. The bolt went right through her leg; she ran for safety; another transfixed her standard-bearer's foot.... The fighting was very fierce on both sides and went on till at least four in the afternoon and still no one could say which were getting the best of it. Shortly after four o'clock the defenders took fresh heart and shot so fast at them, with cannon and other weapons, that they had to withdraw and abandon the assault and get away. Then it was a question of who could get away quickest, for Paris had big guns which could shoot from the Porte St. Denis to well beyond St. Lazare; these threw cannonballs at their backs, which alarmed them very much. Thus they were put to flight, but no one left Paris to pursue them, for fear of ambushes ... they came next day under safe-conduct to get their dead, and the herald who came with them stated on oath to the Captain of Paris that they had suffered at least fifteen hundred casualties, of which a good five hundred or more were dead or mortally wounded....

[1430]

On 23rd May my lady Jeanne, the Armagnacs' Maid, was captured before Compiègne by messire Jean de Luxembourg and his men and by a good thousand Englishmen who were on their way to Paris. At least four hundred of the Maid's men were killed or drowned....

[1431]

On the eve of the Holy Sacrament this year, May 30th in the year 1431, a sermon was preached in Rouen in the presence of my lady Jeanne, known as the Maid, who had been captured before Compiègne. She was standing on a platform so that everyone could see her clearly, dressed in men's clothes. There she was told what great and disastrous evils had through her come upon Christendom, especially the kingdom of France, as everyone knows, and how she had attacked Paris with fire and sword on the day of Our Lady's holy nativity; also what great and terrible sins she had done and caused others to do. How at Senlis and other places she had caused simple folk to commit idolatry, since through her false hypocrisy they had followed her as if she were a holy maiden, because she told them that the glorious archangel St. Michael, St. Catherine, St. Margaret, and many other saints, appeared to her frequently and talked to her as one friend does to another; not by revelation as God has sometimes spoken to those he loves, but bodily, by mouth, as a friend speaks to a friend. She said she was about seventeen; that she was not ashamed that in spite of her father, mother, relations and friends she often used to go to a beautiful well in the Lorraine country—the fairies' and Our Lord's good well, she called it. All the local people used to go there to be cured when they had fevers. This Jeanne, the Maid, often went there, and there, underneath a big tree which shaded the spring, she saw St. Catherine and St. Margaret appear to her. They told her that she was to go to a certain captain, whom they named; she went to him without asking her father or her mother's permission. This captain gave her men's clothes and armour, girded a sword about her, and gave her an esquire and four servants. Thus equipped, she was mounted on a good horse and went to the King of France. She told him that she had come to him by God's command, that she would make him the greatest lord in the world, that it was ordered that all who disobeyed her should be killed without mercy; that St. Michael and many angels had given her a very rich crown for him, and there was a sword in the ground for him too, but she would not give it him till his fighting was done. And she rode with the King every day, amongst very many men-at-arms, no woman with her, wearing men's clothing, points, and armour, and carrying a great stick in her hand. If any of her men did anything wrong, she would wallop them hard with this stick, like a very brutal woman. She says that she is certain she will be in Paradise when her days are done. She says she is completely certain that it is St. Michael and St. Catherine and St. Margaret who speak to her often, whenever she wishes, that she has very often seen them wearing gold crowns on their heads, that everything she does is at God's command and, what is more, that she knows a great deal of what is going to happen. She has several times received the precious sacrament of the altar wearing armour, dressed like a man, her hair cut round, scalloped hood, tunic, scarlet hose tied with dozens of points—certain great lords and ladies reproved her for the mockery of her dress, telling her that she showed little respect to Our Lord, receiving him in such clothes, and she a woman. She answered at once that nothing could make her alter her dress, that she would rather die than stop wearing men's clothes, no matter who might forbid it; that she would produce thunder and other marvels if she liked; that someone had once tried to molest her physically, but she had jumped from the top of a high tower without hurting herself at all. In several places she had men and women killed, both in battle and in deliberate revenge, for she had anyone who did not obey her letters killed immediately without pity whenever she could. She said and affirmed that she never did anything except at God's command, as given to her frequently by the archangel St. Michael, by St. Catherine, and by St. Margaret, who made her do these things—not as Our Lord did to Moses on Mount Sinai, but themselves, personally, told her secret things that were to come; that they had ordered and did order everything that she did, her clothes and everything else.

Such and worse were my lady Jeanne's false errors. They were all declared to her in front of the people, who were horrified when they heard these great errors against our faith which she held and still did hold. For, however clearly her great crimes and errors were shown her, she never faltered or was ashamed, but replied boldly to all the articles enumerated before her like one wholly given over to Satan. This was quite obvious, for she saw the clerks of the University of Paris humbly begging her to repent and recant of her dreadful error and all would be forgiven her through penance, or else she would be burned before all the people and her soul damned to hell. They showed her the writ and the place where the fire would be built to burn her straight away if she did not recant. When she realized that they meant what they said, she asked for mercy; she recanted with her lips and her clothes were changed, she was dressed like a woman. But no sooner did she see herself like that than she fell again into her former error and wanted to have her men's clothing back. She was at once unanimously condemned to death and was tied to a stake on the platform (which was built of plaster) and the fire lit under her. She was soon dead and her clothes all burned. Then the fire was raked back and her naked body shown to all the people and all the secrets that could or should belong to a woman, to take away any doubts from people's minds [none of these dramatic sequences actually took place]. When they had stared long enough at her dead body bound to the stake, the executioner got a big fire going again round her poor carcass, which was soon burned up, both flesh and bone reduced to ashes. There were many people there and in other places who said that she was martyred, and for her true lord. Others said that she was not, and that he who had supported her so long had done wrong. Such things people said, but whatever good or whatever evil she did, she was burned that day....

On St. Martin's in summer there was a general procession to St.-Martin-des-Champs, where a friar of the order of St. Dominic, inquisitor of the faith and master of theology, preached a sermon recalling once again everything that Jeanne, the Maid, had done. He said that she had said that her parents were very poor people, that she had gone about dressed as a man when she was about fourteen years old, that after that her father and mother would have liked to kill her if they could have done so without guilt, and that she had therefore left them, in the devil's company, and had ever since been a murderer of Christian people, full of blood and fire, till at last she was burned. He also said that she had recanted and been given four years in prison on bread and water, but that she never did a day of it but had herself waited on in prison like a lady. There, the devil and two others appeared to her, that is, St. Michael, St. Margaret, and

St. Catherine, as she called them. He—that is, the devil or devils in the shape of these three saints—was very much afraid of losing her and said to her: "Wretched creature, to change your dress for fear of death! Don't be afraid, we will protect you from them all." So she then immediately threw her things off and put the old ones on again that she used to wear on horseback, which she had pushed into the straw of her bed. She trusted this devil completely and told him she was sorry she had ever agreed to change. When the University or those about her saw this and realized her obstinacy, she was handed over to lay justice to die. Seeing herself at the point of death, Jeanne called on those devils who appeared to her as saints, but not one of them appeared again after she was condemned, invoke them how she might. Then she changed her mind, but it was too late.

95. THE UNCONQUERED KNIGHT (c. 1440)

Tales of heroic military deeds are often exaggerated, and it is best to consider them as such. However, if Don Pero Niño did only a portion of what is attributed to him in the late fourteenth- and fifteenth-century wars of Castile, he was a soldier of skill and strength. In this narrative of his fighting, he seems more irritated by the prospect of having to climb stairs and the contenders he had to fight than the pain he was suffering from his numerous wounds. As such, they seem perhaps more believable than similar heroic biographies.

Source: trans. Joan Evans, Gutierre Diaz de Gamez, *The Unconquered Knight: A Chronicle of the Deeds of Don Pero Niño* (New York: Harcourt, Brace, and Co., 1928), pp. 37–38.

While Pero Niño was doing among the enemies of his lord the King as a wolf does among the sheep when there is no shepherd to defend them, it befell that an arrow struck him in the neck. He received this wound at the beginning of the battle. The arrow had knit together his gorget [plate or mail neck armor] and his neck; but such was his will to bring to a finish the enterprise that he had entered upon that he felt not his wound, or hardly at all; only it hindered him much in the movement of the upper part of his body. And this pricked him on the more to fight, so that in a few hours he had swept a path clean before him and had forced the enemy to withdraw over the bridge close against the city. Several lance stumps were still in his shield, and it was that which hindered him most. When he had got so far, the people of the city, seeing the havoc that he wrought, fired many crossbows at him, even as folk worry a bull that rushes out into the middle of the ring. He went forward with his face uncovered and a great bolt there found its mark, piercing his nostrils through most painfully, whereat he was dazed, but his daze lasted but little time. Soon he recovered himself, and the pain only made him press on more bitterly than ever. At the gate of the bridge there were steps; and Pero Niño found himself sorely [put out] when he had to climb them. There did he receive many sword blows on head and shoulders. At the last, he climbed them, cut himself a path and found himself so pressed against his enemies that sometimes they hit the bolt embedded in his nose, which made him suffer great pain. It happened even that one of them, seeking to cover himself, hit a great blow on the bolt with his shield and drove it further into his head.

Weariness brought the battle to an end on both sides. When Pero Niño went back, his good shield was tattered and all in pieces; his sword had its gilded hilt almost broken and wrenched away and the blade was toothed like a saw and dyed with blood. And well do I think that until that day Pero Niño never had been able to glut himself in an hour with the toil he craved: for the truth is that the fight lasted for two whole hours, and that his armour was broken in several places by lance-heads, of which some had entered the flesh and drawn blood, although the coat was of great strength. It had been given him by a great lady; should I say by a queen, I should not lie.

No man should marvel that I should tell of so many feats done by this knight in so short a time, when he was still young in years; for God endows all men with His grace and bestows His gifts on all, according to the measure that it pleases Him and the greatness of His mercy.

F. THE MARGINS OF WAR

96. CAMP-FOLLOWERS WIN A BATTLE (1018)

The death of Vladimir the Great in 1015 set off a war of succession for the leadership of the Kievan Rus between his sons Yaroslav and Sviatopolk. Interceding on behalf of Sviatopolk, who was his son-in-law, Duke Bolesław of Poland marched an army against Yaroslav's Ruthenians in 1018, and the two armies met each other along the River Bug. Sources agree that what followed on 22–23 July—alternatively called the battle of the River Bug or the battle of Volhynia—was a crushing defeat for Yaroslav (even if he would ultimately win the war against his brother), though they widely differ about how Bolesław achieved his victory. Perhaps the most interesting version is that which is related in the twelfth-century Deeds of the Princes of the Poles, *which attributes the turning-point in the battle not to Bolesław's troops but to his camp-followers.*

Source: trans. Paul W. Knoll and Frank Shaer, *Gesta Principum Polonorum: The Deeds of the Princes of the Poles*, ed. Paul W. Knoll and Frank Shaer, Central European Medieval Texts 3 (Budapest: Central European Press, 2003), 31–71.

But let us defer these themes to a later page, and turn to the story of a battle with some unusual features that make it quite memorable. From it we will be able to draw a lesson that humility is better than pride. It came about that, unbeknownst to each other, King Bolesław and the king of the Ruthenians invaded each other's countries at one and the same time. The two armies camped on the banks of a river, each in the other's territory, with the river [presumably the Bug] running between them. The king of the Ruthenians had received word that Bolesław had crossed the river and his army was encamped within the boundaries of his own kingdom, and foolishly he imagined that he and his great host had Bolesław trapped like a netted animal. It is said that the king sent a message memorable in his pride, which was to redound upon his own head: "Let Bolesław know that my dogs and my hunters have caught him like a pig wallowing in the mire." To this the Polish king sent the following reply: "A pig in the mire? Well put, indeed! The hoofs of my horses shall wallow in the blood of the hunters and the dogs, that is, your captains and soldiers, and I shall savage your land and your cities like a wild boar." So passed this exchange between them. The next day a festival was due to be held, and in order to celebrate it King Bolesław put off joining battle till the third day. Now on that day great numbers of animals were being slaughtered as usual in preparation for the king's table at the coming holiday, when he was planning to eat with all his princes. So all the army's cooks, kitchen-hands, servants, and camp-followers were gathered on the riverbank cleaning the carcasses and purging the offal. Meanwhile on the other bank the men-at-arms and retainers of the Ruthenians jeered and hurled abuse, trying to provoke them to anger with their gibes and mockery. They made no reply to the taunts, but instead repaid the insults by hurling in their eyes offal and excrement from the intestines. But when the Ruthenians grew more and more provocative in their taunts, and even began to harry them in earnest with arrows, they left what they were handling to their dogs and birds. They borrowed the arms of the soldiers sleeping in the midday heat, and swimming over the river, Bolesław's army of camp-followers defeated the very sizable host of the Ruthenians. The shouting and the din of the fighting woke the king and the rest of the army, who wondered whatever was going on. When they found out, they doubted that this had been intentional. So they drew up in battle array and went in pursuit of the enemy who were now fleeing in all directions. Thus in the end the glory of the victory did not go solely to the camp-followers, nor were they the sole ones to suffer bloodshed. But the number of soldiers who then crossed the river was so huge that downstream the river did not seem to be water but a dry road. But let this little episode suffice on the subject of his wars, that the record of his life may serve as a model and be a benefit to the listeners.

97. HIRING A FOREIGN ENGINEER (c. 1180)

Warfare has long required specialists—from surgeons to engineers to incendiary makers—many of whom were well-compensated for their skills, and many of whom were itinerant, effectively mercenary contractors. In this apocryphal tale, from a chanson de geste *of the late twelfth century that says far more about its contemporary realities than its Carolingian setting, Charlemagne summons just such a technically advanced engineer to help with his conquest of the fictional castle of Castel-Fort. Aside from the great wealth offered as payment, the fact that Charlemagne affirms their agreement with a chivalric kiss of courtesy says much about the high regard in which such specialists could be held.*

Source: trans. Michael Livingston, from Gerbert de Metz, *Chanson de geste du XIIe siècle*, ed. Pauline Taylor, Bibliothèque de la Faculté de philosophie et lettres de Namur 11 (Louvain, Belgium: Nauwelaerts, 1952), p. 72.

Charlemagne swore it by Saint Paul and Saint Martin,
That he wouldn't rest until the day of his death:
He constructed trebuchets, mangonels, and engines.
Then he sent for Maurin the engineer,
Who was a companion of Constant of Outremer.
He was no more a fool in wood than a clerk is in Latin.
In Alexandria, the Saracens appreciated him very much.
Under Heaven, there is no castle defense—
No ditch, motte, or palisade that is a refuge—
He won't be there but a fortnight
Before he will have burned, levelled, or seized them all.
The king was very pleased when he came;
He made an offer to give him a thousand marks of fine gold,
Thirty fabrics and twenty prize chargers,
Seven cloaks and ten grey furred garments,
If he obtained the surrender of this marble castle.
The engineer responded to him thus:
"I won't take a single penny
Until this marble tower,
Which is more white than ermine,
Sees its stone foundations failing,
And you can see the stones at the top rapidly falling down.
Ogier will kneel before your mercy
With all the other young boys and men."
Charlemagne listened and cracked a smile.
He brought the engineer into his embrace,
Kissed him on the mouth and face, and told him:
"Gold to match your thoughts, young squire,
I will give you as long as we remain friends."

98. SLAUGHTER OF NON-COMBATANTS (1203)

William le Breton, honoring King Philip II Augustus of France in his epic poem Philippide, *was eager to paint his rival King John of England—and those who followed him—in a bad light. Among the supporters of John thus singled out was William Marshal, the earl of Pembroke, who would serve five English kings over the course of his long career. Here, the poet presents King John's plan for the marshal to break the siege of Château Gaillard in Normandy by attacking the non-combatants supporting his enemy. While there is good reason to suspect William le Breton of exaggeration, the slaughter that he describes is nevertheless believable.*

Source: David Crouch, "The Violence of the Preudomme," in *Prowess, Piety, and Public Order in Medieval Society: Studies in Honor of Richard Kaeuper*, ed. Craig M. Nakashian and Daniel P. Franke (Leiden, Netherlands: Brill, 2017), pp. 91–92.

King John, pondering his concerns, sought a way to relieve the garrison, but no means was possible in daylight and he was wary of an attack at night. He discussed his predicament with the Marshal in this way: "O most faithful keeper of my counsels, take a group of 300 elite knights and 3000 mounted serjeants, along with 4000 infantry. Add to these Lupescar's mercenary band. As soon as night falls make a sudden descent on Château Gaillard, since there is no moon tonight. Attack on that side of the river from which King Philip has crossed by a bridge. Nearly all his knights have passed over it with the king along with the knight, [William des] Barres, and the Champenois troops, warlike men whose daring is great. On the bank remain Count Robert [of Dreux], [Louis] the king's heir, Hugh de Châteauneuf, Simon [de Neaufle] and Cadoc's mercenaries. These troops are dug in near the bank, by the efforts of engineers, to safeguard the bridge. Camp followers and riff-raff are scattered across the countryside, along with those people who are to be found selling good round the camps. It may well be that you can satisfy my rage on them, as it is my pleasure to unleash slaughter...."

In just this way King John sent his soldiers into the deepest danger, not deigning to accompany them himself. The king is obeyed, and he drags his feet while the rest make no delay in setting out. The troops arm themselves and the ships slip their moorings. Both forces make haste to the castle, one by water, the other land. Unsleeping, they travel through the quiet and darkness of night; giving up their rest so as to hurry into battle ... The hours are separated by set intervals, and now three times the cockerel is roused to herald the dawn light by its raucous cry. Suddenly the rising sun frees the castle from the gloom of night, and now indeed the Marshal has led his column in haste there by a shorter land route, while the twisting course of the Seine has delayed the voyage of the fleet. The riff-raff, the traders and the unarmed common folk lie about unconscious from their drinking bouts, and they are slaughtered like sheep by the drawn swords of the soldiers. A good few of the crowd of them meet an unexpected end, dead before they can feel the fatal blow. This is the fate of those deeply asleep and dead drunk. Very soon a terrified shouting rings through the camp. The jam at the bridgehead causes the now-roused men to plunge into the river, because the bridge cannot take so many thousands of people at once.

99. PIRACY IN THE ENGLISH CHANNEL (c. 1250)

In the early years of the thirteenth century, the younger son of a minor lord in the county of Boulogne was declared an outlaw by the count, Renaud de Dammartin. The deeds of Eustache the Monk, as he came to be known, passed quickly into legend, but there is little doubt about the real historical impact of the outlaw, who became a mercenary pirate for King John of England: from 1205 to 1212, he and his brothers ravaged the Channel Islands and the coast of Normandy. In 1212, however, Eustache switched sides to support King Philip II of France, now raiding English settlements like Folkestone. In August 1217, the Monk's pirate fleet was devastated by English ships in what would become known as the battle of Dover. Eustache survived, but days later his ship was surrounded in the battle of Sandwich. He was captured and beheaded.

Source: trans. Thomas E. Kelly, in *Medieval Outlaws: Ten Tales in Modern English*, ed. Thomas H. Ohlgren (Stroud, UK: Sutton, 1998), pp. 92, 95–98.

So Eustache became one of King John's retainers and was given command of a fleet of ships. With some thirty galleys given to him by the king, Eustache then set sail. His first destination was the islands of Jersey and Guernsey. But as he approached one of these Channel Islands he found the islanders waiting for him there, armed and assembled with their leader Romerel, the lord of one of the island manors. As he saw Eustache's fleet approaching, the leader said to his men, "Now wait until they've landed. The moment we see them coming ashore, we'll attack and destroy them at once." When Eustache's ships landed, he was the first to disembark. All his companions jumped out after him and the inhabitants of the islands attacked them without delay. Eustache headed straight for the castellan, who was at the head of his troops. Marching well out in front, the leader tolerated no complaints. He boldly led all those under his command right up to the invader's ships. The combat began with an exchange of battlecries: "Godehiere!", "Winchelsea!", "God is with us here," cried Romerel. "St Vincent help us," cried Eustache. Heavy fighting broke out and many men were knocked off their horses. One side attacked fiercely and the other side defended itself very well. After the melee began, it soon became savage, violent and arduous. On the battlefield Eustache held a huge axe in his hands and with it he struck countless heavy blows. He smashed and split many a helmet, and more than one warhorse lost its shoulder. First to his right then to the left he struck blow after blow, making himself lord and master of the battle. Eustache shouted out, "Don't stop striking your blows! They'll all take flight, as you'll soon see." And so the great battle raged on ever more fiercely. That day many coffins were to be made. In the end, Eustache expelled everyone he found there. All the inhabitants of the Channel Islands were sent into exile. In fact, so complete was the destruction he wrought that there was nothing left to burn in any of the castles or manors....

While the Monk was living in England, the Count of Boulogne [Eustache's enemy] appeared on the scene. He had quarreled with the King of France and decided to join forces with King John. When he learned of the arrival of his nemesis, Renaud of Boulogne, the Monk decided his English palace was no longer a safe haven. And so he made up his mind to go back home. But getting there would now be a dangerous adventure, because he had worn out his welcome in England. Moreover, King John gave orders to have the sea watched in order to prevent Eustache from getting across to the French coast.

Eustache, who had a way with words, decided to set off disguised as a minstrel. He first found a bow and a vielle [a stringed musical instrument], then dressed himself properly for his new role. He covered up his short cloak and put on a hood with stripes of orphrey. Picking up a cane covered in leaves, he headed straight for the coast. Once there he saw a merchant ship about to set sail. Everyone had already gone aboard and Eustache waited near the ship, pondering what to do. At last he decided to chance it. He put his feet together and jumped on to the deck. The pilot said, "Minstrel, you'll have to get off, so help me God." Eustache replied, "Yes, indeed, when the ship gets to the other side of the Channel. I don't think you're being very reasonable. To pay for my passage I'll give you the choice: either five silver pennies or my vielle." "And what other fables have you told?" "I'm a very unusual *jongleur* and a minstrel; you'll find very few like me. I know all the songs. For God's sake, fair lord, take me across the Channel. Although I come from Northumberland I've spent the past five years in Ireland. I drank so much good ale there that my face has turned pale and wan. But now I'm going over to drink the wines of Argenteuil or Provins...."

It was evening when Eustache finally arrived in Boulogne. He immediately set off running, now in the guise of a messenger boy. He had with him a large box containing a letter which he was carrying to King Philip. He went straight to the king and showed him the letter. Once the king had read it he learned that the Monk had come to France and was sending his greetings. The letter also explained that the Monk was angry with King John on two counts. John not only killed Eustache's daughter, his cruelty was such that he also had her burned and disfigured. The other reason for his leaving England was because the Count of Boulogne was now there. So Eustache would never be at peace with King John again and that was the main reason why Eustache the Monk had come to France. In his letter he explained that he also had no intention of betraying King Philip, rather he wished to serve him as best he could. The king told the messenger: "If he's on this side of the Channel, get him to come at once and speak with me. I promise that he can come and go in safety. He won't have any difficulty getting here, because no one will be on the lookout for him this far away." With that Eustache spoke up saying, "I'm already here!" "Are you the Monk?" exclaimed the king. "You don't look much like a Frenchman. You're so short! Yet from what I hear, in spite of your size, you're quite brave and bold. You also have a strong reputation for guile and cunning. So apparently you don't need any cat's grease to help you. But you need to be aware that you will not serve me unless you decide to lead a good life from now on." Eustache said, "By St Simon! I promise to serve you well by doing nothing other than good." Thereafter, the Monk proved himself to be a good warrior.

Although the Monk was a great warrior, he was also very bold and cruel. Afterwards he did many devilish deeds in the islands on the other side. He led King Louis and a large fleet of ships across the English Channel, personally capturing the warship known as the *Nef de Boulogne* single-handedly. He took the French king with him to the port of Damme. That was in AD 1213, the year the king lost his ships! They blamed Eustache for having betrayed the king's fleet and he was arraigned on that count. Eustache denied the charge completely and justified himself by claiming there was no man bold enough to furnish proof of such treason. And so they dropped the charges.

Sometime later he again set out on the Channel with a great fleet of ships. With him there was Raoul de Tournelle, along with Varlet de Montagui. When Eustache, the courageous warrior, got out on the open sea he soon encountered more than twenty English ships bearing down on him. The enemy set out in small boats and attacked the ships with longbows and crossbows. The Monk's men guarded themselves against everything thrown at them in the chase by firing missiles and shooting arrows. They killed many Englishmen and defended themselves nobly. Eustache himself toppled many of them with the oar he wielded, breaking arms and smashing heads with every swing. This one he killed, another one he threw overboard. This one he knocked down, another he trampled under foot, and a third one had his windpipe crushed. But Eustache was assailed from all directions with no let up. Battle axes struck his ship on all sides. On the first wave the defenders were able to ward off the attack, preventing the enemy from coming on board. Then the English started hurling big pots of finely ground lime, smashing them to pieces on the ship railings, with the result that great clouds of dust covered the decks. That was what caused the most damage, against which Eustache's men could not defend themselves. To their misfortune the wind was against them, causing even further torment, for their eyes became filled with ash. In the confusion the English leaped on to Eustache's ship and mistreated his men badly, taking all the nobles prisoner. As for Eustache the Monk, he was slain, his head cut off. With that the battle was over.

100. CONTRACT FOR GENOESE MERCENARIES (1337)

This agreement, made by King Philip VI of France to hire the services of Genoese captain Ayton Doria in 1337, is an example of those made frequently between military contractors and mercenary captains during the Late Middle Ages. Sometimes couched within lengthy documents filled with "legalese," these contracts always detailed payment, numbers, and types of soldiers to be provided, how they should be armed and armored, and how booty and prizes were to be divided. Of special note is the requirement that the Genoese provide their own surgeon.

Source: trans. Kelly DeVries and Michael Livingston, from Auguste Jal, *Archéologie navale* (Paris: Athus Bertrand, 1839–40), 2:333–38.

The treaty and accord made between our lord the king and Ayton Doria of Genoa, in which Ayton promises to serve the king, as the king demands, with up to 20 galleys, each at a cost of 900 gold florins a month....

Ayton will serve the king our lord, as it pleases the king or his council, with up to 20 galleys against the king of England and all his allies—however it would, could, or should be against all other enemies of the king of France our lord and his kingdom. Ayton must deliver and maintain in each of these galleys 210 men, all of them supplied and well-armed with breastplates, bascinets, collars that have mail gorgets, and pavises. Of these 210 men, there will be one captain [*patron*], two officers [*comites*], two scribes [*escrivains*], 25 crossbowmen, and 180 sailors to man the oars. And he must deliver and put in each galley 600 crossbow bolts, 300 spears, 500 javelins, short spears, long spears, iron bucklers, along with the maintainers and armorers, as the case may be, for a galley to be well-armed in a time of war.... [Here follows specifics of payments for service, in addition to which Ayton will receive] half of all the prizes that these galleys gain from the enemies of the king of France our lord—except castles, cities, prisoners, and all inheritances, all of which belong to the king.... Ayton must also provide a master surgeon from his country, to whom the king our lord must give and pay 10 florins of Florence each month that Ayton, his captains, his men, and his galleys serve the king.... This is done and accorded on Saturday, 25 June 1337.

101. PAYMENT FOR SPIES (1343)

Little is as vital to a war effort as reliable information. Knowing the enemy's strengths and weaknesses, dispositions and plans, can make the difference between a glorious victory and a disastrous defeat. Spies, whether in the form of local informants or hired professionals, thus have a long history in the annals of warfare. Here, a 1343 French financial account provides insights into the actions and payments of one such intelligence effort that was undertaken during the opening stages of the War of Breton Succession, fought between 1341 and 1364.

Source: trans. Christopher Allmand, *Society at War: The Experience of England and France During the Hundred Years War*, ed. Christopher Allmand, 2nd ed. (Woodbridge, UK: Boydell Press, 1998), pp. 123–24.

Expenses and money paid out by me, Bertrand Jobelin, on the order and commandment of my lords of [the Chamber of] Accounts on certain business concerning our lord the king, mention of which is made more fully as follows;

First, 29th day of November 1342, at the orders of my lords of the Accounts, namely my lord Hugues de Pommart, my lord Fauval de Vaudencourt, Sir Pierre des Essars, and Sir G[uillaume] Balbet, treasurer of France, there being also present my lords Roger de Vistrebec and Bernard Franco, I was summoned and ordered to dispatch messengers to the parts of Brittany as quickly as possible, to find out and ascertain news concerning the situation of the enemies of our lord and king and of the king of England's intentions, and to send frequent news back, by day and night, to my lords of the Accounts, all at the king's expense, according to their will and order thus made to me. For this reason, that very same day, I sent forthwith a messenger on horseback to the country around Dol, to whom I had written; the said messenger returned to me at Pontorson, for which expedition [he was paid] for eleven days, there and back, 4 pounds 10 shillings.

Item, on the 12th day of December, for sending letters from Pontorson to my lords of the Accounts, to make report of the king of England's coming to Vannes in Brittany, of his plans, of the number of men-at-arms and foot soldiers in his service, and of several allies in Brittany whom he had, who were keeping a watch on the roads, namely my lord Olivier de la Chapelle and my lord G[uillaume] de Cadoudal, knights, who, with a large number of men-at-arms, were observing those who were coming into Brittany on my lord the king's behalf; and that my lord Olivier was at Pillemiq, near Nantes, the other in the forest of Villequartier, near Dol and Pontorson.

Item, to inform my lords how the city of Bordeaux had written to the king of England that he should come to its rescue speedily, otherwise it would surrender the city to the king, our lord.

Item, the said Cadoudal was spying out the land so as to gain entry into the castle of Pontorson and into the Mont-Saint-Michel.

Item, to inform the lords of the Accounts how, on the feast of St. Nicholas in winter, the town of Joué, near Nantes, had been taken, and of many other things, so that they should take such steps as seemed to them proper. For this expedition, paid to J. Lambert who travelled on horse for 17 days, going, returning, awaiting and bringing back the reply of my said lords, at the rate of 10 shillings *parisis* ... 11 pounds 5 shillings.

Item, for moneys given to two spies who went from Pontorson to Dinan and elsewhere when the town was burned, to ascertain the situation, being away six days ... 100 shillings.

Item, 24th day of December, for taking letters to my said lords, in which it was reported how the suburbs of Dinan had been burned by the earl of Salisbury, and how it was vital to furnish and defend the castle of Pontorson. Further, how the Cardinals had received letters at Avranches and Pontorson from the king of England, asking that they go to confer with him at Vannes or nearby. For this, paid to a messenger who tarried, went, returned, for twelve days ... 100 shillings.

Item, for moneys given to two spies, to go to the parts of Brittany, both of them to report on what they found at the castle of Saint-Sauveur-le-Vicomte. For this ... 4 pounds *parisis*, worth 100 shillings.

102. ENGLISH MERCENARIES IN ITALY (1361–1364)

Following the Treaty of Brétigny in 1360, soldiers who had been gainfully employed to fight the Hundred Years War, some for two decades, suddenly found themselves out of work. For many, especially the English, prospects at home were neither as remunerative nor as exciting. Some joined bands of other unemployed soldiers to pillage, terrorize, and extort money from areas of France previously untouched by war, while others joined companies of mercenaries, hiring themselves out to whomever would pay for their services. Many made their way into Italy, where some of them became famous as the White Company, eventually to be led by Sir John Hawkwood. In this Florentine chronicle, Filippo Villani (continuator for his uncle, Giovanni, and father, Matteo), describes the mercenaries of the White Company, including the highly polished nature of their armor, which some historians have suggested to have been the origin of their name.

Source: trans. Niccolò Capponi, from Filippo Villani, *Croniche storiche*, vol. 6, ed. Francesco Gherardi Dragomanni (Milan: Boronni e Scotti, 1848), pp. 475–76.

They are all young and for the most part born and raised during the long wars between the French and English—therefore hot and impetuous, used to killing and to looting, quick to arms, not caring about their own safety. In combat, they are ready and obedient to their captains; yet in camp, because of their unrestrained strutting and cockiness, they are disorganized and incautious. A brave army would easily hurt and shame them.

Their armor is almost uniformly a coat of mail [or cloth-covered plate armor] and a steel breastplate, iron plates for the arms, thighs, and legs. They carry strong daggers and swords; all had cavalry lances which when on foot they are happy to use. Each has one or two young pages, and more if in a position of power. When they take off their armor, the pages are tasked to polishing it—so shiny that when they appear in combat their armor looked like mirrors, and thus they are even more frightening.

Others of them are archers, and their bows are long and of yew; they were ready and disciplined, and they were effective. The mode of fighting in the field [of the English] is nearly always on foot, entrusting their horses to their pages. Keeping themselves in a nearly curved formation, they take a lance, wielding it in the same way one would use a spear against a charging boar. So close and packed together, with lowered lances they advance with slow steps and terrible shouts—and their formation can only be pried apart with difficulty.

However, in our experience they are less happy to take the field than to go out at night and raid settlements: they succeed rather by the cowardice of our people than by their own prowess.

103. MERCENARIES DISGUISED AS WOMEN (1388)

Like many other men of war, Bascot de Mauléon was left without direct employment following the signing of the Treaty of Brétigny between England and France in 1360. Bascot turned to what can most favorably be described as a mercenary life: he fought for the highest bidder, or, when none was to be had, he fought for himself. Here, the chronicler Jean Froissart describes Bascot's reminiscences of a particularly memorable stratagem that he used to seize and plunder a small town in France.

Source: trans. Michael Livingston, from *Les chroniques de Sire Jean Froissart*, ed. J.A.C. Buchon (Paris: A. Desrez, 1835), pp. 409–11.

After I had lost the castle of Trigalet, and I had been conducted to the Castelculier, and the duke of Anjou [Louis I] had retreated into France, I determined to do something in which I would profit, or else I would remain in poverty. So I sent men to spy upon the town and the castle of Thurie in Albigeois. That castle has since been of value to me—by pillage, protection-money, and the good fortunes that I have had—one hundred thousand francs. I will tell you how I went and seized it.

Outside the castle and the town is a very lovely spring, where each morning the women of the town had a custom of coming with their pitchers and other vessels. They filled them there and then carried them back to the town atop their heads. In order to seize that place, I joined the company of men that I had sent to assay it, and I took fifty companions from the garrison of Castelculier and we rode all day through the woods and heaths. That night, around midnight, I established an ambush close to Thurie. Then we continued onward—six of us alone, in the clothes of women and with pitchers in our hands—into a meadow close to the town, and we secreted ourselves in a haystack, because it was near the summer Feast of St. John [24 June] and the meadows had been cut and mowed. When the hour came for the gate to be opened and for the women to begin to come to the spring, we all took our pitchers, filled them, and then went back toward the town, covering our faces with kerchiefs. Never would anyone have recognized us. The women that we encountered said, "Wow! By St. Mary, you got up early this morning!"

We responded in their language with fake voices—"So it seems!"—and we passed them by and all six of us walked on toward the gate. When we reached it, we found no one else on guard except a cobbler who was there setting up his lasts and his rivets. One of us sounded a horn in order to summon our companions who were waiting in the ambush.

The cobbler did not care what we were doing, except he heard the loud noise of the horn, and he demanded of us: "Women! Hey! Who just blew a horn?"

One of us responded: "It's a priest who is going into the fields. I don't know if it's the vicar or the town chaplain."

"If it is," he said, "then it's Master Pierre François, our priest. He very much enjoys going in the morning to catch hares."

Right after this our companions arrived, and we entered the town, where we found not a single man who put hand to sword to defend it.

Thus did I seize the town and the castle of Thurie, which has given me more profit and revenue annually, and everyday when it comes, than the castle and all its dependencies would be worth today if they were sold for their very best prices. But I don't know what to do with it right now. I am in negotiations with the count of Armagnac [Jean I] and the dauphin of Auvergne [Beraud II], who have express powers from the king of France to purchase the towns and fortifications from those companions who hold them in Auvergne, Rouergue, Quercy, Limosin, Périgord, the Albigeois, and the Agenais, and from all those who waged war and did so in the name of the king of England [Edward III]. Many have already left me, and they returned their fortifications. But I don't know if I will return mine.

G. DUELS

104. SONG OF HILDEBRAND AND HADUBRAND (c. 800)

Written in a difficult mix of Old High German and Old Saxon on two spare leaves of a ninth-century religious codex, the Hildebrandslied *(*Lay of Hildebrand*) is the* *earliest poetic text in German. Though fragmentary (the full text of the extant poem is translated here), the tale has long fascinated readers for both its antiquity and its tragic power. From analogues and later versions of the story, it is assumed that Hildebrand slays his son Hadubrand at the end of this meeting of champions.*

Source: trans. Michael Livingston, from *Althochdeutsches Lesebuch*, ed. Wilhelm Braune, 14th ed. (Tübingen: Max Niemeyer Verlag, 1962), p. 84.

I heard this told:
That two came together in single combat,
Hildebrand and Hadubrand, between two hosts.
Father and son, they fastened their armor,
Buckled battle-coverings, belted their blades
Boldly over ring-coats as to combat they rode.
Hildebrand spoke, Heribrand's son, he was the more hoary man,
In life more the wiser: he wanted to know,
With few words, who his father was
Among the fighting-folk ...
"... or from which people you come.
If you name only one I'll soon know the others.
Child, in this kingdom I know all the kin."
So Hadubrand spoke, Hildebrand's son:
"This I was taught by these our folk,
Old and wise, who lived long ago,
That Hildebrand was my father, my name is Hadubrand.
Long ago to the east he hasted, he fled Odoacer's hate,
Hence away with Theodoric, and with him went many thanes.
He left in the land little ones lorn,
His bride in her bower a babe at her breast.
Bereft of his rights, he rode hence to the east,
Since this Theodoric was so desperate
For my father, for he was a friendless man.
He was to Odoacer a forever angry foe,
The thane dearest to Theodoric his lord.
Forward in battle he was, for he best loved fighting.
Famed was he among the strongest fighters.
I think he no longer lives."
"God witness," said Hildebrand, "from heaven above,
That you never meet such a manner of man
To fight in battle!"
He turned from his arm a twisted torc,

Crafted from royal coin, that the king had given him,
Ruler of the Huns: "This I give to you in friendship!"
Hadubrand then spoke, Hildebrand's son:
"With the spear a man should take prizes,
Point against point.
You think yourself, old Hun, unbelievably clever.
With words you'll entice me, but then you'll send your spear.
You've survived to such an age by false trickery and deceit.
This was said to me by sea-farers,
West of the Vandal Sea, that in war he was slain:
Dead is Hildebrand, Heribrand's son."
Hildebrand spoke now, Heribrand's son:
"Well I can gather from your war-gear,
That you have at home an honored lord,
That from these lands you've never been expelled.
Well, God save you," said Hildebrand, "Disaster happens!
For sixty summers and winters I wandered far from our lands,
Ever set on the front-line in the army of fighters.
Fate has not brought me death before any fortress,
But now here my own son would strike me with his sword,
Pierce me with his blade—unless I seize his life.
You might easily snap up, if your strength is sufficient,
From such an old man his armor to win,
Robbing booty, if you have any right to it."
"He would be a coward," said Hildebrand, "of the Hunnish east,
Who refused the duel that you so desire,
To struggle together. Let us strive as we like,
To learn which of us two will give up his gear,
And who both byrnies [coats of mail] will bear away!"
Then first they loosed their ash-spears,
Shivering splinters that stuck in their shields.
Then they closed on each other, crashing colored boards,
Bashing harmfully on the hay-white buffers,
Until the linden shields were shattered,
Destroyed by their weapons ...

105. SIEGE, DUEL, AND BATTLE AT HALIDON HILL (1333)

In 1314 the Scot Robert Bruce had won a stunning victory over the English king, Edward II, at the battle of Bannockburn, thus securing for a time Scottish independence. By 1333, however, those two kings were dead, and King Edward III decided it was time for revenge. Personally leading an army north, he besieged the castle of Berwick, then under Scottish control. That prompted a relief effort, and the Scots and English met again on Halidon Hill overlooking the castle. As is reported by English chronicler Geoffrey le Baker, here the young King Edward gained his first battlefield victory.

Source: trans. by Kelly DeVries, from Geoffrey le Baker, *Chronicon*, ed. Edward Maunde Thompson (Oxford: Clarendon Press, 1889), pp. 51–52.

In the year of our lord 1333, the seventh year of King Edward III's reign, on the feast of St Margaret the Virgin, a large number gathered from the whole of Scotland, to relieve the siege [of Berwick]. Divided into three units, it challenged the king's army to battle. An agreement was made between the warring parties that, if the besieged Scots received food from outside on that day, the rebellion would continue; if, however, they were not comforted by food, the town and castle would surrender to the king of England the following day. Therefore four hundred armed men carrying small loaves of bread were ordered to go around the flank of the English army and throw the bread over the walls to those inside; thus, the town technically supplied with bread, would be relieved. But those ordered to supply the town in such a way were intercepted by those at the rear of the besieging army and stripped of their bread.

The English divided their army. Part was to continue the siege; the other were again divided into units and prepared to meet the attacking Scots. There the English, having learned from the Scots to keep their warhorses in reserve to hunt down fugitives, fought on foot, contrary to the tradition of their ancestors.

At the beginning of the battle between the armies on Halidon Hill, a certain Scottish soldier of large stature, called "*Tauri versor*," Turnbull in English, another Goliath, having more confidence in his great physical strength than in God, stood between the armies and challenged a single Englishman to combat. From the opposing side, Sir Robert Benhale, a knight from Norfolk, with a genuflect sought the blessing of the king and attacked the giant with sword and shield. A black mastiff accompanied and helped the Scot; very quickly Sir Robert cut the dog's loins from its back. Consequently the master of the slain dog continued on very quickly but also very angrily, and the knight made a blow to his left and cut off his head.

Immediately the opposing sides came together. The king wisely comforted the English with light banter, but, because of the intense cruelty of the battle, just past midday the Scots, with a large number killed, and their three divisions amassed into one army, finally saw the necessity of flight. The English king and his soldiers, mounted their horses and pursued them quickly, killing, capturing, and driving them into pits and lakes, scattering them for five miles.

106. JOUST BETWEEN ARMIES (1387)

Though the victory of King Juan I of Portugal over King Juan I of Castile at 1385 had ended one phase of the wars over the two thrones, John of Gaunt, the English duke of Lancaster, persisted in his claim to the throne of Castile through marriage. By 1387 he had invaded Castile with the support of the Portuguese. It would accomplish little, and John of Gaunt would be forced to renounce his claim within a year. In the account that follows, the chronicler Fernão Lopes describes how, despite being at war, some "peaceful" jousts occurred between knights in opposing armies during the 1387 campaign.

Source: trans. D.W. Lomax and R.J. Oakley, Fernão Lopes, *The English in Portugal 1367–87* (Warminster, UK: Aris and Phillips, 1988), pp. 247–51.

CII. How Álvaro Gomes and a Castilian Jousted Together

The following day was Easter Sunday. Defenders and besiegers were talking together, as is the custom whenever a safe-conduct is issued, and it happened that Álvaro Gomes, a servant of the Constable, and another squire, a Castilian, challenged one another to a joust. They were to joust on horseback with helmets and mail but without shields, and be limited to three charges only. A similar challenge was made and accepted by Mauburney, one of the Duke's Gascon knights, and Sir Robert, who was in the town. Álvaro Gomes arrived first on the field with his retinue. He wore plate armour, but refused to wear a fauld [armor to cover waist and hips] even though many strongly advised him to do so. He cut a fine, knightly figure, whereas the Castilian certainly did not. At the first charge, Álvaro Gomes caught him in such a manner that he brought him down. Thereupon, the other man remounted and they charged again. This time, having failed to couch his lance as he ought to have done, the Castilian caught Álvaro Gomes low, unintentionally, so that he received a wound from which he later, died. On that day there was no more jousting.

At this time, the King gave safe-conduct to all who wished to come from the town to see the jousting, and, in consequence, many did come. Among them was a squire, a worthy man, well dressed and with a silver chain about his neck. While he was watching and talking to some Portuguese, he let slip insulting words against the King. He referred to him merely as Master and when he wished to be particularly respectful, he referred to him as the Master, your lord, together with further impertinent remarks. Those who heard these remarks were very angered by them. However, nobody dared to reply, because the King had given safe-conduct, and because in any case he was close by, watching like the rest. That night, when the King called for wine and fruit, some people could not refrain from discussing the event and recounting to him what had transpired, and how they had not dared to make a riposte for fear of annoying the King, since he had given the defenders safe-conduct. The King said that he had only given safe-conduct so that they might come to watch and enjoy themselves, but that if someone made remarks that were uncalled for, he would not hold it against anyone who punished him.

CIII. How Mauburney and Sir Robert Jousted

It happened that on the following day that knight called Mauburney and Sir Robert from the town took the field to joust. Both they and their horses were well equipped with protective armour. Mauburney was well built and had jousted many times before; but Sir Robert was smaller and not as expert in this particular accomplishment. When he jousted, Mauburney was armed in the following manner: he wore a helmet without visor, with the rim of his shield held to protect his face in such a way that only the right eye was visible. His horse charged at no faster than a gallop; he did not engage his adversary head on, but at an angle as he passed. The first joust they made, Mauburney caught the other man in the neck; and even though he wore two bacinets one on top of the other, and a throat-piece, the lance passed through and out the other side, hoisting him clean out of the saddle and throwing him to the ground. Everyone feared him dead. Sir Robert remounted and they jousted again, but this time they merely feinted. At the third attempt, they missed each other and the play was terminated.

Now I must emphasize that if, at first, when Álvaro Gomes jousted, many Castilians and other foreigners came out to see how they performed, many more came out to watch the encounters I have just described. Among these spectators was that squire who, as we related, had let slip remarks that were coarse and quite uncalled for. But if his remarks had previously been unseemly, they were now even more so, as well as offensive to the ear. Álvaro Coitado was a fine Portuguese knight from the Constable's company. He was a redoubtable and well-built man; and he had heard what the King had said when people had complained at this lack of courtesy. He had borne the King's reply in mind and therefore was deliberately standing close by to see if the man would say something similar again. When he heard him speaking as impolitely as on the first day, the jousting being almost over, he approached him; and, although the squire was mounted on a mule, Coitado seized him by the necklace with one hand and with the other gave him a heavy punch so that he was momentarily dazed by the blow. Then he pulled so hard on the necklace that he pulled him clean off the mule and the pair of them fell to the ground where Coitado started to rain down kicks and punches upon him, grabbing him by the necklace and telling him to come into the King's presence. There was a general disturbance among the many people from both sides who gathered round to see what was happening. The Castilians said that it was quite unfair that one should come there with safe-conduct for some diversion and yet be dishonoured in this way. The King, who was nearby, hurried up to see what was the matter. Pedro Díaz de Cardoniga, a Castilian knight, acted as spokesman for the rest, saying that it was not right that, given safe-conduct by the King, they should suffer such dishonour at the hands of his men. The King said that he had given them all safe-conduct so that they might come and go freely and stay there to watch and enjoy themselves with the besiegers; but that he had not given them safe-conduct to insult one another. If that squire said things he ought not to have said, then he deserved what had been done to him, and more besides. Then they all dispersed and no more joustings were held in that place.

PART FOUR

THE OUTCOMES OF WAR

A. WOUNDS OF WAR

107. DEATH ON THE FIELD (1289)

While still a young man, although already a celebrated poet, Dante Alighieri fought among Florence's militia cavalry at the battle of Campaldino on 11 June 1289. The Florentines and their allies, Guelphs, fought knights and their retinues from the Casentino countryside, as well as the militia of Arezzo, Ghibellines. Despite facing very experienced soldiers, who initially held significant sway on the battlefield, the more numerous Guelphs eventually gained the victory. Dante was not physically wounded, but the trauma he experienced stayed with him throughout his life. Nowhere is this more effectively shown than in The Divine Comedy: Purgatorio, *canto 5, when Dante comes upon Buonconte da Montefeltro, one of the most renowned of the Ghibelline knights. He was killed in the battle but his body was never found. From his description of Buonconte's death "by bleeding out," though, it seems that Dante likely pursued the wounded knight after the battle.*

Source: trans. Niccolò Capponi and Michael Livingston, from Dante, *Purgatorio*, canto V, verses 88–129.

"I was of Montefeltro, I am Buonconte
... none cares for me.
Thus I drift about with downcast eyes."
And I asked him: "What force or ill luck
dragged you so far from Campaldino,
that none knows your burial place?"
"Oh," came the reply, "at the Casentino's foot
a water runs, by name the Archiano,
amongst the Apennine hermits born.
There, where the Arno river steals its name,
I reached, through my throat a gaping hole,
fleeing on foot and reddening the plain.
There I lost my sight and my speech.
There, gasping Mary's name, I fell,
my flesh alone left upon the shore.

I tell the truth, and you can retell it to the living.
God's angel took me, and the hellish one cried out:
'Oh you, from Heaven, why despoil me?
You deprive me of his immortal part
because he sheds one little tear;
but the rest I will govern in another way.'
You are aware, I'm sure, how vapor in the air
gathers and turns back into water
when it has climbed into the coldest reaches.
There arrived that evil schemer,
and with the strength of his ill-nature
he went to stir the thickening air.
When the day was spent, the valley filled with fog
from the Pratomagno to the Gran Giogo.
The air hung with humid clouds,
pregnant until the waters broke.
The rain fell, and the ditches ran
with what the earth refused.
And when these poured into the streams,
they rushed into the great river,
no force to stem the advancing tide.
At its mouth, the swelled Archiano
found my cold stiff body and shoved
it into the Arno, rending the cross
that my agony-clutched arms had made.
It tossed me over the banks and the depths,
until it buried me, its prey, in the swirling silt."

108. CURING A ROYAL HEAD-WOUND (1403)

The future King Henry V was just 16 years old in 1403 when, leading a wing of his father's forces at the battle of Shrewsbury, he was struck in the face with an arrow. Refusing to leave the field, he reportedly ordered the charge that won the field and saved King Henry IV's kingdom. Afterward, his vicious wound was successfully treated by John Bradmore, a surgeon of London, who recorded his cure in his medical treatise, Philomena. *His account is a magnificently detailed look at the kind of medical practice that was available to men of title and money.*

Source: trans. Michael Livingston, from British Library, Sloane MS 2272, fol. 137r.

And it is to be known that in the year of our lord 1403, and the fourth year of the reign of King Henry IV, on the vigil of St Mary Magdalen [21 July], it happened that the son and heir of the aforesaid most illustrious king—the Prince of Wales, duke of Aquitaine and Lancaster—was at the battle of Shrewsbury struck in the face with an arrow beside the nose on the left side. This arrow penetrated from the side, and the head of the arrow, after the shaft was extracted, stood firm in the back part of the bone of the head six inches deep. Thanks to Almighty God, this noble prince was cured by me—the collector of this present work, *Philomena*—in Kenilworth Castle. Diverse skilled healers came to this castle, saying that they wanted to extract the head of the arrow with potions and other cures, but they failed. Eventually I approached him. At the start I used small tents to probe the wound: made from the pith of an old elder, as long as the wound was deep, dried out and tightly sewn into a clean linen cloth. These tents were saturated in rose-infused honey. Afterwards I made the tents larger and longer and thus continued, ever enlarging these tents until I had a width and depth of the wound that pleased me. After the wound had become so dilated and so deep that in my mind I was certain the tents had reached its bottom, I prepared new tongs, small and hollow, the size of an arrow, and a screw passed through the middle of the tongs. The end of the tongs were threaded inside and out; likewise the end of the screw that passed through the middle of them was threaded around in the manner of a screw so that it held better and more strongly, which is illustrated here [illustration]. These tongs I inserted transversely, following the path of the arrow's penetration. I inserted the screw in the middle. At last, the tongs entered the socket of the arrowhead. Then, wiggling it to and fro, little by little—with the aid of God—I extracted the arrowhead. The diverse gentlemen and the servants of the prince standing by all gave thanks to God. And then with a *squirtillo* [syringe] filled with white wine I cleansed the wound and put in new tents of flax fibers saturated in a cleanser, which is made in this way:

Take white breadcrumbs and boil in clean water and strain through a cloth. Then take a sufficient amount of barley flour and honey and boil it all over a slow fire until it has thickened. Afterwards add sufficient terebentine, and the cleansing ointment is created. The aforesaid flax fibers, saturated in this ointment, I shortened every two days: and so, within 20 days, the wound was perfectly and well cleansed. Afterwards I regenerated flesh with *Unguentum fuscum* [dark ointment]. And note that from the start to the end of this cure, every day, morning and evening, I rubbed him in the neck with *Unguentum neruale* [nerve ointment]. And above that spot I placed a warm poultice bandage, because of my fear of a spasm, which was my greatest fear. Thus—thanks be to God!—he was perfectly cured.

109. CAUTERIZING A WOUND (c. 1440)

This is both an account of military surgery and knightly prowess. Pero Niño was no doubt an unusual soldier (doc. 95), hardy and strong enough to bring admiration from those who encountered him. Was the fan who wrote this anonymous chronicle of Pero's deeds prone to embellishment? No doubt, although the cauterization process he undertook was well known, and sufficient evidence exists—for example, the passage above detailing the process of removing the arrowhead from Henry V's skull—to suggest that many warriors were able to deal with the pain of their wounds with sometimes superhuman efforts.

Source: trans. Joan Evans, Gutierre Diaz de Gamez, *The Unconquered Knight: A Chronicle of the Deeds of Don Pero Niño* (New York: Harcourt, Brace, and Co., 1928), pp. 99–100.

The captain [Pero Niño] already felt very ill by reason of the wound that he had received in the leg before Tunis, and he went ashore. As soon as they arrived the wind had begun to blow so strongly from the east, that for a whole month not a single ship could either enter the Port of Cadiz or leave it. During all this time the captain sojourned there, without its being possible for him to depart. From this delay and from the lack of good surgeons it came about that the wound became very serious. At last the wind fell. Thereupon the captain left Cadiz and went up to Seville, where he was warmly welcomed by as many brave men as there were in the city.

The best surgeons of Seville met to examine the captain's wound. They found it so serious that several desired to cut off the foot, for there was danger of death; and if the foot were cut off, there was a chance of life. The surgeons decided to tell him this, and he answered them: "If the hour when I must die is come, let it befall me as God wills. But for a knight it is better to die with all his limbs whole and united as God has given them to him, than to live wretched and crippled, and to look at himself and see that he is good for nothing." And he said further that they might arrange to perform any other operations that they would, but that as to cutting off his foot, he would never agree. The surgeons decided to cauterize the wound with a burning iron, and they told him that since matters were thus, he must bear this operation, and they would see if it would heal him.

They heated an iron, big as a quarrel, white hot. The surgeon feared to apply it and had pity for the pain it would cause. But Pero Niño, who was already used to such work, took the glowing iron in his hand and himself moved it all over his leg, from one end of the wound to the other. Without stopping, they gave him a second like it, and he applied it for the second time. He was not seen during all this time to give a single sign of pain; no one heard him make any complaint. Thence forward his wound was well dressed, and it pleased God that each day it should mend.

110. AFTER THE BATTLE OF BARNET (1471)

The English civil war known as the Wars of the Roses was one of the bloodiest in the Middle Ages. Lancastrian supporters of King Henry VI and Yorkist supporters of the usurper, Duke Richard of York, offered each other little opportunity for ransom, with a larger number of nobles dying than in any other medieval war. Following the battle of Barnet (doc. 76), on 14 April 1471, Sir John Paston, a Lancastrian, wrote home to his mother to report that he and his brother had survived the battle, although the latter was wounded. Many of his noble friends and acquaintances, however, had been killed.

Source: trans. Michael Livingston, from Letter 774: "Sir John Paston to Margaret Paston," in *The Paston Letters. A.D. 1422–1509*, vol. 5, ed. James Gairdner (London: Chatto & Windus, 1904), pp. 99–101.

Mother, I recommend myself to you, letting you know that, blessed be God, my brother John is alive and fares well, and is in no peril of death. Nevertheless, he is hurt with an arrow in his right arm, beneath the elbow. I have sent him a surgeon, who has dressed him, and he tells me that he trusts that he shall be all whole within a very short time.

It is so that John Mylsent is dead, God have mercy on his soul! And William Mylsent is alive, and his other servants all have escaped in all likelihood.

Item, as for me, I am in a good state, blessed be God, and in no jeopardy of my life, as I consider myself, for I am at my liberty if need be.

Item, my lord archbishop is in the Tower. Nevertheless, I trust to God that he shall do well enough; he has a safeguard for him and me both. Nevertheless we have been troubled since, but now I understand that he has a pardon. And so we hope well.

There are killed upon the field, half a mile from Barnet, on Easter Day, the earl of Warwick, Marquis Montagu, Sir William Tyrrell, Sir Lewis Johns, and many other esquires of our country, Godmerston and Booth.

And in King Edward's party, Lord Cromwell, Lord Say, Sir Humphrey Bourchier of our country, who is a sorely mourned man here, and other people of both parties to the number of more than a thousand.

As for other tidings, it is understood here that Queen Margaret is verily landed and her son in the west country, and I believe that as soon as tomorrow, or else the next day, King Edward will depart from hence to her ward to drive her out again.

Item, I beseech you that I may be recommended to my cousin Lomner, and to thank him for his good will towards me, if I had had need, as I understood by the bearer hereof; and I beseech you on my behalf to advise him to be very aware of his dealing or language still, for the world, I assure you, is right queasy, as you shall know within this month. The people here fear it greatly.

God has shown Himself marvelously like Him who made all, and can undo it all again when He desires; and I can think that by all likelihood shall show Himself as marvelous again, and that in a short time; and, as I suppose, oftener than once in cases such as this.

Item, it is so that my brother is unprovided with money. I have helped him to my power and above. Wherefore, as it pleases you, remember him, because I cannot purvey for myself in the same case.

Written at London on the Thursday in Easter week. I hope to see you soon.

All this letter must be secret. Be not dismayed in the world, for I trust all shall be well. If it thus continues, I am not all undone, nor are any of us; and if otherwise, then, etc., etc.

111. RICHARD III'S DEATH (1485)

Once thought destroyed, the body of King Richard III of England, made justly infamous by William Shakespeare, was recently found under a Leicester parking lot, buried ignominiously after being slain at the battle of Bosworth, 22 August 1485. As the skeleton was found only missing its lower legs and feet, the wounds that disabled and killed him—as well as a couple delivered post-mortem—were easily seen and studied. They confirmed the violence of his death and the desecration of the body that followed as described here by Polydore Vergil in his English History.

Source: trans. Dana F. Sutton, Polydore Vergil, *Anglica historia (1555 version): A Hypertext Critical Edition*, ed. Dana F. Sutton, The Philological Museum, last modified 25 May 2010, http://www.philological.bham.ac.uk/polverg/.

The story goes that Richard could have rescued himself by flight. For those around him, seeing that from the beginning of the battle that their soldiers were fighting slowly and sluggishly, and that others were furtively slinking away from the battlefield, suspected fraud and urged him to flee. And then, when the battle had clearly turned against him, they brought him a swift horse. But he was not unaware that the people loathed him and abandoned all hope of future success, and is said to have replied that on that day he would make an end either of fighting or of his life, such was the man's ferocity and spirit. Because he knew for sure that on that day he would either pacify his realm or lose it forever, he went into battle wearing the crown, so as to make either a beginning or an end of his reign in that battle. And so the wretch quickly suffered that same end that is wont to befall those who equate right, law, and honor with their own will, impiety, and rascality. These are indeed examples which can deter those who keep no hour free of crime, cruelty, and felony, more vividly than can any words. Having gained his victory, Henry [VII] immediately thanked God Almighty with many prayers for the victory he had gained, then, overcome by incredible happiness, he climbed a nearby hill, where, after he had praised his soldiers and ordered the wounded to be tended to, and the dead to be buried, gave his undying thanks to all his nobles and promised he would remember their support. Meanwhile with a great shout his soldiers acclaimed as him as king, and cheered him most willingly. Seeing this, Thomas Stanley [earl of Derby and king of Man, who had changed from the Yorkist to the Tudor side] promptly placed on his head Richard's crown, which had been discovered amidst the spoils, just as if he had been hailed as king in the traditional way in accordance with popular will. This was the first harbinger of his blessedness. After this, Henry took up all his baggage and reached Leicester in the evening, with his victorious army. There he remained for two days, to refresh his soldiers after their effort and prepare for his march on London. Meanwhile Richard's naked body was slung over a horse, its head, arms and legs dangling, and was brought to the Franciscan monastery at Leicester, a sorry spectacle but a sight worthy of the man's life, and there it was given burial two days later, without any funeral ceremony. He reigned two years, two months, and one day. He was slight of stature, misshapen of body, with one shoulder higher than the other, and had a pinched and truculent face which seemed to smack of deceit and guile. While he was plunged in thought, he would constantly chew his lower lip, as if the savage nature in that miniature body was raging against itself. Likewise with his right hand he was constantly pulling the dagger he always wore halfway in and out. He had a sharp, clever, wily wit, fit for pretence and dissimulation. His spirit was lively and fierce, and did not fail him even in death. For when abandoned by his own men, he preferred to take up the steel than to save his life by shameful flight, unsure whether he might soon lose it by disease or by suffering his comeuppance.

B. VICTORY AND SURRENDER

112. CHARLEMAGNE DEFEATS THE SAXONS (804)

Written by Einhard around the year 825, The Life of Charlemagne *is one of the most famous biographies of the Middle Ages, providing a contemporary (if worshipful) account of the man who before his death in 814 had ruled as king of the Franks (from 768), king of the Lombards (from 774), and Holy Roman Emperor (from 800). In a reign of almost constant warfare—he fought in every year but one—Charlemagne created an empire that united much of Western Europe. Here, Einhard describes the end of his king's decades-long campaign to subdue the Saxons, which included mass resettlement and forced conversion.*

Source: trans. Paul Edward Dutton, *Charlemagne's Courtier: The Complete Einhard* (Toronto: University of Toronto Press, 1998), pp. 20–21.

At the conclusion of this campaign, the Saxon war, which had seemed merely postponed, was begun again. No war taken up by the Frankish people was ever longer, harder, or more dreadful [than this one], because the Saxons, like virtually all the people inhabiting Germany, were naturally fierce, worshiped demons, and were opposed to our religion. Indeed, they did not deem it shameful to violate and contravene either human or divine laws. There were underlying causes that threatened daily to disturb the peace, particularly since our borders and theirs ran together almost everywhere in open land, except for a few places where huge forests or mountain ridges came between our respective lands and established a clear boundary. Murder, theft, and arson constantly occurred along this border. The Franks were so infuriated by these [incidents], that they believed they could no longer respond [incident for incident], but that it was worth declaring open war on the Saxons.

Thus, a war was taken up against them, which was waged with great vehemence by both sides for thirty-three straight years [772–804]. But the damage done to the Saxons was greater than that suffered by the Franks. In fact, the war could have been brought to a close sooner, if the faithlessness of the Saxons had [but] allowed it. It is almost impossible to say how many times they were beaten and pledged their obedience to the king. They promised [on those occasions] to follow his orders, to hand over the hostages demanded without delay, and to welcome the representatives sent to them by the king. At different times, they were so broken and subdued that they even promised to give up their worship of demons and freely submit themselves to Christianity. But though they were on occasion inclined to do this, they were always so quick to break their promises, that it is not possible to judge which of the two ways [of acting] can be said to have come more naturally to them. In fact, since the start of the war with the Saxons there was hardly a single year in which they did not reverse themselves in this way. But the king's greatness [of spirit] and steadfast determination—both in bad times and good—could not be conquered by their fickleness or worn down by the task he had set himself. Those perpetrating anything of this sort were never allowed to go unpunished. He took vengeance on them for their treachery and exacted suitable compensation either by leading the army [against them] himself or by sending it under [the charge of] his counts. Finally, when all those who were in the habit of resisting had been crushed and brought back under his control, he removed ten thousand men who had been living with their wives and children along both sides of the Elbe river and he dispersed them here and there throughout Gaul and Germany in various [small] groups. Thus, that war which had lasted for so many years ended on the terms laid down by the king and accepted by the Saxons, namely that they would reject the worship of demons, abandon their ancestral [pagan] rites, take up the Christian faith and the sacraments of religion, and unite with the Franks in order to form a single people.

113. JOMSVIKINGS MEET THEIR END (986)

Between the late eighth and mid-eleventh centuries, Vikings raided Europe. Although Vikings initially attacked from along the coastlines, the many rivers of Europe allowed their low-hulled ships to range inland as well. Among these raiders an elite group of Vikings of the ninth and tenth centuries, the Jomsvikings, are described as the greatest of warriors, whose exploits are detailed in the saga bearing their name as well as in other texts. The Jomsvikings even scared other Vikings. Whether the Jomsvikings were historical or not, in the sagas they represent the embodiment of the heroic ideal. The following passage from Olaf Tryggvason's Saga *in* Heimskringla *shows how they were pulled into the naval battle at Hjorundarfjord in 986. Many Jomsvikings were captured, but this was where the fun began.*

Source: trans. Angus A. Somerville, from Snorri Sturluson, *Óláfs saga Tryggvasonar*, in *Heimskringla*, vol. 1, ed. Bjarni Aðalbjaranarson, Íslenzk fornrit XXVI-XXVIII (Reykjavik: Mál og Menning, 2002), pp. 273–86.

35. King Svein [Forkbeard, king of Denmark] held a magnificent banquet to which he summoned all the important men in his kingdom so that he could honor his father, Harald, with a funeral feast. Shortly before this, in Skane, Strut Harald had also died as had Veseti in Bornholm: he was father of Bui Digri and his brothers. King Svein sent word to the Jomsvikings that Earl Sigvald and Bui, with their brothers, should come to honor their own fathers at the feast provided by the king. The Jomsvikings came to the feast with all their bravest men. They had forty ships from Vendland and twenty from Skane. A huge crowd of men assembled there.

On the first day of the feast, before he mounted his father's high seat, King Svein drank a memorial toast and took an oath that before three years were over he would invade England with his army and kill King Athelred [the Unready] or expel him from the land. Everyone at the funeral feast had to drink that memorial toast. Then the chiefs of the Jomsvikings were served the strongest drink in the biggest drinking horn available. When they had drunk that toast, then everyone had to drink a toast to Christ and again the Jomsvikings were served the fullest horn and the strongest drink. The third toast was to St. Michael and everyone drank it.

After that, Earl Sigvald drank a memorial toast to his father and swore an oath that before three years were out he would invade Norway and kill Earl Hakon [r. 970–95] or drive him from the country. Then his brother, Thorkel the Tall, swore an oath that he would follow Sigvald to Norway and would not flee the battle as long as his brother was fighting. Next, Bui Digri swore that he would go to Norway with them and would not flee from the battle against Earl

Hakon. His brother Sigurd then swore that he would go to Norway and would not run away as long as the majority of the Jomsvikings were fighting. Then Vagn Akason swore an oath that he would go to Norway and that he would not come back until he had killed Thorkel Leire and gone to bed with his daughter, Ingibjorg. Many other chiefs made vows about various other matters. That day, the men drank all through the funeral feast, but, the morning after, when the Jomsvikings were sober, they thought that they had said too much and held a conference to decide how they should proceed. They decided to get their equipment together as quickly as possible and make ready their ships and their army. News of this spread far and wide throughout the land.

36. Hakon's son, Earl Eirik, heard the news when he was in Raumarik. Immediately, he gathered his troops together and then went to Uppland. From there, he continued northwards across the mountains to Trondheim to meet his father, Earl Hakon. Thord Kolbeinsson tells of this in *Eiriksdrápa* [*Eirik's Praise-Poem*]:

From the south there traveled afar
fierce rumors of war
and of armored men. Farm-folk
feared disaster.
The sea-warrior [Hakon] heard
of long-planked ships in the south,
dragged down from the beaches,
Danish ships sent to sea.

37. Earl Hakon and Earl Eirik sent an arrow through the whole Trondelag and dispatched messages to both the Møre provinces and Raumsdal, as well as north to Naumadal and Halogaland. They called for a full levy of both men and ships, as is told in *Eiriksdrápa*:

The skald's praise-poem swells.
The shield-warrior has spread on the sea
his serpent-ships,
his swift vessels under sail;
when the great warrior
went in haste to protect
his father's land with his shield,
many ships lay off the coast.

Earl Hakon immediately headed south to Møre to scout and gather troops, while Earl Eirik assembled the army and moved south.

38. The Jomsvikings made for Limafjord with their fleet and from there they sailed out to sea with sixty ships. They arrived at Agder and immediately steered north to Rogaland. As soon as they reached Earl Hakon's territory, the Jomsvikings began to pillage. They sailed north along the coast, plundering as they went.

A man called Geirmund, traveling with a few men in a fast boat, headed north to Møre where he met Earl Hakon. Presenting himself to the earl, he told Hakon the news that there was an army from Denmark in the south of the country. The earl asked if he knew this for certain and Geirmund stretched out one of his arms, which was severed at the wrist. This, he said, was clear evidence that there was an army in the country. Then the earl asked detailed questions about the army. Geirmund said that they were Jomsvikings and that they had killed many people and pillaged far and wide.

"But they are moving quickly and aggressively," he said. "I'm afraid that it won't be long till they show up here."

Then, traveling day and night, the earl rowed into every fjord, going in on one side and coming out by the other. He sent spies to the uplands around Eid, and south to the Fjords, and also to the north where Eirik had gone with his army. It is told thus in *Eiriksdrápa*:

> The war-wise earl
> had longships at sea,
> launched high prows,
> threats to Sigvald.
> Oars quivered, but the prey
> of the predatory raven
> feared no death,
> divided foam with their oarblades.

Earl Eirik hurried south with his army as fast as he could.

39. Earl Sigvald steered his fleet north to the Stad area. The first place he came to was the Herey Islands. Even though the Vikings came across local people, the locals never told them the truth about what Hakon and Eirik were up to. The Vikings laid waste wherever they went. They lay off Hod, went ashore there and raided. They herded both people and cattle to their ships and killed all the men who were able to bear arms. As they were returning to their ships, an old farmer approached them and drew near to Bui's men. The farmer said: "Driving cows and calves to the shore isn't very warlike behavior. You'd do better to trap the bear, now that you're almost at its den."

"What's the fellow saying?" they asked. "Can you tell us anything about Earl Hakon?"

"He rowed into Hjorundarfjord yesterday. He had only one or two ships, three at the most, and he hadn't heard anything about you," the farmer replied. At once, Bui and his men rushed to their ships, abandoning all their plunder. Bui said, "Let's put this information to good use; we're on the brink of victory."

They reached their ships and rowed out immediately. Earl Sigvald called to them and asked what was up. They replied that Earl Hakon was there in the fjord. Sigvald immediately weighed anchor and they rowed north around the island of Hod.

40. The earls Hakon and Eirik lay in Hallkelsvik where their entire fleet of 150 ships had assembled. They had got word that the Jomsvikings had sailed around Hod. So the earls rowed north in search of them. The two sides met at a place called Hjorungavagr and drew up their fleets for the battle. Earl Sigvald raised his standard in the middle of his troops and Earl Hakon marshaled his fleet for the attack. Earl Sigvald had twenty ships, and Hakon had sixty. In Hakon's army were the chieftains Thorir Hjort from Halogaland and Styrkar from Gimsar. On one wing of Sigvald's fleet were Bui Digri and Sigurd his brother, with twenty ships. Opposite them Earl Eirik, Hakon's son, took up position with sixty ships, and with him were the chieftains Guthbrand the White from the Uplands and Thorkell Leira from Vik. On the other wing of Sigvald's fleet, Vagn Akason positioned himself to the fore with twenty ships, and opposing him was Hakon's son Svein with sixty ships. Among his troops were Skeggi from Uphaug in Yrjar and Rognvald from Ærvik in Stad. As it is told in *Eiriksdrápa*:

Slender ships glided
to sea-battle with the Danes;
the fleet sped
along the sea-coast;
at Møre the earl disabled many
ships of the gold-rich Danes;
the ships drifted,
heaped with the warm dead.

Eyvind Skaldaspillir also says this in *Haleygjatal*:

The meeting was miserable,
the morning grim for the Ynglings' [Norwegians']
foes, when the earls urged their fleet
furiously against the destroying
Danes, when sword-bearing Hakon
drove his sea-riding ships
against the Danish fleet.

Then the fleets joined battle and a fierce fight began. Many men fell on both sides, but far more fell on Hakon's side because the Jomsvikings fought with vigor and daring and their weapons went right through the shields of their opponents. Such a hail of weapons was directed at Earl Hakon that his mail shirt was cut to pieces and he threw it off. Tind Hallkelson says of this:

The splendid mail shirt
that the jeweled woman
had readied for the earl
with her own hands
was riven asunder
in the heat of battle.
There the ringed mail shirt
was stripped from the earl;
(the lord of men still
bears the marks of it).
The warrior threw it off, and the ships
of the mail-clad Danes were cleared.

41. The Jomsvikings' ships were bigger and had higher sides than Hakon's, but both sides fought bravely. Vagn Akason attacked Svein Hakanson's ship so violently that Svein backed up and was on the verge of flight. At that moment, Earl Eirik pressed forward into the battle line against Vagn, who retreated. Now the ships were in the same position as they had been at first. Then Eirik returned to his own ranks where his men had pulled back. Bui had cut the ropes binding his ship to the others in his formation and was bent on pursuing Eirik's men as they fled. Earl Eirik laid his ship broadside to Bui's and a fierce, closely fought battle broke out. Two or three of Eirik's ships came alongside Bui's single vessel.

Then foul weather set in with a hailstorm so severe that a single hailstone weighed an ounce. Sigvald cut the ties between his ship and the others. Then he turned his ship around, intending to flee. Vagn Akason shouted to him and begged him not to go, but Earl Sigvald paid no attention to what he said. Then Vagn threw a spear at him, but hit the steersman. Earl Sigvald rowed off with thirty-five ships, leaving twenty-five behind. Then Earl Hakon brought his ship to the other side of Bui's. Incessant blows fell on Bui's men. Vigfuss, son of Killer Glum, lifted up a pointed anvil which lay on the deck and which someone had just used to rivet the hilt of his sword. Vigfuss was immensely strong. He hurled the anvil with both hands and drove it into Aslak Holmskalli's head so that the point penetrated his brain. Aslak had not been wounded till this moment, but had struck blows to left and right. Aslak was Bui's foster son and was entrusted with the bow position on Bui's ship. Another man there was Havard Cutter. He was the strongest and bravest of men.

During this attack, Eirik's men boarded Bui's ship and headed aft to the raised deck where Bui stood. Then Thorstein Midlang gave Bui a terrible wound across the forehead, shattering his nose-guard. Bui struck Thorstein in the side and sliced him in two at the waist. Then Bui grabbed up two chests filled with gold and shouted loudly:

"Overboard, all Bui's men!"

Bui plunged overboard with the chests and many of his men leapt after him. Many men died aboard the ship because there was no point in asking for mercy. Bui's ship was cleared of men from stem to stern and afterwards the other ships were cleared too, one after another.

Next, Earl Eirik came alongside Vagn's ship. There was fearsome resistance, but, at length, the ship was cleared and Vagn was taken prisoner. He and thirty of his men were tied up and taken ashore. Then Thorkell Leire approached Vagn and said:

"You took an oath to kill me, Vagn, but it looks more likely that I'll kill you."

Vagn and his men sat together on a fallen tree. Thorkell had a great ax and he beheaded the man sitting at the end of the tree-trunk. Vagn and his men were bound together by a rope tied around their legs, but their hands were free. One of them said:

"I have a cloak-pin in my hand. I'll stick it in the earth if I know anything when my head is cut off." When his head was off, the pin fell from his hand.

Next to him sat a handsome man with a fine head of hair. He swept his hair forward over his head and stretched out his neck, saying, "Don't get my hair all bloody."

A man grasped his hair and held it fast. As Thorkell swung the ax, the Viking jerked his head back sharply and the man holding his hair was left in the way. The ax cut off both his hands and embedded itself in the ground.

Then Earl Eirik came up and asked: "Who is this good-looking fellow?"

He replied, "I am called Sigurd and I am Bui's illegitimate son. Not all the Jomsvikings are dead yet."

"For sure, you are a true son of Bui," said Eirik. "Will you accept a pardon?"

"That depends on who's offering it," replied Sigurd.

Eirik answered, "The man offering it is the man with the power to do so—Earl Eirik." "I'll accept," said Sigurd, and he was released from the rope.

Then Thorkell Leire asked: "Earl, even if you mean to give all these men quarter, Vagn Akason isn't going to leave here alive." He rushed forward with his ax raised, but a Viking called Skathi threw himself over the rope and fell in front of Thorkell's feet. Thorkell fell over him, flat on his face. Vagn seized the ax, raised it, and dealt Thorkell his death wound. Eirik said, "Vagn, will you accept a pardon?"

"I will," he replied, "if we all receive one." "Free them from the rope," said the Earl, and it was done. Eighteen men were killed and twelve were pardoned.

42. Earl Hakon and many of his men were sitting on a fallen tree when a bowstring twanged on Bui's ship. The arrow struck Gizur from Valdres, a splendidly dressed landowner, who was sitting next to the earl. Some men boarded the ship and found Havard Cutter on his knees by the ship's side, for the lower parts of his legs had been cut off. He held a bow and when the men reached the ship, he asked, "Who fell off the log?"

They answered that it was a man called Gizur. "Then I wasn't as lucky as I wished to be," said Havard. "You've done quite enough damage, and you'll do no more," they replied, and killed him.

Afterwards, the dead were searched, and twenty-five of the Jomsvikings' ships were stripped. The booty was carried off and divided. As Tind says:

Sword bit limb
when the warlord laid
the sword's edge
on the southern host;
there was danger for the army
until the sword-bearing earl
could clear twenty five
Danish longships.

Then the army was disbanded, and Earl Hakon went to Trondheim. He was not at all pleased that Eirik had given quarter to Vagn Akason. People say that in this battle Earl Hakon had sacrificed his son, Erling, for victory and that, afterwards, the hail storm arose and the tide of slaughter turned against the Jomsvikings.

114. AFTERMATH OF HATTIN (1187)

The Koran held that all had to be given the opportunity to accept Allah and Islam. Even prisoners taken in war could not be executed. In the following account, Ibn al-Athir (1160–1233) details Saladin's policy toward captives from the battle of Hattin (1187; doc. 71). For most, including the king of Jerusalem, Guy of Lusignan, Saladin followed this tradition, eventually granting them freedom. However, Reynald of Châtillon (whom the Muslims called Prince Arnat of Karak) was not to be accorded such favor. Reynald had broken several truces, financed an expedition to conquer Mecca, and robbed caravans traveling outside Karak. Saladin had promised that he would personally execute him, and in a wonderfully theatrical display—for Saladin to offer ice water to these very thirsty men he needed to have large blocks of ice transported from the very tallest of Middle Eastern mountains—the sultan fulfilled his promise. Saladin also judged that, as the Knights Templar and Hospitaller had sworn oaths to die for Christ, they could be executed.

Source: trans. E.J. Costello, *Arab Historians of the Crusades*, ed. Francesco Gabrieli (Berkeley: University of California Press, 1969), pp. 123–25.

[In the final stage of the battle of Hattin] ... the Franks had been suffering terribly from thirst during that charge, which they hoped would win them a way out of their distress, but the way of escape was blocked. They dismounted and sat down on the ground and the Muslims fell upon them, pulled down the king's tent and captured every one of them, including the king [Guy of Lusignan, king of Jerusalem], his brother, and Prince Arnat of Karak [Reynald of Châtillon], Islam's most hated enemy. They also took the ruler of Jubáil, the son of Humphrey (of Toron), the Grand Master of the Templars, one of the Franks' greatest dignitaries, and a band of Templars and Hospitallers. The number of dead and captured was so large that those who saw the slain could not believe that anyone could have been taken alive, and those who saw the prisoners could not believe that any had been killed. From the time of their first assault on Palestine in 491/1098 until now the Franks had never suffered such a defeat.

When all the prisoners had been taken Saladin went to his tent and sent for the king of the Franks and Prince Arnat of Karak. He had the king seated beside him and as he was half-dead with thirst gave him iced water to drink. The king drank and handed the rest to the prince, who also drank. Saladin said: "This godless man did not have my permission to drink, and will not save his life that way." He turned on the prince, casting his crimes in his teeth and enumerating his sins. Then he rose and with his own hand cut off the man's head. "Twice," he said, "I have sworn to kill that man when I had him in my power: once when he tried to attack Mecca and Medina, and again when he broke the truce to capture a caravan." When he was dead and had been dragged out of the tent the king began to tremble, but Saladin calmed and reassured him.

... When Saladin had brought about the downfall of the Franks he stayed at the site of the battle for the rest of the day, and on the Sunday returned to the siege of Tiberias. The countess [of Tripoli, who was held up in the fortress] sent to request safe conducts for herself, her children, companions, and possessions, and he granted her this. She left the citadel with all her train, and Saladin kept his word to her and let her escape unmolested. At the sultan's command the king and a few of his most distinguished prisoners were sent to Damascus, while the Templars and Hospitallers were rounded up to be killed. The sultan realized that those who had taken them prisoner were not going to hand them over, for they hoped to obtain ransoms for them, and so he offered fifty Egyptian dinar for each prisoner in these two categories. Immediately he got two hundred prisoners, who were decapitated at his command. He had these particular men killed because they were the fiercest of all the Frankish warriors, and in this way, he rid the Muslim people of them. He sent orders to his commander in Damascus to kill all those found in his territory, whoever they belonged to, and this was done [although later, in 1188, he would free the king, his son, and the grand master].

A year later I crossed the battlefield, and saw the land all covered with their bones, which could be seen even from a distance, lying in heaps or scattered around. These were what was left after all the rest had been carried away by storms or by the wild beasts of these hills and valleys.

115. EXECUTION OF THE PRISONERS AT ACRE (1191)

The fall of Jerusalem to Saladin in 1187 prompted Holy Roman Emperor Frederick I Barbarossa, and two kings, Philip II Augustus of France and Richard I Lionheart of England, to undertake the Third Crusade (doc. 55). Frederick died en route—although remnants of his troops continued the journey—and Philip and Richard arrived outside Acre, then under siege by resident crusaders. Their numbers reinforced these, and Acre fell. But this did not provoke an attack by Saladin, the desired outcome, although his army was camped nearby. Even Richard's threat of executing 3,000 Muslim townspeople did not bring the sultan to battle. On 20 August 1192, Richard carried out his threat, massacring up to 1,000 of these. The taking of prisoners and the extracting of ransoms were not uncommon military tactics, but it was highly unusual to kill them. Negotiations here had led to no agreement and Richard soon lost patience. A member of Saladin's household, Baha ad-Din offers an insider's view of the circumstances and ponders the reasoning behind Richard's decision.

Sources: trans. C.W. Wilson and C.R. Conder, *The Life of Saladin by Beha ed-Din* (London: Palestine Pilgrims' Text Society 13, 1897), pp. 271–74; revised.

115. Messengers went constantly to and fro between the two armies, engaged in trying to lay the foundations of a permanent treaty of peace. This continued until we had procured the sum of money and number of prisoners we had undertaken to give up to the Franks at the expiration of the first period, in accordance with their demands, that is, that we should give them the cross of the crucifixion, one hundred thousand pieces of gold (dinars), and sixteen hundred prisoners. Commissioners employed by the Franks to examine the instalment we had in readiness for them reported that we had fulfilled the conditions imposed except with regard to the prisoners whom they had specifically named, and who had not all been brought together. They therefore let the negotiations drag on

till the first period had expired. On that day, which was the 18th of Rejeb, they sent to demand what was due to them, and the sultan returned the following answer: "You must choose either one of two things: either send our comrades back to us and accept the instalment due for this period, and we will give you hostages for the performance of the conditions imposed for the periods still to come; or receive the instalment we are sending you today, and send us hostages to be retained until our comrades who are now your prisoners are returned to us." The envoys replied: "We will do neither; send us the instalment that is now due, and accept our solemn oath that your comrades shall be sent back." The sultan rejected this proposal, for he knew that if he were to give them the money, the cross, and the prisoners whilst our men were still detained by the Franks, there would be no guarantee whatever against an act of treachery on the part of the enemy, which would strike a great blow at Islam.

116. When the king of England saw that the sultan was making some delay in the fulfilment of the above-mentioned conditions, he acted treacherously with regard to the Muslim prisoners. He had promised to spare their lives if they surrendered the city, adding that if the sultan sent him what had been agreed upon, he would give them their liberty, with permission to take their wives and children with them and to carry away all their moveable property; if the sultan did not fulfil the conditions, they were to become slaves. The king broke the solemn promise he had made them, openly showed the intentions he had hitherto concealed, and carried out what he had proposed to do as soon as he had received the money and the Frankish prisoners. That is what the people of his nation said afterwards. About four o'clock in the afternoon of Tuesday, the 27th of Rejeb, he rode out with the whole of the Frankish army—infantry, cavalry, and Turcopoles [light-armed soldiers]—and advanced as far as the wells at the foot of Tell el-'A'yadiya, to which place he had already sent forward his tents. As soon as the Franks reached the middle of the plain, between this tell and that of Kisán, which was occupied by the sultan's advance guard, they brought out the Muslim prisoners, whom God had pre-ordained to martyrdom that day, to the number of more than three thousand, all tied together with ropes. The Franks rushed upon them all at once and slaughtered them in cold blood with sword and lance. The advance guard had previously informed the sultan that the enemy had mounted their horses, and he sent them some reinforcements, but they did not arrive until after the massacre had been accomplished. As soon as the Muslims saw what they were doing to the prisoners, they rushed down on the Franks, and a certain number were killed and wounded on both sides in the action that took place and lasted until night separated the combatants. The following morning our people went out to see what had happened, and found all the Muslims who had been martyred for the faith stretched on the ground; they were able to recognize some of them. This was a terrible grief to them. The

enemy had only spared the prisoners of note and such as were strong enough to labor. Various motives have been assigned for this massacre. According to some, the prisoners were killed to avenge the deaths of those slain previously by the Muslims; others say that the king of England, having made up his mind to try and take Ascalon [a port city to the south], did not think it prudent to leave so many prisoners behind in Acre. God knows what his reason really was.

116. EXECUTION OF THE PRISONERS AT NICOPOLIS (1396)

It was not until a lull in the Hundred Years War that France, England, and Burgundy answered the call to crusade against the Ottoman Turks, whose expansion in the eastern Mediterranean had gone unchecked for nearly a century. Led by the young John the Fearless, heir to (and mistakenly called in this document) the duke of Burgundy. Troops drawn from these lands were joined by others from the Holy Roman Empire, including Wallachia, Transylvania, and the Teutonic Knights as they crossed Europe to the Balkan peninsula; together they met King Sigismund I's Hungarian army outside Nicopolis. Sigismund had fought the Turks for several years, but his tactical advice was ignored. The result was a resounding defeat, the Western European soldiers discovering not only that their tactics did not work, but that surrendering resulted in execution rather than ransom. Johann Schiltberger, a Bavarian soldier deemed too young for execution, provides an eyewitness account of this cruel result of the battle.

Source: trans. John Buchan Telfer, Johannes Schiltberger, *Bondage and Travels of Johann Schiltberger, a Native of Bavaria, in Europe, Asia, and Africa (1396–1427)*, ed. Karl Friedrich Neumann (London: Hakluyt Society, 1879), pp. 4–5; revised.

And now when King Bayezid [I] had fought the battle, he went near the city where King Sigismund [I] had encamped with his army, and then went to the battlefield and looked upon his people that were killed; and when he saw that so many of his people were killed, he was torn by great grief, and swore he would not leave their blood unavenged, and ordered his people to bring every prisoner before him the next day, each with as many prisoners as he had captured, bound with a cord. I was one of three bound with the same cord, and was taken by him who had captured us. When the prisoners were brought before the sultan, he took the duke of Burgundy [*sic*] that he might see his vengeance because of his people that had been killed. When the duke of Burgundy [*sic*] saw his anger, he asked him to spare the lives of several he would name; this was granted by the sultan. Then he selected twelve lords, his own countrymen, also Stephen Synüher [likely Stephen Simontarnya, a knight from Transylvania] and the lord Hannsen of Bodem. Then each [Turk] was ordered to kill his own prisoners, and for those who did not wish to do so the sultan appointed others in their place.

Then they took my companions and cut off their heads, and when it came to my turn, the sultan's son saw me and ordered that I should be left alive, and I was taken to the other boys, because none under 20 years of age were killed, and I was scarcely sixteen years old. Then I saw the lord Hannsen Greiff, who was lord of Payern, and four others, bound with the same cord. When he saw the great revenge that was taking place, he cried with a loud voice and consoled the horse- and foot-soldiers who were standing there to die. "Stand firm," he said, "when our blood this day is spilt for the Christian faith, and we by God's help shall become the children of heaven." When he said this, he knelt, and was beheaded together with his companions. Blood was spilled from morning until vespers, and when the sultan's counsellors saw that so much blood was spilled and that still it did not stop, they rose and fell upon their knees before the sultan, and entreated him for the sake of God that he would forget his rage, that he might not draw down upon himself the vengeance of God, as enough blood was already spilled. He consented, and ordered that they should stop, and that the rest of the people should be brought together, and from them he took his share and left the rest to his people who had made them prisoners. I was among those the sultan took for his share, and the people that were killed on that day were reckoned at ten thousand men.

C. PILLAGE AND BOOTY

117. SIEGE OF WORCESTER (1139)

The drowning of King Henry I's only son on 25 September 1120 led to a civil war not long after the king's own death in 1135. Until 1153 England was split between supporters of Henry's daughter and chosen heir, Matilda, and Henry's nephew, Stephen of Blois. The Anarchy, as it came to be called, featured countless atrocities by partisans. Rebellions were some of the most violent and ruthless wars of the Middle Ages. Here, a chronicler recounts the 1139 sacking of Worcester—an English base for Waleran, count of Meulan, a powerful supporter of Stephen—by the earl of Gloucester, who supported the cause of Matilda, and Meulan's vengeful sacking of Sudeley, Gloucester's village. Although this vengeance might be allowed under the so-called Laws of War, it should be remembered that the brunt of these attacks were borne by innocent non-combatants.

Source: trans. P. McGurk, *The Chronicle of John of Worcester*, ed. P. McGurk (Oxford: Oxford University Press, 1998), pp. 275–76.

One morning at the outset of winter, on Tuesday, 7 November, we were engaged in divine service in the church, and had already chanted prime [6 a.m.], when behold a large and strong army which we had expected for many days, approached from the south, arriving from the source of all evil. The city of Gloucester had prepared arms and advanced with an enormous force, both on horse and on foot, to assault, lay waste, and set fire to Worcester. Fearful for the sanctuary's treasures, we put on our albs, and, while the bells tolled, carried the relics of our most blessed patron Oswald outside in suppliant procession, and, as the enemy rushed from one gate to another, we bore them to the cemetery. The enemy gathered together in one body and rushed at first to attack a strongpoint in the southern part of the city near the castle. Our men resisted bravely and manfully. The enemy was repulsed here, and as beacons were lit on the northern side of the city, they sought to break through there. There were no defences on that side, and a mass of raging and uncontrolled enemy forces broke through, and set fires to houses in various places. Alas, no small part of the city was burnt down, though the greater part survived unburnt. An enormous booty of chattels from the city; and of oxen, sheep, beasts, and horses from the countryside was carried off. Many were taken prisoner in the streets and in the townships, and led away, coupled like dogs, into wretched captivity. Whether they had the means or not, they were forced to promise on oath to pay whatever ransom the mouthpiece of their captors cruelly fixed. These things, certainly greatly oppressive to the wretched sufferers, happened on the first day of winter. Now the booty was taken away, numerous houses consumed by fire, the rabid and debauched force retreated, never to return on so degraded an enterprise.

On the thirtieth day of November, the earl of the city came to Worcester. Waleran grieved as he saw the firing of the city, and felt as if the damage had been done to himself. Intent on vengeance, he went to Sudeley with a force of soldiers, for he had heard that John fitz Harold had deserted the king and attached himself to the earl of Gloucester. If you ask what the earl did there, the answer is barely worthy of record for he rendered evil for evil. He seized and carried off a booty of men with their goods and cattle, and returned to Worcester the next day.

118. PLUNDERING RELICS (1204)

As the Third Crusade had failed to retake Jerusalem, Pope Innocent III quickly called the Fourth Crusade. The number of promised crusaders failed to arrive in Venice and, as they owed money for their passage to the Holy Land, the doge, Enrico Dandelo, pressed the crusaders first to attack the Catholic city of Zara and then Constantinople. The "official" reason for going to the Byzantine capital was to help Alexios IV Angelos gain the throne usurped from his father, Isaac, before proceeding to the Holy Land. That the Byzantines also had a monopoly trade agreement with Genoa certainly played a role. The city, which had never before been conquered, was overrun by the crusaders on 12 April after less than a month of siege. For three days the crusaders ravaged the city. As Gunther of Pairis explains, the crusaders did more than pillage and murder the populace: they looted the treasures of the churches, including many of Constantinople's most prized relics. The Fourth Crusade ended there.

Source: "Abbot Martin's Theft of Relics," in *Translations and Reprints from the Original Sources of European History*, vol. 3, published for the Department of History of the University of Pennsylvania (Philadelphia: University of Pennsylvania Press, 1897–1907), pp. 17–19; revised.

While the victors were rapidly plundering the conquered city, which was theirs by right of conquest, the abbot Martin began to cogitate about his own share of the booty, and lest he alone should remain empty-handed, while all the others became rich, he resolved to seize upon plunder with his own sacred hands. But, since he thought it not meet to handle any booty of worldly things with those sacred hands he began to plan how he might secure some portion of the relics of the saints, of which he knew there was a great quantity in the city.

Accordingly, having a presentiment of some great result, he took with him one of his two chaplains and went to a church which was held in great reverence because in it the mother of the most famous Emperor Manuel had a noble grave, which seemed of importance to the Greeks, but which our people held for naught. There a very great amount of money brought in from all the surrounding country was stored, and also precious relics which the vain hope of security had caused the Greeks to bring in from the neighboring churches and monasteries. Those whom the Greeks had driven out had told us of this before the capture of the city. When many pilgrims [crusaders] broke into this church and some were eagerly engaged in stealing gold and silver, others precious stones, Martin, thinking it unbecoming to commit sacrilege except in a holy cause, sought a more retired spot where the very sanctity of the place seemed to promise that what he desired might be found.

There he found an aged man of agreeable countenance, having a long and hoary beard, a priest, but very unlike our priests in his dress. Thinking him a layman, the abbot, though inwardly calm, threatened him with a very ferocious voice, saying: "Come, perfidious old man, show me the most powerful relics you have, or you shall die immediately." The latter, terrified by the sound rather than the words, since he heard but did not understand what was said, and knowing that Martin could not speak Greek, began in the Roman language, of which he knew a little, to entreat Martin and by soft words to turn away the latter's wrath, which in truth did not exist. In reply, the abbot succeeded in getting out a few words of the same language, sufficient to make the old man understand what he wanted. The latter, observing Martin's face and dress, and thinking it more tolerable that a religious man should handle the sacred relics with fear and reverence, than that worldly men should, perchance, pollute them with their worldly hands, opened a chest bound with iron and showed the desired treasure, which was more grateful and pleasing to Martin than all the royal wealth of Greece. The abbot hastily and eagerly thrust in both hands and, working quickly, filled with the fruits of the sacrilege both his own and his chaplain's bosom. He wisely concealed what seemed the most valuable and departed without opposition.

Moreover, what and how worthy of veneration those relics which the holy robber appropriated were, is told more fully at the end of this work. When he was hastening to his vessel, so stuffed full, if I may use the expression, those who knew and loved him, saw him from their ships as they were themselves hastening to the booty, and inquired joyfully whether he had stolen anything, or with what he was so loaded down as he walked. With a joyful countenance, as always, and with pleasant words he said: "We have done well." To which they replied: "Thanks be to God." ...

Therefore "blessed be the Lord God, who only does wondrous things," who in his unspeakable kindness and mercy has looked upon and made glorious his church at Paris through certain gifts of his grace, which he deigned to transmit to us through the venerable man, already so frequently mentioned, Abbot Martin. In the presence of these the church exults and by their protection any soul faithful to God is aided and assisted. In order that the readers' trust in these may be strengthened, we have determined to give a partial list.

First, of the highest importance and worthy of all veneration: a trace of the blood of our Lord Jesus Christ, which was shed for the redemption of all mankind.

Second, a piece of the cross of our Lord on which the Son of the Father, the new Adam, sacrificed for us, paid the debt of the old Adam.

Third, a not inconsiderable piece of St. John [the Baptist], the forerunner of our Lord.

Fourth, the arm of St. James, the apostle, whose memory is venerated by the whole church.

There were also relics of the other saints, whose names are as follows:

Christopher, the martyr.
George, the martyr.
Theodore, the martyr.
The foot of St. Cosmas, the martyr.
Part of the head of Cyprian, the martyr.
Pantaleon, the martyr.
A tooth of St. Lawrence.
Demetrius, the martyr.

Stephen, the proto-martyr.
Vincentius, Adjutus, Mauritius and his companions.
Crisantius and Darius, the martyrs.
Gervasius and Protasius, the martyrs.
Primus, the martyr.
Sergius and Bacchus, the martyrs.
Protus, the martyr.
John and Paul, the martyrs.

Also relics from the following: the place of the nativity of our Lord; Calvary; our Lord's sepulcher; the stone rolled away; the place of our Lord's ascension; the stone on which John stood when he baptized the Lord; the spot where Christ raised Lazarus; the stone on which Christ was presented in the temple; the stone on which Jacob slept; the stone where Christ fasted; the stone where Christ prayed; the table on which Christ ate the supper; the place where he was captured; the place where the mother of our Lord died; his grave; the grave of St. Peter, the apostle; the relics of the holy apostles Andrew and Philip; the place where the Lord gave the law to Moses; the holy patriarchs Abraham, Isaac, and Jacob; St. Nicholas, the bishop; Adelasius, the bishop; Agricius, the bishop; John Chrysostom; John, the almsgiver; the milk of the mother of our Lord; Margaret, the virgin; Perpetua, the virgin; Agatha, the virgin; Agnes, the virgin; Lucia, the virgin; Cecilia, the virgin; Adelgundis and Euphemia, the virgins.

119. RAZING ENEMY PROPERTY (1403)

On 1 April 1403, revealing the seriousness with which he took the Welsh rebellion led by Owain Glyndŵr, King Henry IV of England made his own son, the future Henry V, his lieutenant in Wales. Within a month, the 16-year-old prince reported on a punitive raid he had made into Owain's own country of Cynllaith, in which he attacked the rebel's homes. Despite these scorched-earth tactics, Owain would remain elusive and would lead an enormous assault on South Wales in July.

Source: trans. Rhidian Griffiths, in *Owain Glyndŵr: A Casebook*, ed. Michael Livingston and John K. Bollard (Liverpool: Liverpool University Press, 2013), p. 322.

Dearest and entirely well beloved,

We greet you fully from our whole heart, thanking you very dearly for the good attention which you have for the needs which affect us in our absence; and we entreat you most earnestly for your good and courteous continuance in this, as our trust is in you. And concerning the news from here, if you wish to know, among other things, we have been informed lately that Owain of Glyndyfrdwy assembled his forces of other rebels among his adherents to a great number, with the aim of raiding and also of fighting if English men wished to resist him in his purpose, and thus he boasted to his people; because of which we took our men and went to a place of the said Owain, well built, which was his principal house named Sycharth, where we supposed to find him if he wished to fight in the manner he said; and at our coming there we found no man, and so we set fire to the whole place, and several other houses of his tenants around. And then we went straight away to his other place of Glyndyfrdwy, to seek him there, and there we fired a fine lodge in its park, and all the country around it. And we camped there all that night, and some of our men went out into the country and took an important gentleman of that land who was one of the chiefs of the said Owain. He offered five hundred pounds as ransom if his life were spared, and promised to pay the said sum within two weeks. Nevertheless this was not accepted, but he was put to death; and various others of his companions who were taken on that raid suffered the same fate. And after that we went into the commote of Edeirnion in [...] of Merioneth and there we set fire to a fine and well populated country. And from there we went into Powys, and [because of shortage] of food for horses in Wales, we made our men carry oats with them, and we stayed for [...] days. And to inform you more fully about this expedition, and of all other news from here at present, we are sending this with our beloved esquire John Waterton, to whom please give full faith and credence in what he will report to you on our behalf concerning the above news. And may our Lord have you always in his holy keeping.

Given under our signet at Shrewsbury on the 15th day of May.

D. PRISONERS AND RANSOMS

120. ENSLAVING NOBLE HOSTAGES (511)

Among the many Roman practices that continued through the Middle Ages was the exchanging of hostages—typically the sons of nobility—to ensure good faith between two rival groups: having family members or otherwise high-value individuals in the possession of an enemy that could kill them tended to diminish the likelihood of breaking an agreement—although they sometimes were broken nonetheless. Here, Gregory of Tours relates just such an exchange and the repercussions when the treaty between the king of the Ostrogoths, Theodoric, and the king of the Franks, Childebert I, was broken.

Source: Roy C. Cave and Herbert H. Coulson, *A Source Book for Medieval Economic History* (Milwaukee, WI: The Bruce Publishing Co., 1936; repr., New York: Biblo & Tannen, 1965), pp. 288–89.

But Theoderic and Childebert entered into a treaty and each took an oath that neither would wage war upon the other. They took hostages so that they might the more firmly adhere to what they had promised. Many sons of senatorial families were thus given but when a new quarrel broke out between the kings they were reduced to servitude on the fiscal domains. And those who had taken care of them now made slaves of them. Nevertheless many escaped by flight and returned to their own country, others were kept in servitude; among whom was Attalus, nephew of Saint Gregory, Bishop of Langres, who was made a public slave and put in charge of the horses. He was the servant of a certain Frankish barbarian living in the district of Trier. Finally the blessed Gregory sent his men to inquire about the youth. They found him and offered gifts to his master, but he rejected them, saying, "One of such a family ought to be redeemed with ten pounds of gold."

121. GOSPEL BOOK RANSOMED FROM VIKINGS (c. 800)

The Canterbury Codex Aureus (also known as the Stockholm Codex Aureus) is a splendidly decorated book of Gospels, produced in England (probably at Canterbury) in the eighth century. Stolen by Vikings in the ninth century, the codex was ransomed by Alderman Alfred and handed over to Christ Church, Canterbury. Alfred's pious deed is remembered in this Anglo-Saxon inscription added to the first page of Matthew's Gospel. The codex now resides in the Swedish Royal Library, Stockholm.

Source: trans. Angus A. Somerville, from *A Second Anglo-Saxon Reader: Archaic and Dialectal*, ed. Henry Sweet, rev. T.F. Hoad (Oxford: Clarendon Press, 1978), p. 115.

In the name of our Lord Jesus Christ, I Alderman Alfred and Werburg my wife obtained these books from the heathen army with our money; the purchase was made with pure gold. We did this for the love of God and the good of our souls, and because we did not want these holy books to remain any longer in the possession of heathens. And now we wish to present these books to Christ Church for the praise, glory, and honor of God, and in thanks for his sufferings, and for the use of the religious brotherhood who offer praise to God in Christ Church every day—on condition that they are read every month, as long as God sees fit that baptism should be performed in this place, for the sake of Alfred, Werburg, and their daughter Alhthryth, for the eternal salvation of their souls. Also, I Earl Alfred and Werburg beg and beseech in the name of God Almighty and all his saints that no one should be so bold as to give away or remove these holy books from Christ Church as long as baptism is performed there.

Alfred. Werburg. Alhthryth their daughter.

122. SURRENDER TO BLANCHE OF NAVARRE (1218)

When Henry II, count of Champagne, died in 1197, the title passed to his brother, Theobald III. Four years later, he too was dead, and his widow, Blanche of Navarre, was pregnant with his heir, Theobald IV. Ruling Champagne as regent-countess, Blanche proved enormously adept in securing her son's future title. In 1215, however, Erard of Brienne, married the daughter of Henry II, Philippa of Champagne, and convinced her to press a claim for her father's lands. The result was the War of the Champagne Succession, in which many local barons rallied behind Erard against Blanche and her son. Despite the French king, Philip II Augustus, ruling for Blanche, in 1217 open rebellion was underway and the duke of Lorraine, Thibaut I, had joined Erard and Philippa. Blanche was not to be out-maneuvered, though. Leveraging foreign leaders and papal powers, Blanche isolated her enemies and then attacked them: in May 1218 she led an army that burned Nancy, the capital of Lorraine, and forced Thibaut I into a humiliating surrender, detailed here, that marked the effective end of the war.

Source: trans. Joan Ferrante, "A Letter from Thibaut, Duke of Lorraine (1218, June 1)," *Epistolae: Medieval Women's Latin Letters*, 2014, https://epistolae.ctl.columbia.edu/letter/1338.html.

I, Th[ibaut], duke of Lorraine, marquis, count of Messin and Daubourg, make known to all who will see the present letters, that in the discord which existed between me, on one side, and the lady B[lanche] countess of Troyes and her son, on the other, in the presence of the lord king of the Romans and the lord archbishop of Trier, and many others, such peace and harmony was mediated that I returned to the loyalty which I owed to said countess and her son, namely in the service and justice which my predecessors owed to the counts of Champagne. I conceded also in good faith and swore that not by me nor by my men, those men who are lieges of mine before other lords, would any harm come to the countess or her son or their lands because of war which Erard of Brienne wages against said countess and her son Th[eobald], but we will help them against said Erard and his wife Ph[ilippa] and against the heirs of Henry, former count of Champagne and his allies. But if, let it not be so, any harm were to come to them through me or my men, as was said, I would be held to make amends and to cause amends to be made by my men to the satisfaction and judgment of my dearest uncle, Odo the duke of Burgundy, and John of Arcis, within forty days after I had been asked. If however the duke should die or could not participate, Andreas of Esprisa would take his place. Similarly if John of Arcis dies or cannot participate, the countess or her son may put someone else, whomever she/he wishes, in his place. And if perchance those two could not agree, the bishop of Clermont would be the intermediary, whose judgment about said amends to be made would stand without contradiction. The bishop could also put someone else, whomever he wishes, in place of said Andreas, if Andreas were to die or could not participate.

For these agreements to be held thus, I placed in the hand of the countess and her son the fief which my dearest uncle Henry count of Bar-le-Duc holds from me and the fief which Hugo lord of la Fauche holds from me. Moreover I put in the hand of the duke of Burgundy my castle of Chacenay in such a way that should I fail in any way from making the amends, as was said, the count of Bar-le-Duc and the lord of la Fauche, after forty days in which they had admonished me about making the amends, they would come to the countess and her son, after the forty days were up, with the fiefs which they hold from me, and they would help against me from those fiefs until I had made the amends as stipulated. The duke of Burgundy indeed would render to the countess and her son said castle of Chacenay within forty days after he had been asked. And the countess or her son would hold it until I had made satisfactory amends, as said above.

The agreement on the hostages and the deposit of the castle in the hand of the duke of Burgundy will last, as expressed above, namely from this feast of Pentecost for five years, but I will be held obliged in perpetuity to the loyalty to be observed to that countess and her son, and to helping them in good faith against Erard and the heirs of H[enry] former count of Champagne.

That all the things noted in these letters may remain known and kept in force, I have confirmed with the protection of our seal and I asked my dearest lords, Frederick [II] illustrious king of the Romans, Theodore archbishop of Trier, C. bishop of Metz and Speyer, to confirm them by their letters.

Enacted at Amance in the year of the lord, 1218, on the kalends of the month of June [1 June].

123. ANNOUNCEMENT OF VICTORY (1356)

Despite significant victories over the French at the battle of Crécy and the siege of Calais in 1346, the arrival of the Black Death prevented King Edward III from pressing home his claim to the throne of France—even when the devastating plague took the life of the opposing Philip VI in 1350. It was not until 1355 that plans were put into place for a major assault on France, which was now ruled by King Jean II. The English subsequently launched a massive chevauchée *through France, led by King Edward's son, Edward the Black Prince. When Jean responded in defense, the two armies met on 19 September 1356 outside of the town of Poitiers. In the following letter, addressed to the mayor, aldermen, and commons of London, the Black Prince sends word of his victory over the French, which included the capture of the French king himself. Eyewitness accounts such as this did more than just pass along news of events. By establishing an initial, potentially "official" account of the news, they inevitably had a propagandistic function as well.*

Source: trans. Henry Thomas Riley, "Memorials: 1356," in *Memorials of London and London Life in the 13th, 14th and 15th Centuries*, ed. Henry Thomas Riley (London: Longmans, Green, 1868), pp. 285–88; revised.

Most dear and very much beloved,

As concerning news in the parts where we are, know that since the time when we certified unto our most dread lord and father, the king, that it was our purpose to ride forth against the enemies in the parts of France, we took our road through the country of Périgord and of Limousin, and straight on towards Bourges, where we expected to have found the king's son, the count of Poitiers; and the sovereign cause for our going towards these parts was, that we expected to have had news of our said lord and father, the king, as to his passage; and seeing that we did not find the said count there, or any other great force, we turned towards the Loire, and commanded our people to ride forth and reconnoitre if we could find a passage anywhere: the which people met the enemy, and had to enter into conflict, so that some of the said enemies were killed or taken; and the prisoners so taken said that the king of France had sent Grismotoun [Sir Jean de Blanville], who was in that company, to obtain for him certain news of us, and of our force; and the said king, for the same purpose, had sent in another direction the lord of Craon, the lord Boucicaut [Jean I Le Maingre], the marshal [Jean de] Clermont, and others. And the same prisoners declared that the king had made up his mind for certain to fight with us, at whatever time we should be on the road towards Tours, he meeting us in the direction of Orléans.

And on the morrow, where we were posted, there came news that the said lord of Craon and Boucicaut were in a castle very near to our quarters; and we determined to go there, and so came and took up our quarters around them; and we agreed to assault the said place, the which was gained by us by force, and was quite full of their people, both prisoners and slain, and also some of ours were killed there; but the said lords of Craon and Boucicaut withdrew themselves into a strong tower which was there, and which occupied us five days before it was taken; and there they surrendered. And there we were certified that all the bridges upon the Loire were broken down, and that we could nowhere find a passage; whereupon, we took our road straight towards Tours; and there we remained four days before the city, in which were the count of Anjou and the marshal of Clermont, with a great force of troops. And upon our departing from thence, we took the road so as to pass certain dangers by water, and with the intention of meeting with our most dear cousin, the duke of Lancaster, of whom we had had certain news, that he would make haste to draw towards us. At which time Cardinal [Hélie de Talleyrand-] Périgord came to us at Montbazan, three leagues from Tours, where he spoke to us fully as to matters touching a truce and peace. Upon which parley we made answer to him, that peace we had no power to make, and that we would not intermeddle therewith, without the command and the wishes of the king, our most dear lord and father; nor yet as to a truce were we at that time of opinion that it would be the best thing for us to assent thereto, for there we were more fully certified that the king had prepared in every way to fight with us.

Whereupon, we withdrew ourselves from thence towards Châtellerault, by passage over the stream of the Vienne; where we remained four days, waiting to know for greater certainty of him. And the king came with his force to Chauvigny, five leagues from us, to pass the same river, in the direction of Poitiers. And thereupon, we determined to hasten towards him, upon the road along which he would have to pass, so as to have a fight with him; but his battalions had passed before we had come to the place where we intended to meet him, save a part only of their people, about 700 men-at-arms, who engaged with ours; and there were taken the counts of Auxerre and Joigny, the lord of Châtillon, a great number of others being both taken and slain, both on their side and ours. And then our people pursued them as far as Chauvigny, full three leagues further; for which reason we were obliged that day to take up our quarters as near to that place as we could, that we might collect our men. And on the morrow we took our road straight towards the king, and sent out our scouts, who found him with his army; [and he] set himself in battle array at one league from Poitiers, in the fields; and we went as near to him as we could take up our post, we ourselves on foot and in battle array, and ready to fight with him.

Where came the said cardinal, requesting very earnestly for a little respite, that so there might parley together certain persons of either side, and so attempt to bring about an understanding and good peace; the which he undertook that he would bring about to a good end. Whereupon, we took counsel, and granted him his request; upon which, there were ordered certain persons of the one side and the other, to treat upon this matter; which treating was of no effect. And then the said cardinal wished to obtain a truce, by way of putting off the battle at his pleasure; to which truce we would not assent. And the French asked that certain knights on the one side and the other should take equal shares, so that the battle might not in any manner fail: and in such manner was that day delayed; and the battalions on the one side and the other remained all night, each one in its place, and until the morrow, about half Prime; and as to some troops that were between the said main armies, neither would give any advantage in commencing the attack upon the other. And for default of victuals, as well as for other reasons, it was agreed that we should take our way, flanking them, in such manner that if they wished for battle or to draw towards us, in a place that was not very much to our disadvantage, we should be the first; and so forthwith it was done. Whereupon battle was joined, on the Eve of the day before St. Matthew [21 September]; and, God be praised for it, the enemy was discomfited, and the king was taken, and his son; and a great number of other great people were both taken and slain; as our very dear and beloved knight, Neil Loring, our chamberlain, the bearer hereof, who has very full knowledge thereon, will know how more fully to inform and shew you, as we are not able to write to you; to whom you do give full faith and credence; and may Our Lord have you in His keeping. Given under our Privy Seal, at Bordeaux, 22 October.

124. RANSOM OF A KNIGHT (1356)

A medieval noble, knight, and squire were generally wealthy. When fighting in a battle this not only meant that they wore state-of-the-art armor and wielded state-of-the-art weapons, but also that opponents wished to capture rather than kill them. Ransoms of captured prisoners became a profitable part of victory to those who captured these wealthy men, as can be seen in this record of the ransom of a knight, Thomas de Voudenay, taken at the battle of Poitiers in 1356 (doc. 123). By ransoming him, English knight William de Welesby won a financial windfall.

Source: trans. Henry Thomas Riley, "Memorials: 1356," in *Memorials of London and London Life in the 13th, 14th and 15th Centuries*, ed. Henry Thomas Riley (London: Longmans, Green, 1868), pp. 290–91; revised.

Know all persons who see or hear these letters, that I, Simon de Worsted, mercer and citizen of London, do acknowledge that I have received, on the day of this writing, in the name and behalf of Messire William de Welesby, knight, of England, from Messire Thomas de Voudenay, knight, of the Duchy of Burgundy, by the hands of Turel Guascoin, merchant of Lucca, 300 golden florins of Florence, and a goblet with covercle, of silver, and a ring of gold without stone; in the which the said Messire Thomas was bound unto the said Messire William for his ransom, from the time that he was taken his prisoner at the battle of Poitiers, where the king of France [Jean II] was taken. In the which 300 florins of gold, goblet with covercle, of silver, and ring of gold, aforesaid, I do hold myself to be well and fully paid; and the said Messire Thomas of the same florins, goblet, and ring of gold, and of his said ransom, I do, by these my letters, for ever acquit. In witness of the truth whereof, to these letters I have set my seal, in presence of Henry Pykard, mayor of the City of London, Thomas Dolsely and Richard de Notyngham, sheriffs of London, and Roger de Depham, recorder of the same city, witnesses hereunto especially called and required. Given at London, in England, on the Eve of Christmas, in the year of Grace 1356.

E. THE FALLEN

125. MONGOL DEVASTATION IN HUNGARY (1241)

Perhaps a quarter of the population of Hungary died when the Golden Horde of Batu Khan invaded in 1241. Among the survivors was a cleric, Master Roger, who in a letter to his superiors documented the horrific devastation of his country at the hands of the Mongols, whom he called the Tatars. In the following excerpts, he describes the aftermath of the disastrous battle of Mohi, the fall of the city of Oradea, and his own escape from imprisonment.

Source: trans. János M. Bak and Martyn Rady, Master Roger, *Epistle to the Sorrowful Lament upon the Destruction of the Kingdom of Hungary by the Tartars*, Central European Medieval Texts 5 (Budapest: Central European University Press, 2010), pp. 187–91, 199–201, 217–25.

30 On the Bishops and Other Clerics Killed in the Said Battle

The slaughter among both those fleeing on the broad road towards Pest and those who stayed with the army was so enormous, so many thousand men perished, that one cannot estimate it nor can one very well trust reports as the loss was so huge.... Their bodies were so dismembered by horrible sabers that, though many searched for them, they could not be found after the retreat of the enemy. No mortal may have certain knowledge of the major and lesser laymen who drowned in the marshes and rivers, were consumed by fire, or perished by the sword. Many dead bodies lay on the fields and roads, some beheaded, some dismembered, burnt to death in the villages and churches to which they fled. This disaster, this devastation, this massacre occupied the roads for a distance of two days' walk and the whole earth was red with blood. Corpses lay around as common as flocks of cattle or sheep or pigs standing on open ground to pasture or like stones cut for a building in a quarry. The water had the drowned bodies; these were devoured by the fishes, worms and water fowl. The earth took possession of those who fell from poisoned lances, swords and arrows; they were gnawed away to the bone by flying birds red with blood and domestic or wild animals with sharp teeth. And fire got hold of those bodies that were burnt to death in the villages and churches. Sometimes the fat from such burnings even extinguished the fire so that these took a long time to be consumed. One will be able for a long time to find in many places charred bones wrapped in charred skin but not fully consumed, for these are not favored as food by any animals, unless they perished otherwise. So, as all the corpses became the possession of the three elements, let us see what remained for the fourth one. The air, held to be the fourth element, received the stench of the corpses from the three others; the air was so spoiled and poisoned by the stench that the wounded who remained half-alive in the fields, roads, and forests expired because of the poisoned air, though they might have otherwise survived. In this way, air also participated in this cruel ruin. What may be said of all the gold, silver, horses, arms, garments and other chattels of those who fell in battle or in flight? Horses ran around in the fields and groves with saddle and bridle but without riders, and were so panicked by the noise that they seemed to have gone mad. The terrified animals, unable to find their masters, had to perish by the sword or fall into the hands of others. Their neighing sounded like groaning or crying. The gold and silver vessels, silk garments and other useful things that were thrown away by those in flight on the roads, in the fields and in the woods in order to get away faster from their pursuers were not even collected. The Tatars were [at that time] concerned only with slaying people and seemed to care little for loot....

34 How the Tatars Took Oradea By Storm and How They Pressed On to Tămaşda and Beyond

As we said before, King Qadan, having taken Rodna and captured *ispán* [Count] Aristald, selected the best six hundred armed Germans who were under the said *ispán*. Guided by them, they crossed forests, woods, rocks and gorges and arrived beneath the city of Oradea. The city was very famous in Hungary, therefore many nobles, ladies and peasant women had gathered there. Even though the bishop had left with some of the canons, I stayed there with the remaining people. We had the castle, which we saw damaged on one side, repaired with a strong wall, so that we could find refuge there should we be unable to defend the city. But when one day the Tatars suddenly arrived and my situation in the city was precarious, I did not want to go to the castle, but ran away into the forest and hid there as long as I could. They, however, suddenly took the city and burnt down most of it and left nothing outside the walls of the castle. Having collected the booty, they killed men and women, commoners and nobles alike, on the streets, houses, and fields. What more? They pardoned neither sex nor age. That done, they suddenly retreated, gathered up everything in the retreat, and settled at five miles from the castle. They did not return for days, and those in the castle thought that they had left because of the strength of the castle that was protected by a deep moat and wooden towers on the walls; there were many armored warriors there, and whenever the Tatars came scouting from time to time, the Hungarian warriors chased them on fast horses. When the Tatars did not come to the castle for several days and everyone thought that they had completely withdrawn from there, many of the warriors and others who were in the castle, confident that they had withdrawn, left the castle and moved together into the houses that still remained outside of it. Then, one day at dawn, the Tatars, whose whereabouts they could not know, rushed upon them and killed most of those who did not manage to flee to the castle. Then they immediately surrounded the fortification, set up seven siege engines across from the new wall and bombarded it ceaselessly with stones day and night until the new wall collapsed totally. They did not stop at all, and with the towers and walls demolished the castle was taken by storm. They seized the warriors, canons, and others who had not been killed by the sword in the attack. The ladies, damsels and noble girls tried to escape into the cathedral. The Tatars ordered the warriors to hand over their weapons and from the canons they extorted by the cruelest tortures all that they owned. Because they could not easily enter the cathedral, they set fire to it and burnt the church, together with the women and whatever there was in the church. In other churches they perpetrated such crimes to the women that it is better to keep silent lest people get ideas for most evil deeds. Then they ruthlessly beheaded the nobles, citizens, soldiers and canons on a field outside the city. They violated the saints' graves, trampled upon the relics with their sinful feet, smashed to pieces the censers, crosses, golden chalices and vessels, and whatever else was designed for the service of the altar. They dragged men and women alike into the churches and shamefully mistreated and then killed them there. After they had destroyed everything, and an intolerable stench arose from the corpses, they left the place empty. People hiding in the nearby forests came back to find some food. And while they were searching among the stones and the corpses, the Tatars suddenly returned and of those living whom they found there, none was left alive. And this slaughter was repeated day after day. They finally left for good only when there was no one else to kill....

40 How the Tatars Returned Home Having Destroyed Almost All of Hungary

When they were due to be captured and killed, the better ladies [of the city of Esztergom], dressed as beautifully as they could, gathered in one of the palaces and appealed for an audience with the grand prince. All, about three hundred of them, were led out of the city to the prince and asked for the gift of being left alive under his rule. He, however, in his anger for not having won any booty, ordered them to be robbed and beheaded. And that was done right away.... On the command of the chief kings, we started to retreat across the wastelands with carts loaded with booty and arms, and herds of cattle and sheep, slowly searching all the hiding places and the darknesses of the forests, to find while retreating what they had missed when advancing. Thus, moving back slowly, we reached Transylvania, where many people had survived and where several castles were been readied after the Tatars had been there. What more? With the exception of a few castles, they occupied the whole country and as they passed through, they left the country desolate and empty. Then they left Hungary and marched into Cumania. Now they did not allow, as they had before, that whole animals be slaughtered for the prisoners indiscriminately, but only the intestines, heads, and feet of the animals were given to them. We feared—and heard from the interpreters—that once we left Hungary, we would all be given to their devouring swords. As I had no hope of survival, and a bitter and cruel death was already waiting at the door, I thought it were better to die here than to be tortured by the steady stings [of fear]. Therefore, I left the highway as if following the call of nature, and rushed towards the dense forest with my only servant and hid in the hollow of a creek, covering myself with leaves and branches. My servant hid farther way, so that the chance detection of the one should not cause the unhappy capture of the other. We lay thus for two full days, as in graves, not raising our heads and heard the terrible voices of those who, following the footprints of erring beasts, passed close by in the forest and often shouted after the prisoners who were in hiding. And when we could no more repress in the deep silence of our hearts the very just demands of hunger and the troubling desire for food in the closed silence of our hearts, we lifted our heads and began to crawl like snakes, using arms and legs. We finally met and began in low and feeble voices to utter to each other the sad complaints of our tormenting hunger. We mournfully wept and groaned that it would have been easier to die by the sword than let the bond of our limbs and the unity of body and soul fall apart through starvation. While we were exchanging such words of consolation, a man appeared and as soon as we set our eyes on him, we took to fearful flight and did not turn our sight away [from him] to see whether he was gaining or falling behind us in flight. But we saw that he was not trying to be a roadrunner, for he thought that we might use our advantage to trap him from the side. Thus, when we had mutually observed that we were all fugitives and unarmed, we stopped and made contact with nods and signs. When we had all realized who we were, we discussed in long and friendly conversation what to do. But we were doubly distressed, namely by wretched hunger and fear of death, so that we seemed almost to have lost our eyesight, for we were unable to swallow the sap of the plants of the forest or chew the grass as cattle do. And, although such great hunger beset us and the sting of numbing death threatened, we nevertheless obtained strength from confidence in living, and our hope in escape gave us courage. Thus, taking confidence and strengthened in the Lord, we excitedly reached the edge of the forest. We climbed a tall tree and surveyed the land destroyed by the Tatars that they had not wasted when they first came. What pain! We began to walk across the waste and abandoned land that they had destroyed while retreating. Church towers were our way signs from one place to another and the road they marked for us was rough. The roads and paths had vanished; grass and thorn bushes had taken over. Leeks, purslane, onions and garlic, left in the gardens of the peasants, were, when they could be found, brought to me as the choicest delicacies; the others made do with mallow, houseleek and cowbane roots. We filled our hungry stomachs with these and the spirit of life was revived in our drained bodies.... Finally, on the eighth day after leaving the forest, we arrived at the city of Alba Iulia. There we found nothing save the bones and skulls of the dead, the destroyed and broken walls of basilicas and palaces, soiled by the blood of an enormous numbers of Christians. The earth did not show the blood of the innocent, for it had absorbed it inebriated, but the stones were still cloaked with crimson blood and we could not hurry through them without continuous groans and bitter sighs. Ten miles from there, next to the forest, was a village, called Frata in the vernacular, and here, four miles within the forest, a marvelously high mountain. On the peak of it was a rock, a looming crag, where a great number of men and women had taken refuge. They received us with joy among tears and inquired about the perils we had passed through, all of which we could not tell them in a few words.

126. DESTRUCTION OF THE MONGOLS (1247)

In 1247 at the conclusion of his groundbreaking mission through the lands of the Mongols, John of Plano Carpini presented to Pope Innocent IV a book chronicling his experiences. This report, The History of the Mongols, *is one of the earliest Western European accounts of central Asia. This excerpt—while containing a confused chronology of the Russian campaign of Ogedei (here Occodai), the third son of Genghis (here Chingis) Khan and his successor as great khan, by combining two decades of variously led campaigns into a single effort—nevertheless appears to be accurate in describing the devastation and the unburied dead that the Mongols (here Tartars) had left in their wake.*

Source: trans. Christopher Dawson, *Mission to Asia* (Toronto: University of Toronto Press, 1980), pp. 28–30.

After the death of the emperor, as has been said above, the chiefs assembled and elected in his stead Occodai, a son of the ... Chingis Khan. Occodai held a council of his princes and then divided up his armies. Bati, who ranked second to him, he sent against the country of the great sultan and the land of the Bisermins. These latter were Saracens but spoke the Cuman language. Entering their territory, Bati fought with them and overcame them in battle. A certain city called Barchin held out a long time against him, for they dug a great number of pits around the town and covered them over, and when the Tartars were nearing the city they fell into the pits, and so were unable to take it until they had filled them in.

The inhabitants of another city called Sakint, hearing of this, came out to meet the Tartars and of their own accord surrendered to them. In consequence their city was not destroyed, but many men were killed and others transported. The Tartars plundered the city and filled it with fresh inhabitants; they then proceeded to attack the city of Ornas. This city was densely populated, for there were many Christians there, namely Gazarians, Ruthenians, Alans and others, and there were also Saracens there. The government of the city was in the hands of the Saracens. This city was moreover filled with great wealth for it is situated on a river which flows through Iankint and the land of the Bisermins and runs into the sea, which makes it as it were a port, and other Saracens used to carry on extensive trading with that place. The Tartars, unable to conquer the city by any other means, threw a dam across the river, which ran through the town, and submerged it with its inhabitants and property. Having accomplished this, the Tartars then entered the land of the Turks, who are pagans.

Subduing this country, they attacked Russia, where they made great havoc, destroying cities and fortresses and slaughtering men; and they laid siege to Kiev, the capital of Russia; after they had besieged the city for a long time, they took it and put the inhabitants to death. When we were journeying through that land we came across countless skulls and bones of dead men lying about on the ground. Kiev had been a very large and thickly populated town, but now it has been reduced almost to nothing, for there are at the present time scarce two hundred houses there and the inhabitants are kept in complete slavery. Going on from there, fighting as they went, the Tartars destroyed the whole of Russia.

127. IDENTIFYING THE DEAD (1346)

Colins de Beaumont was, according to this sole surviving work in his name, a herald in the house of Sir Jean de Hainaut when he took part on the French side in their defeat to the English at the battle of Crécy in 1346. In this poem, "On the Crécy Dead," which might well have been written mere days after the event, Colins recounts what he witnessed through a fictive conversation with the personified virtues. He relates not only a harrowing vision of the realities of medieval warfare, but also his despairing efforts to identify the fallen when he was called upon to attempt a listing of the dead from the torn coats of arms and shattered insignia they left behind.

Source: trans. Elizaveta Strakhov, from *The Battle of Crécy: A Casebook*, ed. Michael Livingston and Kelly DeVries (Liverpool: Liverpool University Press, 2015), pp. 37–51.

"Now Fame, tell me, if you would:
When I saw his lords in the fray,
And the standard of Alençon get trampled

To the ground, and the ranks
Of Flanders, of Blois,
Of Harcourt, of Lorraine,
And of Sancerre, and of the good count
Of Salm break in the plain,
Shields and helmets cast upon
On the ground, lords perishing,
Fame, tell me, should I not have been
Guiding him and no one else?"
"Indeed no, lady; but I am weeping
From mourning and for good reason:
For the good count of Alençon
Who is dead, which is a great loss,
Cruel, damaging, and difficult.
Alas! Now the great army
Is deprived of its wages.
The good man who provided them has died.
Now his riches are squandered,
Which were neither of gold nor silver:
They were made up of brave men
And of good knights.
I speak no more of it: if they have been trounced,
It is certainly for good and proper reason.
As for the noble count of Blois,
About this man I could say so much.
I saw him fighting on foot.
Loyalty saw it, she was there.
Indeed, Prowess, so were you.
How did you dare start such an enterprise?
You made him descend from his horse
With a meager retinue of men.
There was his sword bathed in blood;
There I saw him bleeding and wounded,
Going on, fighting on foot,
Always ahead without turning back,
Until he had brought the standard
Of the Prince of Wales all the way to the ground
And held it in his arms
As he died. Lord, what valor!
Ah, me! He was young of age,
Loyal, noble, courteous, and honest.

His death is a great loss.
The same is true of the duke, his brother,
Who was the lord of Lorraine.
And surely one must also consider
The good count Louis of Flanders,
Who died, which is a pity.
Also the man of Sancerre, who is the kind of man—
Though you already knew this, Nature,
For you had guided him
Beyond this region, both near and far:
I produce you as a witness thereof,
For he has always served you well!—
Who merited glory and praise,
And certainly, at the bitter end,
He did not deign to do otherwise
Than as his own battle-cry instructed him.
He did not deign to do otherwise
Than to "attack!"—that was his battle-cry.
Thus he maintained it for as long as he lived,
And he never broke it.
Therefore no one should weary
Of praising him at high court;
And thus also the count of Harcourt,
Who passed away, which is a loss,
Who was so courteous and so capable,
Loyal, noble and of such high status
That he could not have been a better man,
And who died there without assistance.
In the same way you led
The count of Salm to die in the thick fray,
Whom I saw commanding his people so well
That no one could imagine it being better.
May the Lord pardon him all his misdeeds,
For he died there at your instigation.
Ah, Lord! So many fine men died there,
Whom I observe remembered here
That never in the realm of France
Has such a loss occurred as I see here."
"Fame," said Prowess, "I do hear you.
Now, have you spoken your fill?
Indeed I have been listening at length

To Lady Nature and Courtesy,
And Loyalty, and happy Largesse,
Who are all complaining about me
Together. But, surely, it seems to me
That this grief should stay with me
And that I should be mourning the dead and lamenting.
There is good and ample reason for it,
For they were my charges
And they died in my service.
And lest anyone say that I should be at fault
And so that this quarrel may be concluded,
Let us go before the queen,
Lofty Honor, who is our sovereign lady.
If she judges that I might be to blame,
I will not seek to speak about this further.
I see her sitting over there,
Let's go." At that point they all arose
And came before Honor
Who was seated on a throne,
And she gave them much joyful welcome
When she saw them arrive all together.
Nature could not hold back
And renewed her unrestrained mourning.
Weeping, she calls on the queen,
She protests and complains against Prowess,
And each one, as much as she could,
Reiterated her complaint concerning the others.
The queen said: "Is this how
You exercise your grief for him?
From now on, let there be no wailing nor weeping.
It must be abandoned, hard though it is.
I am your sovereign lady,
You are obliged to obey me.
Now I wish to pronounce my verdict.
I am greatly afflicted by their death,
But may you know that I am greatly joyful
That they died in such a manner.
Now it is meet and right that we esteem
Their life, which has thus ended,
And, by their end, their life has been refined
As much as fine gold is.

There can be no end more noble
Than to die for one's true lord.
I have that much more joy for such a death
Than for one hundred men who have remained alive.
And, for the love of God, if you love them
And ever loved them while they were alive,
Be joyful for this death,
For I wish for this kind of death and esteem it."
Then she took Fame by the hand
And said: "Go, Fame, do not tarry;
I command you and so charge you
To go around the mount
To speak praise of those who died
In the battle with such honor,
Who died before their sovereign
And for the maintenance of his honor.
Fame, you should thus not tarry
To proclaim this immediately.
And so you will tell without hesitation
That I have, within my records,
Their names and their deeds and their words."
Then Fame spoke to Lady Honor:
"I will go readily, but, by my soul,
My speech is soon forgotten there;
However, lady, if you so wish,
It would be good that this affair
Be set in rhyme, and not in prose,
For in rhyme is it perceived to be more truthful
And is stamped longer in the memory.
And there is a court musician here,
Who serves high-born men in exactly this.
Colins is his name, born of Hainaut,
And he has many a time exerted great effort
To commemorate the good of good men."
"Fame, go then, find out from him
Whether he might wish to give this a try."
"Yes, in truth, lady, I am certain he would,
For surely indeed he must."
Then Fame came to the door,
Opened it, brought me inside,
And relayed to me in a few words his message

Upon installing me in the room,
He said, "Look around, good friend."
Then I saw the ladies of whom I have spoken,
Saddened, pale, mournful, and afflicted
With lamentation and with suffering.
There I saw cast in the middle of the floor
Many a ragged standard
And many a defouled coat,
And many a shield so shattered and so scratched
That no color nor hue appeared upon them,
And all of this greatly saddened my heart.
I clearly recognized the eight standards
Of a king, a duke and six counts,
In memory of whom this account has been produced.
And I saw anew a whole mount of others:
I saw the standard of the fine man of Chaumont,
Namely of Jean d'Amboise,
Whose death I find unbearably painful;
That of Muretit, whom I mourn;
I saw that of Thibaut of Morveil
And that of Maulévrier.
About Maulévrier, I heard it attested
Before Fame, that he never fell back on his word,
And that he had led in his retinue
Ten knights,
But only one had escaped alive.
Beside the standards were scattered, I saw,
The shields of Guiart of Thouars,
Of Chemillé and of Savonnières
And others of many designs,
All split and all shattered.
Lord! My heart was so afflicted
Over it being impossible to recognize them,
For no distinguishing features appeared upon them.
I turned towards the standards:
I saw the arms of the good
Archbishop Jean of Parthenay,
And of Guillaume of Chalon,
And I also saw, quite close to theirs,
The one of good Jacquemart of Étrelles,

All shattered and all broken;
I saw the surcoat of Hugh of Elcane,
Who was indeed closely bound to Honor.
I saw three more of younger men
Quite close still to the standards:
Of Baussart, of Chamillart, and of Saint-Moré,
For whom Nature mourned greatly,
For she considered it a terrible loss
That she had lost them so young.
Ah, Lord! I was so anguished
That I was seeing so many insignia there
And none that I could recognize,
Whether it were a little pennant or a standard,
A shield, a surcoat, or a pommel ornament:
All were dismantled and all were broken.
In this way I gazed all around,
And I noticed Guillaumes Guenant
Beside his son, all together,
Charros, beside Guillaume Turpin,
And Guy of Laval, brother to Herpin.
I found also Beaumont and Champenois.
But it was with great difficulty that I could even establish
Whether or not these were really them.
Then I turned back towards Fame
And said: "Fame, by the grace of God,
Kindly let me have
Full knowledge of these coats of arms."
"Friend," he said, "by what means
Would you like presently to gain this knowledge?
You may surely well know
That I cannot stay here that long.
Rather, it is high time that I start preparing
To carry out Honor's command.
But tell me now, I ask of you,
Did you see, as you looked from the mount to the valley
The royal standard-bearer
Who carried the royal banner
And was named Regnaut de Saint Marc?
And further Guillaumes Guenars,
Who bore the standard of Thouars,

Aubelluce and that of Crouy,
And Robert and Jean of Picquigny.
Those were prisoners killed there
Because over each occurred such a discord
As to who would have the two, but I note that,
Lest it be forgotten that thus was each killed.
I will say nothing more, in few words,
About the others, but, to my mind,
If you wish to know the truth of it,
Your best source of knowledge
Is Guillaume of Surgères.
That man will be a good guide for you.
Between him and Huet Cholet—
I do not wish to speak about this for much longer—
You will learn through them.
Simon Chamillars was taken prisoner
And Jean of Cayeux-sur-Mer, as well.
But do you know for sure, without any doubt,
That these two were taken together in valor?
They are unable to speak truthfully about this,
Unlike how Guillaume and Huet can.
Because here is what happened:
Each was captured in the combat
And thus, at that point they were led away
Without seeing who was dead or alive
Except those who were still in the fighting.
Guillaume, however, was discovered
Among the dead, wounded in the face and body,
The night after the battle,
And then indeed Huet Cholet, without doubt,
Was found on the third day after the battle,
Which was certainly directly confirmed.
Let Honor have them, I insist,
Ranged with the dead in her records,
For they had been left for dead.
And therefore," he said, "let them both swear there
That it is better for either of them to speak into a sack,
Those who have been ransomed in that place,
Whereas the two who took part in it all,
let them be given full permission
To speak; either will tell it to you truthfully."

With that Fame drew the door
Of the chamber and went out.
And then it came to pass in such a way
That I saw nothing, and thus I lost
Everything that I had just seen before:
The room, the ladies, the accouterments.
As a result, such a great astonishment
Came over me that it forced me to wake up.
Nevertheless I remembered very clearly
What I had seen in the dream,
Which I do not hold to have been a lie,
But surely a vision.
At that very moment I made the necessary arrangements
To render these matters in rhyme.
I have to do this with great speed
Since I could not learn all their names,
And neither could I wait that long,
Until I could speak with either Guillaume or Huet,
In order to know with certainty
All their names in detail.
Thus I offer a more general account,
As my sense bears witness
And so I pray everyone to pardon me
For the lackings of my paltry faculties,
Which are everywhere apparent
In this little work that concludes here.
May the Lord guide us to our ultimate bliss!

128. EXPENSES FOR THE QUARTERING OF HOTSPUR (1403)

On 21 July 1403 Henry "Hotspur" Percy died in a rebellion against King Henry IV of England that was decided at the battle of Shrewsbury. After the battle, his corpse was first buried and then later disinterred, displayed, and then beheaded and quartered. The parts of his body were distributed across the realm as a warning to others who might rebel. The Exchequer Rolls record the following report of William Banastre, the sheriff who was placed in charge of this process: what he had to do, and how much it cost.

Source: trans. W.G.D. Fletcher, "Some Documents Relative to the Battle of Shrewsbury," *Transactions of the Shropshire Archaeological and Natural History Society*, 2nd ser., vol. 10 (1898), pp. 243–45; revised.

The account of William Banastre, sheriff of Salop, of the costs and expenses set forth and paid by him for the transporting of the four quarters of the body of Henry Percy and the head of the baron of Kynnerton, as well as the head of Richard Vernon, knight, who lately made insurrection against the king and his royal majesty and against the debt of their allegiance at Husefeld near Salop on Saturday on the vigil of the blessed Mary Magdalene in the fourth year of this king and by him conquered and sent from Salop: one quarter to the city of London, a second quarter to Bristol, a third quarter to the town of Newcastle-upon-Tyne, and the fourth quarter with the aforesaid two heads to the town of Chester, in the said fourth year, by writ of the king under his Great Seal dated the 26th day of July in the said fourth year to the aforesaid sheriff there directed, and over this account delivered, by which writ the king commanded the aforesaid sheriff, firmly enjoining him that he should receive from the bailiffs of the town of Salop the said four quarters of the body of the aforesaid Henry Percy and the aforesaid two heads, who lately made insurrection against the king and his royal majesty and against the debt of their allegiance, and should send with all the speed that he could by those for whom he would answer one quarter of the body of the aforesaid Henry to the mayor and sheriffs of London, another quarter to the mayor and bailiffs of the town of Bristol, a third quarter of the body to the mayor and bailiffs of the town of Newcastle-upon-Tyne, and the fourth quarter of the aforesaid body together with the aforesaid heads to the mayor and bailiffs of the town of Chester, and deliver the same on the part of the king to be placed over the gates of the aforesaid towns to stay there as long as they were able. And the king commanded the aforesaid mayors, sheriffs, and bailiffs that they should receive the aforesaid quarters and heads in form aforesaid. And the king commanded the aforesaid sheriff to make an allocation of the costs and expenses which appear about the premises in an account to the king's exchequer, etc. And the aforesaid sheriff made an account of his costs and expenses, as below.

The same accounts in 12 rods of cane bought and expended in 4 sacks thence made for the carriage of the aforesaid quarters and heads, and wax and rosin bought and expended for the waxing of the sacks, also cloves, cumin, anise, and other different spices and salt to be placed in the said sacks to keep the aforesaid quarters and heads, on account of their putrefaction and decay, in the said fourth year, and also in parboiling the same 4 quarters, 21s 9d by the aforesaid writs of the king above in the title of this account in the same year as is contained in a certain schedule of particulars here into the treasury delivered. And in money paid to 4 valets journeying from Salop to London for the carriage of one quarter of the aforesaid body, and thence returning to Salop, according to agreement made with them, in gross 53s 4d by the same writs of the king as is there contained. And in money paid to three valets journeying from Salop to Bristol, for the carriage of a second quarter of the aforesaid body, and thence returning to Salop, according to agreement made with them, in gross 40s by the same writs of the king, as is there contained. And in like money paid to 4 valets journeying from Salop to the town of Newcastle-upon-Tyne, for the carriage of a third quarter of the aforesaid body, and from thence returning to Salop, according to agreement made with them, in gross £4 by the same writs of the king, as is there [contained]. And in like money paid to 6 valets journeying from Salop to Chester, for the carriage of the fourth quarter of the aforesaid body and the two heads aforesaid, and thence returning to Salop, according to agreement made with them, in gross £4, by the same writs of the king, as is there contained.

Sum expended: £13 15s. And in account to the same sheriff in the fourth [year] of the king, etc.

F. AN END OF WAR

129. TWO SIDES OF A TREATY (1245)

In 1245 the Moorish leader Abu 'Abd Allah Ibn Hudhayl, known as al-Azraq, surrendered to Alfonso, the son of James the Conqueror, king of Aragon and Catalonia, in northeastern Spain. The unusual documents printed below are two versions of the treaty drawn up on this occasion: one for the Aragonese written in Spanish, and another, for the Moors, written in Arabic. It came at the end of James's 15-year Aragonese campaign to take the territory of Valencia on Spain's east coast; the treaty dealt with one small territory within Valencia. Al-Azraq would rebel in 1248 and 1258, but Valencia remained in Aragonese control.

Source: trans. R.I. Burns and P.E. Chevedden, *Negotiating Cultures: Bilingual Surrender Treaties in Muslim-Crusader Spain under James the Conqueror* (Leiden, Netherlands: Brill, 1999), pp. 36–37, 49–50.

Spanish Version of the Treaty

Let it be known to all present and future: that I Abu 'Abd Allah Ibn Hudhayl, vizier and lord of Alcalá, make myself your vassal, lord Don Alfonso the elder son of the king of Aragon, and I give you eight castles—the one called Pop and the other Tárbena, and Margarida, Cheroles, Castell, Alcalá, Gallinera, and Perpunchent.

These aforesaid castles I give you with their villages, and with districts, and with pastures, and with as much as belongs to them. And of the aforesaid castles, I give you lord Don Alfonso two castles immediately, Pop and Tárbena; and I retain for myself Alcalá and Perpunchent, as an estate for me and for my children and for my family-line, to do with them entirely according to my will. And the other four castles—Margarida, Cheroles, Castell, and Gallinera—these

I keep for three years in such accord that you lord Don Alfonso have half the revenues and I the other half; and those three years having passed, that I give you the castles free and quit, without any litigation, with all their districts and with all their rights just as is said above.

And besides, I make this agreement with you, lord: that of as many castles as I can win from here on through the three years, I give you half the revenues; and the three years having passed, that I give you the castles that I will gain, along with the other four, just as is said above.

And I Don Alfonso by the grace of God prince, elder son of the king of Aragon, receive you Abu 'Abd Allah Ibn Hudhayl vizier and lord of Alcalá as my cherished and much esteemed and very honored and loyal vassal. And I grant and give two castles, Alcalá and Perpunchent, as an estate for you and all your family-line, to give, sell, pledge, or use entirely according to your will.

And I give you the revenues of the two villages Ebo and Tollos for those three years, and after the three years that you release to me those two villages, with the other castles.

Furthermore I swear and contract and grant that all these agreements hold, just as is written above, but in such wise that you be my vassal for the castle of Alcalá and for that which I give you.

Given at Pouet, the sixteenth day of April....

Arabic Version of the Treaty

In the name of God, the merciful, the compassionate. May God bless our lord Mohammed and his family!

This is a noble decree, enjoined by the exalted prince, the heroic, the most fortunate, ... the infante [that is, prince] Don Alfonso, son of the exalted king, the divinely assisted, the ruler of Aragon, upon the most illustrious wazir, the noble, the highest, the most eminent, the most exalted Abu 'Abd Allah b. Hudhayl—may God honor him! [Wherefore] the abovementioned exalted prince makes an agreement with him for three years from the present date, which is stated at the end of the decree, that his [the wazir's] property and retainer['s] shall remain in his castles, and that the abovementioned wazir shall give to the abovementioned exalted prince two castles, namely Pop and Tarbena, which he shall now hand over to him. The rest of the castles shall remain in the possession of the abovementioned wazir, namely Castell, Cheroles, Margarida, Alcalá, Perpunchent, and Gallinera, until the end of the three years. But the abovementioned wazir shall hand them over to the abovementioned prince when the three years have expired, except for the castle of Alcalá with its revenues and the revenues of the villages of Perpunchent, which shall remain henceforth in the perpetual possession of the abovementioned wazir and his descendant for the duration of the reign of the exalted prince. [Furthermore,] the exalted prince shall give to the abovementioned wazir the revenues of Ebo and Tollos for the duration of the three years. When he [the wazir] hands over to him [the prince] the abovementioned castles, namely Margarida, Castell, Cheroles, and Gallinera, he [the wazir] shall [also] hand over to him [the prince] Ebo and Tollos. The exalted prince [also agrees] to give to the *qa'id* [that is, lord] Abu Yahyá b. Abu Ishaq, the ruler of Castell, the village[s] of Espel-la and Petracos to be his perpetually for the duration of the reign of the prince, [both] for himself and his descendant.

[It is further agreed] that the wazir shall give to the exalted prince from the four castles, which he shall hand over to him when three years have elapsed [that is, Margarida, Castell, Cheroles, and Gallinera], half the tithe; and whatever castles the wazir obtains [for] the ruler of Aragon, either by force or by capitulation, the wazir shall have half of the revenue [from these castles] for the duration of the three years. But when the three years expire, he [the wazir] shall hand them over to him [the prince] along with the four other castles.

Written on [15 April 1245].

130. THE BURGHERS OF CALAIS (1346)

After his extraordinary victory at the battle of Crécy in 1346, King Edward III of England marched north and laid siege to the port of Calais, deemed important by Edward as it would give him access both to northern France—for military purposes—and the southern Low Countries—for economic purposes. King Philip VI of France, still recovering from his devastating losses in the earlier battle, arrived with an army outside the English siege camp, made threats and challenges, but ultimately was in no position to dislodge the invaders. The French king would leave, and the town, which had held out for 11 months, would surrender. In this excerpt, French chronicler Jean le Bel recounts what happened next: the story of the burghers of Calais, who would be immortalized by the sculptor Auguste Rodin.

Source: trans. Nigel Bryant, Jean le Bel, *The True Chronicles of Jean le Bel, 1290–1360* (Woodbridge, UK: Boydell Press, 2011), pp. 200–03.

When the people of Calais realised King Philip had gone and all hope was lost, and that they were so stricken with famine that even the strongest could barely go on, they decided it was best to place themselves entirely in the King of England's hands and at his mercy if the only alternative was to starve to death, for most of them were almost deranged with hunger and likely to lose both body and soul. They were all in agreement, and begged their commander Sir Jean de Vienne to open negotiations. He went to the battlements and signalled that he wished to parley. The king immediately sent [Sir William de Bohun] the Earl of Northampton, Sir Walter Mauny, Sir Reginald Cobham and Sir Thomas Holland, and when they arrived Sir Jean said to them:

"You are very worthy knights, sirs, and you know that the King of France, whom we acknowledge as our lord, sent us here with orders to defend the city and castle to avoid any shame to us and loss to him. We've done this to the best of our ability. But now help has failed us, and you've kept us under such close siege that we have no victuals left and will die in agonies of hunger unless the noble king has mercy on us. For pity's sake, dear sirs, beg him to have mercy and allow us to leave, just as we are, and he can take the city and the castle and all its wealth: he'll find plenty!"

Sir Walter Mauny replied, saying: "Sir Jean, we're clear about our lord's intentions because he's made them plain to us. He doesn't intend to let you go as you say; he wants you all to put yourselves entirely at his mercy, and he'll either accept ransoms for those he chooses or put you to death, for you've done him many injuries, caused him great expense and cost him the lives of many of his men: that he is angry is no surprise."

"These terms are too hard to accept!" Sir Jean replied. "We're a small company of knights and squires who've served our lord as faithfully as we could, as you would serve yours in such a case, and we've suffered many hardships; but we'd rather endure the greatest torment ever visited upon man than allow the lowliest fellow in the city to suffer a worse fate than the loftiest! We humbly implore you to beg your king to have pity and accept us at least as prisoners, alive and unharmed."

Sir Walter said they would willingly take this message and do what they could. They told the king all that had been said, but he ignored all pleas and arguments and refused outright to comply with this last request.

"I think that's a mistake, sire," said Sir Walter Mauny. "It wouldn't bode well if you were to send us to one of your strongholds! By holy Mary, we wouldn't be so willing to go if you condemn these people to death as you say, for we'd suffer the same fate in a similar position, even though we were doing our duty."

This reasoning greatly softened the king's heart, and he said: "Fellow lords, I don't wish to be a lone voice in this. Go back and tell them that, for love of you, I shall willingly receive them as prisoners; but I want six of the foremost citizens to come before me in their shifts, pure and simple, with nooses round their necks and the keys of the city in their hands, and I shall do with them exactly as I please."

The lords returned to Sir Jean with this reply and told him it had been hard won. Sir Jean said that, since there was nothing else for it, he would report to the citizens and his companions. So he left the battlements and gave orders for the bell to be rung to summon the people of the city, men and women alike, who were all desperate to hear good news, tortured by hunger as they were. The knight told them what had happened, whereupon they began to howl and lament most piteously. Then the wealthiest of all the citizens—his name was Eustace de Saint-Pierre—stood up and announced to them all:

"Sirs, it would be a grievous pity and calamity to allow all these people here to die, of famine or otherwise, and if any man could save them it would be a great charity and a most worthy deed in the eyes of Our Lord. For my own part, I have such faith in Our Lord that, if I can save these people through my death, I'm sure I shall have forgiveness for my misdeeds. I shall be the first of the six, and place myself at King Edward's mercy, barefoot and stripped to my shift and with a noose at my neck."

At these words they all worshipped him, overcome with emotion, many men and women falling at his feet—and little wonder, for the agonies of hunger they'd endured for more than six weeks are unimaginable. And after the worthy Eustace had spoken as you've heard, another of the richest citizens stood up likewise and said he would be the second. Then a third citizen stood, then a fourth and a fifth and a sixth. I shan't bother to name them all; but they all declared of their own free will that, to save the rest of the people there, they would place themselves, exactly as he'd demanded, at the mercy of King Edward, deemed the most valiant prince in the world. It was a great pity for them and a great service to the people of the city.

Chapter LXXXI

How six burghers of Calais, stripped to their shifts and with nooses at their necks, delivered the keys of the city to the King of England.

... The four knights took these six burghers and led them to the king. The whole army was assembled: there was a mighty press, as you may imagine, some saying they should be hanged directly and others weeping for pity. The noble king arrived, accompanied by his earls and barons, and the Queen—who was pregnant—followed after to see what would happen. The six burghers immediately knelt before the king and said:

"Most worthy king, you see before you six citizens of Calais, great merchants and members of its longest established families. We bring you the keys of the city and the castle, and surrender them to your will. And we submit ourselves entirely to your mercy, in the state you see, to save the rest of the people who have suffered many hardships. We beg you, in your great nobility, to have pity and mercy upon us."

Truly, every lord and knight present wept for pity or was moved to do so; but the king's heart at that moment was so hardened by anger that for a long while he couldn't reply. Then he commanded that they be beheaded at once.

All the lords and knights, weeping, earnestly begged him to have mercy, but he refused to listen. Then that worthy knight Sir Walter Mauny spoke up, saying:

"Ah, gentle lord! Restrain your heart! You're renowned and famed for all noble qualities: don't do anything now to make men speak ill of you. If you refuse to have mercy everyone will say you have a heart full of cruelty, putting to death these good citizens who've come of their own free will to surrender to you to save the rest of the people."

But the king frowned and replied: "Accept it, Sir Walter: I have made up my mind. Call for the executioner. The people of Calais have cost me the lives of so many of my men that these men, too, must die."

[At that the noble Queen of England, weeping bitterly, fell on her knees before her husband and said:] "Ah, my worthy lord! Since I crossed the sea—in great peril, as you know—I've asked for nothing. But now I beg and implore you with clasped hands, for the love of Our Lady's son, have mercy on them."

The worthy king fell silent for a moment; he looked at the Queen on her knees before him, weeping bitter tears, and his heart began to soften a little and he said:

"Lady, I wish you were anywhere but here! Your entreaties are so heartfelt that I daren't refuse you! Though it pains me to say it, take them: I give these men to you."

And he took the six burghers by their halters and handed them over to the Queen, and spared all the people of Calais from death out of love for her. And the good lady bade that the six burghers be freshly clothed and made comfortable.

131. GENERAL AMNESTY TO REBELS (1411)

As the Welsh rebellion led by Owain Glyndŵr was drawing to its end, King Henry IV of England issued a general pardon to the rebels for the peace of the kingdom on 22 December 1411. Those excepted from this offer of amnesty were the rebel leader Owain and Thomas Ward of Trumpington, who was reportedly impersonating the usurped (and dead) King Richard II.

Source: trans. Kelly DeVries, in *Owain Glyndŵr: A Casebook*, ed. Michael Livingston and John K. Bollard (Liverpool: Liverpool University Press, 2013), pp. 143, 145.

The king to the sheriff of Kent, greetings.

When, out of reverence for God, and by special request of the lords, both spiritual and temporal, and of the Commons of our Kingdom of England, in the last Parliament, and for the peace and quiet of our people, we pardon each and every liege of our Kingdom of England, with the exception of Owain Glyndŵr of Wales, Thomas of Trumpington, and our other adversaries, both in England

and France, or elsewhere, except those who joined it falsely, our surety of peace, that pertains to us against them, for all kinds of treasons, insurrections, rebellions, felonies, kidnappings, offenses, assaults, transgressions and contempts, made by them, before the nineteenth day of December, recently past, done or perpetrated (except for murders and the rape of women) provided that our lieges themselves did not support brigands, robbers or plunderers or were in prison for banditry, or robbery, without owing writs for or surrendering bail and are not convicted of or held for a felony of record. However, we do not wish that officials, our ministers or any others who are debtors or otherwise accountable to us, by debt or in possession of an aforementioned benefice, have any part of the present pardon. We command that this pardon be proclaimed publicly in every place in your bailiwick where it is more expedient or necessary, and that you notify each of our lieges that the letters be filed separately by them from before the upcoming Feast of the Nativity of St. John the Baptist, if they wish to obtain the benefit of such pardon.

Witnessed by the king at Westminster, on the 22 December on behalf of the king by the grace of his parliament.

Similar letters are directed to each sheriff in England, and to the chancellor of the king in the County Palatine of Lancaster.

132. AFTER THE FALL OF CONSTANTINOPLE (1453)

Angelo Giovanni Lomellino was the podesta (governor) of the colony Pera, opposite the Golden Horn from Constantinople. Largely populated by European merchants, mostly from Genoa—Lomellino was both—the colony officially took a neutral stance during the Turkish siege of the city in 1453, although Lomellino admits that, with his permission, several inhabitants assisted in the vain attempt to keep Constantinople from Ottoman capture. Pera would come to a similar agreement of neutrality with the Ottoman sultan, Mehmed II, as they had previously with the Byzantines, but as can be seen in this letter from Lomellino to his brother, the community was greatly worried that they would be included in the Ottomans' post-siege wrath.

Source: trans. J.R. Melville Jones, *The Siege of Constantinople 1453: Seven Contemporary Accounts* (Amsterdam: Adolf M. Hakkert, 1972), pp. 132–36.

My noble and beloved brother. You must forgive me, if I have not written before, and if even in this letter I do not answer yours. I have been so constantly filled with sorrow and distress, that at the present time I wish I were dead rather than alive. You will have heard by now, I am sure, of the unexpected fate of Constantinople, captured by the Turkish Sultan on the twenty-ninth of last month [of 1453], a day which we longed for, because it seemed to us that our victory was assured. The Sultan attacked from all sides throughout the night. As morning came, Giovanni Giustintiani [in command of the city's defenses] received a ... [manuscript damage] and left his gate, and went towards the sea, and by this same gate the Turks entered, finding no resistance, and this was the end of it; one would not expect to lose even a single house so cheaply. I can well believe that it came about because of our sins.

Now, my dear brother, you see my position, may God give me strength to bear it. They put the city to the sack for three days, and you never saw such suffering; the extent of their plundering cannot be calculated. I sent to the defence of the city all the mercenaries from Chios, and all those who had been sent from Genoa, and a great number of the citizens and burghers from here, with my nephew Imperiali and members of my own establishment. For my part, God knows that I did whatever was possible, since I knew that once Constantinople had fallen, this place was also lost.

They captured most of the city. A few terrified persons managed to reach here, and other merchants and citizens were able to escape, and most of them rejoined their families. Some were captured by the palisade [protecting Pera's landside], because the masters of the ships were so overcome by fear that they would not wait for anyone. With the greatest of difficulty I brought back some of those who were by the palisade; you never saw such a terrible sight.

Seeing the position I was in, I thought it better to lose my life than desert the city; if I had gone, it would have been sacked at once. I decided, on the contrary, to take steps for its safety, and at once sent ambassadors to the Sultan with fine gifts, saying, 'We have a good pact between us,' and asking in submissiveness that he should be willing to continue it with us. But no answer was given. The ships dragged themselves to a place where they could raise their sails. I sent a message to the masters, that for the love of God and for pity's sake they should stay the next day, since I was sure we would reach an agreement with the Sultan. They would have nothing of it, but made sail in the very middle of the night. In the morning, when the Sultan heard the news that the ships had gone, he told our ambassadors that he wanted the city thrown open to him, and we were barely able to keep our persons and our possessions safe; he said that we had done as much as we could to save Constantinople, and that we had stopped him from capturing it on the very first day. Here indeed he spoke the truth, and we were in the greatest danger. To escape his rage, we had to do what he wanted, as you will see from the enclosed; everything was done in the name of the burghers. I thought it best not to take part in anything, but afterwards I visited the Sultan, who came here twice. He caused destruction everywhere. The towers on the walls were broken down, and much of the moat filled in, and he had the Tower of the Holy Cross pulled down; also part of a curtain wall inside the barbican, and part of the barbican. The sea walls were left standing. He took all our cannon, and intends to take all the weapons and means of making war which the citizens have. He has also had lists made of all the property belonging to the merchants and citizens who have left here, saying, "If they return, they shall have them back, and if not, it will all belong to me."

Because of this, we arranged for a message to be sent to Chios, to tell all the merchants and citizens who had left here that they could come back; and if they did, they would have their property. With the Sultan's messenger we sent Antonio Cocca, and told all the merchants how the Venetians had left all their stocks of goods here. As to our own citizens who had gone away with their families and households, this letter informed them in the same way that all Genoese could travel on business in these parts.

That night the Sultan went back to Adrianople ... At this time ... he had the Bailo of the Venetians decapitated, with his son and seven other Venetians, and also the Catalan consul with five or six other Catalans. Now you can see whether we were in any danger. He looked for Maurizio Cataneo and Paolo Bocchiardi, who went into hiding, and sent one of his officers here to guard the place; while he sent other officers to Constantinople with about fifteen hundred janissaries. He sent an officer to Chios, as it is said, to demand that a transit tax should be levied, and it is said that he is sending one here, and intends to do the same in Caffa and all the larger ports. He also demanded from the Despot of Serbia certain territories which had been held by his father, and the Despot was most unwilling to hand them over. In sum, he has become so insolent after the capture of Constantinople that he sees himself soon becoming master of the whole world, and swears publicly that before two years have passed he intends to reach Rome; and by the One True God, unless the Christians take action quickly, he is likely to do things that will fill them with amazement. On the other hand, if they make the necessary preparations, Constantinople will be the beginning of his ruin.

For your information, the terms of the agreement which has been made are that our citizens can appoint a senior official to administer justice among them. When this agreement had been made, I planned to leave the Residence, and find a house for myself. But the citizens asked me to stay in the Residence and continue governing them until such time as it was possible for me to leave. For a number of reasons I was happy to agree to their request, although not, you will understand, because it included any salary.

The Sultan does not propose to levy any taxes, except for a poll-tax; but the *Compere* have lost the places which belonged to them. I would most strongly recommend to our Doge that he should arrange for a full-scale embassy to come here, to discuss everything that applies to our places of business; at the same time he should not relax his efforts to organise the Christian nations, and should do what has been done up to now. We are continually looking for aid; our forces now consist of one small vessel with a hundred and forty-eight men, such as they are. I can see the hand of God in this whole affair, because no one played his part properly, neither the Greeks nor the Venetians. By the One True God, unless some action is taken by the Christians, the Sultan will surprise them; all his aspirations are in the direction of further wars.

My nephew Imperiali was captured, and I have done everything possible to get him back. His identity was discovered, and they would not allow him to be ransomed. Then the Sultan heard of him, and took him, and another, a Venetian, with him; the reason being, that he wants to have some Latins at his court, which has thrown me into such melancholy that I scarcely know how to go on living.

I have done everything I could for the present, but could not get him back. I hope it will not take too long, if I keep up my efforts; money will not stand in the way, even if I am left with nothing but my shirt. Whichever way I look, I see trouble. Forgive me if I am not writing very clearly; my mind is so disordered that I hardly know what I am doing. For the last eighteen months I have had nothing but work and worries, and in one day all our labours went for nothing, because of our sins, I can readily believe.

My deepest respects to our master the Doge; I am not writing to him, because my spirits are so low. My respects too, if you please, to my father-in-law, to whom I have not written for the same reason, and you can read this letter to him. Commend me to my father and your wife, and give my greetings to the others.

133. OTTOMAN TREATY WITH THE VENETIANS (1478)

The Ottoman Turkish conquest of the Byzantine Empire in 1453 left the Venetians in a precarious position. With the Ottomans now in control of the eastern Mediterranean land from the Balkans to Syria, islands laying off these coasts became their next target. Several of these, including Crete, were held by Venice and integral to their ability to trade with the Persians, Mamluks, and Knights Hospitaller. This led to almost continuous war between the Venetians and Turks between 1463 and 1478, with the Venetians faring poorly and losing numerous territories and colonies in the Balkans and along the Adriatic to the Ottomans. In 1478 the two enemies reached a truce agreement that, not surprisingly, considering the military situation, favored the Ottomans and their sultan, Mehmed the Conqueror.

Source: trans. Diana Gilliand Wright, "When the Serenissima and the Gran Turco Made Love: The Peace Treaty of 1478," in *Reading the Middle Ages: Sources from Europe, Byzantium, and the Islamic World*, ed. Barbara Rosenwein (Toronto: University of Toronto Press, 2006), pp. 497–99.

I, the great lord and great emir, sultan Mehmed-Bey, son of the great and blessed lord Murad-Bey, do swear by the God of heaven and earth, and by our great prophet Muhammad, and by the seven *mushaf* which we Muslims possess and confess, and by the 124 thousand prophets of God (more or less), and by the faith which I believe and confess, and by my soul and by the soul of my father, and by the sword I wear:

Because my lordship formerly had peace and friendship with the most illustrious and exalted signoria of Venice, now again we desire to make a new peace and oath to confirm a true friendship and a new peace. For this purpose, the aforementioned illustrious signoria sent the learned and wise Sir Giovanni Dario, secretary, as emissary to my lordship so we might make the said peace with the following old and new provisions. For this my lordship swears by the above written oaths that just as there was formerly peace and friendship between us, namely, with their lords and men and allies, I now profess good faith and an open peace by land and sea, within and without the straits [the Dardenelles], with the villages, fortresses, islands, and lands that raise the banner of San Marco [Saint Mark is Venice's patron saint], and those who wish to raise the flag in the future, and all those places that are in their obedience and supervision, and to the commerce which they have as of today and are going to have in the coming years.

[Confirmation of Previous Agreements.]

[1] First, no man of my lordship will dare to inflict injury on or opposition to the signoria of Venice or its men: if this happens, my lordship is obligated to punish them according to the cause: similarly, the most illustrious signoria is obligated toward us.

[2] Further, from this day forward, if either land or other goods of the most illustrious signoria and its men is taken by the men of my lordship, it will be returned: similarly, they are obligated to my lordship.

[3] Their men and their merchandise may come by land and by sea to every land of my lordship, and all the merchandise and the galleys and the ships will be secure and at ease: they are similarly obligated toward us in their lands.

[4] Similarly, the duke of Naxos and his brothers and their lords and men with their ships and other boats are in the peace. They will not owe my lordship any service, but the Venetians will hold them just as it all used to be.

[5] Further, all ships and galleys, that is merchantmen and the fleet of my lordship, wherever they may encounter the Venetians, will have good relations and peace with them. Corsairs and klefts, wherever they are taken, will be punished.

[6] If any Venetian incurs a debt or commits other wrong in the lands of my lordship, the other Venetians will bear no responsibility: similarly, the signoria of Venice [vows the same] to our men.

[7] If any Venetian slave flees and comes into Turkish hands and becomes a Muslim, they will give his master 1000 aspers: if he is a Christian he will be sent back.

[8] If any Venetian boat is wrecked on the land of my lordship, all the men will be freed and all the merchandise returned to their agent: they are similarly obligated to our men.

[9] If any Venetian man dies in the lands of my lordship, without a will or heir, his goods are to be given to the Venetian *bailo* [Venetian diplomatic representative to the Ottomans]; if no *bailo* is found, they will be given into Venetian hands. Venice will write what to do.

[10] Further, the most illustrious signoria will have the right and authority specifically to send a *bailo* to Constantinople, with his household, according to custom, who will be able to dispense justice and administer Venetian affairs, according to their custom. The [Ottoman] governor will be obligated to give him aid and cooperation.

[New Provisions and Conditions for Peace.]

[11] If the said *bailo* wants to secure his position during this time, he is obligated to give my lordship every year a gift of 10,000 Venetian florins from the commercial transactions.

[12] Further, the most illustrious signoria of Venice is obligated for every debt lying between us and for all debts whether common or private or of certain of their men, for all the past time before the war until today, to give to my lordship 100,000 Venetian ducats within two years. Further, my Lordship cannot look for past debts, either from the most illustrious signoria of Venice or from its men.

[13] Further, the most illustrious signoria of Venice is obligated to hand over to my lordship the fortress called Skodra in Albania, except that it may remove the lord who is *rettor* [governor], and the council, and all the other men who wish to depart, specifically, with their merchandise, if they have any. The signoria will take the equipment and all other military matériel or whatever is found in the fortress at present without any opposition.

[14] Further, the most illustrious signoria of Venice is specifically obligated to transfer to my lordship the island of Lemnos, except that they will take the *rettor* and the Venetian citizens. The other men who want to go will take whatever they have to go wherever they want. Those who want to remain on the island will be pardoned for what they did up to this point.

[15] Further, the most illustrious signoria of Venice will hand over to my lordship the present fortresses and lands which were taken in the war

from my lordship, that is, the lands in the Morea [southern Greece], except that the men in their authority may go wherever they want with whatever they have. If any want to remain in the present territories and fortresses they will have complete pardons, specifically, for every act, if they did anything up to now.

[16] Further, my lordship is obligated to hand over to them the occupied lands, that is, to the former borders of their fortresses which abut the lands of my lordship on all sides.

The above-written provisions are confirmed and ratified and sworn.

The present writing was done in the year 6987 [1478], the 12th indiction, the twenty-fifth of the month of January, in Constantinople.

134. SURRENDER OF RHODES TO SULEYMAN (1522)

There are several eyewitness accounts of Suleyman the Magnificent's siege of Rhodes in 1522. However, only one, this badly damaged letter, written from Messina, Sicily, on 15 May 1523 by an English Knight Hospitaller Nicholas Roberts, to the earl of Surrey, describes the meeting where the young Ottoman sultan offered conditions of surrender to the Knights Hospitaller after they had defended Rhodes for nearly six months. The Knights were especially impressed by the determination of Suleyman, who despite losing 103,000 troops—confirmed by other sources as unexaggerated—was willing to continue his assaults on the city, and seemed to have countless numbers of replacements to do so. The Knights would accept the conditional surrender and, on 1 January 1523, leave the city.

Source: trans. Michael Livingston, from Whitworth Porter, *A History of the Knights of Malta*, vol. 1 (London: Longman, Brown, Green, Longmans, and Roberts, 1858), pp. 515–18.

Regarding the destruction and seizure of Rhodes, I advised your lordship by my letters, dated this past February, that with my next letter I would send your lordship an account of all such things that took place between the Great Turk and us during the siege.

I believe since the time of the Romans as far as I have read in [history that] there was never a town besieged with so massive an army, both by sea and by land, as [Suleyman] besieged with all. For by the sea he had ... of 5 sails not lacking 15,000 seamen; and by land, 100,000 fighting men, and 50,000 laborers with spades and pikes, there with the intent of seizing Rhodes in the space of four months. They brought a mountain of earth before them to the walls of the town, which was as high again as the walls of the town, which ... the destruction and death of many a man, [woman] and child. At all such times as they would give us any battle, they would put 400 or 500 cannoneers upon that mountain, that the people for a man could not go in the ... of that mountain.

I was one of those whom the Lord Master [of the] Religion [Philippe Villiers de l'Isle Adam] sent to the Great Turk for ... such time as the pact was made between the Turks and him. The Great Turk is of the age of [28] years. He is very wise, discrete, and much ... both in his words and also in his ... being of his age. I was in his court ... at such time as we were brought first to make our reverence unto him we found ... a red pavilion standing between two ... lines, marvelous, rich, and sumptuous. [Suleyman was] sitting in a chair, and no one else sat in the pavilion. That chair was of ... work of fine gold. His guard standing near his pavilion were 22 in number [and] they are called Sulaky, these number [and they are] continually about his person. He has [Janissaries in the] number of 11,000 of them; they wear on their heads a long white cap, and on the top of the cap a white ostrich [feather], which gives a great appearance.

[Suleyman's] army was divided in four parts, the captains [of which parts] were called as follows: the Grand Vizier is called Pir Mehmed Pasha, the second Mustafa Pasha, the third Ahmed Pasha, the fourth [Qasim, the] Beylerbey of Anatolia. These are the four governors under the Great Turk; every one of them had 50,000 men under his banner, and they encamped at four different places around the town. Every one of them made a breach in the wall of the town, such that in some places 500 men on horseback might come in at once.

After the wall of the town was down, they gave us battle often upon even ground, so that we had no manner of advantage upon them. Yet thanked be God and Saint John [patron saint of the Hospitallers], at every battle they returned without their purpose. Upon last Saint Andrew's eve [29 November] was the last battle between the Turks and ourselves. At that battle 11,000 Turks were slain, and of our part, 100 and ... score. After that day the Turks decided to give us no more battle, but to come into the town by trenches. As a result they made ... great trenches, and by the space of a month did come almost into the midst of our town, in so much that there lay nightly within our town ... thousand Turks. The trenches were covered with thick tables, and holes in them for their cannons, so that we could not approach them ... and a month after that we saw precisely that the town was lost that we had refused to surrender in hope of relief: at that time we saw that no relief was coming, nor was any relief prepared to come, and considering that most of our men were slain, we had no power nor ... manner of ammunition, nor victuals, but all lived by bread and water. We were as men desperate ... determined to die upon them in the field, rather than be put upon the stakes, for we doubted he would give us our lives, considering there were slain so many of his men.

But in the end of the season they came to parley with us, and demanded to know of us whether we would make any agreement and said that the Great

Turk was content if we would give him the walls of the town. He would give us our lives and our goods. The commons of the town, hearing this great proffer, came ... to the Lord Master, and said that considering that the wall and strength of the town was taken, and the ammunition spent, and that most of your knights and men slain, and also seeing there is no relief ready to come, they determined ... this offer of terms from the Great Turk gives us the lives of our wives and children. The Lord Master, hearing that the opinion of the whole commons was resolved to take that offer, fell down almost dead; after he had recovered himself a little, seeing them continue in the same, he at last consented to the same.

During the siege the Lord Master had taken part in every battle, often as the most humble knight of the religion. Knights there were slain 703, of the Turks 103,000. They gave us 22 battles. [Twenty-fourth of] September was the general battle, from the beginning of the day to high ... without ceasing. They gave us battles in five different places of the town, and there were slain, by their own confession, at that battle 22,000. The Great Turk was there in person, and in the battle we had slain three score ... upon our walls, before ever we were ready to ... them. There were slain of our part 6,000 and ... during the siege time. May the Lord have your lordship in his merciful keeping.

G. MEMORIALIZATION

135. BATTLE OF BRUNANBURH (c. 955)

Sometime late in the year 937, somewhere in Britain (a leading contender in scholarship is near the town of Bromborough in the Wirral), a remarkable coalition army of Scots, Britons, and Hiberno-Norse came together to meet the Anglo-Saxon King Athelstan and defeat him. The Battle of Brunanburh, a 73-line poem written within living memory of the event and preserved in four of the surviving manuscripts of the Anglo-Saxon Chronicle, *is undoubtedly the most famous accounting of their defeat: a testament to the brutality of the fighting and the glory of the victory that the Anglo-Saxon poet believed had been earned.*

Source: trans. Michael Livingston, from *The Battle of Brunanburh: A Casebook*, ed. Michael Livingston (Exeter, UK: University of Exeter Press, 2011), pp. 41, 43.

Here King Athelstan, lord of earls,
ring-giver of men, and his brother also,
Prince Edmund, age-long glory
won in strife with swords' edges
near Brunanburh. They split the shieldwall,

hewed the battle-wood with hammer-beaten blades,
Edward's sons, as it was their
birthright that they often in battle
against every enemy defended the land,
treasure, and homes. Their enemies perished.
The men of the Scots and the men of the sea,
fated, they fell. The field darkened
with the blood of men, from the rising of the sun
in the morningtime, when that glorious light
glided over the ground, bright candle of God,
of the eternal Lord, until that noble creation
sank to rest. There lay many warriors
destroyed by spears, men of the north
shot over shield, and so, too, the Scots,
weary, sated with war. The West Saxons thence
the length of the day in troops
pursued the hated peoples,
hewed the fugitive harshly from behind
with mill-sharpened swords. The Mercians did not deny
hard hand-play to any heroes
who with Anlaf over the sea-surge
in the belly of a ship had sought land,
fated to fight. Five lay still
on that battlefield—young kings
by swords put to sleep—and seven also
of Anlaf's earls, countless of the army,
of sailors and Scotsmen. There was put to flight
the Northmen's chief, driven by need
to the ship's prow with a little band.
He shoved the ship to sea. The king disappeared
on the dark flood. His own life he saved.
So there also the old one came in flight
to his home in the north; Constantine,
that hoary-haired warrior, had no cause to exult
at the meeting of swords: he was shorn of his kin,
deprived of his friends on the field,
bereft in the fray, and his son behind
on the place of slaughter, with wounds ground to pieces,
too young in battle. He could make no boast,
that gray-haired warrior of the sword-slaughter,
the old deceitful one, no more than could Anlaf.

With the remnant of their army they had no reason to laugh
that they were better in the work of war
on the battlefield, of the clashing of banners,
of the meeting of spears, of the meeting of men,
of the exchange of weapons, when they on the field of death
played with the sons of Edward.
Departed then the Northmen in their nailed ships,
dreary survivors of the spears, on Dingesmere,
over deep water to seek Dublin,
back to Ireland, ashamed in spirit.
Thus the brothers both together,
king and prince, sought their home,
the West-Saxons' land, exultant from war.
They left behind to divide the corpses
the dark-coated one, the black raven,
the horn-beaked one, and the dusk-coated one:
the white-tailed eagle, to enjoy the carrion,
that greedy war-hawk, and that gray beast,
the wolf of the wood. Never was there more slaughter
on this island, never as many
folk felled before this
by the swords' edges, as those books tell us,
old authorities, since here from the east
the Angles and Saxons came ashore.
Over the broad salt-sea they sought Britain,
those proud war-smiths. They overcame the Welsh,
glory-eager earls, and took hold of this land.

136. LAMENT FOR JERUSALEM (1099)

While Europe rejoiced at the news of the fall of Jerusalem to the crusaders in 1099, this was not a sentiment shared by the majority in the east, especially those in the Holy Land. Muslims, Jews, and Middle Eastern Christians had all been horrified by the brutality of the campaign and the indiscriminate slaughter of men, women, and children by the triumphant crusaders. The Iraqi poet Abu l-Muzaffar al-Abiwardi was living in Baghdad at this time and may well have been aware of the pleas for aid made by those Muslims living in the Holy Land to the caliphs of Baghdad. His poem is one of many from this period lamenting the loss of life and land to the crusaders.

Sources: trans. E.J. Costello, *Arab Historians of the Crusades*, ed. Francesco Gabrieli (Berkeley: University of California Press, 1969), p. 12.

We have mingled blood with flowing tears, and there is no
room left in us for pity.
To shed tears is a man's worst weapon when the swords stir up
the embers of war.
Sons of Islam, behind you are battles in which heads rolled at
your feet.
Dare you slumber in the blessed shade of safety, where life is as
soft as an orchard flower?
How can the eye sleep between the lids at a time of disasters
that would waken any sleeper?
While our Syrian brothers can only sleep on the backs of their
chargers, or in vultures' bellies!
Must the foreigners feed on our ignominy, while you trail
behind you the train of a pleasant life, like men whose world
is at peace?
When blood has been spilt, when sweet girls must for shame
hide their lovely faces in their hands!
When the white swords' points are red with blood, and the iron
of the brown lances is stained with gore!
At the sound of sword hammering on lance young children's
hair turns white.
This is war, and the man who shuns the whirlpool to save his
life shall grind his teeth in penitence.
This is war, and the infidel's word is naked in his hand, ready to
be sheathed again in men's necks and skulls.
This is war, and he who lies in the tomb at Medina seems to
raise his voice and cry: "O sons of Hashim!
I see my people slow to raise the lance against the enemy: I see
the Faith resting on feeble pillars.
For fear of death the Muslims are evading the fire of battle,
refusing to believe that death will surely strike them."
Must the Arab champions then suffer with resignation, while
the gallant Persians shut their eyes to their dishonor?

137. DEFEAT OF IGOR (1185)

Igor Svyatoslavich was prince of the Rus' principality of Novgorod-Seversk (the modern town of Novhorod-Siverskyi, Ukraine) when he launched a campaign against the nomadic Cuman (or Polovetsian) peoples along his border, who were led by Khan Konchak. The raid proved disastrous, as the Cuman forces surrounded and wiped out almost the entirety *of the Rus' army. Igor was taken captive, though he would manage to escape a few months later. Defeats often make good literature (*The Song of Roland, The Charge of the Light Brigade*), and Igor's failure near the river Donets in 1185 gave rise to a powerful epic:* The Tale of Igor's Campaign*—a powerful, nationalistic recounting in Old East Slavic. The excerpt here memorializes the climactic moment of the defeat.*

Source: trans. Robert C. Howes, *The Tale of the Campaign of Igor* (New York: Norton, 1973), pp. 36–38.

From morning unto evening
And from evening unto morning
The tempered arrows fly.
Swords ring against helmets
And kharalug lances crash
On an unknown plain
Amidst the Polovetsian Land.
And the black earth under horses' hooves
Was sown with bones,
And watered with blood,
And from these bones
There sprang up sorrow
Throughout the Russian Land.
What sound do I hear,
What rings in my ears,
Far away, early, before the dawn?
Igor turns back his troops;
He fears for his dear brother Vsevolod.
They fought for a day,
They fought for another,
And on the third day, towards noon,
Igor's banners fell.
Here brothers were parted
    from one another,
On the shore of the swift-running Kayala.
And here the blood-red wine ran out,
Here the brave Russians finished their feast:
Having brought their kin to drunkenness,
They themselves lay down
For the Russian Land.
The grass bows in pity
And the trees, in sorrow,

Bend to the ground.
For now, O brothers,
A time of sorrow has come,
And desolation covers our troops.
Obida [Injustice] has risen up
In the army of the grandson of Dazhbog.
As a maiden she stepped forth
Into the Troyan Land;
With her swan's wings
She splashed the Blue Sea by the Don.
And, splashing, she banished
The times that were fat.
The wars of the princes
Against the heathen
Have ended.
For brother said to brother:
"This is mine, and this too is mine."
And the princes began to say of small things:
"This is great."
And they began, among themselves,
Discord to forge.
And the heathen, from all directions,
Came into the Russian Land in war.
O far has the falcon flown,
Killing birds, to the seals
But Igor's brave army will not be raised!
Lamentation shrieks for it,
And Sorrow gallops through the Russian Land,
Hurling fire at the people from flaming horns.
And the Russian women wept, saying:
"Now we cannot think of our dear husbands
with our thoughts,
Or dwell on them in our minds,
Or gaze on them with our eyes.
And gold and silver we shall never wear again."

138. SONG OF THE BATTLE OF THE GOLDEN SPURS (1302)

By the end of the thirteenth century, the urban cloth-making industries of the county of Flanders relied entirely on English wool. Frequently this meant that the economic interests of Flemish townspeople clashed with the military policies of the kingdom of France.

A crack-down by King Philip IV (the Fair) led to the imprisonment of Guy de Dampierre, the count of Flanders; French soldiers were then garrisoned in the larger towns. In a well-planned attack on the night of 18 May 1302, the citizens of Bruges rose up and murdered their French garrison. The revolt spread like fire, and Philip sent his most experienced general, Count Robert II of Artois, and a large number of other nobles and knights to end it by force. On 26 June, outside the town of Courtrai, this army encountered an army that was for the most part made up of inexperienced Flemish militias. In a stunning upset, the Flemings emerged victorious, with the battle becoming known as the battle of the Golden Spurs due to the hundreds of knightly spurs that were recovered from the slaughtered French (doc. 73). News of this defeat was welcomed in England, as reliant on the Flemish towns for their economic interests as the Flemings were on them, and this song honoring the victory was composed shortly thereafter.

Source: trans. Michael Livingston, from *Political Songs of England*, ed. Thomas Wright (London: Camden Society, 1839), pp. 187–95.

Listen, lords, both young and old,
About the French so proud and bold,
How the Flemings utterly destroyed them
    upon a Wednesday.
Better off they'd have been to stay back in their land,
Than to seek the Flemings by the sea-strand,
For which many a Frenchwoman wrings her hands
    and sings wellaway!
The king of France made new statutes
In the land of Flanders, between them all,
That the commons of Bruges did very much rue;
    they said among themselves:
"Let us gather together our strength in the evening,
Let us take the bailiffs by twenties and by tens,
Lop off their heads upon the green,
    and toss them in the fen."
The weavers and the fullers assembled together,
And made their council in their common hall;
They took Pieter de Coninck to be called their king
        [de Coninck means "the king" in Medieval Flemish],
    and be their chieftain.
They took their chargers out of their stalls,
And closed the town within the wall;
Sixty bailiffs and ten they took down,
    and many another man.
Then the bailiffs, who had come from France

Drove out the Flemings who made the disturbance;
They turned against them with sword and with lance,
as men both strong and nimble.
I tell you in truth: despite their prowess,
Despite their patronage from the king of France,
Four hundred and five there had mischance
by day and also by night.
Sir Jacques of Saint-Pol heard how it was:
Sixteen hundred knights he assembled on the grass;
They traveled toward Bruges, road by road,
with a massive host of men.
The Flemings heard word of the case,
They began to clink their basins of brass,
And shattered them to pieces as stone does to glass,
and threw them all to the ground.
Sixteen hundred knights there had their end;
They lay in the streets, slaughtered like swine;
There they lost their steeds, and many a charger,
through their own pride.
Sir Jacques escaped by a cunning trick:
Out from a postern where they sold wine,
He fled from the fight back home to his bed,
in very great dread.
When the king of France heard this, at once
He assembled his peers of the realm every one:
The proud count of Artois, and many another,
all to come to Paris.
So the barons of France went there,
Entered the palace paved with stone,
And judged the Flemings should be burnt and slain,
by power of the fleur-de-lis.
Then said King Philip, "Listen now to me,
My counts and my barons, gentle and free,
Go, fetch me the traitors in bonds to my knee,
hastily and quickly."
Then swore the count of Saint-Pol: "From the mouth of God!
We shall fetch the scoundrels wherever they might be,
And draw them with wild horses out of the country,
by five thousands."
"Sir Ralf Devel," says the count of Boulogne,
"We'll leave alive neither canon nor monk,

Let us go forth at once, without any excuse,
  for no man shall live!
We shall flay the rabbit, and roast his loins;
Word of the deed shall spring as far as Cologne,
And even as far as Acre or Saxony,
  and make them full pale."
Seven earls and forty barons all told,
Fifteen hundred knights proud and quite bold,
Sixty thousand squires between young and old,
  go to take on the Flemings.
The Flemings bravely came to face them,
These proud French counts, their knights, and their men;
They killed and slayed over the hills and the plains,
  all for their king's sake.
These French came to Flanders as light as the hare;
Before it was midnight there fell upon them care:
They were trapped in the net like a bird in a snare,
  with charger and with steed.
The Flemings strike them on the bare head;
They will exchange them for neither ransom nor pay;
They chop off their heads, happen what may,
  and for this they have cause indeed.
Then said the count of Artois, "I yield to thee,
Pieter de Coninck by name, if you are gentle and free,
That I will suffer neither shame nor disgrace,
  and that I will not be dead."
Then swore a butcher, "By my honor!
You will never again see the king of France,
And you won't be imprisoned in Bruges:
  You'd eat too much bread!"
There they were heaped by the pit-full,
These counts and barons and all their knights;
Their ladies will await them in bower and in hall
  for far too long.
In their place must their king call other knights,
And take other steeds out of their stalls:
For they have drunk something more bitter than gall,
  upon the dry land.
When the king of France heard the news,
He cast down his head, his hands he began to wring.
Throughout all France the news began to wing;

and woe it was for them all!
Much was the sorrow and the weeping
That was in all France among old and young;
The greatest part of the land began to sing,
"Alas! and wellaway!"
Away, you young pope! What will be your counsel?
You've lost your cardinals when you need them most;
You'll never get them back, no matter the reward,
this truth I tell you.
Go forth to Rome to atone your misdeeds;
Pray to good saints that they will let you do better:
Unless you work wiser, you'll lose land and people,
the crown fell well to you.
Alas! simple France, it may seem a shame to you,
That a few fullers can so tame you;
Sixty thousand in a day made the trip often,
with count and knight.
From that the Flemings make a very good game,
And swear by Saint Omer, and also by Saint James,
If the French return, they'll get nothing but shame,
if with them they fight.
The war thus began, I tell you in truth,
Between France and Flanders, and they became foes:
For the French had put the count of Flanders in prison,
for treasons untrue.
Unless the Prince of Wales is given his life,
What the king of France gets will be more bitter than soot;
Unless he makes proper amends for his deeds,
he'll regret it anew.

139. THE FOUNDING OF BATTLEFIELD CHURCH (1406)

In 1406, three years after his defeat of the rebellious Henry "Hotspur" Percy at the battle of Shrewsbury, King Henry IV of England granted this license to Roger Ive and John Gilbert to establish a chapel that would provide intercession for the dead upon the site of his victory. Later, in 1410, Henry would reconstitute the chapel into a college of priests dedicated to Saint Mary Magdalen, and it today stands as Battlefield Church, a memorial to the battle and its dead.

Source: trans. W.G.D. Fletcher, "Battlefield College," *Transactions of the Shropshire Archaeological Society*, 3rd ser., vol. 3 (1903), pp. 179–80; revised.

Henry, by the grace of God king of England and France and lord of Ireland, to all to whom these present letters shall come greeting. Know that of our special grace we have granted and given license for us and our heirs, so far as in us lies, to our beloved Richard Hussey esquire that he can give and assign to our beloved Roger Ive chaplain and John Gilbert chaplain, two acres of land with the appurtenances in Albright Hussey in the county of Shropshire, lying in a certain field called Hayteleyfeld in which there was a battle between us and Henry Percy lately our adversary deceased and his adherents, which are not held of us in captivity as it is said. To have and to hold to the same Roger and John and their successors, in pure and perpetual *frankalmoign* [church property held in perpetuity in return for prayers for the donor and his heirs], to celebrate forever divine service daily in a certain chapel by them there to be newly made, built and constructed, for our safe condition so long as we shall live, and for our soul when we shall have departed from this life, and for the souls of our progenitors, and of those who were slain in the same battle, and there are buried, as also for the souls of all the faithful departed according to the ordinance of the same Roger his heirs or assigns on this behalf to be made. And likewise, by tenor of these presents, we have given special license to the same chaplains, that they can receive and hold to them and their successors, from the aforesaid Richard, the aforesaid land with its appurtenances, to celebrate forever divine service daily in form aforesaid, as is aforesaid, notwithstanding the statute passed concerning lands and tenements not to be put in mortmain, being unwilling that the aforesaid Richard or his heirs, or the aforesaid chaplains or their successors, by reason of the statute aforesaid, should thence be hurt molested or damaged by us or our heirs, justices, escheators, sheriffs, or other our bailiffs or officers, or those of our heirs. In witness whereof we have caused these our letters to be made patent. Witness myself at Westminster, 28 October in the 8th year of our reign.

SOURCES

J.L. Baird, trans. *The Chronicle of Salimbene de Adam*, 542–43. Renaissance Texts and Studies 40. Binghamton, NY: Center for Medieval and Early Renaissance Studies, University Center at Binghamton, 1986. Copyright © 1986. Reprinted with permission from Arizona Board of Regents for Arizona State University.

János M. Bak and Martyn Rady, trans. "Epistle to the Sorrowful Lament upon the Destruction of the Kingdom of Hungary by the Tartars," in *Anonymus and Master Roger*, 187–91, 199–201, 217–25. Central European Medieval Texts 5. Budapest: Central European University Press, 2010. Reprinted by permission of the publisher.

Jean le Bel. *The True Chronicles of Jean le Bel, 1290–1360.* Trans. Nigel Bryant, 200–03. Woodbridge, UK: Boydell Press, 2011. Reprinted by permission of Boydell & Brewer Ltd.

James A. Brundage, trans. *The Crusades: A Documentary Survey*, 31–36, 97–98, 100–03, 121–22. Milwaukee, WI: Marquette University Press, 1962. Reprinted by permission of the publisher.

R.I. Burns and P.E. Chevedden, trans. *Negotiating Cultures: Bilingual Surrender Treaties in Muslim-Crusader Spain under James the Conqueror*, 36–37. Leiden, Netherlands: Brill, 1999. Reprinted by permission of Koninklijke BRILL NV.

Niccolò Capponi and Kelly DeVries. *Castagnaro, 1387: Hawkwood's Great Victory*. Trans. Niccolò Capponi. London: Osprey, forthcoming. Reprinted by permission of the translator.

Linda L. Carroll, trans., Patricia H. Labalme and Laura Sanguineti White, eds. *Venice,* Cità Excelentissima*: Selections from the Renaissance Diaries of Marin Sanudo*, 214–15. Baltimore: Johns Hopkins University Press, 2008. Copyright © 2008. Reprinted with permission of Johns Hopkins University Press.

Adam Chapman, trans. "Indenture between Henry V and Sir Thomas Tunstall, 29 April 1415." *University of Southampton Humanities Research Blog*, 26 October 2013. http://blog.soton.ac.uk/humanitiesresearch/history-2/2013/10/indenture-between-henry-v-and-sir-thomas-tunstall-29-april-1415/.

Geoffroi de Charny. *A Knight's Own Book of Chivalry*. Trans. Elspeth Kennedy, 55–59. Philadelphia: University of Pennsylvania Press, 2005. Reprinted with permission of the University of Pennsylvania Press.

E.J. Costello, trans., Francesco Gabrieli, ed. *Arab Historians of the Crusades*, 12, 123–25, 129–37. Berkeley and Los Angeles: University of California Press, 1969. Copyright © 1969 Routledge & Kegan Paul. Reproduced by permission of Taylor & Francis Books, UK; reprinted by permission of the University of California Press.

David Crouch. "The Violence of the Preudomme," from *Prowess, Piety, and Public Order in Medieval Society: Studies in Honor of Richard Kaeuper*. Ed. Craig M. Nakashian and Daniel P. Franke, 91–92. Leiden, Netherlands: Brill Press, 1999. Reprinted by permission of Koninklijke BRILL NV.

Anne Curry. "Disciplinary Ordinances for English and Franco-Scottish Armies in 1385: An International Code?" *Journal of Medieval History* 37, no. 3 (2011): 293–94. Copyright © 2011. Reproduced by permission of Taylor & Francis Books, UK.

Charles Wendall David, trans. *The Conquest of Lisbon: De Expugnatione Lyxboniensi*, 53–59, 101–05, 137–39. New York: Columbia University Press, 2001. Copyright © 2001. Reprinted with permission of the publisher.

Ralph Henry Carless Davis and Marjorie Chibnall, eds. and trans. *The Gesta Guillelmi of William of Poitiers*, 115–17, 123–41. Oxford: Clarendon Press, 1998. Reprinted by permission of the publisher.

Christopher Dawson. *Mission to Asia*, 28–30. New York: Sheed & Ward, 1955. © 1955 Christopher Dawson, *Mission to Asia*, Sheed & Ward. Used by permission of Bloomsbury Publishing Plc.

George T. Dennis. "'Woman Repeals Pirates': Note in a Florentine Manuscript." *Byzantine and Modern Greek Studies* 23 (1999): 256–57. Copyright © 1999 Centre for Byzantine, Ottoman and Modern Greek Studies / Cambridge University Press. Reprinted with permission of the publisher.

Kelly DeVries. *Guns and Men in Medieval Europe, 1200–1500: Studies in Military History and Technology*. Volume 2. Trans. Peter Binkley and Kelly DeVries. Aldershot, UK: Variorum, 2002. Reprinted by permission of Kelly DeVries.

Kelly DeVries, trans. *Owain Glyndŵr: A Casebook*. Ed. Michael Livingston and John K. Bollard, 143, 145. Liverpool: Liverpool University Press, 2013. Reprinted by permission of the translator.

H.B. Dewing and Glenville Downey, trans. *On Buildings: Procopius, Vol. VII*, 97–115. Loeb Classical Library Volume 343. Cambridge, MA: Harvard University Press, 1940. Loeb Classical Library ® is a registered trademark of the President and Fellows of Harvard College.

Paul Edward Dutton, ed. and trans. *Charlemagne's Courtier: The Complete Einhard*, 20–21. Toronto: University of Toronto Press, 1998. Reprinted with permission of the publisher.

Joan Ferrante, trans. *Epistolae: Medieval Women's Latin Letters*. 2014. https://epistolae.ctl.columbia.edu/home

David Frendo and Athanasios Fotiou, eds. and trans. *John Kaminiates: The Capture of Thessaloniki*, 41–63. Perth: Australian Association for Byzantine Studies, 2000. Reprinted by permission of the translators.

Rhidian Griffiths, trans. *Owain Glyndŵr: A Casebook*. Ed. Michael Livingston and John K. Bollard, 322. Liverpool: Liverpool University Press, 2013.

Robert C. Howes, trans. *The Tale of the Campaign of Igor*, 36–38. New York: W. W. Norton & Company, Inc., 1973. Copyright © 1973. Used by permission of W. W. Norton & Company, Inc.

Hilda Johnstone, trans. *Annales Gandenses: The Annals of Ghent*, 26–30. Oxford: Clarendon Press, 1986. Reprinted by permission of the publisher.

J.R. Melville Jones, trans. *The Siege of Constantinople 1453: Seven Contemporary Accounts*, 132–36. Amsterdam: Adolf M. Hakkert, 1972. Reprinted by permission of the publisher.

Thomas E. Kelly, trans., Thomas H. Ohlgren, ed. *Medieval Outlaws: Ten Tales in Modern English*, 92, 95–98. Stroud, UK: The History Press, 1998. Reprinted by permission of the publisher.

Hugh Kennedy. *Crusader Castles*, 190–98. Cambridge: Cambridge University Press, 1994. Copyright © Cambridge University Press, 1994. Reproduced with permission of Cambridge University Press through PLSclear.

Paul W. Knoll and Frank Shaer, eds. and trans. *Gesta Principum Polonorum: The Deeds of the Princes of the Poles*, 31–71. Central European Medieval Texts 3. Budapest: Central European Press, 2003. Reprinted by permission of the publisher.

Kritovoulos. *History of Mehmed the Conqueror*. Trans. Charles T. Riggs, 41–52, 55–77. Princeton, NJ: Princeton University Press, 1954. Copyright © 1954, renewed 1982. Reprinted by permission of Princeton University Press.

Henricus Lettus. *The Chronicle of Henry of Livonia*. Trans. and ed. James Brundage, 144–47. New York: Columbia University Press, 2003. Copyright © 2003. Reprinted with permission of the publisher.

Michael Livingston, ed. *The Battle of Brunanburh: A Casebook*, 41, 43. Exeter, UK: University of Exeter Press, 2011. Reprinted with permission of the editor.

Fernão Lopes. *The English in Portugal 1367–87*. Trans. D.W. Lomax and R.J. Oakley, 247–51. Warminster, UK: Aris and Phillips, 1988. Reprinted by permission of the publisher.

P. McGurk, ed. and trans. *The Chronicle of John of Worcester*, 275–76. Oxford: Oxford University Press, 1998. Reprinted by permission of the publisher.

Jo Ann McNamara, John E. Halborg, and E. Gordon Whatley, eds. "Radegund, Queen of the Franks and Abess of Poitiers (ca. 525–587)," from *Sainted Women of the Dark Ages*, 60–105. Durham, NC: Duke University Press, 1992. Copyright © Duke University Press. All rights reserved. Republished by permission of the copyright holder.

Charles Christopher Mierow, trans. *The Deeds of Frederick Barbarossa*, 202–04. New York: Columbia University Press, 1953. Copyright © 1953. Reprinted with permission of the publisher.

Alec R. Myers, ed. "Parliamentary Roll III, Document 50," in *English Historical Documents, Volume IV: 1327–1485*. Copyright © 1996 Routledge & Kegan Paul. Reproduced by permission of Taylor & Francis Books UK.

Christine de Pizan. *The Book of Deeds of Arms and of Chivalry*. Trans. Sumner Willard, and ed. Charity Cannon Willard, 115–16, 171–72. Philadelphia:

Pennsylvania State University Press, 1999. Reprinted by permission of the publisher.

John C. Rolfe, trans. *Ammianus Marcellinus*, vol. III, 463–83. Loeb Classical Library Volume 331. Cambridge, MA: Harvard University Press, 1939. Loeb Classical Library ® is a registered trademark of the President and Fellows of Harvard College.

James Bruce Ross and Mary M. McLaughlin, eds. *The Portable Renaissance Reader*, 65–69. Harmondsworth, UK: Penguin, 1953. Copyright © 1953, 1968, renewed © 1981 by Viking Penguin Inc. Used by permission of Viking Books, an imprint of Penguin Publishing Group, a division of Penguin Random House LLC. All rights reserved.

Janet Shirley, trans. *A Parisian Journal, 1405–1449*, 233–34, 240–42, 249, 253–54, 260–65. Oxford: Clarendon Press, 1968.

Angus A. Somerville, trans. "Gospel Book Ransomed from Vikings (ca. 800)," from *A Second Anglo-Saxon Reader: Archaic and Dialectal*. Ed. Henry Sweet and rev. T.F. Hoad, 115. Oxford: Clarendon Press, 1978.

Angus A. Somerville, trans. "Jomsvikings Meet Their End." From Snorri Sturluson, *Óláfs saga Tryggvasonar*, in *Heimskringla*, vol. 1. Ed. Bjarni Aðalbjarnarson, 273–86. Íslenzk fornrit XXVI-XXVIII. Reykjavik: Hiðíslenzka fornritafélag, 2002.

Elizaveta Strakhov, trans. "Identifying the Dead," from *The Battle of Crécy: A Casebook*, 37–51. Ed. Michael Livingston and Kelly DeVries. Liverpool: Liverpool University Press, 2015. Reprinted by permission of the translator.

Dana F. Sutton, ed. and trans. Polydore Vergil, *Anglica historia (1555 version): A Hypertext Critical Edition.* Birmingham, UK: University of Birmingham, 2010. Copyright © 2010. http://www.philological.bham.ac.uk/polverg/25eng.html.

Craig Taylor and Jane H.M. Taylor, trans. *The Chivalric Biography of Boucicaut, Jean II Le Meingre*, 29–31. Woodbridge, UK: Boydell Press, 2016. Reprinted by permission of Boydell & Brewer Ltd.

J.M. Upton-Ward, trans. *Rule of the Templars*, 21–22, 35, 58–60. Woodbridge, UK: Boydell Press, 1992. Reprinted by permission of Boydell & Brewer Ltd.

Richard Vaughn. *John the Fearless: The Growth of Burgundian Power*, 60–62. London: Longmans Green and Co., 1966. Reprinted by permission of Boydell & Brewer Ltd.

Diana Gilliand Wright, trans. "When the Serenissima and the Gran Turco Made Love: The Peace Treaty of 1478," from *Reading the Middle Ages: Sources from Europe, Byzantium, and the Islamic World*. Ed. Barbara Rosenwein, 497–99. Toronto: University of Toronto Press, 2006. Reprinted with permission of the translator.

INDEX

Topics are listed by document number. The index is intended to be used in tandem with the table of contents.

READINGS IN MEDIEVAL CIVILIZATIONS AND CULTURES

Series Editor: Paul Edward Dutton

"Readings in Medieval Civilizations and Cultures is in my opinion the most useful series being published today."
—William C. Jordan, Princeton University

I—Carolingian Civilization: A Reader, Second Edition
edited by Paul Edward Dutton

II—Medieval Popular Religion, 1000–1500: A Reader, Second Edition
edited by John Shinners

III—Charlemagne's Courtier: The Complete Einhard
translated & edited by Paul Edward Dutton

IV—Medieval Saints: A Reader
edited by Mary-Ann Stouck

V—From Roman to Merovingian Gaul: A Reader
translated & edited by Alexander Callander Murray

VI—Medieval England, 500–1500: A Reader, Second Edition
edited by Emilie Amt & Katherine Allen Smith

VII—Love, Marriage, and Family in the Middle Ages: A Reader
edited by Jacqueline Murray

VIII—The Crusades: A Reader, Second Edition
edited by S.J. Allen & Emilie Amt

IX—The Annals of Flodoard of Reims, 919–966
translated & edited by Steven Fanning & Bernard S. Bachrach

X—Gregory of Tours: The Merovingians
translated & edited by Alexander Callander Murray

XI—Medieval Towns: A Reader
edited by Maryanne Kowaleski

XII—A Short Reader of Medieval Saints
edited by Mary-Ann Stouck

XIII—Vengeance in Medieval Europe: A Reader
edited by Daniel Lord Smail & Kelly Gibson

XIV—The Viking Age: A Reader, Second Edition
edited by Angus A. Somerville & R. Andrew McDonald

XV—Medieval Medicine: A Reader
edited by Faith Wallis

XVI—Pilgrimage in the Middle Ages: A Reader
edited by Brett Edward Whalen

XVII—Prologues to Ancient and Medieval History: A Reader
edited by Justin Lake

XVIII—Muslim and Christian Contact in the Middle Ages: A Reader
edited by Jarbel Rodriguez

XIX—The Twelfth-Century Renaissance: A Reader
edited by Alex J. Novikoff

XX—European Magic and Witchcraft: A Reader
edited by Martha Rampton

XXI—Medieval Warfare: A Reader
edited by Kelly DeVries & Michael Livingston